DEATH VALLEY

DEATH VALLEY

The Summer Offensive, I Corps, August 1969

Keith William Nolan

PRESIDIO

To April and C. C., and my family

Copyright © 1987 by Presidio Press
Published by Presidio Press
31 Pamaron Way, Novato CA 94947

Library of Congress Cataloging-in-Publication Data

Nolan, Keith William, 1964–
  Death Valley.

  Bibliography: p. 316.
  Includes index.
  1. Vietnamese Conflict, 1961–1975—Campaigns—
Vietnam—Hiep Duc Valley.   2. Vietnamese Conflict,
1961–1975—Regimental histories—United States.
3. United States. Marine Corps. Marines, 7th—
History.   4. United States. Army. Infantry
Brigade. 196th—History.   5. Hiep Duc Valley
(Vietnam)—History.   I. Title.
DS557.8.H54N65   1987   959.704'342   86–30478
ISBN 0–89141–287–5

Printed in the United States of America

Sometime after August of 69, a grunt walked through the American Division Headquarters compound in Chu Lai. He wore no helmet now that he was in from the bush, and his hair was dirty and uncombed. He had unauthorized sideburns and a handlebar mustache. He held his M16 rifle over his shoulder like a tramp stick, and his faded, grimy fatigue shirt hung open. A green sweat towel was draped around his neck, and his trouser cuffs were rolled up, exposing muddy and cracked jungle boots. A starched major approached and questioned his unmilitary appearance. He smiled, "The war's over. We've got to start acting like garrison soldiers now." The young grunt pulled a grubby envelope from his pocket. He shook it at the major. "What do you mean the war's over? Three months ago, seven of us were at LZ Baldy and now five are dead!" But the major was still smiling, "Well, let's say it's slowed down quite a bit."

Contents

Preface

This is my third and probably last book on the subject of the American fighting man in Vietnam. This unplanned trilogy recounts, in varying detail and coherency, the high time of the U.S. military (as typified in my book on the 1968 Battle of Hue), the period of disillusion (1969 Summer Offensive), and the final act when drugs and internal strife were almost as much a problem as the communists (1971 Laos Incursion).

I've written not from any personal experience in the world of hurt and pride described to me by the veterans I've interviewed. I am one of the sheltered, conservative middle class (only because of the hard-working, American Dream–style success of my parents). What prompted my writing then—other than the personal satisfaction in crafting words—was to investigate for myself the one-sided pontifications on Vietnam by my high school and college teachers. With rare and much-appreciated exception, the classroom was not a place for discussing Vietnam as the complex situation it was; instead, the professors—many of whom were student protesters in the 1960s—presented the subject as if from an unbending Leftist manual. The leaders of the Saigon regime are tarred in the most corrupt terms, probably accurately, but Ho Chi Minh glows through as an unblemished nationalist hero. South Vietnamese soldiers terrorized the rural population, while the only civilian victims of the National Liberation Front were, of course, corrupt government officials. My Lai is discussed with the inference that this was only a more bloody example of U.S. tactics, while no mention is made of communist atrocities or of the systematic abuses by the Hanoi and Pol Pot regimes since the "liberation." One pamphlet passed out in my high school history class raised the question of personal morality by discussing the decisions made by Germans assigned to Nazi concentration camps and American pilots assigned to fly as forward observers for air strikes in Vietnam.

At certain points, I was almost sick with frustration at the mindless repetition of such cliches and—worse—the unknowing acceptance of them as the whole truth by the students around me. That's what prompted my interest in the subject. Vindication of the Vietnam veteran sustained the effort. I hoped simply to write about the war as the soldier saw it. And the soldier experienced things which reflected badly on the war effort and the men involved. It would be an injustice for me to combat those Leftist myths by substituting a set of equally unrealistic Rambo myths. I could not ignore the mistakes and weak moments but, despite what some senior officers have suggested to me, I find absolutely no joy in reporting them.

The topic of this book—the 1969 Summer Offensive—was discussed by the media at the time in terms of "the 37-year-old Marine battalion commander killed leading a charge" and "the Army company that refused to fight." There was much to tell about these actions and, in the telling, I hope to present what the "average" grunt experienced in Vietnam.

Thank you to those vets for telling me.

Marine Corps veterans who helped are: LtGen Ormond Simpson, Ret.; Colonels Robert Beeler, Brian Fagan, Ray Kummerow, Ret., Jon Rider, P. K. Van Riper; Lieutenant Colonels Ray Hord, Marvin Lugger, Ret., John Pidgeon, USMCR, Jim Steele, Ret., Allen Weh, USMCR; LCdr Roy Black, USN, Ret.; Maj William Peters; Capt James Webb, Ret.; ex-Lieutenants Larry Orefice and Bill Schuler; SgtMaj Charles Awkerman, Ret.; First Sergeants Chester Richards, Ret., and William Yohe, Ret.; MSgt John Bradley; PlSgt N. W. Crowe, NG; SSgt George Blake, Ret.; Sgt Charles Zotter, NG; ex-Sergeants Eugene Brodie, Nick Cominos, Bill Lowery, Ralph Sirianni; ex-Corporals Carson Bartels, Lee Dill, Roger LaRue, and Don Wells; ex-Lance Corporals Charly Besardi, Lorne Collinson, John Ellison, Robert Mercati, Charles Norton, Rolf Parr, Craig Russell, Patrick Smith, and Ron Smith.

Army veterans who helped are: LtGen Thomas Tackaberry, Ret.; MG Lloyd Ramsey, Ret.; Colonels Roger Lee and Cecil Henry, Ret.; Lieutenant Colonels Gary Allen, NG, Harvey Browne, William Gayler, NG, Steve Maness, and Norman Mekkelsen; Majors Jerry Downey, USAR, David Grieger, Ret., Barry Parsons, NG, Joel Thomason, and

John Whittecar, Ret.; Capt Joe Loadholtes; ex-Captains Ernie Carrier, Phillip Kinman, Bill Robinson, Eugene Shurtz, and William Wilson; CW4 Ken Fritz, NG; SgtMaj Ed Crain, Ret.; SFC Rick Allison; ex-SSgt Jim Lynch; ex-Sergeants Charles Brown, John Curtis, Al Holtzman, Ray Keefer, Mike Kosteczko, and Billy McWhirter; ex-SP5 Joe Kralich; ex-SP4s Ralph Brantley, Jerome Colburn, Robert Davis, Bob Hodierne, Robert Ferris, Charles Jandecka, Robert Kruch, Roland Lasso, Jerry Samftner, Eric Shimer, and Calvin Tam; and ex-PFC Tom Goodwin.

Government departments and personnel who helped are: Col John Miller, Mr. Charles Smith, Mr. Benis Frank, and Mr. Danny Crawford of the Marine Corps Historical Center, Washington Navy Yard, Washington, D.C.; F. B. Anthony of the Decorations and Medals Branch, Headquarters Marine Corps, Washington, D.C.; Col John Greenwood and Mr. Ronald Lyons of the Marine Corps Association, Quantico, Virginia; Mr. Jeffrey Clarke of the U.S. Army Center of Military History, Washington, D.C.; Col Morris Herbert, Association of Graduates, and Mr. Alan Aimone, Military History Librarian, U.S. Military Academy, West Point, New York; Col David Lemon of the Chief of Military History and the Center of Military History, Washington, D.C.; Col Denis Mehigan, USA, Commander/Editor in Chief, *Pacific Stars & Stripes,* Tokyo, Japan; Mr. John Slonaker, Chief, Historical Reference Branch, U.S. Army Military History Institute, Carlisle Barracks, Pennsylvania; and the offices of Senators Robert Byrd, Charles Grassley, and Edward Kennedy.

Private agencies or individuals who helped are: Mr. Richard Pyle (Associated Press); Mr. James Sterba (*The New York Times*); Mr. Nick Mills; Mr. Robert and William Powell; and Ms. Suzanne Westgaard, Executive Assistant, *Soldier of Fortune* magazine, Boulder, Colorado.

Keith William Nolan
Columbia, Missouri
June 1986

PART ■

The Grunts

Chapter One

You Could Feel the Ghosts

On the afternoon of 17 June 1969, LCpl Roger T. LaRue, of D Company, 1st Reconnaissance Battalion, 1st Marine Division, sat against the canvas seat of his helicopter. The interior of the CH46 Sea Knight was vibrating. LaRue's seven partners sat facing each other. They wore camouflaged fatigues and bush hats; their hands and faces were streaked with green and black paint. K-Bar knives were taped upside down on shoulder harnesses for easy reach. Weapons were locked and loaded.

No one was saying much.

They had lifted off from Camp Reasoner, Da Nang, and they touched down—briefly—on the long spine of Charlie Ridge. The Recon Marines disembarked quickly, then crouched in the deep brush as the Sea Knight pulled out. The noise faded, the ship disappeared, and the silence and heat of the jungle took over. Sweat was already beginning to stain LaRue's fatigues. He kneeled with the others, eyes flicking into the hillside of trees, hands tight around his stocky M79 grenade launcher.

Any North Vietnamese in eyeshot would have seen their hovering chopper, so the recon team moved out quickly. Their job was not to fight the enemy on this canopied mountain, but to find them and call in the firepower. This ridge line belonged to the North Vietnamese Army. That's why the Marines travelled small and light. There was no room for slack, and the battalion had a catch phrase: If you can't pack the gear, don't ask for the job. LaRue fit in well. He was nineteen and dedicated. Most importantly, he was able to tune out most of his fear until the chopper set them back down at Camp Reasoner. There he would chain smoke; there he would drink himself numb.

On the third day of this patrol, they found it.

The point man led them down a two-hundred-foot escarpment. LaRue was the third one to the bottom. A thin stream cut through a ravine choked with vegetation. The point started towards the sound of running water and suddenly froze, silently raised his shotgun, and glanced back. LaRue caught the look in his eyes. He signalled the fourth man in line, the team radioman, to freeze. Then LaRue edged forward and crouched with the point and deuce among some creekside boulders. He peered through the overhanging foliage. Jesus! There were five North Vietnamese soldiers downstream, talking and laughing as they sunned themselves on a large, flat stone. Beyond them, the Marines could hear the singsong chatter of more Vietnamese. LaRue's heart was pumping furiously. We've just stumbled into a goddamned base camp! The NVA on the rocks, casting a few glances in our direction, must think we're some of their buddies coming back to camp, LaRue reckoned.

There was no way to climb back atop the ridge without being recognized, and little chance that the others could come down to help. Then LaRue noticed that the radioman was trying to do just that. The radioman— a quiet guy due to rotate home soon—carefully picked his way into the trap, propelled by some unspoken loyalty. He crouched behind their boulders, then calmly whispered into his handset, giving the NVA's location and requesting immediate air support. The radioman's name was Kiev Zoller, and LaRue had nothing but admiration for that Marine.

The radio hissed its answer: air on the way.

Minutes crawled by. The NVA sunning themselves kept looking in the Marines' direction. Finally one picked up his AK47 automatic rifle and disappeared in the direction of the base camp. He came back accompanied by an NVA officer in gray fatigues and polished leather gear; the two strode directly towards the boulders, the officer in front drawing a 9mm Soviet pistol from its holster. The four Marines sucked air. The point gripped his shotgun, the deuce his M14 rifle; LaRue sighted down the stub barrel of his M79. Corporal Zoller held the radio mike with his left hand, his right hand sweaty around the pistol grip of his M16 rifle.

When the North Vietnamese were thirty feet away, the point man suddenly sprang into view, blasting off four incredibly quick shots from his pump gun before the NVA even realized what was happening. The NVA officer bounced off his feet and crashed back down into the brush six feet away, his chest and head pulverized. In the same instant, LaRue squeezed the trigger, felt the grenade launcher buck hard against his shoulder, saw the other North Vietnamese collapse.

The jungle erupted with return fire. LaRue tried to break open the M79 to reload, but his mind choked with panic. He could hear NVA moving at them. Oh God, no, we're going to die. No way out. His hands shook uncontrollably; the breech wouldn't budge. The point and deuce were firing furiously. LaRue finally slammed the weapon against his knee, pulled out the spent casing, dropped in another round, and snapped it shut. The safety stuck. He dropped the M79 in a panic and grabbed at his Colt .45, but the pistol holster was twisted around behind him. He couldn't reach it. He grabbed the stock of Zoller's M16, but Zoller refused to give it up. LaRue picked up the grenade launcher again, forced the safety off, aimed at the noises, and fired. The round spun from the barrel, but exploded short and blasted shrapnel back over the Marines' heads. He reached into his ammunition bag and pumped off two more rounds. His terror began to evaporate as he got the M79 working. He became resigned to the fact that they were going to be overrun and killed, that there was no reason to fear the inevitable. All they could do was make themselves expensive; so, while the radioman calmly maintained his vigil calling for air support, the other three laid down enough fire to sound like a small army. LaRue pounded two rounds into a thick tree trunk above a gulley; the NVA who'd been sunning themselves had ducked there when the shooting started, and they did not reappear.

Over the cacophony, they distinguished the propeller buzz of two OV10 Bronco observation planes. Then the cool, reassuring drawl of a pilot came over the radio, "Coffee Time, Coffee Time, this is Cowpoke Three. I hear you got some problems with the little brown people. Well, just mark your pos with an airpanel and we'll throw around some shit." The Broncos came in under Zoller's direction, strafing across the creek with 40mm automatic cannons and 7.62mm machine guns. On their last pass, they laid a grouping of white phosphorus rockets into the NVA camp. Behind them, a flight of F4 Phantom jets rolled in on the hot, white smoke curling up through the green canopy. The Marines hugged earth, palms tight against their ears, under the supersonic scream of dives and the convulsion and concussion of hundreds of pounds of exploding bombs.

In the confusion, the Marines who'd been atop the ridge during the firefight slipped down and they all headed down a trail away from the exploding chaos of the camp. They moved for five hours without rest, exhausted bodies spurred on by the knowledge of what would happen if they stopped. They paused once to fill canteens from a creek. They finally stopped when it was too dark to see. Every hour throughout the night they could hear the NVA firing single shots as signals between the hunting parties. When the first fuzz of daylight appeared, the team moved out again. From a field of green elephant grass, razor-sharp and reaching above their heads, they could see the sky become dotted with helicopters. A Sea Knight descended into the waving blades with its back cargo ramp down, door gunners tight behind their fifties. In moments, the recon team was aboard. Then they were up and out.

■ From December 1968 to December 1969, MajGen Ormond R. Simpson was commanding general, 1st Marine Division, headquartered on Hill 327 three kilometers west of the coastal city of Da Nang, Republic of Vietnam. General Simpson was described by one of his battalion commanders as ''. . . a tall, rawboned Texan who loved his Marines, passionately. He loved to shake their hands, talk to them, find out where they were from and how they were getting along. His warmth was very real. I know he took the casualties hard, and he chose to sign off personally on a letter to every Purple Heart awardee. Some of his nights were very long.''

Simpson was a thoughtful man. When he looked at his rice paddy infantrymen, he reflected that Tarawa had been a nightmare but one that lasted ninety-six hours. And when it was over, it was over. Not so in Vietnam, and that was the peculiar hardship of this war. The young riflemen—the grunts—were not always fighting, but they were always out in the bush where the danger was omnipresent, the privations constant.

In 1969, the four regiments of the 1st Marine Division maintained a brutal routine of 1,000 patrols every twenty-four hours in their Tactical Area of Responsibility of the I Corps Tactical Zone.

The enemy could be anywhere at anytime.

Mostly, though, by the summer of 69, the ground war in South Vietnam had become most actively focused in the southern sector of the 1st MarDiv TAOR; this was where the border between Quang Nam and Quang Tin Provinces ran horizontally across the Que Son Mountains. The 1st Marine Division occupied Quang Nam, while the 23d Infantry

Division (Americal), U.S. Army, occupied Quang Tin. In the mountains between them lived the *2d NVA Division*. The mountains belonged to the enemy; from there, they kept the pressure on and the cost was almost constant. The area exacted a daily tax from the Marine battalions assigned to patrol it in the form of Viet Cong booby traps and snipers, a cost accentuated every month or two by clashes with battalions and regiments of North Vietnamese regulars.

The killing ground north of the Que Sons was called the An Hoa Basin. The Marine Corps had first landed at Red Beach, Da Nang, on 8 March 1965. It took until early 1966 to stabilize the villages around the city's airfield sufficiently; then elements of the 3d Marine Division began pushing ten miles southwest into the fringes of An Hoa. Paddied flatlands stretched in from the coast, but mountains rose around the Basin; the Que Sons formed its western and southern frontiers, a spur called Charlie Ridge its northern. In October 1966, the 3d MarDiv HQ displaced north to Phu Bai from Da Nang, and the 1st MarDiv HQ moved north from Chu Lai to their vacated command bunker on Hill 327. In the An Hoa arid basin, it was a war of attrition, one operation always followed by another. Georgia. Liberty. Macon. Independence. Newcastle. Mameluke Thrust. Allen Brook. Henderson Hill. Taylor Common. Pipestone Canyon. The *2d NVA Division,* and the numerous battalions that supported it, proved a tough adversary, but—although one could barely perceive it in those glaring, hot paddies—the Marine Corps was accomplishing its mission.

The U.S. Army, which had first moved into I Corps in April 1967 to reinforce the thin Marine line, was also solidly in place by 1969. The lowlands on the southern side of the Que Sons—the Hiep Duc and Song Chang Valleys—were protected by a string of fire bases manned by the 196th Infantry Brigade, Americal Division. Consequently, Hiep Duc was the Americal's westernmost advance, as was the An Hoa Basin for the 1st Marine Division.

In 1969, the Arizona Territory, in the southern corner of the Basin, was the war's bloodiest arena. At a time when the political watchwords were Vietnamization, Pacification, and Troop Withdrawal, the grunts in the Arizona were still operating Search & Destroy. Their's was a stagnated war of attrition which, by 1969, was responsible for most of their casualties (USMC casualties in Vietnam would eventually exceed USMC casualties in WWII). The object was to keep hammering at the communist strongholds, and to maintain whatever gains had been made

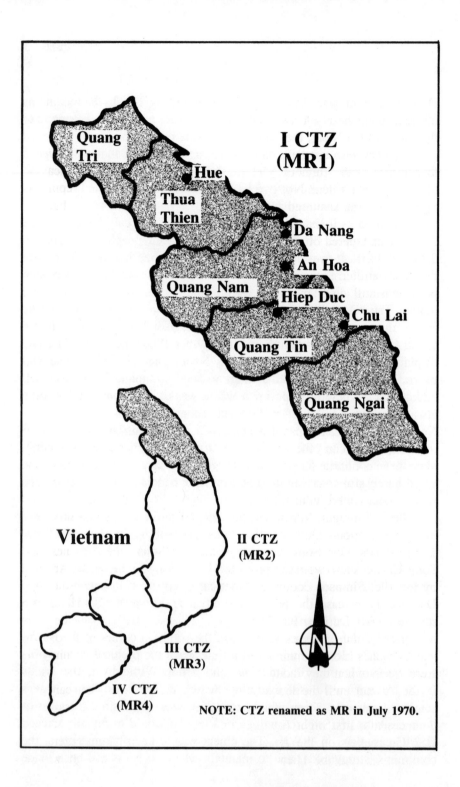

in four years of war. Da Nang had become the rear in the continuing effort to push the NVA away from the populated coastal lowlands. The farther from Da Nang, the more dangerous it became.

The latest encounter in the Arizona was with the *90th NVA Regiment* in mid-June 1969. Elements of the 5th Marine Regiment suffered heavily, but they found a dead NVA battalion commander and a dead company commander; the shattered NVA regiment left more than three hundred bodies behind as it limped back to its mountain havens.

Contact tapered off dramatically after this battle. In fact, an unusual calm had settled over most of South Vietnam even before then, and newspapers referred to the Summer Lull. U.S. combat operations continued, men still died, but the NVA were not meeting them punch for punch. The NVA drifted back to their hideaways, and the meaning of this became a topic of political debate. On 8 June 1969, President Nixon had announced the gradual phase-out of U.S. units from the war zone. The discussions centered around dissecting the communist response: was the lull a sign from Ho Chi Minh that the Hanoi regime was more amiable to the new U.S. policy, that the stalled Paris peace talks had a chance for new life?

Major General Simpson would have begged to differ.

The 1st Recon, the eyes and ears of his division, was probing, slipping into Charlie Ridge and the Que Sons. The Recon Marines were more successful than Simpson had first imagined they could be, and their findings were vital (although not surprising)—the NVA were regrouping in strength. In response, in July 69, General Simpson launched another operation—Durham Peak—which saw the 5th Marines helicoptered into the Que Sons. To pick up the slack, the 7th Marines (Col Gildo S. Codispoti) were shifted south from their AO to cover the Arizona; meanwhile, Simpson coordinated with the Americal to screen the Hiep Duc Valley in case the NVA retreated from the 5th Marines in that direction. But Durham Peak was a dry run; the NVA disappeared into their honeycomb of caves and tunnels, even abandoning many of their supply caches and mountain base camps to avoid battle. The communists fought only when they thought they had the advantage.

It was not until the second week of August that the NVA came out of the woodwork. There was a flashpan of fighting all across South Vietnam that first night (including sappers in the wire at 1st MarDiv HQ and rockets on the Americal HQ); then the struggle centered on the Arizona and the Hiep Duc and Song Chang Valleys. It was an eighteen-day campaign (12–29 August), blandly labelled the 1969 Summer Offensive.

The 7th Marines were attacked in the Arizona.

Fire bases of the 196th Brigade, Americal, were hit by sappers.

Outnumbered 196th companies were surrounded in Hiep Duc and Song Chang, and the 7th Marines were committed to assist in halting the offensive, then in pursuing the retreating enemy.

U.S. firepower once again stymied the NVA.

The 1969 Summer Offensive would be another hard-fought American victory but, perhaps, not a resounding one. For one thing, the Marines were gradually committed to the battle. General Simpson noted, "Had we been able to turn the *entire* 1st Marine Division south, there would have been a far different and far better story to tell. However, this was never considered since we could never leave Da Nang uncovered."

And there were some battlefield failures.

The NVA goal was, of course, to keep blunting the slow advance into their territory. And they hoped to make trouble extending beyond the battlefield: to kill and to keep killing Americans at a time when Nixon was talking Vietnamization, so that the national confusion and horror over the continuing body bags and amputees would finish what the North Vietnamese Army could only start. In 1969, the commanding general of the NVA admitted that more than a half-million men had been killed, ten times the total U.S. death list. The statistic was offered with a shrug: the number of dead meant nothing; the sacrifice was palatable, because motivation was what really counted. Washington had decided on a war of attrition to combat the communist invasion because they thought Hanoi would blink first. They were wrong.

The 1969 Summer Offensive was unlike many Vietnam campaigns only because of its mood. It was the first major engagement after the announcement of U.S. withdrawals. A new slogan was heard: Why be the last man killed in Vietnam? Such sentiments were rarely expressions of cowardice or antiwar protest. More simply, a cynicism that always had existed among the grunts about the validity of attrition tactics became crystallized. They knew they were leaving, and they knew the job wasn't done. A spiritual malaise began to affect the entire war effort. "Nothing much of anything was decided by the summer campaign," commented SP4 Bob Hodierne, U.S. Army combat photographer. "I don't believe any Medals of Honor or court-martials for cowardice were its fruits. It, in fact, could be seen as painfully typical of the whole damn experience.

Pain, death, little private acts of heroism and cowardice, individuals changed forever, and when it was done—what? As the GIs said, 'Fuck it, it don't mean nothin.' ''

The grunts who fought the 1969 Summer Offensive were the smallest part of the Green Machine, the slim end of a funnel that yawned wide at the top. Only a relative handful did the actual fighting. For every grunt in the bush, there were from five to ten men supporting him in base camps. For this campaign, there were two anchors of command and support and both were located along Highway One on the coast: Da Nang for the 1st Marine Division and Chu Lai for the Americal Division. Both sites had been secured by the Marines in 1965; by 69, they were insulated by miles of barbed wire and guard towers, and within, living was physically comfortable. And boring.

An arc was drawn around Da Nang to indicate the maximum range of NVA 122mm and 140mm rockets; the 1st and 26th Marines conducted saturation patrols in this Rocket Belt. Base camps of the 5th and 7th Marines were sprinkled across the flatlands between Da Nang and An Hoa, bridges between the rear and the bush. Hill 55 (7th Marines Command Post) sat east of the northern tip of Charlie Ridge; the villages there were replete with guerrillas and the Marines jocularly nicknamed the area Dodge City. Rivers running down from the Que Sons twisted in several directions towards Hill 55, and numerous battalion base camps for the 7th Marines were constructed near the banks: Hill 10, Hill 37, Hill 65. A dirt road called Route 4 (or Thunder Road) ran west from Highway One to Charlie Ridge; smaller convoy roads radiated from it to connect the various bases.

Four miles south of Hill 55, the rivers isolated a stretch of land called Go Noi Island; it was a bleak, desperately hot place which resembled a moonscape covered with tall elephant grass. It had a bad reputation and there were no permanent positions on it. Nor were there any in the Arizona Territory. The Arizona was isolated too, blocked by the Que Sons to the south and west, the Song Thu Bon River to the east, and the Song Vu Gia River and Charlie Ridge to the north. Directly east across the Song Thu Bon was the An Hoa Combat Base (5th Marines Command Post); it was a red clay hill, circled by wire and bunkered in with four million sandbags. Since it sat at the base of the Que Sons, it was called Little Dienbienphu. Route 537 ran north from An Hoa to

Dodge City, crossing a curve of the Song Thu Bon over Liberty Bridge. The bridge was the work of Navy Seabees; the perimeter compound, called Phu Lac 6 after a nearby hamlet, was an artillery fire base for the 11th Marines.

Morale in these cantonments was better than in places like Da Nang and Chu Lai. There were frequent rocket raids and infrequent sapper attacks, living conditions were more spartan, and there was enough to dispel complacency and forge some comradeship. But these base camps were also hot, boring, and dusty, and an occasional problem did crop up. A platoon leader noted some of the reasons:

> The nature of the war dictated that there would be numerous fortified strongpoints, surrounded by no-man's-land. Most of the rear echelon Marines were eighteen to twenty years old, surrounded by barbed wire with nothing to do except mundane, boring jobs. There was little entertainment or diversion, so oftentimes there would be problems in the rear. These could be booze, drugs, or racial. More often than not these problems resulted from boredom and idleness rather than viciousness or premeditation. By this I mean few people enlist in the Marines during wartime to smoke dope or raise hell in a little American island surrounded by barbed wire and rice paddies. But idle minds are the devil's workshop. Now add to this the fact that the rifle companies dumped their pot heads and troublemakers back in the rear. To protect lives in combat, it was easier to send malcontents back to be supervised by the companies' first sergeants and gunnery sergeants, who were generally less than sympathetic to any complaints that these castoffs would have. This is what usually caused fraggings.

Fragging was the nickname for assaults on superiors, usually with a fragmentation hand grenade. But such incidents were few and far between, and the real problem for the Marine Corps in 1969 was an undercurrent of black militancy. There existed a terrible frustration among many blacks that their deaths in Vietnam would serve no purpose, and that their place was really with the civil rights movement—or The Revolution— back home.

When LtCol Ray G. Kummerow assumed command of 3d Battalion, 7th Marines in August 1969, he encountered a smattering of this discontent. Kummerow, who was unusually attuned to the social revolution being exported to the battlefield, noticed the young black Marines arrived already extremely sensitive to any real or imagined discrimination. The battalion operations officer had created a Watch & Action group to investigate all charges of prejudice. Most were unfounded, but a few were not; for example, some officers and staff NCOs would not allow Black Power bracelets, made from woven bootlaces, but ignored the peace medallions worn by white grunts. To a certain percentage of blacks in 3/7 Marines, these incidents became their excuses for malingering.

For others, though, their alienation with the war effort was very real. For example, in November 1969, 3/7 was at LZ Ross preparing for an operation in the Que Sons. Prior to this, the battalion had been reduced to 600 men due to battle casualties and malaria, and Lieutenant Colonel Kummerow—himself a casualty of the Summer Offensive— had just hitchhiked back to Ross after recuperating on a hospital ship. Trouble was in the air. The battalion had just received 300 replacements from the 3d Marine Division, and half these men were black; they were bitter about being sent back to the bush while the rest of their former division sailed for Okinawa as part of the withdrawals. These were the Marines who organized a show of protest in one of the line companies. This particular company was known as a "brother killer"—during Operation Oklahoma Hills, a black grunt had to be dragged aboard a helicopter, and after landing in the bush he accidentally ran into the chopper blades and was killed. As this company formed up to go into the Que Sons again, sixteen blacks didn't answer muster; a few even crept off to far corners of LZ Ross and disappeared in empty bunkers. Kummerow told the company commander to stand down and round up his missing men. The next day, they held a meeting in the fire base chapel. Kummerow noticed some of these blacks were the finest infantrymen in the company, and he had no doubt they were sincere. They felt that blacks were not only overrepresented in the bush,* but were given the most dangerous assignments by the company leaders—there was only one black officer in the entire battalion and he had no tolerance for such complaints— and that whites received most of the promotions and safer rear jobs. At this time, all Kummerow could do was to ". . . assure them that if they truly had a grievance it would be heard out by their chain of command,

---

* This was true for these men, and many blacks concluded from such personal observations that their sacrifice was out of proportion to their numbers in society. Many thought this was no accident; however, of those who died in Vietnam, 12.5 percent were black while 86.3 percent were white. This corresponded roughly to racial demographics in the United States.

and if they didn't get satisfaction, they had recourse at any level to request mast. I told them they were in trouble, but if they didn't carry out their orders, they would be getting into deeper trouble. They believed and trusted me.'' The company humped off LZ Ross that evening with these men back along.

On one hand, appropriate action was taken regarding specific charges made by the black Marines, and on the other, Kummerow handed out reductions in rank and fines to some of those involved. He discussed the case with General Simpson and Colonel Codispoti, and they agreed ''. . . it was a tough problem and one for which there were no easy solutions. After the company went back to the field, Codispoti recommended no disciplinary action. I think he feared a reaction that would engender a situation worse than that which occurred, and wanted to cool it. I felt I had to do what I did to maintain the status of discipline in the battalion. There were many other Marines, white and black, who didn't relish the hardships and dangers of patrol, and I didn't want to invite anyone else to seek an easy out.''

Kummerow saw no other such incidents.

Mostly the men simply did their jobs. ''Like going to work in the morning'' is how Cpl Lee Dill put it. He was a tank commander with B Company, 1st Tank Battalion, and he spent the summer of 69 escorting supply convoys and minesweeps on the road between An Hoa and Liberty Bridge. He didn't have much time to worry about anything but doing it right. When they burned down the road, which impregnated everything and everyone with red clay dust, Dill threw power to the black Marines and peace signs to the white Marines.

They had good team spirit and what problems occurred were usually the kind that seem funny later. Like the time in August of 69 when they were supposed to sweep to Liberty Bridge. Dill's tank, Naturally Stoned, and another tank, Funky Ride, rolled to the An Hoa gate to pick up their infantry support and the minesweep team. They were late and, instead of the team, a staff sergeant showed up drunk and mumbling that ''fuck it, we don't need no support!'' He climbed into the lead tank and ordered them to hit the road. Dill reluctantly followed in the second tank. They hauled ass as the sergeant did three-sixties in his turret. Over the radio, his crew sounded mortified. Off the road were some figures who turned out to be Marines but who, in the distance, looked like ARVN. The sergeant suddenly opened fire in their direction with his cupola-mounted .50-caliber machine gun. Dill gulped. Oh shit.

He toyed with the idea of shooting the crazy man, but dismissed it. They finally reached the Phu Lac 6 compound, but old sarge didn't even slow down. A truck was headed in their direction on the camp road and they passed just as the sergeant rotated his turret again, broadsiding the truck windshield with his 90mm gun tube. They parked on the perimeter and the battalion commander came on the radio, wanting to know what the hell was going on. Dill told him the truth, nervous about being involved with the colonel, even more concerned about the sergeant leering at him, drunk and pissed, his hand resting on his holster. Dill had a .45 on his hip too, and he was thinking, oh man, I ain't believin' this! Thankfully, though, sarge only stumbled back to his tank and fell asleep.

The next day he was busted and sent to the rear.

But no one was immune to the real war. One morning the supply convoy brought in new treads to the An Hoa tank park. The men stripped to the waist and spent the day sweating the treads into place with the same care and concern, Dill thought, of pit crews working on Indy cars. They took a break to cook steaks and drink warm Pepsis, and Dill talked with a tank driver named Schreckengost. He started walking away, had gone ten steps, when the air began screaming and he bounded for his tank. The Marine lying across the driver's hatch was clutching at his bloody legs, and the tarp over the .50-cal. ammo in the gypsy rack was on fire. Goldstein put the fire out as Dill scrambled into his turret, screaming for a corpsman. In seconds, the 122mm rockets had stopped falling. That's when they found Schreckengost, sprawled unconscious right where Dill had been talking with him; he had a hole in his chest. Jellerson bandaged the wound and they picked up Schreckengost to put him on the stretcher. They saw his back then. It had been blown wide open at the exit of the white-hot chunk of shrapnel. He died on the medevac.

Finally, there were the infantrymen, the grunts, the few who actually lived in the bush. It was not uncommon for rifle companies in the An Hoa Basin to go ninety days straight in the field, their only connection to the world the resupply chopper which came every four days. It was a dehumanizing existence where man became part of the wilderness, subject to the killing heat and chilling rains, to leeches, mosquitoes, and ringworms, where feet rotted and men died. Everyone hated the bush. Yet, it was the real Marine Corps out there. It was all in the bush. The chicken-shit harrassment fell away; the racial problems and the dope were put away for other places and other times. Some men became brothers, and virtually all had the solidarity of shared suffering and shared victories.

The grunts had a saying: For those who have fought for it, life has a flavor the protected can never know. There was pride, cynicism, fatalism, comradeship.

Morale was at its best and worst in the bush.

In many ways, the grunts of the summer of 69 were the same manchildren who took Iwo Jima (the average age of Marine riflemen in WWII and Vietnam was nineteen). The courage was the same, but it was a vastly different war they were fighting. Sometimes the absurdities were all too plain, like the day 2dLt Bill Peters of D Company, 7th Marines, was pinned down with his platoon a klick west of Hill 65. They huddled behind the paddy dikes as a machine gun fired from the village ahead. Peters radioed for a mortar fire mission; a voice said negative, friendly ville in the area. Peters asked for the map coordinates of the village, then exclaimed at the answer, "That's where they're shooting at me from!" Too bad. The platoon pulled back then, and it left a bad taste in their mouths. Why are we so stupid, Peters asked himself in frustration; why do we force ourselves to fight like this?

It was a strange war and even though the grunts of 69 were proud, they were children of their times. And by then, the waters were very muddy. Sgt Bill Lowery joined C Company, 7th Marines in May 1969; he'd already pulled a 1966–67 tour in the An Hoa Basin, but it was like returning to a whole different war. The enthusiasm had drained like air from a tire, but everything was still pounding away, grinding viciously, but going nowhere. It was as if the machine was running for no other purpose than its own aggrandizement. It was a sick joke, Lowery thought. He looked at his new company commander, a precisely polished lieutenant, and had no doubts about the officer's personal courage. But it was obvious he was building a career here; he wanted to win a medal and a promotion, so his radio talk was always formal and when the colonel was around he laid it on thick. When the lieutenant put Lowery in for the Silver Star, Lowery dismissed it as a ploy for the lieutenant's own Silver Star to be approved.

All we did was our jobs, he thought; now everybody wants to window dress it.

He heard scout dogs in the Americal got Bronze Stars.

It seemed in 1969 that the second string had come to continue a game no one wanted to play anymore. The new grunts seemed hip to the farce and waste. Their hair was longer; the smell of marijuana drifted in the rear. Discipline was beginning to corrode. No one was fighting for God and Country anymore, they just wanted to survive. At least that was the opinion of Sergeant Lowery, and an emotional flak jacket formed around his soul. A dead Marine didn't affect him anymore; it was more like a blown television tube that needed to be replaced. But he kept humping. To the powers that be it didn't matter what went on under a man's helmet, only that he do his duty. And, even in 1969, most never quit.

In this strange, controversial war, there was one constant which tied the grunts of 69 together with every generation of American soldier. Combat. The tools were slightly different, the emotions were not. S. L. A. Marshall once observed that combat most closely resembled a tumultuous playground in a tough neighborhood. A sense of order appeared only when the commanders, or the historians, pieced together all the fragments into an understandable package. When it was actually happening, no one really knew what was going on from one minute to the next.

Peters, a baby-faced second lieutenant with brown hair in a high crewcut, lost his first man eight days after getting his platoon. It was on a routine squad ambush near the Da Nang Rocket Belt, on a pitch-black night that poured a noisy rain. Peters joined them as they left the platoon perimeter and walked parallel to a brushy riverbank. Out of nowhere, there were hurried, jolting shots from the point, then a continuous exchange.

Peters clawed into the wet grass.

Everyone seemed to be on automatic. The platoon sergeant was up in moments, organizing a hasty defense. The grunts triggered return bursts through the rain. Peters crouched with his radioman, calling in support fire. He had always made a mistake with it at Basic School, had never done it for real before, but now he snapped all directions out correctly. He talked with the chief of the 81mm mortars on Hill 37, giving him his observer target line in degrees.

"What's that in mils?"

"Seventeen-sixty," Peters answered instantly. It was 100 degrees with 17.6 millimeters per degree. All his training was clicking right and he suddenly flashed to the time at Basic School when he complained to a captain that they did the same things over and over. The captain said that was so no matter how physically or mentally exhausted you were in combat, the things you needed to know to keep your people alive would be gut reactions. He was right. Peters brought the 81mm rounds in even as the VC firing died down; at the same time, he directed in artillery airburst rounds on the likely avenue of enemy withdrawal.

Their casualties were dragged back then and a Navy corpsman with an enormous mustache approached Peters. "Lieutenant, we got one dead, six wounded, and Doc Flashpool got shot in the chest. If we don't get him out right now, he's gonna die 'cause I can't stop the bleeding." The point man, a black kid, lay dead in the mud among the wounded. Peters crouched over Doc Flashpool, a nice, skinny kid, the only man among the casualties he really knew. "Doc, it's the lieutenant. Are you okay?"

Flashpool suddenly grabbed the front of his T-shirt, pulling him closer. "Lieutenant, don't let 'em do it. Don't let 'em do it to me."

"Do what, Doc?"

"Don't let 'em bury me as a sailor. I'm not a fucking sailor. I'm a Marine! I want to be buried in a Marine uniform!"

"Doc, you're not going to die. We've got a chopper inbound. We're going to get you out of here." Peters was saying what he was supposed to, but what he was thinking was—God, I'm twenty-one years old and I've got a nineteen-year-old kid hanging on me, giving me his death wish. Oh Christ, don't let him die! He didn't.

A medevac helicopter was overhead within minutes. Peters's radioman walked into an open paddy to signal the orbiting chopper with a strobe light. That made him an outlined target to any enemy who might still be lurking, but someone had to do it. Among the grunts, bravery was often routine. No one opened fire, but the Sea Knight pilot said he had *three* lights in his sights. The radioman set a second light and the pilot responded, "Roger that." The chopper touched down in the soggy, black paddy and in seconds it was lifting off, nose down, and disappearing into the rainy gloom with the dead and wounded aboard.

The platoon returned to the perimeter. Lieutenant Peters wrapped himself in his poncho. He did not allow poncho hootches at night for they presented a silhouetted target; so he lay in the rain, his head on his pack. Like every grunt in the platoon, his pack was ready to be shouldered at a moment's notice, and his M16 rifle was beside it, semidry under another poncho. He listened to the drizzle, and he reflected. He was nervous as hell. But he also felt a certain calm, a realization that he had not panicked, probably would never panic. The job never got easy but Peters was beginning to realize what most Marines come to know: I can hack it.

■ The border between Quang Nam and Quang Tin Provinces ran a twisting but generally horizontal line from Laos to the South China Sea. The TAOR of the 1st Marine Division ended on the northern side of this line. The TAOR to the south was the responsibility of the U.S. Army and, in the summer of 69, that meant the 196th Infantry Brigade (Col Thomas H. Tackaberry) of the Americal Division (MG Lloyd B. Ramsey). The 196th had four line battalions: 2–1 Infantry to the north on LZ Ross and to the east near the coast on LZ Baldy; 3–21 and 4–31 Infantry in the center of the brigade area on LZs East, Center, West, and Siberia; and 1–46 Infantry to the south on LZ Professional. The other two brigades of the Americal Division operated even farther south in an area of guerrilla ambushes and booby traps; it was the 196th which made the nose-to-nose contacts with the communist regulars. There were two main areas of NVA infiltration in the 196th AO—both valleys below the Que Sons. Hiep Duc Valley consisted of cultivated rice fields with a Que Son spur (the Nui Chom ridge line) to the north and an unnamed spur to the south. This second spine provided the northern frontier for a deserted area called the Song Chang Valley for the river that ran through it.

Hiep Duc was the AO of the 4th Battalion of the 31st Infantry, Song Chang the AO of the 3d Battalion of the 21st Infantry; the battalion rears were at Landing Zone Baldy (along Highway One on the coast) but the grunt companies operated from small, bunkered hilltops along the southern ridge. They were situated successively inland across the forested spine: East, Center, West, and the fourth and newest fire base, Siberia, named in deference to its isolation and to the 31st Infantry Regiment's combat expedition during the Russian Revolution. LZ Siberia was the last outpost into the Que Son Mountains, and it overlooked the Hiep Duc Resettlement Village. It was beautiful land, undulating down from the canopy of lush greenery to the artfully terraced rice fields. Everything was brilliantly green and alive and, because of its rambling thickness, very dangerous for men on ground patrol.

"It was forbidding terrain, the most scary I was ever in," commented Capt Jerry Downey, a company commander and staff officer in the 196th InfBde. "One could feel the presence of the enemy or the ghosts of those who had gone before whenever one moved through. It was positively eerie."

Many new ghosts would come in the summer of 69.

The hamlet where the Hiep Duc Resettlement Village was eventually erected had been overrun by the VC on 17 November 1965. Communist revolutionary justice took effect; as one reporter noted, "Officers who flew over the town Wednesday saw no sign of life. They saw the bodies of the district officials impaled on tall spikes around the headquarters building." ARVN troops retook Hiep Duc after tough fighting, but due to a lack of manpower, they abandoned the prize.

It wasn't until November 1967 that Operation Wheeler/Wallowa began finally to destroy the enemy stronghold. The push was spearheaded by the 1st Squadron, 1st Armored Cavalry, Americal Division, and supported by infantrymen of the 196th Brigade. Elements of the 1st Air Cavalry and 101st Airborne Divisions were also committed. Casualties were heavy but Hiep Duc was finally "pacified" in November 1968 after a final action along Nui Chom involving the 4–31. In March 1969, the civil affairs section of 4–31 had the Resettlement Village constructed in the ashes the NVA had left behind. LZ Siberia was also bulldozed out of the nearest hilltop for the village's security, and the former inhabitants were trucked and helicoptered in from refugee camps at Tam Ky and Nui Loc Son. Others were forced in from the tiny hamlets that still dotted the valley. There were 4,000 residents and the place garnered the nickname Tin City because the bamboo huts were sided with U.S.-made tin sheets. For the first time since 1965, the farmers of Hiep Duc returned to their fields. The communists' opinion of all this was made clear in May 1969, when sappers infiltrated the village and killed fifteen civilians. After that, enemy activity dropped to a low ebb and the 4–31, operating off LZ West and LZ Siberia, found little evidence of their presence. Direct defense for the village came from a small ARVN garrison on LZ Karen (located between West and Siberia on the ridge). The area, at least in MACV briefings, was being showcased as a model pacification zone.

That was overly optimistic; the NVA wanted this advance halted and the 1969 Summer Offensive would be one of the Americal's toughest battles. The division had a spotted history. Among the men who wore the Southern Cross patch of the Americal Division were many brave and dedicated ones, but there were those who said the Americal was the worst component of the U.S. Army, Vietnam. The three brigades of the division had arrived piecemeal and the first in-country, the 196th InfBde, began its new war on a sour note. In its first major engagement—in War Zone C of Tay Ninh Province, III Corps—the brigade commander lost control of the heavy fighting and was removed from command. That was in November 1966; in April 1967, the 196th was airlifted to Chu Lai, where it operated under the auspices of Task Force Oregon with a brigade each from the 25th and 101st Divisions. In October, the 198th arrived by air and sea to Duc Pho, and in December, the 11th joined them. At this point, TF Oregon was dissolved and the union of the 11th, 196th, and 198th Infantry Brigades heralded the uncohesive rebirth of the Americal Division. The 11th had made an emergency deployment from Schofield Barracks, Hawaii, and its officers were generally marginal performers. The 198th had worse problems. It had been hastily formed from the armored divisions at Fort Hood, Texas; when unit commanders were instructed to release men for the new unit, they reportedly purged their worst troops.* The conglomeration became known, derisively, as the Dollar Ninety Eight Brigade.

SP4 Hodierne, U.S. Army photographer during the 69 Summer Offensive, was in 1967 a civilian reporter on hand for the Americal's introduction to war. He wrote:

> They were frighteningly green. I remember choppering in to some makeshift LZ near one of their first fights late one afternoon. The place was chaos, guys walking around in the open, supplies dumped everywhere. I headed up the trail where I was told the contact was. About fifty meters up the trail, guys are coming my way, running, dropping gear, just running full tilt. Retreat would dignify what they did. The next morning, we all went back up the trail to where they had been hit. I don't remember

---

* Captain Downey noted another initial problem. "There was a rumor, one I was never able to substantiate, that the Americal had received the bulk of McNamara's Hundred Thousand, troops of very low IQ who had been drafted to take the place of those able-bodied men who had run to Canada and Sweden." To carry this further, these were the men most prone to getting themselves killed and committing atrocities.

much more than the body of a medic on top of a wounded guy he had been treating. It was clear to me they had fled, leaving their wounded behind. I didn't have much use for the Americal Division. It scared me to go out with them.

Such a characterization does injustice to most of the men in the Americal. Still, the division operated with a sense of disorder and dispirit which set it apart from the rest of the U.S. Army. Continued Hodierne, "The Americal had conscripted enlisted men, rookie NCOs, ROTC and OCS platoon leaders who planned to do their three years and out, company commanders with little more experience than their platoon leaders, and field grade officers all looking to get their tickets punched in the hole that read, 'combat command.' It could not have been a starker contrast to the units I saw in 1966, outfits like the 101st Airborne or the 1st Air Cav. In those days, fully half the enlisted men were volunteers, the NCOs were seasoned pros, and the company commanders knew what they were doing."

In addition, the Americal operated in one of the areas of South Vietnam where the population did not try to sit out the war, but where the people were the enemy. It was a brutal war of snipers, ambushes, and old women who planted booby traps—and where the Search & Destroy doctrine was most cruelly interpreted by frustrated and inexperienced U.S. forces.

My Lai tainted the entire division.

By 1969, the Americal Division was improved, but not shining. It now received its replacements like any other unit, and an effort was made to infuse better leadership; still, first impressions are lasting and the division's initial reputation turned away many of the Army's most ambitious and talented men. And, turning specifically to 4th Battalion, 31st Infantry, 196th Infantry Brigade, to the men out on LZ West and LZ Siberia who would bear the brunt of the 1969 Summer Offensive in Hiep Duc Valley, there was another dilemma—stagnation. Since reclaiming the valley in November 1968, the Polar Bears, as the battalion called itself, had encountered little resistance. June of 69 had seen sappers in the wire at the 4–31 Rear on LZ Baldy, and the line companies had made a ten-day foray into the adjacent Song Chang Valley. That had been about it, though. Their patrols were generally quiet and, thus, routine; and routines are very dangerous in war.

They were to bleed for their rustiness.

PFC Charles Jandecka, who joined Bravo Company 4–31 in August 1969, began his tour at the Americal Division Combat Center on the beach at Chu Lai. He hated it. Their hootches were overcrowded and scurrying with rats. The days were occupied with introduction classes, but the nights were hot, loud with rock music, depressing, and menacing. Throngs of GIs roamed about looking for diversions; some were stoned, some drunk; troublemakers hunted for other troublemakers or for scared kids. Fistfights broke out. Grunts called these men REMFs. Rear Echelon Mother Fuckers.

But there was camaraderie out on LZ West and LZ Siberia. There were also men who arrived with a sense of duty. PFC Robert Bleier, who came to Charlie 4–31 in May 1969, was one of them. A Notre Dame football star and a professional with the Pittsburgh Steelers, he hadn't joined the reserves fast enough to beat his draft notice. Mouthing the right cliches, he could have resisted it fashionably, but he didn't. Instead he thought, how could I explain shirking out to a son I may someday have? The battalion surgeon on LZ West remembered him for what he did not do. Of all the GIs lining up at his medical bunker looking for a way out of the field, Rocky Bleier, who had good reason to bitch, was never one of them. Such devotion could be tempered. The first afternoon Bleier arrived at LZ West as a replacement on a resupply bird, several GIs took him aside. They asked if he was a head or a juicer. Bewildered, he answered, "Well, I like to have an occasional martini, you know, on the rocks with an olive." They laughed. They said marijuana was on the decline, although at a recent pot party in the perimeter bunkers interrupted by NVA sappers, several American soldiers had died because they let their boring surroundings override their common sense.

The NVA regulars were trying to avoid a fight and Charlie Company's sweeps found little action. The men looked at patrolling as hot, trudging, and useless. Bleier saw more than one GI drop his rucksack during a rest break and kick it, screaming helplessly, "You goddamn green monkey! You sonuvabitch, you've been kicking my ass all day, now I'm going to kick yours!"

That was good for a laugh, good for morale. Other forms of catharsis were not. Bleier's platoon chased a running figure into a tree line. There they found several hootches and some people—one of the little groups that lived free of the wire-enclosed Resettlement Village—who probably supported the local NVA and VC with rice and places to hide. The

GIs exploded. They fragged the family bunkers, then started burning the thatch hootches; the women wailed hysterically as their few belongings were consumed in the fire. Bleier could only think, this is absurd. One of the GIs grabbed an old papasan, kneed him in the crotch, then bashed him on the head with the butt of his M16. The man dropped to his knees in agony, and the kid screamed at him, "You motherfucking, slant-eyed dink! You're the reason we're over here!"

Some of the Polar Bears were getting flaky. Patrols were faked. GIs assigned to listening posts off the LZs often just holed up in an empty perimeter bunker. Men fell asleep on guard duty in the bush even though sometimes when they moved out the next morning, they found their claymore mines turned around to face them and the trip handles of flares secured with string. Ammunition was quietly tossed into the brush on patrols to lighten the load. Shamming became popular because it was mildly punished at best; GIs could stretch out R and Rs for days by hanging with buddies in the rear. So could men who dreamed up any excuse to get out of the bush for awhile.

"It was a ludicrous way to run a war," Bleier wrote.

SP4 Barry Parsons rotated to Alpha 4–31 in April 1969, after three months as a security guard in Chu Lai. He described ten of their hard, drab days in and around Landing Zone West in his pocket diary:

Beginning to hate Jim Dean more everyday. Matt is a pain in the ass too. If he doesn't watch him he'll be walking around with a busted mouth. . . . They sure do like to hassel you up here on LZ West. The CO jumped in Sticks shit & mine. Told us both to shave off our side burns. They finally had memorial services for those two fellows who were killed. . . . We're walking a little over 6 klicks one way. Down Nui Liet. What an ass kicking walk it was. All of us are burning up from the sun. When we were at the top of Nui Liet the CO told us to go back down the hill again to the same place. 3 Dinks were spotted there. Boy was everyone mad about it. A lot of us didn't want to go at all, and LT Rice almost had a mutiny on his hands. CO wouldn't even drop us in water or food either. That really gave everybody the ass. Walked down and everybody is either sick or getting there. Got almost to our position when guys started falling out left and right. . . . Our squad almost got caught not going out on LP last night by LT Rice and Top Price. They walked right pass Sticks and didn't see him. I thought it was all over for us. . . . Pat and I are taking out the LP tonight. Probably go to Bunker 29 too. We waited for Pat to show up but at 9:00 we went down to B-29 without him. Finally he came down all fucked up on pot. Rayborn crashed on guard twice last night which gave me the ass. He could have gotten us all in trouble. . . . By the way they act you'd think it was stateside up on a LZ. . . . Today is just another detail like always, and we're still working on wire laying. . . . Sometimes a fellow can get real depressed over here in Nam. It's the same routine every day.

These men were draftees, but they were not antiwar. They saw problems in their units but did not consider them on the verge of collapse. Sure, we smoke Mary Jane on the LZs, Parsons reckoned, but there's a time and place for everything. He saw only one man in his platoon smoke grass in the bush; some GIs caught him and punched him around.

SP5 Joseph Kralich, a conscientious objector and senior battalion medic, noted that once the battle started, malingering stopped. He saw only one patient on LZ West who was not physically injured: the man's best friend had been killed with him in one of the first, violent contacts, and he was in a trance. As for the rest, Kralich commented, "Most were tired and in physical and emotional pain, but still resolved to survive. Out of water, ammo, and medical supplies, they were forced to survive on instinct and training, but with solid leadership being there when called upon."

Combat finally turned many of them into real soldiers.

"Considering the conditions and horrendous odds," Private Jandecka wrote after the summer battles, "the men of 4–31 performed markedly well. In spite of their battle weary condition, the men followed orders faithfully. Oh yes, often with much grumbling but always as ordered."

■ On 23 February 1969, the NVA staged a midnight sapper attack on the 1st MarDiv HQ and 26th Marines CP on Division Ridge. They breached the wire and captured several bunkers, but were driven off after a night of close combat. At the same time, NVA and VC units attempting to sever Highway One were beaten back by the 1st Marines and the 1st Military Police Battalion. Other NVA units approaching Da Nang under cover of these attacks were intercepted by the 7th Marines and routed after a brutal, three-day battle which included hand-to-hand combat.

On 19 March, NVA sappers and infantry breached the wire at Liberty Bridge, manned by a company of 1/5 and an artillery battery of 2/11, and gutted three bunkers with flamethrowers before a heroic, hasty counterattack plugged the gap and artillery fire was brought to bear at pointblank range.

On 31 March, the 7th Marines began Operation Oklahoma Hills, an eight-week foray into and around Charlie Ridge. At the same time, on 29 April, B and D Companies of the regiment conducted a bloody foray into the Arizona.

On 9 May, the 5th Marines executed an expert deployment around a large NVA unit moving through the Arizona, then devastated them with air and arty. ("We caught them with their pants down," said 2dLt James Webb, platoon leader with D/1/5. "Our FO was calling for artillery on four hundred NVA and he was sixth on the priority list!" After recovering, the NVA struck back at the isolated companies; this was later immortalized in Webb's novel, *Fields of Fire,* and it was the day his Marine called Snake posthumously won the Navy Cross for dragging wounded men through a withering crossfire.) The battle lasted three days.

On 7 June, the *90th NVA Regiment* attacked 1/5 Marines in the Arizona, sparking a week-long battle. The NVA retreated to Charlie Ridge.

What followed those four months of sustained activity was called the Summer Lull. It was during this time that the 1st Battalion, 7th Marines, 1st Marine Division, under the command of LtCol John A. Dowd, crossed the Song Vu Gia into the Arizona Territory. Their operation continued through the last six weeks of the lull; then the 1969 Summer Offensive almost buried them.

Chapter Two

The Arizona

It was almost twilight when Delta Company moved down a weathered railroad trestle without tracks. Nicholas Cominos looked back over his shoulder. It was another hot night in the Arizona flatlands, and in the fading light the company was moving to a new night position to disorient enemy mortarmen. The column was perfectly spaced, everyone silhouetted, faces hidden in the shadows of helmet brims. This is really beautiful, Cominos thought; this is what the poet sees sometimes.

It became his lasting mental portrait of the operation.

The 1st Battalion, 7th Marines entered the Arizona Territory on 1 July 1969 as part of Operation Forsythe Grove. The op had been hastily organized after reports of an impending attack on Hill 65 by six hundred NVA believed to be massing in northern Arizona. To preempt this, 2/5 Marines took up blocking positions in western Arizona, 1/5 Marines in eastern Arizona, and 1/7 Marines were to sweep south between this cordon. Alpha 1/7 (Capt Edward T. Clark III) was helicoptered into southern Arizona at first light to form the final block for the sweep. They took some fire, but gunships quieted it. The assault companies staged on the banks of the Song Vu Gia below Hill 65: Bravo 1/7 (1stLt Allen E. Weh), Delta 1/7 (Capt Brian J. Fagan), and attached Lima 3/7 (Capt Jon K. Rider). Charlie 1/7 (1stLt Raymond A. Hord) was the reserve on Hill 65.

The river crossing commenced at 0600 in a rolling barrage of two thousand tank and artillery rounds. The tanks were firing from atop Hill 65, over the heads of the troops in the river, devastating the tree lines hundreds of yards inland with high-explosive and white phosphorus shells. The arty worked across terrain features which offered good firing vantages and into likely avenues of enemy retreat. Amphibious tractors ferried Bravo and Lima Companies across the Vu Gia; however, loose sand, variations in water depth, and mechanical difficulties left most of the amtracs stuck at midstream. Cables were attached to tow them out. Bravo and Lima fanned out from the opposite beach line, securing it, while Major General Simpson helicoptered to the starting point to confer with Lieutenant Colonel Dowd. Dowd approved of the contingency plan to use helicopters and, within thirty minutes, the remainder of the battalion assault force was across the river. Ahead of them and on their flanks, Phantom jets plastered the countryside with bombs and napalm. The artillery continued to pound in. There was virtually no return fire. The sun was the enemy this day. Alpha Company, the southern block, had deployed on a small ridge called the Hot Dog and it was an eight-klick hump from the Vu Gia to link up with them.

The following day, Operation Forsythe Grove was terminated. Intelligence had been faulty. No large NVA force was detected and "only" five men had been killed: a man from L/3/7 hit by a short U.S. 8-inch howitzer round, and four NVA who were caught in the sweep. At this point, 1/7 Marines withdrew to the corridor between Charlie Ridge and the Arizona; they secured Route 4 as combat engineers reopened it all the way to the Thuong Duc Special Forces outpost deep in the mountains. Then, on 17 July, the battalion conducted a second river crossing. The 5th Marines were leaving An Hoa for Operation Durham Peak in the Que Sons, and 1/7 was left virtually alone to police the Arizona. Their continued operation had no name, but it lasted four more weeks. The Battalion CP set up on the Hot Dog, and the four rifle companies scoured the Arizona flatlands, constantly hunting, moving at least every two days, repeatedly crisscrossing the area. Chasing phantoms.

It was no different from the dozens of continuing Search & Destroy missions being conducted throughout South Vietnam on any given day, all of which could be described with one word: miserable. Every day—every single day—the companies broke up into platoon patrol bases from which the squads went out hunting. The thermometer hovered above 100 degrees, the dust from the paddies covered everything, and the men moved listlessly under eighty pounds of gear: helmet, flak jacket, frag grenades, CS tear gas grenades, M16 bandoliers, extra M60 ammunition, claymore mines, trip flares, an M72 LAW rocket, pack, rifle. At night, they went on ambush patrols. There was little rest from the heat and the humping and, while men looked fit and tanned, their eyes were sunken, their faces drawn. The U.S. Army prided itself in getting a hot meal to the troops every day, even in the field. The U.S. Marine Corps did not have the helicopters or the troops for such a logistical luxury. They got helicopter resupply only every fourth day, usually enough C rations for two or three days, and enough water to drink only sparingly, none to shave. The water was shipped to the field in 155mm artillery canisters and reeked of chlorine. Guys wrote home for Kool Aid just to kill the taste. Bomb crater water was even worse.

Miserable, just fucking miserable.

For Corporal Cominos, a squad leader in Delta Company, the worst thing about the days were the fields of shoulder-high, razor-sharp elephant grass. The men emerged from those briars with their arms and hands bleeding and the leather of their jungle boots peeling. The worst thing about the nights were the mosquitoes. They rose in swarms in the hot night air, and Cominos always slept with his poncho wrapped around him like a cocoon.

One had to find ways to endure. Morale in the battalion was never such that Cominos ever seriously considered bagging a patrol, but he did discard his shirt and T-shirt. He wore his flak jacket over a bare chest, and he shit-canned most of the vest's fiberglass plates; he left only four—one over his heart, his chest, and two in back over his kidneys. He also threw away his Marine-issue pack and used a captured NVA rucksack; it was more comfortable and utilitarian. The most-used piece of gear was his green towel, tucked between neck and flak jacket collar, to wipe the sweat from his face every couple minutes.

It was a brutalizing existence, made even worse by stagnation. During its weeks in the Arizona, 1/7 Marines made no solid contacts with the enemy. Their prize kept eluding them; mostly what they found were booby traps and stolid, unanswering villagers who populated the few hamlets still left in this free-fire zone. Frustrations simmered in the grunts, but they did not become murderers. Sergeant Lowery noted:

We definitely did not go over and just blow civilians away for no reason at all. We never did that. All these stories you hear about search and destroy where they went through and they killed every man, woman, and child is a bunch of bullshit. We did kill every duck, chicken, and water buffalo that we came across. We poisoned all the wells. We burned all the hootches with the old Zippo lighter. These hootches would go up and you could hear all kinds of stuff popping inside of them—it was ammunition they had hidden inside the straw. These people were all supporters of the NVA and VC, and they deserved whatever happened to them. But unless a gook had a weapon we didn't kill him.

Still, the psychological pressures of Search & Destroy could be intense. There were too many gray areas. On his first tour, Lowery had taken out a night ambush near a ville. He set his M60 team in atop a small hill, then was placing the ambush below the mound when he noticed the girl—a Vietnamese woman was squatting in the brush, peering intently at the machine gun pos. Lowery ran towards her, shouting, "Halt! *Dung lai, dung lai!*" The woman bolted and he triggered a hurried burst; her arm jerked, but she kept running. Lowery crammed a fresh mag into his M16, braced, and emptied it into her back. They gathered around the mamasan. She was a pretty girl, they all commented, clean, her teeth unstained by betel nut. And she was still alive, breathing in labored gasps. Their new corpsman looked at her in horror, mumbling, "What do I do?" "Fuck it," Lowery said, "put her out of her misery." The corpsman pulled out his .45 automatic and started shooting. He kept pulling the trigger until the slide locked back, and he kept mumbling, "What do I do, what do I do!"

Was that an atrocity? No, it was necessary.

But you gotta understand, Lowery continued, the new corpsman didn't give a shit what happened to these worthless gooks; and in that, he spoke for a certain percentage of all grunts.

Most did what they had to do to survive in an alien, hostile environment.

Most men didn't have time for much thinking. Cominos, from a solid Greek Orthodox family, had joined the Marines after college graduation, a rarity in the grunts. What was also rare was that he volunteered for the bush not only because he wanted to prove something—but because he believed. Deep down, though, the only thing that seemed pertinent were the men in his squad. The only questions he asked were how many klicks we going today, which squad's got point, who's taking out the ambush tonight? The most lasting impression Corporal Cominos had of the operation in the Arizona was not the daily pain or the occasional cruelties, but the quiet courage of the grunts. They endured and they endured and they endured, he thought. Everyone bitched and cursed, but they had a job to do and they did it. He always remembered his

M79 man, "Carbo" Carbahal from California. The man was in intense pain for days, but only when he could barely walk did he report his injuries. He was medevacked and it turned out he had stress fractures in his shins. He had kept his mouth shut because he didn't want to let his buddies down.

On 16 July, 1st Battalion, 7th Marines walked from Hill 37 to the vicinity of Hill 65, from which they would cross the Vu Gia back into the Arizona. It was a dreary, hot, dusty day as the grunts walked down Route 4, one column on either side of the dirt road. Lieutenant Peters of Delta Company plodded along with his platoon. He had his M16 in the normal bush position: sling over shoulder, weapon hanging at the waist pointed left, left hand gripping the plastic stock, right hand on the trigger guard, thumb on the safety catch ready to push it to semi.

Peters was in the righthand column as they passed a hootch. He turned to his left to tell something to the man behind him just as a figure ran to the gateway in front of the hootch and threw something. In one movement, Peters whipped around into a squat, left hand thrusting the barrel in the direction of the movement, and he found himself a second from firing with his M16 in the face of a four-year-old boy. The kid had run out to throw a rock at the Americans. He stared terrified at the rifle. Embarrassed, Peters walked on.

The next morning, the men helicoptered into the Arizona.

They moved with a steady drumroll of air and arty prepping their path but, like before, they found little except for blood trails. Lieutenant Peters's platoon was walking point for Delta Company and they paused in one tree line while arty was processed into the next one. When the fires lifted, the platoon started across on line, more concerned about the incredible heat than the remote chance of anybody still being in the tree line. They were about forty meters from it when one of the M79 grenadiers got bored. He called to Peters, "Hey, can I bloop 'em?"

"Yeah, go ahead." The old recon by fire.

The kid fired a grenade into the tree line—and the woods suddenly erupted with the jackhammering of a dozen AK47 assault rifles. Everyone scrambled towards the dike ahead. Peters was distinctly aware that he was buckling the chin strap on his helmet; that was something he instinctively did when things seemed bad. Heavy fire snapped overhead and the Marines could only shove their M16s over the berm and fire blind.

Peters's heart was racing. He had only one clear thought: where are the bastards! The tree line was a briar patch.

His radioman lay beside him; his shouting snapped Peters back to the business at hand. "It's the captain! He says pop the gas!"

That's right, Peters suddenly thought, we can do that. Each platoon carried an E8 launcher which fired CS tear gas. He called up his gas man and told him to fire into the trees. The grunt was on his knees, unshouldering the launcher. "It won't work 'cause one of the legs is broken."

"You mean to tell me you've been carrying this sonuvabitch for a month, and now you tell me it doesn't work!" Peters shouted in frustration. "Give me that!" In a rash moment of anger, he hefted the launcher and scrambled over the berm. He became the lone target and dust kicked up around him as he ran to the next dike. He dropped his pack and rested the launcher against it; then he removed the top, yanked the lanyard, and the vials of CS began popping from their foam rubber mounting like champagne corks. The launcher bucked backwards from the recoil, until it was almost shooting straight up. Peters heard one of his grunts yelling, "Lieutenant, you gotta lay on top of it or it's going to kick back in your face!" He jumped on it, very aware that his nose was six inches from the shells zipping out. He couldn't hear the M16s or AK47s anymore—he was too engrossed, too scared, almost laughing, you gotta be kidding me, what am I doing!

At the last shot, he suddenly noticed there was a pause. He looked up. Tear gas covered the tree line and the paddy ahead. His first thought was to charge and the hand-and-arm signal to fix bayonets flashed in his head; then he remembered they didn't carry bayonets. He dropped to his knees and twisted around, raising his hand to wave his platoon forward. He meant to shout let's go!, but he got only the first word out and the platoon was instantly coming over the dike. They ran right towards the tree line, shouting, coughing from the gas, firing from the hip. Peters—almost aglow with pride—joined their frantic rush and they crashed into the trees with only one man taking a minor graze wound across his arm.

There were no NVA, only more blood trails.

Meanwhile, the battalion command group was being lifted into the area aboard Sea Knights. Air strikes were run to suppress enemy fire and the door gunners pulled long bursts into the dried out tree lines. Still, more than a few AK47 rounds slashed through the elephant grass and thudded into the dirt around the CP Marines as they unassed the birds and organized. No one dove for cover—there really was no place to hide. The platoon finally moved out as the fire petered out. Once again, the sweep's objective was the Hot Dog and the battalion pushed through the initial, evaporating resistance only to be rubbed raw by the sun and the distance. Lieutenant Peters, for one, had to reach into himself to keep going. The firefight had exhausted them, and they stumbled like drunks under their packs. They bunched up. When the column halted, they could only stand in a sweaty daze; they were supposed to drop to one knee and watch the flanks. Peters and his platoon sergeant walked the line, yelling themselves hoarse.

The CP column was moving slowly too. They were burdened under radios and mortars, and some men wished they would take fire just so they could lie down. As it was, they paused only to put the torch to any hootches in their path. Guys heaved rice baskets and work benches into the fires, and took photographs. The CP finally set up on the Hot Dog before nightfall, and Alpha Company dug in around them. The Hot Dog became the CP's home for the remainder of the operation. They moved every two days from knoll to knoll so the NVA could not zero in on them, until by the end of the op they had humped up and down the Hot Dog three times. Even in the bush, it was mostly a routine.

Every day was the same, but a little different.

On their sixth day back on the Hot Dog, General Simpson helicoptered in for a brief visit. That night, LCpl Donald R. Wells, the new battalion radioman, saw his first North Vietnamese regulars. He and a buddy were sitting on a boulder on the perimeter, checking out the lowlands with a GreenEye night scope. About four hundred meters away they spotted six figures crossing a paddy, hunkered under packs, AKs, and B40 rocket-propelled grenade launchers. They quickly radioed the CP but it took fifteen minutes to get the 81mm mortars ready. Their first shot was way off, and Wells watched disgusted as the NVA ran and disappeared into a tree line. A few more rounds impacted into the paddy and finally the battalion liaison officer, a mustang lieutenant, got an M14 rifle with a night scope and opened up. It was impossible to tell if he hit anything.

They moved out the next night in a drizzle. Wells humped the PRC25 radio behind Lieutenant Colonel Dowd, M16 muzzle down over his shoulder, the radio handset wrapped in plastic to keep out the rain. They left a crew with their 106mm recoilless rifle on the hill, dug in and hidden by brush; Dowd planned to double back and catch any NVA who might move into the area after their apparent departure. As soon as they began hiking downhill, villagers—mostly women and kids who'd been congregating from the moment the Marines began saddling up—swarmed into the perimeter. The Marines burned their trash pits so the enemy couldn't use anything, but a few C ration cans always survived. The CP humped a thousand meters through the paddies, and it was pitch black when a call came over Wells's radio: the group on the hill had twenty NVA moving near them. Dowd grinned widely and told Wells to pass the word that they were turning around and heading back. A second call came: the NVA had disappeared before they could sight the 106. They were almost back to the Hot Dog when the group called again: four NVA had just reappeared. The black stillness was suddenly cracked by a quick roar and flash from the 106, then the explosion of a beehive round shredding foliage. The subsequent patrol found heavy blood trails.

Bravo Company took a few RPGs and Chicoms that night; they medevacked six wounded in the morning, then moved on. The CP moved in after them, setting up for two days and one night in their old foxholes; Lieutenant Colonel Dowd split the CP and took a dozen men in a "jump" group to Charlie Company. They moved out at night through the thick mud of the paddy lowlands. A killer hump, Wells thought; the muck extracted much energy. The area was pocked with shell craters, thirty feet across and deep with muddy water, and they skirted along their rims. Wells was deathly afraid of them. Cripes, he thought, with this radio and pack and ammo, batteries, and junk strapped to my back, I must weigh 250 pounds. If I fell in, I'd drown before they could pull me out.

The men finally got across and were setting up in a tree line when the point men trotted back with five Vietnamese males they'd surprised. The radio reported other successes that night: Delta spotted fifty NVA with a GreenEye moving in a wood line, called in artillery airbursts, and Bravo swept in to count a few bodies. In the morning, Dowd set his jump CP into position, then took Wells and a few grunts on a hike to Charlie Company. Lieutenant Colonel Dowd and Lieutenant Hord were talking, and Wells waited and munched on some wild sugarcane. One of the daylight patrols moved past; a skull was affixed to the back of a grunt's pack, its jaw bouncing as he walked so it looked like the skull was talking. Wells and the grunts shouted their approval.

The jump CP spent four days with Charlie Company, the last day being the only eventful one. Wells was sitting around on the perimeter when a Vietnamese appeared from a far tree line. There were shouts, then a grunt opened up with his M60 and the man dashed away with rounds kicking up dirt all around him. There were hoots and laughs when the man jumped, unscathed, into some trees. Later that day, Lieutenant Hord radioed the CP to complain that a certain scout-sniper was zeroing in his rifle by shooting water buffalos. The sniper had a good reputation; Dowd cracked a grin and told Wells to radio back that they must be enemy transport. The day after the execution of the buffs, Lieutenant Colonel Dowd took his jump CP back to the main group on the Hot Dog. That afternoon, a helicopter from battalion rear dropped off a small generator and electric hair clippers. Lance Corporal Wells spent the day making himself scarce. His hair was long by Marine standards and he intended to keep it that way. Besides the peace symbol drawn on his helmet cover, it was the only symbol of his minor rebellion against the lifers.

Captain Clark of Alpha and Captain Fagan of Delta were both calm professionals on their second tours. Lieutenant Hord of Charlie was also good but, in comparison, an eager youngster. Weh of Bravo was also a lieutenant, but of a harsher cut. An aggressive and blunt man, he had originally enlisted at seventeen; after college and OCS, he'd spent three months in 1967 as a platoon leader with 3d Recon before being wounded and evacuated. He rotated back in September 68, spent four months as an air observer, then requested infantry duty again. Weh prided himself in melding his company into a well-oiled killing machine, and his diary notes from the Arizona operation sound as if in war, he had found his natural state:

I planned a platoon ambush about 400–500 meters down the trail west of our pos the night we set up (July 20th). At dark the platoon moved out and within 45 min had a meeting engagement with four gooks— result 1 dead NVN and about 4 of my Marines wounded by grenades they threw. I sent a squad out to pick up the casualties and bring them back so they could continue to establish an ambush. We called a Medevac and waited. About 2330 the chopper came in and with his lights on came down right outside our lines. As it settled it was hit by mortar and an RPG rocket and concurrently automatic weapons fire opened up on us from all over. The chopper took off (luckily he made it) and as he did his trigger happy gunner raked our position with a burst of .50 cal M.G. fire. . . . We then took some mortar rounds, RPG rockets, and AK47 fire that was exceptionally well placed grazing fire for the next two hours.

Bravo and Delta Companies usually worked in unison, so it was on 25 July that Lieutenant Peters made a mildly horrified note in his own diary concerning Bravo. Three NVA had been killed in one of Bravo's ambushes; the grunts ripped one's shirt off and carved "B 1/7" in his back. The head was hacked off another corpse. Peters had never seen anything like it. The rumor was that the NVA had treated some of Bravo's dead in a like manner, and the frustrated grunts were taking their payback. That was how the Marines put it: Payback is a Mother Fucker.

Morale among the grunts could not have been described as enthusiastic. The sweat and dust of the Arizona did not allow for that. But the men of 1/7 were remarkably untouched by the problems beginning to plague other units and they performed the mean task at hand professionally and, on occasion, with elan. They were one of the best battalions in the division.

The character of a unit begins at the top, and that was most clear with John Aloysius Dowd. He looked like a football tackle and was the father of six; he'd put in two years with the Merchant Marines and at age twenty joined the Corps; he was commissioned via OCS after enlisted boot camp. Vietnam was his first war and one of his company commanders, Weh, described him as a "hound straining at the leash." Dowd took over the battalion after seven months on the staff at 1st MarDiv HQ, and he literally revelled like a Patton in his first combat command: toting a grease gun, unflappable under fire, a shamrock drawn on his flak jacket. He led from the front.

That was one side of Dowd, the tough-guy image. To his company commanders, he was known as Uncle Jack and they appreciated his style of delegating and supervising. He did not ram orders down his captains' throats, but assigned a mission, offered a positive attitude and motivation, and let them run their own shows. Dowd appreciated the stress the men were under and he made an effort to appear relaxed and to keep everyone informed and involved. He spent a good portion of his time with the line companies, talking with the captains and lieutenants, but mostly with the grunts, just shooting the breeze and quietly trying to get a feel for morale.

He appeared a happy man.

Lieutenant Colonel Dowd took over in March, and on 21 April 1969, he won a Silver Star. When a night listening post spotted two hundred NVA preparing to cross the Vu Gia in sampans, Dowd joined the small group and helped direct the subsequent barrage. The NVA unit disintegrated in confusion and by morning light, the Marines counted seventy-one bodies in the streambed weeds. One Marine had been slightly wounded. Eight days later, Dowd took B Company into the Arizona. Captain Fagan's D Company had led that first foray, conducting a quiet night crossing of the Vu Gia and securing the shore for the arrival of Dowd and B Company the next morning. B Company immediately kicked off towards a suspected NVA concentration. Intelligence was right this time and, in short order, Bravo was bogged down under automatic weapons and mortar fire with heavy casualties. Fagan led Delta on a flanking attack which overran the mortar site and an NVA battalion camp. They consolidated for the night and weathered a mortar raid. At dawn, the NVA were still around them. The air and arty were brought in Danger Close and drove off the enemy.

The April operation had solidified Dowd's standing in the battalion. It had much the same result for Captain Fagan of Delta Company. He had taken over only weeks earlier from a steely and effective commander, but by the time D Company walked out of the Arizona, he had won the trust of his men and the first of his Bronze Star recommendations. The harshest review of commanders comes from the grunts on the firing line, but most echoed the appraisal of Lieutenant Peters and Corporal Cominos. They thought Fagan was the absolute best; he was a concerned man with a dry wit who, most importantly, had mastered tactics and supporting arms.

Fagan was twenty-five years old. He was from Warren, Ohio, one of seven children of an insurance salesman whom the WWII draft had sent to Patton's army and who came home with a battlefield commission. Fagan went Navy ROTC in college and received his gold bars and degree the same day in 1963. He married right out of Basic School and took his wife to Hawaii for his first duty station. In the spring of 65, his unit deployed to Da Nang as part of the buildup. He completed that tour as a battalion staff officer with the 4th Marines and, in 1967, was prepared to leave the Marine Corps. He had a wife and three children and had already lined up a civil engineer position; but for reasons he could not fully articulate, Fagan turned down the job and stayed in the Corps. He was training the new lieutenants at Quantico when he made the decision, and everything in his upbringing told him his place was really with the young Marines in combat. To temper such idealism with the cynicism of Vietnam, he should have felt alienated from the rest of the war effort. Unfortunately for the novelists, Fagan happened to be an exceptional leader with compassion for his men who also believed in the cause. His only complaints were those typical of hawks.

Captain Fagan had a good company in a good battalion. Still, there were occasional problems. Marijuana had been an unknown his first tour. It was not apparent in Delta Company, but occasionally the company gunnery sergeant would report that a man was not ready to go on an operation. They'd leave him in the rear and only later would Fagan hear that the man's buddies had caught him smoking grass and refused to have him along. Fagan had Delta for six months and they were in the bush for five and a half; he volunteered to keep them out precisely because he didn't want them exposed to the corruptions of the rear. The grunts bitched about his enthusiasm for the field and, if he'd been a marginal performer, there might have been problems. As it was, most grunts seemed proud of their reputation. It was a matter of risking death in combat but having a common goal versus disintegrating in rear-area squabbles. A third of Delta Company was draftees, but Fagan couldn't tell them from the volunteers. They did their best and he tried to do his best by them. They were youngsters, he thought, unlettered kids, tough, humorous, sarcastic, faithful, and loyal to each other. And vulnerable. He'd seen men cry with hurt and frustration after the frenzied efforts to patch up and medevac a grunt who'd just lost his leg to a booby trap; then they'd pick up their rifles and keep going.

LCpl John G. Bradley, of Charlie Company, was the eternal kid Marine: skinny, red from the sun, impatient with the boredom and sweat of humping, exhilarated in a way, though, with the unshakable feeling of adventure.

Bradley grew up in Marysville, Washington, living off and on between his divorced parents and graduating from high school as a Boy Scout and the All American Boy. In 1968 when he graduated, the counterculture hadn't yet made an impact on his hometown, and his reactions to the campus protesters on television were traditional. He had no sympathy for the messages on the placards held by his peers, and all he saw was anarchy. All in all, though, the war seemed very distant until that summer after graduation when a local boy was killed. Bradley was a supporter of the war but, most of all, he was young and curious; two months out of school, his mother signed the papers so he could enlist at age seventeen.

He volunteered for Vietnam and reported to C Company in February 1969; it was still an adolescent adventure at first and, although mortars hit the battalion rear his first night, excitement overrode fear. His first firefight was an adrenaline high. Such spirit was soon rubbed raw in the unglamorous sweat and dust of the repetitious patrolling and ambushing. Fatigue became the byword. Bradley made his first kill in April; walking point for his squad down a paddy trail as they returned from a night patrol, he saw something hunched over the path in the dawn light. He shouted to halt, then pumped his M16 into the figure when it bolted. He approached the body, rushing with the thrill of getting a confirmed kill; then he almost vomitted when he saw it was an unarmed mamasan. They found a booby trap on the trail, which they blew in place, and Bradley's mind flashed between excitement and revulsion, finally clearing the slate with the thought: fuck it, if we'd gotten here fifteen minutes later, the bitch would have blown my legs off.

He never told his parents the truth about the kill.

There was only one saving grace out in the mud—the professionalism and camaraderie of his squad. Harvey Peay, the squad leader, was sharp. A tough Kentucky boy, he ignored rules and regs and talked mostly about going home, buying a GTO, and marrying his girl friend. He also seemed to thrive in the bush. Mouse Cullen, his fire team leader, was saving his money so he could go to college. Schaffer was a big guy who loved good times and, deciding that Australia beat Vietnam, never came back from R and R. Dutch Sterling, a grenadier, was a mustached kid from California who loved to bullshit about surfing and who had a peace medallion around his neck (taped to his dog tags so it wouldn't jingle on patrol). Buttons just wanted to finish his tour and get back to the farm.

They were a little world unto themselves, bound together, as far as Bradley was concerned, by an unspoken sense of friendship and dedication as Marines. They never discussed the war. Between patrols, they played cards in the dirt and talked of hunting trips; past contacts; some lifer who pissed them off; and girls—those they'd screwed, those they wanted to screw, those they wanted their buddies to think they'd screwed. Just plain old good guys, Bradley thought. They were typical of all Marines, he reckoned, their ambitions honed to a few essentials: killing gooks in the bush and, in the rear, figuring ways to sneak into the ville to get laid.

The new operation was more of the same—hot and plodding. Lance Corporal Bradley made cryptic notes in his diary, an eighteen year old's view of the Arizona Territory:

July 5th: The damn gooks are raising a storm shooting the hell out of the birds. tracer all over. and we go next hope this isn't my last entry. I love you mom and dad and be proud of me if something goes wrong. Gotta sky now here come our birds love John.

July 10: Gues what an asshole I must have been worried to death. "Orders" kill & destroy every moveing body shoot. We had light contact yesterday and got a gook. Burned our first vill were to serch and burn all hootchs and food. Good thing we packed loads of chow. Water is going to be a hassle though.

July 11th 1969: Change of orders again. question the people and don't destroy there homes. What the hell is this war comeing to. We had a good thing going now there fucking it up. Thats officers for you.

July 13th: Got hit last nite and a real mess. mortars and hit from 3 sides. We had security for the bn CP when at about 8:30 we got hit. I was sitting with pay & sterling have some chocolate when they hit. We started thoughing out some shit when sterling started to run out of Bluper rounds. I ran from cover to get some more when a 30 opened up. The rds were flying all around. I could see and feel the tracers. When I got the rds then got to cover. Sgt Schick said he was putting me up for the bronze star the next morning. That be great the kid will even have a medal when he gets home. We didn't take any casualties which is fine! Well gotta go. Miss you all so very much.

Aug 2: Haven't had much to write till today. Last nite when we came off our ambush I popped a green pop up and it started a fire. We were up till about 3 in the morning putting the damn'd thing out. Yours truly got chewed out roally. But I give a fuck. Were not doing much except moveing continuelly to keep the gooks off-balance.

Aug 3rd: Schick though a gas gernade into a hotch today and mouse and sterling got the gas in the face when a change of wind came up. funnist thing in a good while.

August 5: Rocky hit a booby trap today. Messed him up pretty bad. Rodriguey had a hell of a concusion an shrapmetal in the leg. wish it had been me god I'd love to get off this operation.

Lance Corporal Bradley saw living North Vietnamese only once during the operation, near the end of July. He'd been walking point that day, leading the platoon down a narrow trail in a thick tree line. They stopped for a break and Bradley gave his camera to Peay and posed, leaning against a boulder, sweaty blond hair on his forehead, cigarette dangling, sweat towel and undershirt soaked under his flak jacket, his M16 resting on his thigh in one hand, his helmet in the other. No sooner had Peay snapped the photo than Bradley surged with adrenaline—four NVA, in fatigues and bush hats and toting AKs, walked unaware from the bamboo. They were right over Peay's shoulder, maybe seventy yards away, and Bradley shouted and opened fire the same time Dutch Sterling did. Peay instantly spun and fired too, as one of the NVA fell heavily in the brush. Two comrades grabbed him under the arms and ran back into the tree line as Bradley, Peay, and Dutch sprinted after them. It was incredible, Bradley unable to describe it: heart pounding, sweat glistening on his arms as he fired on the run, and the NVA running, right there in the open on the trail, bobbing in his gun sights. Dutch halted long enough to drop two M79 rounds amid the fleeing NVA; the explosions were on target but they disappeared into some thick vegetation around a bend. The Marines halted, wary of an ambush, and were suddenly exhausted, coming down from the adrenaline. The rest of the platoon jogged up, asking what the hell was going on, and they checked out the only signs that the North Vietnamese had even been there—a splash of blood and a dropped canteen where the first man had fallen.

■ In the seven weeks that 2dLt Lawrence H. Orefice commanded a platoon of Mike Company, 3d Battalion, 7th Marines, three of his men were killed and six wounded. All the casualties came from booby traps.

That's how it was in the An Hoa Basin. It could change a man. Orefice learned that on his first night patrol. His platoon had palace guard for the regiment on Hill 55 when movement was detected; it appeared that a mortar tube was being set up in the tree line near the local ville. They reconned by fire from the bunker line; then Orefice took out a squad. They found nothing. The squad leader entered the nearest hootch and dragged out a young papasan, shaking him by his shirt front, slapping him, shouting questions in his face. The Vietnamese did not resist, nor did he whimper. He just kept repeating, "No VC, no VC." Orefice shouted to stop it. The young corporal did, then said simply and without sarcasm, "We gotta do this, lieutenant. They're all a bunch of VC sympathizers out to get our ass. And if we don't get rough with them, they're not going to do anything for us."

The corporal was a good Marine and Orefice looked at the stoic papasan. He knows, Orefice thought with a burning frustration that would become a daily pill; this gook knows exactly who was here and he won't tell us!

Lieutenant Orefice had few answers.

Orefice had come to the Marines out of Windsor, Connecticut, for the same reasons many of his generation joined the Peace Corps: the patriotic challenge evoked by JFK, the desire to help. He went to Vietnam, though, with doubts, not about the validity of that country's goals, but about the realism of attaining them. Can the ARVN carry the ball? Such thoughts evaporated once he joined his platoon. He was now directly responsible for thirty lives and the daily pressures of that allowed for little reflection. He thought his company commander, Captain Stanat, was good, as was his platoon sergeant, Staff Sergeant Hebert, as were the grunts. His total allegiance was to them.

If Orefice never stopped feeling sympathy for the plight of the common villager, he also grew to view them all as potential threats. One of his sergeants carried a few Chinese Communist grenades in his pack in case they accidentally killed an unarmed Vietnamese; place the grenades on the body, radio in a confirmed kill, avoid a hassle. They never had occasion to do this, but it seemed judicious.

The enemy was all around and invisible.

In July, they evacuated the Chau Son Village and resettled the people in a controlled zone near Hill 55. Without the support of the populace, coerced or voluntary, the local VC would dry up. It sounded good on paper. An Army captain from civil affairs, a gangly fellow with glasses, was put in charge of the project. Orefice's platoon was teamed with the captain's Vietnamese militia to do the legwork. They cordoned off each hamlet and marched the people to Hill 55. The villagers carried what they could, showing no emotion. They're pawns, Orefice thought, they have to go whichever way the wind is blowing; and today we're the wind. The resettlement ville was surrounded by wire and guarded by the captain's militia; every morning, the people were allowed to return to their fields under the watch of the Marines. This was all well and good, except for the local VC who relied on their nighttime visits to hamlets for food and shelter. One night, finally, a VC sapper squad crept expertly into the resettlement ville; the men wore only loincloths and carried only wire cutters and sacks of U.S. M26 grenades. They sprinted through, tossing grenades into the hootches, and in the time it took Orefice and a squad to rush down and link up with the militiamen, everything was over. All that was left was to call the medevacs. Orefice walked among the smoking huts. It had been a slaughter. About ten people were dead; others with limbs shattered or blown off stared in shock. The survivors were wailing, crying, staring in hate. Orefice could almost smell the anger: the Marines had put them in such a position and then not defended them.

Within days, the experiment disintegrated. People did not return at the end of the work day and others crept off to return to old homes, more concerned with what the VC could do to them than what the Americans could do for them. A few days later, the inexperienced captain walked onto a bouncing betty mine.

He was medevacked minus one leg.

Not long after that, on 28 July, Lieutenant Orefice became a casualty himself. His platoon was manning an observation post on the river below Hill 55; there were bunkers, a watchtower, and concertina wire. Just before dawn, it was Orefice's turn on watch. It was incredibly boring and, at first, he thought his eyes were playing tricks on him. There was something in the paddies two hundred meters away. He stared harder and the scene suddenly focused. Gooks! They appeared to be setting a booby trap. Orefice radioed for a fire mission but Captain Stanat went by the book: it was a restricted fire zone because of the villages, and he needed a clearer sighting to ensure the silhouettes were actually VC before 81mm mortars or artillery could be employed. Within minutes, though, another platoon in M Company took sniper fire and the radio net became crowded with their requests for fire support. Orefice took the opportunity to employ his platoon's own 60mm mortar. Then he took out a squad. A hundred meters from the kill zone, they paused to recon by fire with M16s and M79s; there was still no response. When they finally swept in, they found a mortar round and two booby traps abandoned in the field.

The squad set up a hasty perimeter so they could destroy their finds. No sweat, Orefice thought; whoever was here is long gone. The squad leader, Corporal Smith, wasn't so sure. He was a sharp, young man with much time in the bush and he checked out a nearby path with his M16 at the ready.

Orefice walked after him, calling, "Hey, Smitty, don't go out there. Come on back inside here. Cool it, will ya."

In that instant, Orefice saw the filament wire, barely visible in the dawn light, just in front of Smith's foot. He knew exactly what it was: a trip wire staked across the path, connected in the roadside brush to a grenade tucked inside a C rat can, pin removed, safety spoon held in place by the can. Tug the wire, knock the frag from the can, and the spoon pops. Smith was right on it and Orefice was shouting and diving at the same time. "Booby trap!" There was an explosion, then Orefice jumped back up, shaking, and quickly patted himself for wounds. He found none. He rushed to Smith. His legs were shredded and he was dying. Behind them, the radioman was screaming. Orefice rushed back to him as others bent over Smith. The radioman's flak jacket was hanging open and a piece of shrapnel had slashed his stomach. A loop of intestine squeezed out and the kid was wide-eyed and mumbling. The corpsman knelt beside him, talking him out of his shock and pouring a canteen of water over the exposed guts so they wouldn't dry out.

They were waiting for the medevacs when one of the grunts told Orefice there was blood running from his cheek and mouth. He tentatively touched his face and discovered that a pellet-sized piece of shrapnel had pierced his cheek, chipped a tooth, and lodged in his tongue. Orefice joined his two casualties on the Sea Knight and ended up at the 1st Medical Battalion in Da Nang. The doctor stitched his cheek, left the shrapnel in his swollen tongue, and gave him a bottle of antiseptic to gargle with.

Within twenty-four hours, he was back in the bush.

Three days later, on 2 August, his platoon was detailed to conduct a predawn cordon around Chau Son 2. At daybreak, another platoon would escort in an intelligence team to question the villagers. Everything went smoothly, so well, in fact, that a VC sleeping in the ville didn't realize he was surrounded until the intelligence team strolled in. He shot the team leader with a pistol, then bounded off into the brush.

The terrain swallowed him. Orefice heard the hurried exchange of fire, then was radioed to move in and secure an LZ for the medevac. By the time he arrived, the team leader, a black warrant officer, had been bandaged and he was smiling. The wound was small, a clean shot through his arm, and it was the man's second tour. Million dollar wound, he was saying. The medevac landed near the village, in and out without problem, then Orefice's platoon searched the place. They found the opening to a small tunnel. They dug around it a bit but it was too small for Torres, their tunnel rat, to get into so they could only pop in a few CS grenades and move on.

Torres took the point as they left the ville, the platoon following in file. It was just another hot day. They were walking up a grassy knoll when an explosion came out of nowhere, enveloping Orefice in a sudden blast of noise, concussion, hot wind, and pain. His M16 was blown from his hands, but after the explosion he realized he was still on his feet, wobbly, singed, but still standing. Pain pulsed through his body. His left arm hung useless, a piece of the forearm suddenly gone, the bone broken. A chunk of shrapnel the size of a golf ball burned fiercely in his lower right leg. Smaller bits of metal had nicked his arms, legs, and face, and some of the red-hot pieces were embedded in his flak jacket, smoke curling from them. Thank God I had it buttoned up, Orefice thought through the haze; then he felt something warm and wet in his crotch. A corpsman and a grunt helped Orefice to the top of the hill, where Staff Sergeant Hebert was deploying the men into a hasty perimeter. They helped him sit down; then the corpsman unbuttoned his trousers. Orefice stared horrified as the doc wrapped gauze around his penis. A chunk of flesh had been torn off, and it was like trying to patch a garden hose. Each layer of gauze instantly soaked crimson.

Within the hour, Orefice and Torres were medevacked to the U.S.S. *Repose,* anchored in Da Nang Bay. The Sea Knight landed on the deck pad, corpsmen hustled them off on litters, and they ended up side by side on stainless steel tables. The air conditioner was on full, the steel was like ice, and the two naked grunts, used to hundred degree heat, couldn't help but shiver violently. They started talking to keep their minds off the pain and the cold, joking about having a good vacation in the hospital. Orefice liked Torres. He was a little guy with dark skin and curly hair—a quiet, respectful, gutsy kid. Whenever they found a tunnel, he was the one who stripped off his helmet and flak jacket, got a .45 and a flashlight, and climbed in. He was small enough to fit into the Vietnamese tunnels, so small, in fact, that his flak jacket hung low even when it was zipped up. That's where he'd been hit, a single piece in the upper chest. It didn't look too bad.

The next day, Orefice was stitched up and in bed. He asked the doctor about seeing Torres; the doctor said he was dead. Orefice could feel something drain in him. Why had Torres died? It had been only a single piece of shrapnel in the place where his flak jacket didn't fit.

■ On 5 August 1969, things began happening to the 1st Battalion, 7th Marines in the Arizona. At twilight that evening, Lieutenant Colonel Dowd and his radioman, Lance Corporal Wells, sat in the trampled grass of the CP, quietly monitoring the radios. Wells was down to his blue jean cutoffs and his jungle boots in the night heat, finally relaxing. The day had been another bummer of humping to a new location on the Hot Dog, then unpacking and digging in. Poncho hootches were up, fighting holes ringed the perimeter, and everyone was unwinding, eating Cs, smoking, sleeping in the raw earth.

The first explosion impacted right to their front.

Dowd and Wells bolted up, and the colonel turned to him, "Call Charlie Company and find out what's going on." Wells picked up the hand mike and, thirty feet behind him, a mortar round exploded—the same instant that AK rounds began zipping overhead. For a second, everything seemed paralyzed. Then in an unthinking lunge, Wells hurled himself into a slit trench in front of them. He instantly realized he'd left his radio and jumped up, grabbed it, and slammed back into the trench. He became tangled in a bush but couldn't even feel the stickers. Lieutenant Colonel Dowd bounded into view within seconds, jumping, hitting the edge of the trench, and tumbling in. Right behind the colonel, the rest of the battalion staff clambered in.

Dowd took the radio, so Wells crawled back to his foxhole, grabbed his M16 rifle, and put on his flak jacket and helmet.

The firing had stopped.

The NVA must have had the CP knoll mapped out because, in one quick volley, they placed twenty rounds of 60mm mortar, RPG, and M79 fire, and several hundred AK47 rounds right into it. Just as quickly, Marines on the perimeter fired at muzzle flashes, the mortar crews pumped out illumination, and it was quickly ended. Men on the hill were shouting now. There were moans. Wells's poncho hootch was blown down. The one beside his, the corpsmen's, had taken a direct hit and torn ponchos, helmets, plasma bottles, and gear were scattered in the dirt. Three corpsmen were sprawled in the wreckage. Wells and a sergeant named Herb, also from the Communications Platoon, carried one of the corpsmen to a trench. He was hit in the ass and grazed in the head; a surviving corpsman patched him up by flashlight. Wells and Herb held a poncho over them so no NVA marksman could zero in on the light.

A Marine turned on a strobe for the medevac, and the Sea Knight came in lights off, as gunships fired into the tree lines as cover. Wells held up one end of a poncho litter and hustled towards the cargo ramp, convinced the NVA were going to cut loose with an RPG any second. A supply man, peppered with shrapnel, was in the poncho and a corpsman trotted beside them carefully holding up a plasma IV. The Sea Knight pulled out, the NVA did not fire, and Wells suddenly noticed it was pitch black.

It had gone from dusk to dark in a flash.

Two hours before midnight the next night, a couple Chicom grenades were tossed into Alpha Company's lines, wounding two Marines. Their injuries were minor enough so they could wait until daylight for medevac. Several hours later, a Marine from Alpha was killed. He'd been on guard in a two-man hole when he had to take a piss. He walked a few yards into the brush and was coming back when his sleeping buddy startled awake and fired his M16 at the noise on the perimeter. The man who'd done the shooting was walked up to the CP by some grunts. Wells awoke to hear the Marine hysterically sobbing that he'd killed his buddy.

He too was slated for a medevac.

On the evening of 10 August, PFC Charly Besardi and PFC Tom Bailey were walking point for 3d Platoon, Lima Company, 3d Battalion, 7th Marines. They were in Dodge City, following a path below Charlie Ridge. The sun was setting behind the mountain and, in the hazy silhouettes of twilight, Besardi suddenly noticed the movement. A hundred meters ahead, men were crossing the path, north to south, one right after the other; he could just make out the outlines of pith helmets, packs, AK47s, and RPG launchers. It seemed there were hundreds of them.

Besardi and Bailey hustled back to the rest of the platoon. The

platoon leader, 2dLt Jeff Ronald, quickly got the men on line across
the dirt road and everyone cut loose at the same time. Red tracers whizzed
towards the silhouettes and, instantly, the NVA on the road bolted and
disappeared. In seconds, fire was being returned from deep within the
roadside thickets. Explosions began bursting about forty feet ahead of
them. Besardi noticed his buddy Vaughn to his right, firing an M79.
He called to him in his clipped Massachusetts accent, "Vaughn, shoot
that seventy-nine out farther, man! You're shootin' 'em too short!"

Sergeant Fuller, the platoon sergeant, shouted back amused, "You
stupid asshole, Besardi, those are RPGs being thrown in on us!"

In the middle of it all, Marines started laughing.

The firing lasted maybe thirty minutes, a noisy exchange that claimed
no Marine casualties. It finally ended when the last of the NVA fell
back into the night. A flare ship droned overhead, turning the fields
into a stadium, and word was passed for Besardi's squad to sweep forward
and make the body count. He almost balked in fear: nine Marines strolling
into hundreds of North Vietnamese! They waded forward through the
thick brush under the weird light, and Besardi noticed that Lieutenant
Ronald and Sergeant Fuller were with them. His fear did not evaporate
then, but his hesitation did. He looked upon them much like older brothers
he wanted to impress. They always did right by the platoon, took more
than their share of chances, and, although Besardi was convinced they
were all going to be killed, the idea of refusing them was unfathomable.

No one died. The NVA were gone, leaving only a few pith helmets
and packs. In the morning, the platoon searched along the road and up
into the foothills of Charlie Ridge. They found at least part of what
they were looking for: three NVA stragglers sitting in the brush of a
creek bed, eating rice, their packs unshouldered beside them. The lead
squad opened fire and, in that screaming instant, one of the NVA lurched
violently while the other two rolled, grabbed their AK47s, and bounded
into the brush. Besardi saw one dash down the creek, splashing through
the shallow water, and he lunged after him. Besardi wasn't thinking; it
was all just go, go, go, get the bastard! The NVA lost his helmet as
he tried to clamber over the creek berm and into the thickets. He was
forty feet away. Besardi halted in the middle of the creek, firing his
M16 madly at the scrambling figure. The NVA slammed face first into
the embankment, dropping his AK. Besardi's M16 suddenly jammed.
He frantically tugged at the bolt, trying to clear it.

The terror lasted only seconds. Lieutenant Ronald had been just behind him, and he sprinted past Besardi and pumped his M16 into the gook until he stopped moving. They policed up the area, searching the bodies and the three packs left behind. It didn't make a whole lot of sense to Besardi. The NVA had many people on that path and they'd been fully equipped. Why did they retreat from a platoon?

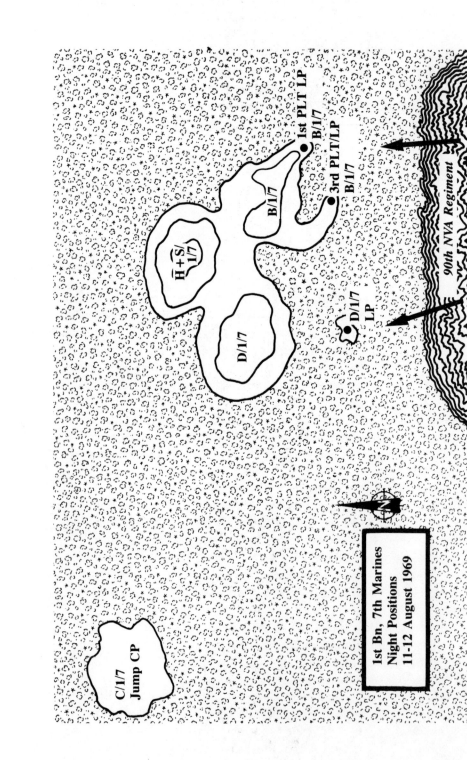

C/1/7
Jump CP

H+S/
1/7

D/1/7

B/1/7

1st PLT LP

3rd PLT/LP
B/1/7

B/1/7

D/1/7
LP

90th NVA Regiment

N

1st Bn, 7th Marines
Night Positions
11-12 August 1969

Chapter Three

Contact

Lieutenant Weh, commanding officer of Bravo Company, 1st Battalion, 7th Marines, 1st Marine Division, stood on a knoll of the Hot Dog as the sun sank on 11 August 1969. He was looking south. Paddy fields encircled his hilltop and rambled south for several hundred meters to a tree line. It sat like an island in the untilled rice paddies, overgrowing an abandoned village. Weh tried to peer into it. In the fading light, he was doing what he'd done a hundred times before, accessing the terrain, gauging likely avenues of enemy attack. He had an intuitive feeling that night, absorbed from six years as an enlisted Marine, three years of commissioned service, and from fourteen months in Vietnam.

He could feel the enemy in that tree line.

There was no logical explanation. Working in tandem with Delta Company that afternoon, they had picked the wood line clean. They found nothing. But now Weh could feel them watching from in there. If they were going to attack, this would be their last chance. The battalion was preparing to move north in the morning, a final one- or two-day sweep to the Vu Gia, then out of the Arizona and back into Dodge City.

That last night, Bravo was on an eastern knoll.

Delta was on another knoll a hundred meters west.

Charlie was almost three kilometers farther west.

Alpha was already north along the Song Vu Gia.

The Battalion CP and H&S Company were set up near Bravo and Delta on a third knoll of the Hot Dog; from above, their independent but nearby perimeters looked like the points of a triangle. A jump CP was with Charlie.

Everyone was working under standard procedure.

Lieutenant Weh's headquarters occupied a space perhaps ten square yards atop a twenty-meter mound; it was the center of his company's perimeter and holes were spaced in the scrub brush for himself, his gunnery sergeant, a company radioman, battalion radioman, and his forward observation lieutenant and radioman (the FO teams were attached from the 11th Marines). Weh had his three rifle platoons deployed in a tight circle at the bottom of his hillock, where the slope meshed with the rice fields. The soil was hard, dry, and rocky; the grunts chipped out small foxholes, no more than three feet deep, and shallow sleeping areas in case mortars hit while they were off watch. 1st Platoon (Lieutenant Campbell) faced south; 3d (Lieutenant Schirmerhorn) faced south and east; 2d (Lieutenant Albers) faced north. Each platoon had a hundred-yard frontage, ten yards between foxholes, two men to a hole. Trip flares were rigged and claymore mines faced forward, detonating cord reeled back to the foxholes.

Two tree-lined fingers jutted from the knoll and pointed at the tree line. The shorter of the two extended from the eastern rim of the perimeter (Campbell), the longer from the western (Schirmerhorn); Weh had both send out squads after dark to avoid detection. They set in as listening posts at the tips to watch that murky tree line and to protect the concealed approaches that these fingers of land provided an enemy.

Bravo's hillock fell into a saddle which rose to a second hillock some hundred meters west. Captain Fagan's Delta Company dug in around it. They also were in a tight perimeter, and Fagan too was suspicious of the tree line to the south. A brushy mound sat about seventy-five yards in front of Delta's lines, and he dispatched a fire team and an M60 team to it.

The saddle between Bravo and Delta rose gently to a third hillock a bit to the north, still on the Hot Dog ridge. The battalion command post, supervised by Maj Robert B. Alexander, the S-3 operations officer, was dug in there with Capt J. W. Huffman's H&S Company. The CP and H&S personnel performed their own security, but the grunts usually bitched if they had to set up near them. The cluster of radio aerials was an irresistible target to NVA mortarmen; and the H&S Marines were more likely to make noise in the dark—talking, coughing, walking around, opening soda cans and C rations, even having cooking fires. At least the grunts said so.

Lieutenant Hord's Charlie Company was about two-and-a-half klicks west of the Hot Dog, dug in around a tiny abandoned ville in another tree line island. Lieutenant Colonel Dowd and his jump CP were with them. Captain Clark's Alpha Company was even farther from the Hot Dog, helicoptered north to positions along the Vu Gia. They were to be the block for the next day's battalion sweep. This was to be their last night in the infamous Arizona.

Nerves were clicking. It had been too easy.

The tension became real sometime after midnight when all three listening posts from Bravo and Delta began whispering into their radios. There were noises . . . then murky figures just visible in the paddies . . . then hushed Vietnamese voices. In the dark, it was impossible to tell what was approaching them, and the teams were instructed to remain in place to further gauge the situation. Sometimes the few are sacrificed to alert the many. At 0415, it happened: a trip flare suddenly popped in the paddies near Bravo Three's LP on the long finger, followed by a hasty exchange of fire. Lieutenant Weh, half-asleep in a hole with his radioman, instantly rolled out from under his poncho and took the radio handset. He asked the squad leader with the LP what was going on. The response was a strained whisper, "I don't know, but there's a lot of people moving out here."

What was out there was the 8th and 9th Battalions, *90th NVA Regiment,* reinforced by a battalion from the *368B NVA Rocket Regiment,* and their plan was to completely overrun the 1st Battalion, 7th Marines.

The Marines knew none of this yet.

Moments before the LP was hit, the 81mm Mortar Platoon of H&S Company was alerted. They had four tubes up and their section leader, SSgt "Flash" Gordon, had his radios in a poncho-covered foxhole. He stuck out his head and called to Gun Number One, "Zotter, we got movement in front of us." LCpl Charles Zotter was on watch at the time; he was a nineteen-year-old high school dropout who'd been given the choice of the Marine Corps or jail because of his street gang activities. He'd been in-country thirteen months, and he moved quickly. He roused his partners in the shallow mortar pit, then picked up an illumination round and clicked the time fuse on the nose to three seconds. That meant the shell would burst before it reached its highest point, before the NVA who heard the pop of the round leaving the tube could run to cover.

Then came that first burst of fire. Zotter instantly dropped the illum round down the tube, and the black hill was bathed in white light. The next second, the H&S Marines opened fire—a frantic downhill sweep of M16 and M60 fire, a virtual wall of red tracers. There were North Vietnamese all over their hillside. They were NVA sappers, wearing only shorts, coming uphill with satchel charges and grenades and unreeling detonation cord behind them. Someone had jumped the gun, though, for they were only halfway up. They ran back, some tumbling in the fire from the foxholes. Zotter saw one clearly; he was running, clawing at his back as bullets thudded into it, stumbling, finally collapsing on his face.

In moments, the NVA disappeared.

The firing continued, most of it concentrated near that long finger in front of Lieutenant Schirmerhorn's platoon in the Bravo line. After that first conversation with the LP, Weh had gotten his FO out of his hole. Within fifteen minutes, artillery from the 11th Marines in An Hoa was slamming into that southern tree line and around the listening post. Weh also contacted battalion to scramble air support. That took longer, but within an hour, a USAF C119 prop plane was orbiting, pouring fire down from its electric-powered miniguns (a variation of the old gatling gun).

The grunts called these gunships Spooky; each minigun fired 6,000 rounds a minute, which was good because, by the time it came on station, Weh was up against an NVA force larger than he dared admit. Weh had not initially ordered the LP back, because it had taken nearly thirty minutes of cat 'n' mouse in the pitch dark before it began to focus: a large NVA force was closing in on Bravo Company, bypassing the LP until they were only an island in the stream of enemy soldiers. Weh finally radioed the squad leader to bring his team in, then radioed Schirmerhorn to send men to guide them back into the lines.

Then the LP's radio went dead.

The squad sent out by Schirmerhorn took fire as soon as they advanced from their foxholes. At the same time, Campbell's LP came under fire. Then came a barrage of RPG and AK47 fire against Schirmerhorn's side of the line, then a scrambling rush of North Vietnamese into their perimeter.

The listening posts had served their purpose: the lines had been put on a 100 percent alert before the NVA could finalize their attack, and artillery was already up. When the Bravo LP abruptly disappeared from the radio net, Fagan was in the process of calling back the Delta LP. They too had begun to take fire. The LP was from the 2d Platoon under 2dLt Denny Taylor (replacing Lieutenant Peters who had rotated to the rear two weeks earlier); as the LP began moving back under fire, Fagan radioed Taylor to send out a squad to help them in. The squad managed to link up with the listening post, but the NVA were almost on them. They flung grenades at each other on sound. AK rounds snapped past in the blackened brush until, finally, PFC Cornelius J. Cashman dropped to one knee. He cradled his M60 butt against his hip, sling over his shoulder, and told the others to get moving. He would cover them. Cashman was not an inexperienced new guy or a renegade looking for trouble; if any stereotype fit, it was of the All American Boy. Cashman shouted, "I'll be right there, I'll be right there," as he scythed the brush with his sixty, keeping the NVA back long enough for the rest to slip back. Inside Delta Company's perimeter, Lieutenant Taylor made a quick head count. Cashman was not there. His M60 was silent. Taylor's radio report to Fagan was emotional, but Fagan would not allow a search party. He was probably dead, the NVA were still coming, and they could not afford such a gap in their lines. Fagan made a mental note to put Cashman in for the Navy Cross, and only hoped that if the kid were still alive, he would keep his cool and hide in the bushes until dawn.

Charlie Company was also under fire from RPGs and AK47s; it was sustained, but seemed designed only to keep them in place. The grunts sat tight in their holes, suffering only a few shrapnel wounds, awaiting the assault that never materialized. Lieutenant Hord's hole was near where Lieutenant Colonel Dowd was hunched over his radios. They could hear Weh desperately calling his LP. No answer. A squad of Marines was missing and, in the middle of it, Dowd was getting inquiries from regiment and division. Everyone feared the worst and Hord could see the anguish and frustration in Dowd's eyes. The colonel was a fighter, but this was not a battle of his design. No one really knew what was happening. The only option was to hunker down and weather it out. As they waited for dawn, Dowd told Hord they'd march over to the

Hot Dog at first light and take it from there. His voice was charged with one desire—swift retaliation.

Lance Corporal Wells was half-asleep in his foxhole after the initial melee on the H&S Company hill. An RPG or mortar exploded nearby. It showered him with dirt and sent him scurrying for their trench. The slit trench was only three feet deep, and there were a dozen Marines crouched in it. The firing was creeping closer and there was an air of high-strung anticipation as the men fingered their weapons and strained their eyes. No one was firing, though; there were other Marines down the hill and, even in the flare light, things were indistinct.

An M60 crew was set up in front of the trench in a little scooped pit. Wells kneeled with them and squinted through their GreenEye; it cast an eerie lime fuzz across the battlefield, but individuals stood out. To their left, he could see grunts from Bravo Company. There were NVA right up with them; farther to the right, there were more still. These NVA seemed to be milling around. The assistant gunner took back the scope and used it to adjust the gunner's fire. The Marine cranked a few tracers into the milling group, locked on the target, then started pumping his M60 around that spot. Wells and the rest in the trench opened fire too, triggering M16 tracers into the spot where the M60 tracers were bouncing.

Wells really couldn't see a thing.

Nearby, the 81mm mortars were pumping out a constant barrage. High explosive, white phosphorus, illumination. An occasional line of green tracers punched across the hill. Mortars impacted; a few RPGs whirl-banged in. Zotter caught fast glimpses around his mortar pit. Illum rounds floated down on parachutes and tracers arched through the black. A corpsman was shouting, "Bring your wounded over here!" Four silhouettes at a time moved towards the shout, a fifth Marine invisible between them in a poncho. There were moans. An officer shouted, "Keep your eye on that body!" There was a dead NVA near the perimeter, naked except for shorts, lying on his back with one knee up. A gangly, crazy hillbilly named Pridemore took up a position near the mortar pit. He had a night scope mounted on his rifle and shot an NVA creeping up to retrieve the body. Zotter saw Pridemore in the morning; he had the scope carefully wrapped and he nodded to it, grinning, "That makes nine."

These actions constituted the dangerous periphery of what had become a focused attack on Bravo Company and, more specifically, Lieutenant Schirmerhorn's platoon. He and his acting platoon sergeant, a black corporal, had their men on a hundred-yard line at the base of the hill.

From atop the hill, all Lieutenant Weh could see of their fight was tracers and flashes from fragmentation grenades. Weh reckoned that the LP had broken the momentum of the attack before being swallowed up, and that the quick artillery barrage had shattered the following waves of troops. But the first wave was sizable and Schirmerhorn was glued on the radio to Weh; Schirmerhorn said it was a free-for-all, gooks all around. As long as the young lieutenant was on the radio, Weh felt secure that the line was holding. But things were tense. For one thing, the 105mm battery supporting them from An Hoa reported running low on ammunition. To deplete an artillery battery's stock and still have NVA coming at you meant many bad guys, and Weh was praying for daylight.

With the sun came the Phantoms and the rest of the battalion. Weh was thankful that the NVA hadn't launched their assault just one hour earlier. It was 0600 by then; given an extra hour, he thought the NVA could have forced their way all the way up to his CP before dawn. They seemed to have the numbers for it.

Weh radioed Albers to send one of his squads up to the CP. He was also on the horn with Fagan; Dowd had directed Delta to come to Bravo's aid. They decided that at first light, one platoon from Delta would physically tie in with Schirmerhorn's besieged platoon, thus containing the NVA and allowing the jump CP and Charlie to sweep in. From there, they could retake the finger where the listening post had disappeared.

With dawn, the NVA were ebbing away.

There were still stragglers in the line, and Lieutenant Weh wanted to get down to 3d Platoon with the attached squad. Time, he thought, to let them know they were not all alone.

A fire team went down the hill first, followed by Weh and his two radiomen, then the rest of the squad. The sight of a Marine carrying only a .45 and flanked by two waving radio aerials was an irresistible target. As soon as they reached the base of the hill, Weh could see in the gray twilight the North Vietnamese soldier getting up from behind a paddy dike twenty feet ahead. It was like slow motion to Weh as he instantly dove to his right, the AK47 emptying the thirty-round banana clip in one burst, Weh able to see green tracers snapping past his left leg. He crashed to the ground at the same time that two grunts ahead of him sprang to their feet; they suddenly realized there was an NVA only feet from them, and they shot him down.

Weh's senior radioman, Cpl John Constien, was sprawled facedown just behind him. He was moaning and Weh turned him over. His eyes rolled back, blood spilled from his mouth; he was gut shot. Weh bellowed, "Corpsman, corpsman up!" then used his K-Bar to cut Constien's pack suspenders. He pulled the pack and radio off, trying to make the kid comfortable. A corpsman jogged over, and Weh jumped back up. He told the squad leader to report to Lieutenant Schirmerhorn, then grabbed one of the grunts rushing past. "You're my radio operator!"

Corporal Constien died in the minute that took.

Weh helped his new radioman get the PRC25 on his back. Schirmerhorn was shoring up his ruptured line and, in the dawn haze, they could see the re-act platoon from Delta Company coming across the paddy. With that, Weh wanted to get over to Lieutenant Campbell's side of the line, where the gun battle was continuing. They clambered back up the hillock, the new radioman, bewildered and excited, following. As soon as they cleared the crest, the antennas drew another burst of AK fire, but they made it down unscathed. Campbell told Weh that most of the NVA had skyed out; there were only two left, stuck behind a dike and still firing.

They finally silenced those two.

It was 0700 by then, and the last shots were heard within the next thirty minutes. The Delta platoon tied in with Schirmerhorn's platoon and they moved onto the wooded finger. Anxious to find out what happened to the LP, Weh joined the sweep. There were wounded Marines, dead Marines, dead North Vietnamese. Navy corpsmen followed the skirmish line, attending to the casualties. They'd advanced only some fifty feet when Weh came across a doc bandaging a young, wounded NVA. Weh exploded, "Get the hell away from him, we've got Marines who need help!"

The sweep found the lost listening post. Except for a couple of wounded, the entire squad was KIA. Killed In Action. The squad leader had survived; he later told Weh that he had had no idea what was happening. When the NVA finally swarmed over their position, he had taken cover and sweated out the night convinced he was going to be discovered and killed any minute.

Bravo and Delta Companies shored up the battered perimeter while the jump CP and Charlie Company marched in from the west. Lieutenant Colonel Dowd was so explosive that he outdistanced his infantry escort and arrived at the Hot Dog first. The area was being policed up then. Among other things, one LP from Bravo, which had stayed low during the battle, trotted back to their lines, scared shitless and overjoyed to still be living.

Bravo had eight dead, twenty-four wounded.

Delta had one dead, seven wounded.

Charlie and H&S had a handful of wounded.

There were more than fifty dead North Vietnamese littered around Bravo Company's perimeter; there were also mounds of equipment and weapons left behind, most of it of recent Chinese Communist make. There were pith helmets, web gear, automatic rifles, carbines, machine guns, grenades. Marines held up empty RPD machine gun ammo drums and half-fired ammo belts. It was only then that they realized how many NVA had been involved; they estimated that two infantry battalions had hammered into Bravo Company. Black communications wire was also found around Bravo's perimeter. It had been unreeled during the night as guides so the NVA infantrymen leaving their tree line could navigate forward in the dark. Some strands ran straight from the NVA position to the Marine position. Other strands were laid across those lines to indicate staging points for the various NVA units; a final strand marked the line of departure.

These Marines were part of the best-educated and informed army in history. They knew about the withdrawal plan and the discussion it had caused. They were also hearing on the radio that their hill was only one of many places the NVA had hit. As his men policed up that morning, Lieutenant Weh wrote a letter to his wife of one year on some 1st MarDiv stationery:

They came at us from two sides and we had gooks in the open, gooks in the trees, and gooks everywhere. . . . By the time you read this the enemy offensive will be old news, but they really hit everyone today, everywhere! Rockets, ground attacks, mortars, you name it. I can't figure those God Damn dinks out. If they wanted Nixon to pull out troops they're sure not making it easy for him. To hell with them all they can keep coming down and we'll keep killing the stupid, indoctrinated SOBs.

Lance Corporal Zotter stood along the crest of the hill, watching other Marines stack up the captured gear and lay the dead NVA in a line. One grunt stood over the dike where the last two had gone down fighting, and hollered up, "Hey, this one's still alive!"

Dowd answered from the hill, "Where's he hit?"

"He's shot right in the ass!"

The Marines along the hillock burst into rough laugher and shouts. Dowd hollered to bring the prisoner up, and the grunts reached down and effortlessly hefted the little NVA like an empty sack of oats. Three others helped carry him up by his arms and legs, and they tossed him down almost at Zotter's feet. The NVA had a battle dressing placed on his buttocks and tied around his leg, and he was stiff, frightened, and in a lot of pain. Two Vietnamese scouts crouched beside him and began firing off questions. The NVA gritted his teeth in a grimace of pain, and shook his head no, no, no. One of the scouts slid his knife up the prisoner's anus, then twisted. The man's eyes almost popped from his head. He talked.

Lance Corporal Wells did not see this torture. He did, however, notice more than one grunt veer from his path across the hill to give the NVA prisoner an angry kick.

Zotter thought Dowd was a scrappy old bird, and decided to sit near where the colonel was conducting his business. Dowd was on the radio and it sounded like he was arguing with someone who didn't quite believe him. ". . . But I've got fifty dead gooks out here!" Zotter got the impression Dowd was trying to convince some rear staff officer when he ordered the dead NVA piled up on a cargo net. They folded the edges up, hooked them to a ring at the top, then secured the net to the underside of another Sea Knight. The chopper took off with the stuffed cargo net swaying below it, arms and legs sticking through the rope weave. It wasn't much later that Zotter witnessed another example of the colonel's grit. Dowd was resting, leaning back, when a Vietnamese voice suddenly shouted over the radio. Dowd grabbed the handset and answered his foe's cocky shout with, "Come and get me, motherfucker!"

In accord with standard operating procedure, the initials and last four numbers of each dead man's serial number were radioed to battalion rear on Hill 55. Lieutenant Peters, XO, D/1/7, choked when he deciphered their KIA report. Cashman had been in his platoon for three months.

He was tall and handsome, blond hair, blue eyes, with a little teenage grunt mustache. A good guy, a damn good Marine. His body had been found where he'd been firing from, and was choppered to Graves Registration in Da Nang. Peters and an enlisted man who'd known the deceased were detailed to formally identify the body.

Cashman lay in a drawer at the 1st Med morgue, naked, hands stiffly crossed against his chest from their position in the poncho litter. His eyes were open, eyebrows arched, mouth in a circle of astonishment. There was only one mark on him, a single bullet hole right below his navel. Six inches of intestine hung from the hole.

Peters went through his gear. There was a high school graduation photo of Cashman's girl friend and her last letter to him, talking marriage. Oh, this sucks, Peters thought, feeling ill. No one else's death—and he'd lost four men as a platoon leader—had affected him like this. His mind was churning. Cashman was a handsome, smart, squared-away Marine. He's dead. He was going to get married. He volunteered. He's dead. His parents were immigrants; it's not even their war. He's dead. He's an only son and he could have gotten out of going to Vietnam. And he's fucking dead.

For what!?

The company clerk typed up the formal condolence letter to Cashman's parents for the company commander to sign. Peters also wrote. He received a reply from the father, a sad letter with one message. Why *my* son? Peters wrote back that Cornelius Cashman was a Marine fighting for his country, which is how Peters always saw things. He didn't hear from the father again until Christmas; there was ten dollars in the envelope and a note to buy some booze for his son's platoon. Peters sent the bottle out to them in a mailbag. It wasn't until ten years later that he worked up the courage to fulfill a promise he had made to himself. Mrs. Cashman answered the phone; he was very nervous, had no idea what to say, but she was a kind woman who remembered his letters. She made it very easy to talk.

That was all for later. When Peters returned to the company area, he told First Sergeant Headley, "Top, I can not hack this. Anymore IDs, you got it. I can't hack this stuff."

Chapter Four

What Marines Do Best

It took Charlie Company and the Battalion CP two hours to reach Bravo Company's hillock, after having moved out at first light on 12 August. In the rising heat spreading across the dead paddies, Lieutenant Hord saw the most startling sight of his year in Vietnam. It was the black communications wire that the NVA had strung, the guides for the NVA infantrymen as they crept in the dark towards the Marines. Bodies were clustered stiffly along the guides, some of the dead NVA still clutching the wire. Lieutenant Hord examined the dead as the company filed past. He could see thirty of them. They had new green fatigues, pith helmets, full web gear, two canteens, AK47 automatic rifles, and a few SKS carbines. Some had whistles and pistols. But what hit Hord hardest was how diminutive and young they looked. He would have sworn some couldn't have been more than thirteen years of age.

Hord glanced at his own men. They were looking at the bodies too, their faces filled with looks of surprise, fear, retribution, anticipation. Hord could feel it. It was electric. They all knew what was waiting.

This is finally it, he thought.

Atop the low knoll, Hord joined the huddle of commanders and radiomen. Lieutenant Colonel Dowd quickly sketched out a counterattack scheme. B Company was to secure the Hot Dog and the Battalion CP. C Company was to sweep the several hundred meters south into that tree line island; it was dense with thickets of bamboo and elephant grass, beaten-down hootches, and old trails, and it seemed the likeliest place for the NVA to have retreated to. D Company was to stand by to reinforce C Company.

By 0900, Charlie 1/7 stepped off in the attack.

The men moved with two platoons on line, one platoon back, and with Lieutenant Hord's command group twenty meters back in the seam between the two lead platoons. They had barely reached the paddy when the far tree line erupted into an absolute roar of sustained, concentrated fire. At first, most of it was too high or too low, and the Marines pressed on. Then the whole tempo increased as the air cracked with close AK rounds and dust kicked up in the paddy. Grunts collapsed as they ran for cover. Hord was on the horn, his radiomen trotting alongside, urging on the platoons fifty more yards to the cover of a large dike.

Hord too was jogging for it in a crouch—seconds seeming like hours—when his company radioman abruptly collapsed. He was dragged up to the high dike, an AK round in his chest. Lieutenant Hord crouched beside him, helping get the radio off and shouldering it himself. The radioman was scared but composed, talking with Hord as a corpsman taped a compress bandage over the sucking hole. He was an Irish kid from New York and he mumbled, "I guess I just bought my ticket home."

"Yeah, you sure did. Take it easy."

But the air was already escaping from his lungs, his breathing labored, his lips turning blue. The radioman was dying.

And the rest were taking a regiment's worth of fire.

From the Hot Dog, Lieutenant Colonel Dowd had a panoramic view of the fight; no NVA could be seen retreating from the tree line. They had found their attackers all right, and they too wanted another solid confrontation. Artillery from An Hoa was up again shortly, and the C/1/7 FO adjusted it into the wood line. Several sorties of Phantoms roared in, napalm canisters wobbling down in their wake. But the AKs kept firing, and the NVA lobbed a few mortar rounds onto Charlie Company and the Battalion CP. Lieutenant Hord and his group stayed pinned to the dusty ground and pinned to their radios. He ordered his two lead platoons to unpack the E8 gas launchers they'd been humping around for months without using; the wind was perfect and they fired the gas right into the trees. The NVA fire became disoriented for a moment, and the lead squads were able to advance a quick jog to the next series of dikes. That was the pattern for the afternoon.

When Charlie pushed off, Lieutenant Colonel Dowd radioed Captain Fagan to be prepared to assault south, then east, if Charlie Company bogged down.

Fagan sat down with his headquarters group, going over the maps. They planned to attack in a standard skirmish line, two up and one back, and they would split the CP element between the two lead platoons. Captain Fagan would accompany one platoon, GySgt C. C. Richards the other. The gunny was Fagan's unflappable alter ego in running the company; he was a hard taskmaster and looked like a Marine NCO down to the shaved head, stocky build, and snarls. During that April foray when Lieutenant Peters's platoon had been pinned down with two dead, his stalwart, Cpl R. L. Gibson, had run back for help. Gunny Richards had rounded up a group and, with Gibson, led a wild charge that allowed Peters to drag their casualties back. Such casual bravery had its price. Gunny Richards's tour ended during a November operation in the Que Sons, when he charged a 12.7mm machine gun that had pinned down a platoon; he was shot in the face, his cheek and lower jawbone splintered.

Captain Fagan would join the other platoon with 1stLt Bob Allan, his FO, and with his three radiomen. They were his constant shadows. Corporal Brundage, chief radioman, was a savvy guy who kept Fagan abreast of the mood among the grunts. Lance Corporal Nelson, backup radioman, was a friendly guy known as the Lurch; he was tall, wiry, and always so loaded with extra batteries and C rations, in addition to his pack and radio, that each step looked like it would be his last. PFC Frenchy Paris, battalion net radioman, was a quiet young draftee with a wife back home. Fate had not treated him well, from draft board to Marine grunts, but he simply and quietly did the best job he could.

They were a good team. The company had a lot of heart, and Fagan's instructions to them were simple. They already knew their jobs; he just let them know when it was time to go.

About two hours into Charlie Company's slow advance, Frenchy handed the handset to Captain Fagan. Major Alexander was on the other end; he was quick and blunt, "Hey, Charlie's not moving. How fast can you go?"

"We can move out in ten minutes."

"You're sure of that?"

"Yeah, I'm positive."

A bit later, battalion called again: Delta Company was to come in on Charlie Company's right flank and assault into the tree line. Captain Fagan had already been on the horn orienting his platoon leaders, and in short order they moved out as planned. First downhill to the south—

over the area where Cashman had died—then up a small rise. With Fagan and Richards constantly on the radio to keep them spread out and on line, the platoon crested the hill which was blanketed by elephant grass, then pivoted left (east) and swept down the gentle slope.

At five hundred meters, they could see the tree line island; at three hundred meters, the AK47 and RPG fire began raining down on them.

Corporal Cominos unconsciously threw himself into the dirt. He found himself in a shallow depression, pressing, pressing down, his back so exposed he knew it would be ripped open any second. He raised his M16 to fire back. The air above him seemed electrified. He couldn't see a thing, only smoke and trees. He worked on impulse, pulling ammunition magazines from his claymore pouch and emptying five.

All along the line, everyone was doing the same, but Delta Company was halted. Captain Fagan, crouching with his radiomen behind the lead platoons, tried to assess the situation. His machine gun teams were firing, but he was reluctant to use anything heavier, not even mortars, for fear of shelling Charlie Company. He didn't know the exact location of their advance; Gunny Richards was over in that direction to ensure they didn't shoot at each other, but the smoke grenades that Charlie Company had popped at their request were not visible in the bramble. Well, it can only get worse, he thought, and with that, Fagan radioed his platoon leaders to assault into the tree line. That's exactly what they did, using fire and maneuver, progress measured from dike to dike, until finally the Delta line was in the fringes of the woods.

And there they bogged down again.

Delta Company was assaulting the forested island from the west, gaining a tenacious foothold in the edges. Charlie Company was assaulting from the north. They were still pinned down in the open paddies when Lieutenant Hord, the company radio strapped to his back, got on the horn to his reserve platoon. They were to move up to the firing line.

The platoon advanced through the cover of some high brush and tied in with a squad on a knoll of burial mounds. Lance Corporal Bradley's squad took up positions on a berm at the edge of the knoll, on line, Mouse to Bradley's left and the first man of the next squad to his right. They were separated from the North Vietnamese by only forty yards of paddy. Bradley flattened himself behind a grassy burial mound, pack dropped to his left, helmet still on, cranking through mags. He snapped with adrenaline and just happened to be looking at the right place when a bare head popped into view through the vegetation. The NVA was rising up to fire. Bradley and the Marine to his right instantly fired and the head snapped out of sight.

"Didja get him, didja see anything!"

Then Bradley got his, an RPG slamming into the dike several yards to his left, knocking him unconscious the same instant he heard the blast. He came to a few minutes later, head throbbing, dimly aware of a man shouting from behind asking if he was okay. He moved slowly, still flat in the grass of the mound, still under fire, covered by ruptured earth. He checked for wounds. His left ear was bleeding and his right arm burned from a piece of shrapnel, but his gear had taken most of the rocket-propelled grenade. His pack beside him had a large piece of shrapnel lodged in it, his helmet was dented, and the hand guard of his M16 was cracked.

For a moment, Bradley could only lie dazed and hurt. That's when his best friend, Harvey Peay, rose up to fire over the dike and took an AK47 round in his head. He collapsed onto Wendell Wright, the squad radioman, who could only stare for a horrified moment; then Wright calmed down and, under the steady fire, dragged Peay back over the hill to where the corpsmen were working. Lance Corporal Peay lay in the dirt for more than an hour before the medevac could get in; he died before they reached the hospital.

Litter teams used ponchos to get the wounded back to the Hot Dog, where medevacs were being worked off the slope opposite the tree line. When he later thought about it, Lieutenant Hord was mightily impressed at the courage it took to carry a wounded man back across that paddy. But in the din of firing, he didn't see or hear a single helicopter. His attention was zeroed in on the enemy tree line ahead.

Fire and Maneuver.

By the fourth hour of the assault, Hord had made it to within a hundred feet of the woods. He hunkered against a three-foot dike with his command group. The air inches above their heads screamed with passing rounds. To his left, several Marines were sprawled in the scrub brush, the dead frozen into stillness under flak jackets and ammunition, the wounded rocking in pools of blood, moaning to themselves. The sun beat down on them. To Hord's right, more men were sprawled. Medevacs were impossible. The NVA were right in front of them. Hord could see them. They were in a trench at the edge of the trees, wearing pith helmets, bobbing up to fire. The Marines facing them ducked and popped up to fire too.

Hord watched a Phantom roll in on the trench line and release its bombs. He pressed behind the dike as the explosion rocked the ground and slashed the air with whizzing chunks of hot metal; then he quickly peeked back up as the jet pulled out. An NVA stood up in the trench, firing his AK at the departing Phantom. That was a beautiful air strike; Hord almost screamed, why are you still alive?

Lieutenant Hord radioed battalion, "Youth Six, this is Charlie Six. If we can get going now, I think we best because I'm sure we're just going to lose some more men sitting here."

Lieutenant Colonel Dowd okayed the frontal assault.

Hord keyed the company radio. He told the reserve platoon to lift their fires in two minutes as the two lead platoons made their rush. Then he got his squad leaders on the horn: fix bayonets, we're charging in one minute; a green-star cluster flare will be the signal. Around him, grunts who still had bayonets began fixing them to M14 and M16 rifles. Hord was moving on a combination of training and terror.

He pulled the flare from his web gear.

The line erupted—guttural yells over the cacophony, the cracks of passing bullets. The men ran crouched, engulfed in smoke and noise. It was a slow-motion nightmare, but this time running into a real live monster.

In seconds, the company was on the trench line. Hord bounded into it, terrified, trying to get out of the fire, almost landing on a North Vietnamese soldier. The man was slumped motionless against the trench wall with what looked like a dagger in his forehead. Hord looked closer. It was a large chunk of shrapnel. God, he thought, this is surreal, like a corpse springing from its grave. The whole world was erupting around him. The NVA were rushing back deeper into the woods, except for a few stragglers or diehards. A bunker opened fire from a slight rise amid the trees, and Hord saw one of his Marines charge right at it. The kid was shirtless, had three or four grenades cradled in his arm like footballs, and he sprinted up to the bunker, pitching them overhand, underhand, lobbing them into the opening. He dove as they exploded, then instantly sprang to his feet and lunged to the opening, firing his M16 into the bunker.

The assault continued on its own momentum. Hord scrambled from the trench with his .45 still in its holster, and carrying an M16 taken from a casualty. He never fired the rifle; the radio was his tool. He walked in a crouch down the general skirmish line of his two platoons, pausing every few yards to kneel and get his bearings. Around him, Marines were hurling grenades, screaming, changing magazines. Twenty feet away, he could see NVA ducking among the trees. Hord had never seen anything like it, was too scared to be afraid. He was amazed that the North Vietnamese seemed to be looking right at his radio but none paused to shoot. Dead NVA lay at his feet, bark and leaves blasted onto them.

The NVA disappeared into a second slit trench in the woods, and their firing grew more intense. Hord had one thought stronger than all others: will I live?

Then Delta Company swept in from the right flank.

Delta Company had been pinned in the fringes of the trees, taking heavy casualties. The situation was intolerable. Captain Fagan finally left his command group back with the reserve platoon and worked his way up to the point of contact with Gunnery Sergeant Richards and Lance Corporal Nelson. First they walked in a crouch, then on all fours, and finally they crawled when they noticed everyone else was down. Fagan could see dead Marines, four or five of them, and a dozen wounded sprawled around the farthest point. A young corpsman, loaded down with extra bandages and water, scrambled among them, seemingly unaware of the heavy fire. Everyone else was down, firing and throwing grenades, but pinned in place.

Fagan lay in the brush, quickly sizing up the situation. The company had to renew the momentum of the assault, and quickly. LAW rockets and M79 grenades were not knocking out the family bunkers dug near the hootches. Fagan radioed his platoon leaders to set up their E8 gas launchers and to fire the CS over their heads into the ville area. He did not pass the order to don gas masks; the wind was behind them, and the men looked too hot and tired to fight in them.

If all went well, they'd follow the gas in.

The CS exploded in white clouds, then dissipated in invisible gusts. A bit off-target, Fagan noted, but a gentle, steady breeze carried it like a carpet over the hootches and bunkers. It must have been incredibly hot and stuffy in the bunkers. The NVA fire became disorganized, and Fagan shouted into his radio to his lieutenants.

Someone near Corporal Cominos began screaming, "Stand up, get on line!" The men charged automatically, simple and straight ahead. They were up and in the open for thirty yards. The air snapped and cracked around Cominos's head.

God, oh God, go, go, go!

Dirt kicked up around them. The air itself was screaming.

Faster, shit, move, move!

Cominos burst into the thicket ahead, almost tripping over several North Vietnamese slumped in and around their spider holes. The fire from ahead was still fierce, but he hurried on, M16 up from the waist, pouring sweat. He passed a dilapidated, old hootch, then an awful sensation suddenly hit him. Something was wrong. The hootch! In his haste, he hadn't fragged it. He jogged back, just as two grunts following him popped grenades into the family bunker. One cranked his M16 into the hole, then peered in. He shouted that two dead NVA were inside. Oh Lord, Cominos thought, they could have wasted me so easily when I went past. He joined the two Marines, suddenly laughing, "Oh boy, I gotta get my act together!"

Cominos rushed into the next brush line. There was Captain Fagan, standing in the fire and casually turning as Cominos's squad staggered in hollow-eyed and sweating. Fagan pointed. "Take your Marines and put them over there." Cominos was incredulous; how'd the Skipper get here so fast! Cominos would follow that man anywhere.

The squad hit the dirt, and an NVA cut loose on them from a spider hole twenty yards ahead. A Marine instantly charged past Cominos.

He emptied his M16 into the hole.

All along the Delta line, men were charging wildly. Captain Fagan could see the backs of NVA as they ran, could see Marines storming after them, firing on the run, screaming, rolling grenades into bunkers and spider holes. Fagan's heart was pumping wildly. He saw one NVA hop from a hole seventy-five meters ahead. He already had his .45 out and he fired a couple of rounds at the man, laughing with relief. He thought, when you can finally see the NVA, you know they're losing. Gunny Richards fired his .45 also, laughing with the release of tension, then laughing with Fagan because they couldn't hit a thing.

They calmed down and returned to their radios to get the grunts back under control before they completely overran the battalion line.

To their left, C Company was still fighting for its life.

Sergeant Lowery—acting platoon sergeant and already scratched up from a close RPG back at the burial mounds—was firing his M16 at the second NVA trench. His lieutenant hollered at him to link up with Delta Company, and he took off to the right in a running crouch, holding his helmet down. Something exploded beside him and shrapnel stung his legs. He could feel nothing, kept moving. He stumbled upon what he thought was Delta Company's flank—a lieutenant and some grunts crouched amid a tree grove. An AK47 was cracking from a family bunker ahead. The lieutenant looked at him incredulously and shouted that he'd just run through the NVA. It didn't mean a thing, didn't even click with Lowery. He was high on adrenaline. He pumped his M16 towards the bunker. One of the men slam-banged a LAW at it. Lowery could see the bunker in the elephant grass, its front smashed down from the explosion. An AK jammed out a side port and ripped off a blind burst. You are waxed, motherfuckers, Lowery almost laughed as he rushed forward. He dropped beside the opening, tossed a grenade in, rolled aside. Boom! The NVA stuck the AK out again, emptying the magazine wildly into the dirt and grass. He ducked back to reload and Lowery jumped up again with several grunts who had come up after him. They tossed more frags in, then chattered their M16s into the dugout.

Two dead North Vietnamese soldiers were inside. Lowery suddenly noticed the whole battlefield was quieting.

Between Charlie and Delta, the NVA had been broken up. Lieutenant Hord was crouched with his radio when he saw Delta Company approaching through the trees in a disciplined line, weapons in the assault position. There were only two platoons, but they looked like a thousand Marines to him. The survivors around him began shouting in wild elation that it was over, that they were still alive—that they had won!

The two companies consolidated what they had, then swept through the tree line end to end, reconning by fire, fragging each and every bunker, using Chicoms when they ran out of U.S. grenades. There was little, if any, resistance. The NVA retreat was complete. It was then that Charlie Company's reserve platoon came in. They didn't know what to expect, so they quickly measured their ammo, fixed bayonets because they didn't have enough, then charged. It was anticlimactic.

Lance Corporal Bradley paused at the first trench to look at the spot where he and the other Marine had fired. A North Vietnamese was slumped with his back against the earthen trench wall and an AK47 beside him. A small hole was in his forehead and the back of his head was blown out. Another dead NVA was sprawled beside him in the slit trench.

Got you!

After what they had been through, it felt great. Lieutenant Hord could see the exhilaration on every face. For weeks—months—they had sweated and kicked booby traps. This was their reward. A life experience, he thought, flooding with emotions. They had taken on the North Vietnamese Army on their terms, and they had emerged victorious. The jungle floor was literally smoking. Marines foraged through it, laughing, taking photographs, picking up souvenirs, inspecting the bodies. There were stacks of equipment left behind: rifles, grenade launchers, mortars, stick grenades, radios, ammunition, packs, web gear, dozens of bicycles used for transportation. They even found an old bathtub with claw legs, which they imagined the NVA regimental commander had used.

By dusk, Charlie and Delta Companies were humping back towards the Hot Dog. Lieutenant Hord walked in front of his column, suddenly aware of the heat and his own fatigue, but still swimming in the victory. He was a regular officer, the son of a career sergeant, and he had literally demanded infantry duty. This is what he'd always wanted. It had been as perfect as combat could get. Dowd, whom he greatly respected, had orchestrated a classic attack. His Marines had carried it out with stunning courage. And Fagan, his Basic School instructor, had rounded it out, coming in like the cavalry. He looked at his Marines, filthy and quiet as they trudged up the hill. They weren't trained to freeze when a booby trap exploded on a trail; they'd been trained to close with and kill the enemy. And they'd done it. They were warriors, Hord thought; morale was higher than it ever had been or would be, and it was the proudest moment of his life.

Lieutenant Colonel Dowd greeted them on the hill.

He was beaming and they shook hands, congratulating each other. If we could pop champagne, Hord thought, we would.

The battalion staff and company commanders held their meeting. Spirits were still running high, and Dowd had to take control so they would address the present situation. Even from their vantage point on the Hot Dog, no one had been able to tell in which direction the NVA had retreated after their tree line had been seized. If they had fled to the south or west, the Que Son Mountains offered a sanctuary their battalion could not tackle alone. If they had gone east, they would run into the 5th Marines AO around the An Hoa Combat Base. Dowd decided their only option was to sweep north towards Alpha Company's encampment on the Song Vu Gia. Prospects did not seem likely that they'd find anything, though. Plans were sketchy, intelligence was nonexistent, everyone was exhausted. Lieutenant Colonel Dowd finally ended the meeting, ''Go ahead and get some rest. We'll reconvene in the morning, and we'll put the rest of this together.''

Chapter Five

Hounds Too Fast on the Hunt

Before dusk on 12 August, reinforcements moved into the vicinity of the Hot Dog: India Company, 3d Battalion, 5th Marines (Capt Robert A. Beeler), which humped in from An Hoa; and two platoons from Lima Company, 3d Battalion, 7th Marines (Capt Jon K. Rider), which choppered in from Hill 37. Lima's 3d Platoon was on patrol when the warning order came, so Rider was attached a platoon from Kilo Company for this operation.

By nightfall, these two companies were dug in within sight of 1/7's hillside of foxholes. The night was free of combat, but not of commotion. The 81mm mortar crews fired H&I most of the night, and some of it exploded too close for comfort near India Company. Captain Beeler had only recently lost some of his Marines to friendly fire—from misplotted 3/5 H&S fire in the Que Sons during Operation Durham Peak—and he was quickly on the horn to 1/7's operations officer. The fires were shifted farther out into the paddies. Later, one of India's listening posts captured a North Vietnamese. He was alone, presumably lost, and the grunts just reached out and grabbed him when he walked past their hiding place in the bushes.

At first light, the battalion came alive again.

The mission for 13 August was pursuit of the bloodied NVA regiment, and Lieutenant Colonel Dowd held a predawn huddle at his command post. His three company commanders were there, along with Colonel Codispoti, who stood in camouflaged fatigues, hands firmly on his hips, silver eagles shining from his collars and from his starched fatigue cover. The regimental commander had choppered in the previous day and now was going to accompany the sweep. Only the most cynical were not impressed by this style of leadership; but Lance Corporal Wells and the other radiomen on the fringe of the meeting were young and salty, and they hid their astonishment by mumbling among themselves how bad the colonel's cigar stunk.

Codispoti was a definite piece of work. He had replaced a more calm—some thought a more professional—colonel. Codispoti himself was short and stocky; with white hair; enormous eyebrows; and a gruff, Brooklyn clip. He was prone to temper tantrums even over trivial matters, and he had many idiosyncrasies. He'd already been passed over for brigadier general, so he was not afraid to run things the only way he knew how—his way. Colonel Codispoti was there to kill communists. Period. He allowed himself little slack as he constantly helicoptered among his units, looking, conferring, writing orders on the backs of old envelopes; he hammered at his battalion commanders for results, pushed his grunts to the edge of exhaustion. Some understood that the only way to save American lives was to keep the Vietnamese on the run. Others were not so charitable towards him. One weary staff officer in 2/7, for example, wrote of an upcoming operation hard on the heels of the summer battles, ". . . regiment had a crumby scheme-of-maneuver designed to kill and wear out the maximum number of Marines. But we got it changed. It was another of those fight up the hill deals."

But most thought Codispoti knew what he was doing. At one regimental briefing, the S-4 (supply) officer got up to report on the amount of food and ammunition each of the twelve rifle companies would have that night. He said one company was down to zero or one can of C rations per man, and Codispoti immediately stopped the briefing to ask why. The supply officer said the company hadn't sent in a ration request form. Codispoti went apeshit, "I don't give a damn if they don't ever send anything! It's your job to keep track of how many rations they have and make sure they have food to carry on and fight out there. And, goddammit, if this ever happens again, I'll pack the rations on your back and you'll walk 'em out to them!''

It made the right impression on everyone.

Not surprisingly, Codispoti and Dowd hit it off well and the regimental commander always smiled on 1st Battalion. The company commanders of 1/7 respectfully likened him to Vince Lombardi and referred to him as Coach Codispoti or the Bear. He was not a grandstander. He'd choppered in to see how his Marines were faring, and to be on hand to provide any outside support that might be needed.

It was still Dowd's ball game, and they moved out as the boiling sun rose. The first skirmish line was formed with D/1/7 on the left, then C/1/7, I/3/5, and L/3/7 on the right. The CP entourage followed Delta Company. The rest of the battalion followed in a second line. The hastily sketched plan was to sweep south from the Hot Dog, then east through the bombed-out tree line. On the other side, they were to pivot north and continue until their hammer met A/1/7's anvil on the banks of the Vu Gia. The artillery batteries at An Hoa and Hill 65 had their tubes up, and Broncos were on station overhead to direct the support fire.

At first, the battalion was like a hound against its leash. They kept stumbling into things in the tree lines—dropped gear, blood trails, an occasional NVA body—and the forward observers with the point platoons reconned each wood line with arty and mortars before the line swept in. They met only token resistance; the NVA were running north. Lieutenant Hord was stunned. He thought they'd kicked ass the day before and didn't expect any resistance today, but the aviation net on his radio was alive with excited Bronco pilots. "They're runnin' all over the place, there's gooks everywhere!" The NVA were breaking up into small groups, but the pilots kept the artillery on them. That was the view from the air. At ground level, it was not so well-defined. Although four Marine rifle companies were spread out on a line stretching for a kilometer, it was not like walking the parade deck. The intersecting tree lines and paddy dikes blocked the view and the enemy was invisible, pausing only to snipe and run. Most men just trudged along, dripping sweat under helmet, flak jacket, and pack; not firing a shot because no targets were visible; and taking some satisfaction in the abandoned NVA packs and ammunition bandoliers dotting their route.

The line finally paused in a tree line facing a large paddy. It was several hundred meters across, as flat and open as a pool table, and the artillery was processed into the opposite tree line. Battalion passed word to continue the sweep. Captain Fagan was wary: the paddy seemed a perfect ambush spot. It would have been wiser first to secure the flanks of the opposite tree line and clear it before walking right into the open. We're in too much of a hurry, he thought. As the men resumed their advance, Fagan glanced to his right; for hundreds of yards, he could see hundreds of Marines materializing from the woods into the sun-blasted and wide-open rice field.

India Company was in the center of the line as it advanced, and Captain Beeler also had a headful of worries. For one thing, his men were exhausted. They'd spent the last three weeks humping the mountains and had returned to the An Hoa Combat Base only the day before; within hours, they were on the move again, this time into the Arizona. Additionally, Beeler didn't know his platoon leaders: his only two experienced officers had to remain at An Hoa, one taking over the exec slot, the other assigned as pay officer. Consequently, 1st and 3d Platoons had untested second lieutenants. 2d Platoon had a career staff sergeant, but Beeler was wary of him; he seemed worn out to the point of being timid.

Their sweep had begun to get strung out almost immediately. 3d Platoon had lagged behind to police up a pile of enemy equipment; at the same time, the rear security of 2d Platoon tripped a booby trap. Beeler radioed 3d Platoon to drop the captured gear and secure an LZ for the medevac.

Only 1st and 2d Platoons entered the open paddy.

Halfway across, a pair of explosions burst near them, a harmless shower of shrapnel and dirt clogs. Everyone instantly dropped flat, looked around, then got moving again when nothing else developed. No one had seen the source of fire or heard anything except the explosions. Beeler figured it had been mortars, until he looked at the tree line facing them. RPGs? He didn't like the way things were shaping up and requested 1/7 to shell the woods again. Forty meters from the trees, he could feel the NVA. The paddy rolled up a three-foot berm to the tree line island; a thick cluster of bamboo sat along the edge of the embankment. 1st Platoon was right in front of the bamboo screen, having just crossed the final paddy dike. Beeler suddenly ran to that dike, hollering to open fire.

Two grunts looked back at him quizzically, then the platoon line triggered a few bursts into the brush.

The next second, the NVA opened fire.

It was an instantaneous eruption, an RPD machine gun jackhammering from within the bamboo clump, a dozen AK47s joining the scythe. The eruption murdered 1st Platoon. The point man, LCpl James Norris, charged the bamboo but was shot dead in his tracks. The new lieutenant dropped with a round in his shoulder, and the squad leader was killed. A dozen others fell wounded, and the survivors squeezed into the ash. Rounds cracked the air inches above their backs. Only a few could or would raise their M16s to fire back. The platoon sergeant, Sgt John Valdez, had saved the day in a similar situation when India Company was in the Que Sons. Pitching smoke grenades to form a screen, he had been able to drag their casualties back under fire and won a Silver Star recommendation. He tried to repeat the success.

Valdez was shot to death as soon as he moved.

Sergeant Valdez had been on his second combat tour, but reportedly had not told his family. He wanted to spare them the worry. His completely unexpected notification of death was followed by posthumous awards of the Silver Star, Bronze Star, and Purple Heart.

In seconds, 1st Platoon had been decimated. 2d Platoon, however, had been out of the line of fire and had jogged into the tree line. Captain Beeler, huddled behind the last dike, radioed the staff sergeant in command to hit the machine gun position from the flanks. As far as he was concerned, all he got from the tired sergeant was a token effort. When the platoon got up to attack, a new man was killed and several were wounded, and the platoon hunkered back among the trees. That is where they sat the rest of the battle.

1st Platoon was pinned down, 2d Platoon was paralyzed, and 3d Platoon was far back in the last tree line. Typical, Beeler thought: the NVA can hide in the trees, but the Marines have to expose themselves in the paddies between the wooded islands. Then the NVA ambush you when you're too close to them to call in supporting arms. Beeler reckoned there was only one NVA platoon in the tree line, a delaying party centered around the machine gun. They had excellent fields of fire, were willing to die in place, and they were accomplishing just what they had intended.

When the ambush began, Captain Fagan was very glad to be on the left side of the skirmish line. There was a tree line there leading to the enemy woods and narrow, shimmering Snake Lake. This lake formed the western boundary of the sweep and gave Delta Company a protected flank.

Delta was in the middle of the paddy when the shooting started, and they caught some stray rounds. Their response was to double-time down the dikes and into the trees, which was done without casualties. They were hastily securing in the wood line when Codispoti approached Fagan. The gruff, old colonel was a bit winded and excited from their run under fire and, not being very formal anyway, he asked for a report. "Holy cow, what's going on?" Fagan was not at all sure, but with all the company commanders on the radio, they pieced it together.

D/1/7 had secured the left flank of the enemy tree line.

L/3/7 had done likewise on the right flank.

I/3/5 was pinned down in the middle.

C/1/7 had pulled back to the woods from which they'd left, joining B/1/7 and H&S/1/7.

Meanwhile, the battalion command post was pinned down in the paddies behind Delta Company. A couple of snipers fired on them from the trees on their left, and stray rounds from the hornet's nest on the right also cracked past. It was the second time that day that the CP had come under fire; saddling up that morning, the NVA had dropped a few mortar rounds on them and SgtMaj Charles C. Awkerman narrowly escaped injury. He'd just finished a C ration breakfast in his foxhole and had moved away when the mortars hit; his pack left beside his hole had been punched through with shrapnel. Now, Sergeant Major Awkerman was down along a dike with Lieutenant Colonel Dowd. Word came on the radio that the CO of India Company had been hit. Dowd told Awkerman to get the CP into Delta Company's position in the woods; then the colonel tagged his radioman and they scrambled over the dike on the right flank. Dowd had never even met the India CO, but such was his professionalism.

The bamboo clump in front of India Company had quieted down: the NVA let go only a burst when a Marine moved. Captain Beeler, still crouched behind the dike, saw a black-haired head pop from a spider hole within the bamboo. He appeared to be spotting for the machine gun. Beeler took an M14 rifle from a sniper—a Scout-Sniper team from 5th Marine Regiment had been travelling with his CP group—and sighted in on the spot. When the head popped up again, he opened fire but the NVA kept dropping back into his hole.

The exchange was going nowhere. The sun was blazing and wounded men were dying in the paddy. Beeler finally decided they'd have to rush the embankment, duck against it out of sight of the bamboo, and toss fragmentation grenades up into the machine gun pit. It was insanely simple: Captain Beeler and his radiomen, Corporal Valley and Lance Corporal Ray, dropped their backpacks and went over the dike, shouting, shooting, running as fast as they could. The RPD suddenly opened fire and Beeler dove to the bank, rolling flat against it. The burst had grazed him—a tear across his left hand, another across the side of his neck which permanently lodged a piece of his flak jacket collar into the wound. Beeler glanced to his right. Corporal Valley and a few others had made it with him and also hugged against the berm; Lance Corporal Ray was clutching his wounded hand. Beeler started lobbing grenades up into the bamboo; the response was a Chicom tossed down at him. It landed beside him and in a reflexive lunge from the prone position, he sprang five feet, then curled with his back to the grenade. The explosion kicked him in the butt—where he had an asspack full of C rations—but there was no pain and he rolled back.

The exchange continued. It was taking forever, and a grunt named Williams was going crazy. Top point man with Spanky Norris, who lay dead in front of the bamboo, he raged with grief and anger. Beeler could see two grunts holding him down to keep him from charging.

The Marines and North Vietnamese were within yards of each other, which is why there was no madhouse of firing. In fact, from a distance, little appeared to be happening. Lieutenant Colonel Dowd and his radioman hiked across the paddy right up to the shooting, until an India Marine hollered to get down because the machine gun hadn't been knocked out yet. Dowd paused, but everything was quiet, so they popped over the next dike. A burst from the machine gun instantly knocked them back down. Lieutenant Colonel Dowd was shot in the head and chest.

He never knew what hit him.

With the battalion commander suddenly vanished from the radio waves, there were a lot of confused calls. Fagan finally got Major Alexander, S-3, 1/7, on the horn. Alexander said, "This is the Six."

"Where's the Actual?"

"He's a Kilo. I'm the Six."

That's how the company commanders were informed that the colonel was dead. Lieutenant Peters, XO, D/1/7, was not very surprised when he heard the news. He'd always thought Dowd was too gungy for his own good. One of the first things Peters learned as a combat officer was to try to look like an enlisted man in the bush. He packed away his gold bars, wore simply an o.d. undershirt under his flak jacket, and traded his .45 pistol for an M16 rifle. One day in July, Peters's platoon had been on an isolated hillock when, from out of nowhere, Lieutenant Colonel Dowd and Sergeant Major Awkerman had come walking towards his perimeter with two riflemen. Not only had they been walking through the Arizona with such a small party, but there had been Dowd in all his glory, cigar jutting from his jaw, walking stick in his hand, and a silver oak leaf on his cover. It had shone in the sun. As far as Peters was concerned, Dowd had been begging for a sniper to hit him. He wondered, with little sympathy, if the colonel had let his macho streak kill him.

Lima Company on the right flank was trying to push through the tree line to assist India Company. When the ambush was first sprung, Lima had been in the paddy with two platoons up and their attached platoon from Kilo back. Lieutenant Colonel Dowd had instantly come over the battalion command net to tell Captain Rider to press the attack into the tree line. Rider gave the order to his two lead lieutenants.

They made an assault right out of the book.

The forward observer crouched behind a burial mound with Rider, calling in more artillery, while the M60 teams jogged to the far right flank and pumped grazing fire across the company's front. The reserve platoon was moved to refuse the right flank, while grunts in the paddy fired cover for fire team and individual rushes. From dike to dike, they edged towards the invisible snipers in the tree line. Everything was going so smoothly that Rider felt more like an observer than a participant, and he found himself standing atop the burial mound more closely to watch his Marines attack; he was beaming.

To understand why the company commanders in this battle were so proud of their riflemen, some background is necessary. In 1965, Rider was a platoon leader in the 7th Marines when they deployed to Vietnam from Camp Pendleton. At that time, most of the senior officers and sergeants had experience ranging from Gaudalcanal to Inchon. Almost all the staff NCOs were veterans of the Korean War, and most of the new corporals and sergeants had at least four years in the Corps. When Rider returned to the regiment in 1969, his company was a body of teenagers. The grunts were mostly new graduates or dropouts from high school, and most of his NCOs had been promoted early due to the manpower drain of Vietnam. He had sergeants who weren't old enough to drink beer legally. His platoon leaders were all Rice Paddy Lieutenants, rushed through a shortened version of Basic School for only one use.

But now these young lieutenants and grunts—with bullets snapping over their heads, but with a tangible enemy finally materializing in this sweaty hell—were charging right at the North Vietnamese.

They were Marines.

Captain Rider was finally chased off that burial mound when his new gunnery sergeant, Gunny Martinez, shouted at him, "Goddammit, skipper, you better get off there or we're going to bury your ass in that bloody mound!" Lima Company got into the trees without casualties, but then took several wounded as they cautiously advanced towards India and Delta Companies: the NVA were firing from spider holes and, with the arty turned off now, snipers had clambered up into the trees.

It was about then that Dowd was killed.

Soon after, Captain Beeler finally got a grenade into the machine-gun pit. The RPD was silenced and he brought 3d Platoon across the paddy to secure the area. They found a dozen dead NVA in the bamboo. The rest were retreating into a cane field behind the tree line, exchanging a few more grenades and rifle shots with Lima Company as they pressed right to left through the trees. Lima tied in with Delta and the firing evaporated. The battalion line consolidated in the woods and medevacs were called in. Captain Rider noticed in particular one wounded man. He couldn't even remember the kid's name because he was a cook at the battalion rear on Hill 10; whenever a company rotated to the base camp, he pestered its CO about going to the bush with them. Rider finally went to the BnXO and got permission to take him on one operation. This was the one and the happy cook accompanied the assault platoons; once in the bush, though, an NVA in a tree dropped a grenade which hit the cook's helmet and exploded. Blood leaked from his ears and nose. When Rider saw the Marine heading for the medevacs, he was deaf, stunned, and looking rather pleased with himself.

Lance Corporal Wells usually carried the primary radio for Dowd. This morning, though, he'd been made the spare operator and a wireman from the comm section went with Dowd. The sweep had been easy going at first; the sun was warm, spirits were up, and a thudding of artillery led the way. Wells was feeling excited and he and a buddy humped along, laughing and humming the latest Beatles' tune: "Happiness is a Warm Gun." Things began slowing down when India Company tripped two booby traps. They paused while a Sea Knight dropped in;

when they resumed the march, everyone closed into a file trying to walk in the footsteps of the man ahead. The rifle companies were moving too fast to collect all the NVA gear in their path, so Wells and a Marine from H&S supply were sent down a footpath to police up what they could carry. The CP kept moving as they ambled down the trail into some thick brush, getting a little lost but not too worried since the NVA were on the run. The small forest seemed deserted by the time they found the NVA 82mm mortar rounds; there were twelve of them, three tied to each end of two sticks to be carried over the shoulder. The men didn't have any explosives to destroy the rounds and the water in the paddy was too shallow to sink them. Reluctantly, they shouldered the enemy ammunition and continued their casual, disoriented stroll.

They finally got to the edge of the woods and rested on a dike. Ahead of them, the grunts were already far into the paddies. That's when the machine gun opened fire.

Wells and his buddy quickly rolled behind the dike as high rounds clipped the woods behind them. The noise was incredible as they watched the fight. Finally, they saw figures run into the trees. Wells was amazed at such bravery. It was the Marine Corps discipline, he reckoned, instilled from boot camp—don't think, just do it! The firing petered out soon after; that's when he noticed the NVA mortar rounds. They'd dumped them atop the dike when they first sat down and they'd laid there during the entire fight; one round could have disintegrated the two spectators.

They shouldered the rounds again and trudged up to where Delta Company and the Battalion Command Post were consolidating. Wells looked for Dowd but he was nowhere in sight. Grunts said he'd been shot. Wells kind of liked the Old Man and gulped, "Oh, Geez!" as he dumped the mortar shells and jogged to where the casualties were being collected. Dowd was right there among the other dead, a poncho over him and a hole in his head. The casualties were being carried to a clearing for medevac, so Wells took the poncho, rolled Dowd into it, then called for some guys to help. Wells toted the colonel's pack and grease gun with the two magazines taped end to end.

In the LZ, Wells noticed the colonel's radioman was waiting in the grass; his face was contorted in great pain from his machine gun wound. On the way back from the LZ to the CP, Wells passed a wounded Marine heading towards the medevac. There was dried blood on his arm and flak jacket, and he was holding his bandaged arm; but he was grinning broadly, "I finally got one confirmed. It's all mine and I got him. I got an NVA to my credit now!"

Lieutenant Hord passed within yards of Dowd's body as he brought Charlie Company into the wood line. His eyes teared. He loved the colonel and had to look away; he couldn't go over and touch the body for fear he would break down.

Medevacs began coming in. There was no fire.

In India Company, corpsmen were finally getting to the men who'd been stuck for hours in the parched field. One, Cpl James Castor, was gravely wounded and they worked frantically on him. Besides him, four men from India had been killed and sixteen others wounded. Captain Beeler's hand was bleeding and swollen, and he tucked it in his flak jacket so the troops wouldn't see it as he moved about. He made sure their prisoner was still alive and had him placed aboard one of the medevacs. Then he turned over command to the new lieutenant leading 3d Platoon, the only officer left. He made sure to have a talk with 3d Platoon's sergeant first, though; this staff sergeant was the only seasoned leader left and Beeler told him to stick with the lieutenant and make sure everything was okay until they got their two experienced lieutenants back in the field.

At 1800, Beeler went out on the last Sea Knight. Corporal Castor was also aboard and corpsmen kept up their efforts to save him all the way to the 1st Medical Battalion, 1st MarDiv, Da Nang, where he was quickly loaded onto a stretcher and rushed inside. The 3/5 Navy chaplain met them there, and Beeler handed him his asspack full of C rations; he was surprised to discover all the cans had been opened by the Chicom shrapnel. He also asked the chaplain to check on Castor—he died on the operating table.

A Navy surgeon gave Beeler a local, sutured up his neck and hand, then sent him to a ward. He didn't feel too badly, at least not until a corpsman noticed he was still bleeding from the neck and had him rushed to intensive care. He lay on a gurney and noticed one of his men, Lance Corporal Stewart, beside him. Stewart had tripped the booby trap that morning, but Beeler had not seen him before the medevac came; he was shocked to see that the young man's leg was gone. After surgery, the Division inspector general and a young Marine came through the ward with a Polaroid camera. The IG presented Captain Beeler with his Purple Heart and the Marine snapped a photo. The IG suggested he send it home as soon as possible to let his relatives see him smiling from a hospital bed. Hopefully, it would allay some of the fears the telegram would bring. Beeler thought that was a good idea and so did his wife; she still carries the photograph.

In the tree line, Major Alexander had assumed command of the battalion. He'd been with 1/7 only about two weeks, but was on his second tour; three years earlier as a company commander with the 4th Marines he had won the Silver Star. Compared to Dowd, he was a taciturn, businesslike man.

Colonel Codispoti, of course, outranked Alexander but, as was proper, Codispoti let the chain of command take effect. Codispoti was still an observer and a helper, and it was now Alexander's ball game. He got on the radio to clear up any confusion and to get the battalion moving again. "Youth Six is Kilo. I am Oscar India Charlie. The plan is this: continue to march and we will make it to the river." There was only token resistance. A few NVA were visible moving through the tree line and Lieutenant Hord, a student of military history, had thoughts of Dunkirk. Alpha Company was waiting for them on the banks of the Vu Gia. As it turned out, the conclusion of the chase more closely resembled one historian's characterization of the cavalry pursuing the plains Indians: ". . . like an amoeba each band would divide, divide, and divide again, and again, and once again, leaving a less and less distinct trail, with the result that his blue-jacketed cavaliers never could catch anybody to punish."

Captain Clark's Alpha Company did not have the opportunity to machine gun the retreating swarm. In their three days as block along the Vu Gia, they had spotted the NVA only once: a party of six the morning after the initial attack. They killed one. Besides that, all they'd found were booby traps: one USMC KIA, one USMC WIA.

The *90th NVA Regiment* melted into Charlie Ridge.

This was all the victory the North Vietnamese could claim against Dowd's battalion; to kill fewer than thirty Marines, they had left almost three hundred of their own in the paddy fields. The five companies of the sweep consolidated with the one company along the river before dark. There they dug a huge perimeter. The grunts stripped to the waist to scrape out foxholes amid the high, bright green elephant grass; and there they hunkered down, spent, depressed, elated, glad it was over.

Around them, the sky was a pale twilight blue, clouds streaked low on the horizon; and the river was a wide, crystal blue reflection of the green shore.

Fagan stood with Hord at dusk and said simply but, to Hord, very profoundly, "We'll never forget this."

However, it wasn't quite over.

The night was a Disneyland of pyrotechnics. There was illumination from dusk till dawn, a constant succession of poppings and airborne spotlights floating down. In this stark, flat landscape of black and white elephant grass, an NVA sapper unit crept up to the perimeter. Sergeant Lowery of Charlie Company picked up his second Purple Heart in two days in the first volley: he was sitting with his lieutenant in their little poncho shelter when a Chicom thumped into the ground beside them. There was a brilliant flash, then the realization that almost everyone in the hootch had been peppered with little pieces of metal.

Charlie Company killed two NVA in front of their foxholes, but most of the shooting was on Bravo Company's side of the line. Lieutenant Weh figured there was a platoon of NVA in the brush, but it was a relatively quiet fight. The NVA only threw grenades and Weh's Marines sat in their holes under the continuing illum, firing only single shots when heads or backs rose above the grass. Weh was impressed by his men's cool marksmanship. So were the NVA. They pulled back and Bravo found seven of their dead at dawn.

■ On 14 August, 1/7 Marines crossed the Song Vu Gia without incident. The river was wide and shimmered fiercely under the sun, but it was only knee-deep and the grunts forded it in a long, snaking file. They rested their weapons over their shoulders like tramp sticks, let their flak jackets hang open, secured their helmets to packs, and put on covers or bush hats. They were headed home. A dozen Marines dropped their gear on the opposite side and helped their heavily burdened comrades up the bank. Behind them, a contingent from 3/7 Marines had secured Route 4 and was waiting with amtracs and trucks, and food and water. Among them were combat photographers from the Information Services Office, 1st Marine Division, and a dozen civilian journalists with minicams and microphones. By the time Charlie Company crossed the river, they had to file between two columns of Marines to reach the road. The reporters were behind that line, shouting questions about the number of casualties and the dead colonel, but word was passed not to talk with them until after debriefing.

Lance Corporal Bradley looked at the reporters as if they were vultures. He never saw one in the bush, and was convinced they twisted things to fit their own political perceptions. One kept shouting questions louder than the rest.

"Fuck off!" Bradley snapped.

The convoy on Route 4 deposited the weary battalion to Hill 55. It was time to unwind, rehab, and, for the officers at least, complete the administrative side of every battle. Witness statements for personal decorations were taken; there was talk of a Medal of Honor for Dowd. A score of other recommendations were typed up, and the battalion as a whole was submitted for a Meritorious Unit Commendation, which was later approved. Other duties were less pleasant; there were wounded to be visited.

The detail which came last was the most painful. On 17 August, the battalion held a formation in an outdoor ceremony honoring their dead. American and Marine Corps flags, a forest of battle streamers hanging from the standard, flapped beside a wooden platform. There was a row of M16 rifles in front of the platform, bayonets in the dirt. Twenty-two rifles, twenty-two helmets, twenty-two pairs of jungle boots. Sergeant Major Awkerman—whose father had served with the Marine Corps in WWI, and who himself had landed at Gaudalcanal, Saipan, and Okinawa—read the honor roll.

LtCol John A. Dowd (CO, 1/7)
Cpl John R. Constien (B/1/7)
HM3 Alan W. Brashears, USN (H&S/1/7)
LCpl Joseph G. Sands (B/1/7)
LCpl D. P. Quinlan (B/1/7)
LCpl Fred J. Delarenzo (D/1/7)
LCpl Charles J. Garity (C/1/7)
LCpl Harvey Peay (C/1/7)
LCpl James Cashman (D/1/7)
PFC James R. Rice (A/1/7)
PFC Charles A. Hood (B/1/7)
PFC Benjamin W. Stone (B/1/7)
PFC Joseph Colorio (D/1/7)
PFC Gerald Rios (D/1/7)

PFC Tilmen Bartholomew (D/1/7)
PFC James Braham (D/1/7)
PFC Phillip Guzman (B/1/7)
PFC Stephen Kelly (B/1/7)
PFC Ronald Ray (B/1/7)
PFC G. D. Tate (B/1/7)
PFC W. R. Wilson (B/1/7)
PFC Carlos Baldizon (A/1/7)

The next day, 1st Battalion, 7th Marines got what everyone who'd survived what they'd seen deserved: a rest. One company at a time, the battalion was rotated through Stack Arms, an in-country R and R center within the compound of the 3d Amtrac Battalion on China Beach north of Da Nang. Stack Arms had been opened in June exclusively for the infantry, a labor of love by General Simpson. His motivations were expressed on the wooden sign that hung above the compound gate: ". . . in recognition and appreciation of the tremendous load these Marines are carrying for Corps and country."

D Company was the first to Stack Arms and Lance Corporal Wells went with them. They filed in, handed over their weapons, ammunition, gear, and faded jungle fatigues, and getting undershirts and tiger-stripe shorts. Then a gunnery sergeant herded them to an outdoor theater and mounted the stage. The gunny pointed to fifty-five-gallon drums filled with ice and beer and shouted, "Okay, everybody go get a beer!" Wells was swept forward in the pandemonium; then the men settled back onto the wooden benches. The gunny surveyed them tight-lipped. "What's wrong with you, you're not really Marines! You only have one beer! I want to see a beer in each hand!" The grunts exploded, shouting, spraying beer—laughing.

Stack Arms lasted three days, three whole days without any duties or lifer harassment. The grunts loved it. They watched movies all night. They showered and shaved in hot water. They played football on the beach. They telephoned home via a communications unit. Some got drunk. Some got stoned. They slept on cots. They ate steak, chicken, hot dogs, hamburgers, drank can after can of beer the first day and opted for soda the next two days. Most overdid it, but it smoothed out the wrinkles. Wells ate so much the first day, he barely ate afterwards. Bradley got drunk for the first time and his buddies dragged him to bed. He woke up, put his trousers on backwards, and ran into the ocean. He managed to wash up before the lifeguards had to dive in. Zotter watched a buddy careen drunkenly towards a general who was shaking hands and talking with the grunts. The kid stumbled and crashed at his feet. He looked up, ''Goddamn, I never got to shake hands with a fucking general before!''

The officer reached down. ''Well here's your chance, son.''

They both laughed, everyone loved it, and the next morning, Zotter found his section leader, Staff Sergeant Gordon, passed out in the barbed wire.

The 1st Battalion, 7th Marines came out of the Arizona on 14 August and rotated its companies through Stack Arms from the 18th to the 25th; on the 20th, Delta Company led the incremental move south to LZ Baldy for another combat operation.

The Americal Division was in trouble.

The command had been trying to preempt this trouble since 20 July, the day Operation Durham Peak began. Three battalions (2/1, 2/5, and 3/5) had been sent into the Que Sons south of the An Hoa Combat Base to draw the *2d NVA Division* into a fight. The op lasted three weeks and claimed the lives of fifteen Marines and seventy-six North Vietnamese. There were numerous important finds, including a large and hastily evacuated NVA hospital equipped with Swedish surgical instruments of the highest quality. The 5th Marines regimental report wrote it up as a victory: ''. . . Although large scale enemy contact was not experienced, Operation DURHAM PEAK was considered highly successful in that it denied the enemy freedom of movement in his normally natural haven. The presence of a multi-battalion force caused the enemy to abandon his numerous base camps and flee to the lowlands north and south. . . . Numerous large base camps and caches were discovered and destroyed. In addition, valuable intelligence information was gained concerning the Que Son Mountains, e.g. trail networks, base camps, and caves. . . .''

General Simpson agreed, but had his reservations. The whole point had been to pin the *2d NVA Division,* to cripple them before they could choose the time and place for their offensive. The enemy had not been pinned. Simpson was impressed at how quickly and completely the NVA could fade away; more than once, his Marines had found warm cooking fires in deserted camps.

Simpson was also frustrated. At the start of the operation, he had coordinated with General Ramsey, CG, Americal Division, whom he knew and liked, about providing a block south of the Que Sons. That was the AO of 4–31 Infantry, 196th Brigade; but tied down with the protection of LZ West, LZ Siberia, and the Hiep Duc Resettlement Village, they had been able to deploy only C and D Companies. Two companies to screen the eight-mile northern frontier of the Hiep Duc Valley.

The NVA walked right past them.

One of the Americal's gravest problems was that they were stretched too thinly and simply could not afford the units and material required for every mission (the joke among the grunts was that an airmobile combat assault in the Americal was one helicopter making fifteen trips). In addition, the demarcation line between the Marines and the Army was right down the Que Sons, making neither division wholly responsible. U.S. units were instinctively wary of AO borders and the NVA knew this.

Then came the night of 11–12 August 1969, when the *2d NVA Division* was able to bring the war down from the mountains on their own terms. While the 1st Marine Division was fighting around Da Nang and An Hoa, the Americal Division had been fending off another series of attack. Within days, Simpson and Ramsey conferred, and Ramsey then approached the commanding general, III Marine Amphibious Force; they wanted to expand the 1st MarDiv south to assume LZ Baldy, LZ Ross, and (finally) the whole of the Que Sons. That would take the pressure off the Americal and provide reinforcements for the counterattack.

PART ■ ■

Gimlets and Polar Bears

Chapter Six

Landing Zone West

S P4 Ray Keefer was feeling good. He was shooting the shit with his buddies, a beer in one hand and a joint in the other. They were a dusty, coarse, loud crew. Their unit, A Troop, 1st Squadron, 1st Armored Cavalry, Americal Division, was preparing positions at Chu Lai in preparation for the arrival of the rest of the unit from Hawk Hill. Chu Lai was a quieter area and for Keefer—a nineteen year old who'd been wounded four times—this was cause enough to get loaded. Which is exactly what he and his buddies were doing in the warm evening air—until the radios in their vehicles came alive.

It was the night of 11–12 August 1969.

C Troop reported incoming fire; they were still on Hawk Hill (on Highway One between Tam Ky and LZ Baldy), providing security for an Americal infantry battalion that was assuming their old squadron base camp. Then they reported NVA in the wire. A second call for help came in; two tanks from A Troop were providing security on a hill outpost, and the commander of tank two-nine reported RPG fire.

The 1st Regiment of Dragoons had the reputation not only of being professional heads, but professional killers; in response to these calls, the men at Chu Lai scrambled to their vehicles. Keefer had heard no order to do so, but they pulled up to the post gate. Men were standing on the decks of their tanks and tracks, flak jackets over bare chests, frag grenades and smokes hanging across gun shields, and they broke out the ammunition for the machine guns as they argued with the MPs on duty to open the fucking gate! The adrenaline was pumping, but an officer appeared and simmered them down. The only way to Hawk

Hill, he explained, was up Highway One. The NVA were attacking throughout the area and they most likely had set up along the road to ambush the re-act; plus, the highway was hemmed in by rice paddies and their vehicles couldn't maneuver well in them. The men returned to their bunkers, pissed off, and frustrated. They could only sit and monitor the jumbled conversations coming over the radio. NVA inside the wire at Hawk Hill. Artillerymen firing their 105-point blank. A GI from tank two-nine shouting that they'd taken two RPG hits and needed a medevac for two men seriously wounded with shrapnel in the chest and face. Medevacs kept away by the ground fog and ground fire. Automatic fire and explosions came through the buzz of the radio.

Little else had been as painful to Keefer as listening to buddies dying and not being able to do a damn thing to help.

■ That night was the beginning of the 1969 Summer Offensive. More than a hundred locations, both military and civilian, including hospitals, were shelled or attacked by the communists; most attacks were ended or repulsed by dawn. One assault, however, was to be the start of something bigger. The target was Landing Zone West, base camp of the 4th Battalion, 31st Infantry, overlooking the Hiep Duc Valley. Sappers and infantrymen of the *3d Regiment, 2d NVA Division* crept up this jungled mountainside under the cover of darkness, toting satchel charges and automatic weapons, their skin blackened with charcoal. In addition, three Soviet-manufactured 12.7mm antiaircraft guns had already been dug in at the base of LZ West to hamper medevacs and gunships.

Thus, 12 August was the official beginning of the battle for Hiep Duc Valley; but it was really on 8 August that the troubles began for the Polar Bear battalion.

Delta 4th of the 31st Infantry had made that contact.

Delta Company was commanded by Capt Norman B. Mekkelsen, a soft-spoken West Pointer. The company's premature contact with the NVA occurred in Happy Valley. This populated rice bowl—named because it was sniper-infested and everyone was damn happy when they left it—was north of LZ West and south of LZ Ross. It sat at the eastern tip of Nui Chom, the rugged ridge line defining the northern frontier of Hiep Duc Valley. C and D Companies had been sent in to screen for the USMC's Operation Durham Peak.

On 8 August, a platoon from Delta under a new lieutenant surprised five NVA at a lowland stream. They gunned down four, then hastily chased the survivor as he disappeared up a brushy slope of Nui Chom. It was rough going and one of the platoon's best soldiers was near the front of the uphill chase. As he climbed over a huge boulder, an AK47 suddenly opened fire from only yards away, nailing the grunt in the chest. He fell dead as heavy NVA fire erupted. At the time, Captain Mekkelsen was about two kilometers away with 1st Lt Juan Gonzalez's platoon. Mekkelsen tried to raise the platoon in contact, but no one answered. The RTO finally responded, then gave the mike to his lieutenant. This was his first firefight and—with AK rounds snapping just overhead and Chicom stick handle grenades bouncing down at them—he reported he was pinned down. The NVA were above them on the mountainside, concealed in spider holes burrowed under boulder outcroppings.

Mekkelsen radioed back that he'd better get his platoon organized and moving, or they'd die in place.

The new lieutenant said they couldn't move.

Exasperated, Mekkelsen told Gonzalez to be ready to move immediately if needed. He then gathered his weapon and ammunition, took his FO and RTO, and told Gonzalez to get his two M60 teams and come with them. Gonzalez was one of their more able platoon leaders, and Mekkelsen wanted him up front so he would know the score if they had to call for the entire platoon.

This small group jogged towards the pinned-down platoon and, via radio, got the general location of the GIs and NVA. They decided to hike up the mountainside some four hundred meters to the right of the NVA dugouts, then hit them from that flank. Going uphill, they passed an area of flat boulders that had recently been used as an NVA latrine. Most of the shit was in loose piles—Mekkelsen wasn't unhappy to note the enemy was suffering from diarrhea—but there was too much of it, indicating that, as was later estimated, Delta had run into an NVA company.

They were close to the sound of shooting when they were faced with the choice of exposing themselves by climbing over more boulders or continuing along a crevice in the rocks with their backs against one side, their feet against the other, and a ten-foot drop below them. They opted for the latter alternative and, after getting an M60 positioned to cover them, Captain Mekkelsen led the way down the crevice with Lieutenant Gonzalez coming next. An NVA suddenly fired down the channel.

Mekkelsen felt something slam into his left knee, the one facing the enemy, and in the next moment the M60 gunner was returning fire and the rest were throwing grenades. It was over quickly but Mekkelsen noticed that Gonzalez was leaning forward. He said he thought he'd been hit in the back, but there were no apparent marks when Mekkelsen pushed up his sweaty undershirt. "Well," said Gonzalez, "I guess I'm not hit."

"If you're not," Mekkelsen answered, "I am!" The M60 gunners hauled them up, and they got a bandage around his seriously damaged knee. Mekkelsen did not report his wound to battalion—it was his company and he'd handle this mess. He leaned against his radioman as they continued up. At their advance, the NVA disappeared. They linked up with the ambushed platoon, recovered the dead GI, and arranged to medevac the one or two wounded men. The RTO also finally reported their wounded captain.

That's when the 4–31 Command & Control Huey came in. Aboard were LtCol Cecil M. Henry, BnCO; Maj Roger C. Lee, BnS-3; and Capt Phillip Kinman, Bn-Surgeon (he was exceptional for a draftee doctor, practically fighting his way onto the command ship whenever there was a report of wounded GIs in the field). They launched from LZ West and were orbiting Nui Chom in minutes. The platoon was near a ravine formed by the erosion of a long-dried-up waterfall. This looked to be the best LZ on the forested ridge, so the grunts popped smoke and the pilot homed in. The Huey glided to a hover along the eroded hole, one skid against a rock ledge, and Major Lee stood on the other skid to give Mekkelsen a hand up. The North Vietnamese opened fire again as they pulled up. Lieutenant Colonel Henry was crammed behind the pilot's seat with headphones on as the pilot shouted to his copilot, "Slump down in your armored seat 'cause we're taking beaucoup fire!" The NVA were shooting down on the rising chopper from their mountain perches. The Huey was only yards from the slope. A Chicom was flipped in the open cabin door and, just as quickly, Major Lee reflexively kicked it out the opposite door. The grenade exploded beneath them. The pilot finally got them over the peak—actually it took only seconds—then banked the Huey around and got the hell out.

As they headed for the medical station on Hawk Hill, Henry radioed Delta Company to pull back from their untenable position and regroup on the valley floor. He then switched frequencies to get air and arty support for them. It was a five-minute flight to Hawk Hill, and they just had the chance to wish Mekkelsen well before the medics carted him off. Then the C&C hopped back over to where Delta had regrouped. The platoon leader was a senior first lieutenant, so Henry passed command to him.

The C&C also picked up Lieutenant Gonzalez; three AK47 rounds had punched into the M16 bandolier around his waist, smashing the ammunition magazines, but only bruising him. Gonzalez handed Lee some wild peppers he'd picked, while Doc Kinman plucked out fragmented metal slivers that had pierced his skin. Lee put the peppers in his pocket, and they raised a welt on his thigh through the cloth. Gonzalez had been eating those monsters. He hailed from Durango, Mexico, and he was a tough hombre.

He joked about his good luck in the ambush.

All in all, Delta Company was in a foul mood. Besides losing Captain Mekkelsen, they'd lost their first KIA since November 1968. This was significant since Delta was rated the best in the battalion, a fact due to their fine company commanders. Capt John A. Whittecar, a hard-core professional on his second tour, had taken over Delta after the November battle along Nui Chom. Before rotating to a staff position on LZ West, he had shaped his listless draftees into a proud company. Captain Mekkelsen, the son of a sergeant major, took over the reins in June after serving as a platoon leader under Whittecar.

Bravo Company, under Capt William H. Gayler, and Charlie Company, under Capt Thomas L. Murphy, were a notch below. They were colorless companies whose performances ranged from mediocre to workmanlike depending upon conditions; they were typical of the Americal Division. Then there was Alpha Company, which was especially short of experienced NCOs (the battalion was lucky if it could muster one or two Regular Army NCOs per company; most were "shake 'n' bakes" going from private to sergeant after a ninety-day course). In addition, Alpha's cautious and popular commander, Capt Stanley Yates, had recently rotated; the new CO, Capt James G. Mantell, and an unhealthy number of troopers were FNGs, or Fucking New Guys. One indicator of the low morale in Alpha Company was that, by Doc Kinman's count, the company harbored a disproportionate number of malingerers.

This is, of course, all subjective.

So is a discussion of the battalion staff, whose members were as diverse as the companies they led. Lieutenant Colonel Henry and Major Lee both had previous tours as ARVN advisors under their belts and were professionally respected. Despite very different personal backgrounds, they meshed well and they drove their battalion hard in what was generally a complacent, quiet time. Henry—a man with a big, bald dome and a friendly face—was a product of the hardscrabble farms and two-room schoolhouses of Rome, Georgia. He had enlisted soon after his eighteenth birthday, served in the rear during the Korean War, then earned an OCS commission. He was almost a fatherly figure, hard when he had to be, consoling at times, a man who did not take the deaths of his troopers lightly. He had come to LZ West in July and was considered a rock under pressure.

Major Lee was not as well liked. A high school wrestler from Omaha, Nebraska, he had graduated from West Point only after some academic difficulties. He was an Airborne Ranger who stood stern-faced and crewcut in his fatigues. Many considered him a ticket-puncher, too harsh and spit-shined; but he was a fighter. In June, when sappers penetrated LZ Baldy and raised hell, Lee had been serving as battalion executive officer. He saw one NVA crawl down a drainage ditch and duck under a culvert, and GIs screamed that another had gone under a hootch. Major Lee shot them both to death, and caught some light shrapnel in the stomach when the satchel charge of the one under the culvert detonated. He and a captain then ran to the part of the perimeter manned by the brigade LRRPs, and reorganized those men who'd been stunned into inaction when one of the first RPGs demolished a bunker and killed the two men inside. For that, Lee won a Bronze Star recommendation. He was aggressive, but he was not unyielding. Early in his tenure on LZ West, he assigned the line companies a fierce schedule of humping six klicks a day and then patrolling. Captain Gayler, a Texas volunteer, finally told him, "What you should do is grab your rucksack and come out in the bush, because you've lost touch with the realities out here." Major Lee maintained a hard stare in return and Captain Gayler gulped, but then Lee grinned, "Maybe you're right."

Battalion SgtMaj Hoss Gutterez, a Mexican-American, was big, crass, boastful, and an all-around gutsy soldier.

Comments on these men came chiefly from the commanders above them and the company commanders below them. Most of the grunts in the 4th of the 31st Infantry didn't really know who the staff members were and either routinely saluted them or routinely dismissed them as chicken shit lifers. Such feelings are not hard to understand. A young grunt living in the mud was bound to be less than charitable to those who saw the war mostly from helicopters. Such feelings are common in any war, but it is important to note that there were no fraggings during Henry's command. Most of the grunts just reluctantly resigned themselves and kept humping. As far as Gayler was concerned, the men were lucky that under Henry and Lee, battalion headquarters was not as far removed from the bush as it was under some other officers.

9 August saw the second contact in two days.

The Polar Bear's part in the screening operation was terminated and Lieutenant Colonel Henry and Sergeant Major Gutterez dropped into Charlie Company's perimeter to supervise their airlift from Happy Valley to LZ Siberia. The men planned to go out with the last squad; that was all they had left on the ground when a higher priority mission arose elsewhere and division yanked their helicopter support. The stranded group decided to hump to LZ West, and they were on the trail below the camp when firing erupted. Everyone dropped in the bushes. Gutterez led several men around the flank and fired towards the NVA, who immediately broke contact and disappeared into the vegetation. The fight lasted perhaps five minutes, but the squad stayed put another thirty until a detachment from Bravo Company humped down from West.

It wasn't until 2000 that the squad finally got to LZ Siberia. They were pissed off and shaken. One of them launched into a fabulous story for his comrades who'd missed the skirmish, which reflected the knee-jerk cynicism of the grunts.

. . . Our point man came face to face with three NVA. I'm telling you, he could see the dinks' faces. They were twenty-five yards away. Our guy raised his gun and—click—nothing. The round didn't chamber. So our second guy came up to support, and we were in a damn firefight. Bullets were flying everywhere. I don't know how we missed each other. Most of us took cover behind stumps and trees. The colonel tried to dig himself a hole, he was so scared. But the sergeant major was a big dude, maybe six-three, two hundred and fifty pounds. Everybody's sergeant—toughass, part Indian, World War II hero, and probably hadn't been in one of these things for thirty years. He was so excited, I thought he was going to have a heart attack. He pulled his handgun, a forty-five—a forty-five, mind you—and started hollering, 'Come on, you guys, let's go get those bastards. Fuckin' gooks. This is what we're here for. You on the right, when I say charge, you charge. On the left, when I say pin 'em down, you open fire.' The son of a bitch almost got us killed. What's worse, we missed dinner, so that's two nights in a row without anything to eat.

On 9, 10, and 11 August, LZ Siberia was mortared.

When Alpha Company 4–31 was choppered to LZ West on the morning of 11 August, they had a collective case of the ass. The new colonel was stressing aggressive patrols and night ambushes, but the new captain didn't seem to have the experience required. Among those pissed off grunts, Specialist Parsons was probably dragging the most. He'd been out of the bush for twenty days—extending his R and R by shamming with some buddies in the rear—and the last six days back in the field had been grueling. His load of M60 machine gun, ammunition, and rucksack had been kicking his ass like a new guy again. He was mighty glad this morning as Alpha Company replaced Bravo Company on the LZ West bunker line for their week of palace guard. The Bravo GIs weren't enthusiastic about returning to the bush; when Parsons's gun team took over one of their bunkers, they found a lot of machine gun ammo and grenades stashed under the cots. That much less to hump on patrol.

LZ West was no different from hundreds of fire bases dotting the Vietnamese wilderness. It rambled for several hundred yards across the humps of the ridge. Thirty bunkers, constructed of metal culvert halves, timber, and sandbags, ringed the LZ; each looked like a miniature sandbag castle. Chain-link fence circled most of the post, and in the brush creeping downhill was concertina and tangle foot wire. In the center of the perimeter, the 4–31 Tactical Operations Center was bunkered in under heavy layers of sandbags. More barbed wire twisted around it. Several radio aerials were stiff above these bunkers, and an American flag hung from one. A PP55 ground radar unit was installed beside the TOC. Dug in at the south end of the LZ were three 155mm pieces (C Battery, 3–16 Artillery), and an M55 truck mounted with .50-caliber machine guns (G Battery, 55th Artillery) sat at the northeast and southwest sides of the mountain base.

The LZ was hot, dusty, and boring—very boring. The big diversion was killing rats or, if you were so inclined, finally breaking out the marijuana stashed at the bottom of your ruck. Mostly, the LZ offered the line grunt a place to relax.

Which is just what Barry Parsons wanted. Along with Tom, Bubba, and Shorty from the weapons squad, Parsons was assigned to Bunker 30, the point position on the western side of the line. The men were sitting around when their platoon leader, 1stSgt James F. Price, and their platoon sergeant, Sgt O. J. Causey, came in to pass the word.

They were to be on alert that night because of the recent contacts, and in the morning they would be making a sweep of the LZ mountainside. Tom and Shorty were FNGs so they didn't bitch as loud as Parsons and Bubba; nevertheless, they pulled their watches. Parsons had the second shift, from 2230 to 0030. He woke up Tom to take his place, rolled onto a cot, and the next thing he knew Sergeant Causey was waking them up.

Causey, a shake 'n' baker, was worked up and, as he usually did when he was excited, he stammered hard, "Th-th-there are d-dinks in front of y-your bunker!"

Parsons sat up on his cot. "Sure, O. J. Don't feed us this shit, I want to get some sleep."

"I'm n-not kidding!"

Parsons got up and peered into the black. Their artillery was firing and, in the flashes, he suddenly saw the silhouettes. A figure was visible a hundred yards downhill; he was standing and pointing. Six figures crouched behind him, carrying what looked like Bangalore torpedoes— wide bamboo poles packed with explosives.

"Holy shit, there they are!"

Parsons was rattled. The day before in the bush, the platoon had reconned by fire and a bullet had sheared apart in the barrel of his M60. The barrel had been taken to the battalion maintenance hootch. He was without his pig gun and quickly cranked the internal land line to the company command bunker. First Sergeant Price answered. Top Price was an older man, called to active duty from the national guard, and he was something of a father figure to the platoon. He was also respected, especially in comparison to the inexperienced young guys with the instant stripes who populated the battalion. Typically, Top Price told Parsons not to get excited.

"Excited hell! I have dinks in front of my position with Bangalore torpedoes and God knows what else, and I need some firepower!"

Top Price said wait one, and cut to B-TOC.

The officer who answered said to calm down.

Parsons was instantly pissed. Fucking lifers! He shouted to Top Price, "Tell him to come look for himself!"

More than one officer had, in fact, come to look for himself. Earlier, the GI manning the radar had picked up movement at three thousand meters. Lieutenant Colonel Henry, falling asleep on his cot in a room adjacent to the TOC command bunker, quickly pulled his clothes back on; in response to the warning, he put the base on 100 percent alert and got the artillery and mortar crews to their pieces. Artillery began thundering into the pitch-black. This had been going on for some time with no response to indicate anyone was really out there. Henry and Lee joked, "For all the rounds we're expending, there better be at least one dead dink in the wire!" Major Lee casually strolled down to the bunker line—wearing a T-shirt, a pair of blue jeans, and shower sandals, and carrying no weapon—and peered through one of the Starlite Scope mounts. Flares were fired and, in the yellow glow, nothing was visible; then the flare burned out and the sea of elephant grass around the hill seemed to move in his night scope. Lee peered at one of the fingers coming off the hilltop, he could see figures darting from boulder to boulder.

At the same time, Captain Whittecar (recently rotated from D Company to serve as air operations officer) had trotted down to one of the quad-fifty gun positions. He too saw nothing at first, until a vague impression of movement prompted him to tell the gun crew to recon by fire. They ripped off a burst and a Bangalore torpedo suddenly shrieked up like a deflating balloon with a rooster tail of fire trailing it. Whittecar shouted to fire a flare and, in the sudden glare, they caught some NVA in midstride, slithering through the high grass and shoving torpedoes under the wire to blow pathways. The gun crew started sending a stream of red tracers at them.

Doc Kinman was in the TOC when the .50-calibers suddenly erupted; someone joked, "Aw bullshit, nothing's out there. He's always smoking marijuana."

That's when Lee and Whittecar jogged back.

And that's when the defense of Landing Zone West really began. Within a minute, a nervous GI ran down to Bunker 30. He handed Parsons an M60 machine gun, then ran back towards the TOC. From the bunkers, Alpha Company and Echo Recon sent M16 and M60 tracers into every noise or movement; M79 grenadiers fired dozens of rounds. From the center of the perimeter, the 81mm and 4.2-inch crews of the Echo Mortar Platoon had their tubes angled almost straight up, pumping out illumination rounds. Artillery was being fired from LZ West itself, and from LZ Siberia, LZ Center, and LZ Ross.

The hill was lit up like a Christmas tree.

Parsons was on the M60, while Tom, Shorty, and Bubba fired their M16s from the bunker and tossed grenades downhill. The ammo stash left by Bravo Company was coming in very handy. The quad-fifty fired tracers like red cigars across the clearing, and Parsons could see NVA flop like rag dolls. Six panicked under the fusillade and took off downhill. Parsons saw them on the main trail, heads bobbing above the brush, headed towards a slight open rise on the path. He quickly sighted his M60 on the spot and cut loose when they ran into view. They all appeared to collapse amid the tracers.

The North Vietnamese were trapped on the slope between the firing from the bunker line and the howitzer fire from Siberia, which blocked their escape routes. The result was chaos. Some NVA tried to hide; others tried to run away. They did not return any fire; at least the only NVA fire that could be heard above the racket was a single mortar round. Realizing that everything was clicking into place and that the battle had turned into a turkey shoot, Lieutenant Colonel Henry and Major Lee ambled out to the bunker line. They spent the remainder of the night atop a bunker, watching the show. GIs were out of their bunkers too, laughing, shouting to one another.

By 0630 it was over. There were no U.S. casualties.

That's when Parsons noticed that his M60 barrel was red-hot and the floor of the bunker was covered with expended brass and links.

With dawn, reinforcements were choppered atop LZ West and gunships homed in on the NVA parties moving away from the base of the hill. Delta Company had been in the bush when the attack began; they conducted a forced march, found a clearing, and Chinooks lifted them to the base at first light. Delta swept out from the bunker line Alpha was still holding, M16s anxious in their hands, looking over the NVA bodies and equipment strewn in the grass with fear, surprise, and excitement. Eventually, SP4 Robert Ferris and SP4 Barry Harper lit up cigarettes and took a break, sitting back-to-back on a boulder. Right in front of Ferris, a North Vietnamese sat up in the tall grass as if waking from a concussion.

Their eyes locked for a second; then, simultaneously, the NVA reached for a basket of Chicoms as Ferris snapped his M16 to his shoulder. It jammed. In the time it took Harper to twist around and fire, Ferris rapped the butt of his M16 against the boulder, thus sliding the bolt back, ejecting the jammed round, and chambering the next one. He opened fire too.

The NVA was blown full of holes where he sat.

When Alpha Company made its sweep, Parsons was unnerved by what they found. Some of their claymores had been turned around to aim at them, and their trip flares had been secured with string. Split bamboo poles, white side up, had been laid uphill through the grass as guides to the infantrymen following the sappers. Directly in front of their bunker, maybe seventy yards down, two NVA were hunkered dead with an RPG. We were the point bunker, he thought—that was meant for us!

Besides the piles of weapons and equipment, there were bodies— fifty-nine that they could find. The sweep also came up with six prisoners, all wounded and left behind in the chaotic morning retreat. They were quickly interrogated; why had they not returned fire or retired when it was still dark? They said they were under strict orders not to attack until twilight, when they thought the Americans would be changing guards and be least prepared. When the firing began in the dark, some of their officers were killed; others disappeared. No new orders were received. Such inflexible discipline was not uncommon in the North Vietnamese Army.

The NVA dead were buried in shell craters as helicopters arrived, bearing General Ramsey, Colonel Tackaberry, and a cabinful of reporters.

The lull was definitely over for the Polar Bears.

That evening, Lieutenant Colonel Henry and Major Lee requested the brigade aviation officer to take them on a night recon flight. From LZ West they flew north to Nui Chom, from where Henry thought the sappers had come. As they cleared the crest of the mountain, they saw campfires on the northern slope some distance away. Henry radioed the artillery battery on West and, in short order, white phosphorus rounds were bursting around the dots of light. They were quickly extinguished. The men flew back to the mountain pass between LZ West and Center. There were more lights and these too were hastily doused as the noise of the helicopter echoed down to the enemy bivouac area. These sightings prompted Henry to send Bravo Company north into the Hiep Duc Valley, and Delta Company south into the Song Chang Valley. Search & Destroy. But, once again, the enemy was choosing to evade them.

■ On the morning of 11 August, the Marines began their move south into the AO of the Americal Division. The advance group was a team of liaison and communications personnel from 2d Battalion, 7th Marines off the Da Nang line. It was a routine move and 1stLt John H. Pidgeon, XO, C Company, 11th Motor Transport Battalion, 1st Marine Division, was assigned as convoy commander.

Pidgeon was just getting off his truck after an An Hoa run when he was told to report to the BnS-4; the supply officer didn't know what was up, but lent him a jeep to report in to Division. Pidgeon was briefed at 1st MarDiv HQ. A lieutenant from 2/7, whose rifle platoon would perform convoy security, provided most of the details. It was not complicated. Pidgeon would have thirty-five trucks (every fourth one with a cab-mounted .50-cal.) plus a wrecker to tow any damaged vehicles; they'd be carrying mostly ammunition. An aerial observer would be on station in case fire support was needed. There was also a briefer from the Americal Division, a lieutenant colonel from LZ Baldy, who painted a rosy picture. The roads were swept every day without incident, he said; the area was a model pacification zone. No sweat, Pidgeon thought, straight down Highway One, unload, then head for home.

It was a quiet trip. The only thing unusual he noticed on the way to Baldy was that the Vietnamese along the road didn't wave. He wasn't sure what to make of it. Were they being watched? Their final destination was LZ Ross, a small outpost northeast of Nui Chom; it was fifteen klicks west of Baldy down an old colonial road named Route 535. The convoy was cutting through a large, flat expanse of sand and brush when the truck ahead of Pidgeon with a grunt squad aboard rounded a curve in the road. There was an explosion, a geyser of sand on the shoulder. Then silence. Everyone kept rolling, per procedure, and Pidgeon looked at the crater as they passed. No truck treads were near it. It had been a command-detonated mine.

The enemy was out there all right.

Their mine had done no damage because the Marine truck driver had remembered his training. The VC planted their mines in the shoulder of the roads to take advantage of lazy drivers who cut the corners at curves. Pidgeon credited his four, hard-nosed sergeants with drilling those lessons into the young Marines. They proudly called themselves the 11th Mothers.

Landing Zone Ross was a small, lonely-looking place, Pidgeon thought. There were two, low knolls off the road separated by a hard-packed saddle—ARVN on one knoll; a small detachment from 2–1 Infantry, Americal, on the other. The Marines ended up in the saddle. They circled their trucks for the night, fifties outboard, men on watch in the ring mounts and under the vehicles. Lieutenant Pidgeon didn't have to replace the infantry platoon leader on watch until 0200. He climbed into his truck and fell asleep on a stretcher. Suddenly he was wide awake—not aware he'd heard the incoming mortars—and scrambling under his truck. The first round had hit five yards away, splattering his truck with shrapnel, but the only damage was Pidgeon's ringing ears. More rounds impacted around the LZ, and a Marine in a gun mount hollered he'd seen the tube flashes about five hundred meters out. It was a populated area, and they could not get permission from the Army to return fire with their fifties.

It was a frustrating night for the Marines; by daybreak, they were all ready to go home. The truckers were waiting for the Army to sweep the road when one of the sergeants hollered from his truck, "Lieutenant, look at this shit!" Pidgeon climbed up with him. The sweep team—which should have consisted of at least four men with minesweepers and an infantry squad on the flanks—was only an old truck being backed slowly down the road. It was loaded with sandbags to set off any mine that had been planted during the night. Christ, he thought, these guys are crazy!*

The grunts from 2/7 were staying on Ross, but the truckers were heading back for Baldy right after the sweep. Pidgeon huddled with his sergeants. It was quick. "We're going out of here fast, gents. Fifteen second intervals at no less than thirty-five mph. If there is a gook out there holding two wires, we'll make it tough on him. If you must abandon your truck, get under the rear duals. Stay on the road. Lock and load your M16s and good luck." They hauled ass all the way to LZ Baldy, trucks empty, infantry security gone. A command-detonated mine boomed and a couple of AK47s sniped from within the roadside brush. No damage, no casualties.

They didn't even slow down to return fire.

At Baldy, they received word from 1st MarDiv to remain overnight: a bridge on Highway One north of Hoi An had been dropped. They headed north the next morning and stopped at the juncture of Highway One and Route 4, which ran west into Dodge City. They were to meet a sweep team. The eastern leg of Route 4 had been closed for months due to heavy losses; this latest sweep was hours late. Lieutenant Pidgeon

---

* They or their commanders were indeed crazy. WO Ken Fritz, who flew medevacs that summer with the 176th Helicopter Company, Americal, commented, "That was a real bad road. I can recall picking up people who had been blown up as a result of numerous mines. Guys sweeping the road for mines with a deuce-and-a-half loaded full of sandbags, and it didn't quite turn it over but it just about wasted all the guys on the deuce-and-a-half."

waited under the broiling sun, thinking that once you've seen one group of a hundred Vietnamese villagers, you've seen them all! They crowded the halted convoy. The Marines bought soda from the villagers, who were friendly until a sale was rejected; then a sarcastic, "Number ten!" The kid Marines told them to fuck off. Some children were selling marijuana, and their older sisters were selling themselves. The girls were friendly, pouting and acting hurt if turned down. After the sergeants made sure the villagers stayed away from the rigs, it was rather relaxing to talk with the children. Pidgeon wasn't totally at ease, though; this was always too vulnerable a situation.

The sweep finally came on the radio: ETA of twenty mikes. The southern voice was familiar, and Pidgeon recognized the face when the sweep came trudging in. It was a classmate from Basic School. There were no smiles or handshakes. Roads are cleared by technique or accident, Pidgeon thought; this was a case of the latter. An engineer had missed a mine in the road, which totalled the truck following them. A medevac was called.

Two days later, on 15 August, they headed back to LZ Baldy, trucking in the remainder of 2/7 Marines from the Da Nang Rocket Belt. It was a large convoy, more than two hundred trucks, and Lieutenant Pidgeon was dual convoy commander with 1stLt Al Fabizak. Pidgeon rode up front; Fabizak brought up the rear; and it was a typical, quiet, hot, dust-caked run to LZ Baldy. The night was different, though. The Marines were on the airstrip, truckers and grunts sleeping in the vehicles and under them, when the mortars began coming in and the sapper teams were spotted in the wire. The Marines squeezed under the trucks, weapons trained on the airstrip. Ahead of them, the GIs in the perimeter bunkers were on their M60s, slicing the black night with red tracers low to the ground. Flares popped over the base, their parachutes eerily floating down to drape themselves over hootches and wire. Pidgeon crouched beside his truck watching a couple of gutsy Huey gunship crews lift their birds off the strip amid the sporadic fire. They buzzed the wire, then made strafing passes behind a mass of huge boulders to the south. The boulders faced the arty section of the perimeter, and an NVA mortar crew was lobbing shells from the cover. Sappers were moving forward in the wire and an artillery crew dropped their tube to ground level. Then came the weird rush of a beehive flechette round screaming into the night.

At first light, GIs and Marines stood on the perimeter photographing the NVA bodies in the wire. Lieutenant Pidgeon thought back to that briefing from the Americal colonel. Model pacification? He thought it smelled more like peaceful coexistence. The attitude of the Americal Division, or at least of the GIs he talked to, was: what you don't find can't hurt you. Which was all well and good, considering the confused and confusing politics of the war. But you can't sit out a war when the other side is still out to kick your ass.

Pidgeon was glad his duties took him back to Da Nang. He was glad to be done with the Americal.

Chapter Seven

Ambush

In the late morning of 17 August 1969, the 110 men of Delta Company, 4th Battalion, 31st Infantry, 196th Infantry Brigade, Americal Division, began moving back towards Landing Zone West. They humped single file, moving like sleepwalkers under a ferocious sun. It was 110 degrees in the Song Chang Valley and the grunts were humping a heavy load. They had the full rucks they'd left LZ West with four days before, and a full complement of ammunition: their searching had not uncovered the enemy.

The company "zapper" squad was on point. They were the elite of the outfit, all with at least six months in-country, who had volunteered to conduct the scouting and night ambushes. Their radio call sign was Destroyer 6. They followed a trail near the base of LZ West. Specialist Ferris was about three men back from the point, with the squad's PRC25 radio strapped to his back. It weighed twenty-five pounds, a hefty addition to his rucksack and bandoliers, and Ferris trudged listlessly, dripping sweat. It was nearly 1700.

The point man suddenly opened fire.

Ferris snapped forward. There they were—three North Vietnamese with khaki fatigues, packs, and AK47 assault rifles. He got a quick look at their backs as they bounded down the trail. The two groups had almost walked into each other. The squad gave chase; Ferris jogged with the handset to his mouth, telling the company commander what was going on. The NVA kept running, pausing only to fire quick bursts, dashing deeper into the brush. The squad moved in behind them and was lucky enough to spot one crouched along a stream.

The NVA died in the abrupt explosion of several M16s.

GIs checked the body as others fanned out to secure the area. Ferris casually watched the grunts walk down a berm towards a thick tree line. Then those trees erupted. Ferris instantly dropped, shoving himself into the dirt behind a dike. He'd never experienced such concentrated fire. He forced himself back up, hand tight around his M16 pistol grip, spent shells flying out. He could see muzzle flashes and smoke. The rest of the company was in a grove back across the paddy. Some of them were firing too. Ferris and a buddy low-crawled to them along a dike, chins in the dirt. They shouted for ammunition and grenades from the guys, then started back. Ferris jumped off a berm and landed wrong; his back throbbed. The crawl under fire seemed to take forever. They finally bellied into position along the last berm and slung the bandoliers through an opening in the brush where the rest of the squad was pinned down and returning fire.

They shot it out for almost an hour before the shadows of dusk allowed them to crawl away. They got back to the company perimeter in the trees in absolute wonderment that they were still alive. One GI had been wounded; one had been killed. He was a tall, skinny country boy; his best buddy Harper, another quiet country kid, was an emotional wreck.

The body of James Hurst had been left.

It was already dark as Delta Company dug in. It was a small perimeter with a roofless hut in the center, nicknamed the French Hootch because it had cement walls. The shooting had petered out when the zapper squad pulled back and a resupply chopper, Rattler 26 out of Chu Lai, made its approach; as soon as it came within range of the tree line across the paddy, there was another torrent of fire. Both pilots were wounded in their armored seats, but managed to limp the Huey to LZ Center. Then, at 1900, the NVA made a probing attack on Delta Company. The blind exchange in the dark didn't last long, but another GI was killed and two more were wounded. From the amount of enemy fire, it seemed they had walked into a NVA battalion. To say the grunts were stunned, tired, and scared would be barely to scratch at the surface of their emotions.

It was a long night.

In the morning, 18 August, Lieutenant Colonel Henry and Sergeant Major Gutterez stood on a bunker at the edge of LZ West with the crew assigned to fly the 4–31 C&C that day. They were charting their flight down to Delta's position in the valley and, since it would be under fire, they were being very precise: "Okay, we'll go around that tree, then. . . ." Delta Company was running low of ammunition. After an emergency resupply of it was stacked in the Huey, the men climbed aboard and the helicopter bore down the jungled hillside. There was not much fire on the way in—Henry thought the NVA were too stunned—and the Huey hovered quickly over a clearing beside the French Hootch. The crew shoved out the ammo, then the Huey orbited around and sailed uphill. This time, they took heavy fire. Henry had told the two door gunners not to fire since Delta's perimeter was not well-defined in the bramble of trees and bushes; so he and they could just sit white-knuckled as several rounds punched loudly through the floor and out the metal roof. Back on Landing Zone West, they counted bullet holes in the rotor blades.

Henry was very concerned about Delta Company's situation. The new company commander, the senior first lieutenant who had taken over ten days earlier, was too green. From monitoring the radio transmissions within the company net, Henry got the impression that the platoon leaders and troopers did not have the same confidence in him that they'd had in Whittecar and Mekkelsen. Captain Whittecar was having the exact same thoughts. From the LZ bunker line, he'd watched the entire action with binoculars and, since he knew both the terrain of the valley and the men of Delta like the back of his hand, he had been in radio contact with the new lieutenant throughout. The man sounded like he was in over his head and knew it: his voice cracked with fear, confusion, almost shock. The company had frozen in place. The North Vietnamese now had the upper hand.

That's when Henry asked Whittecar to resume command of Delta Company. He eagerly agreed. Whittecar then radioed the lieutenant, noting that he'd be pulled back to LZ West as soon as he could get the helicopter in.

The sigh of relief in his response was obvious.

Whittecar had a Huey on the LZ West pad loaded with ammunition and water containers; then they made the short hop down the mountain. They kicked out the supplies in that grassy clearing beside the hootch, then he hopped out and headed for the command post. He walked fast, helmet on, M16 in his hands, pumping adrenaline. He was only vaguely aware of the lieutenant passing him to board the helicopter. Whittecar didn't trust him enough for a situation report and they didn't even exchange glances.* Whittecar, who wore eyeglasses and had an angular jaw and was thirty-one years of age, was something of a hero to the nineteen-year-old grunts of Delta Company; as he strode through the high elephant grass, the looks of dejection turned to astonishment and relief.

One trooper was young enough, scared enough, and proud enough to exclaim, "My God, I'm glad you're back!"

"Well, let's get this damn show on the road!"

John Whittecar had grown up in Glenrock, Wyoming, the son of an oil field worker. His early years were routine. He graduated from high school, did a hitch in the Navy, then joined the men in the oil fields. It wasn't the life he wanted, so in 1961 he reenlisted, this time in the U.S. Army. His company commander in West Germany recommended him for OCS, and he was commissioned a second lieutenant in 1965. Whittecar was soon leading a rifle platoon of the 1st Infantry Division in III Corps, north of Saigon. That was a 1966–67 tour, and afterwards he contemplated taking his Silver Star and Purple Hearts and quitting the service. Things just didn't make sense. The national leaders did not seem able to come to grips with what was necessary to finish the job they'd started. His platoon had operated near the Cambodian border and their observance of that imaginary line had aided only the enemy. That was just one example of their self-imposed restraint, and the enormous waste of it ate at him like acid. What hurt even worse was his homecoming; if he wore his uniform in public, there were strangers who'd call him a baby-killer and his wife a whore.

Whittecar stayed in the Army. He focused on doing a job and in November 1968 he was rotated back to Vietnam with captain bars and orders for HQMACV in Saigon. He pulled strings for another combat command in the Big Red One. The night before he was to ship out to them, an allotment came down from the Americal Division for captains, and he found himself on a transport plane to Chu Lai.

Whittecar had never even heard of the Americal, but he did know about the 196th Infantry Brigade. In 1966, his battalion of the 1st Division

---

* The lieutenant was very concerned that his career was ruined. On the assumption that the man was not incompetent, only unprepared for such a fierce fight, Henry later gave him command of B Company and noted that he did "an excellent job."

had been rushed in to bail them out after their disastrous operation in War Zone C. He was not impressed when he joined his new company in the bush, initially viewing his reluctant draftees with the thought: you guys aren't going to get me killed, and I'm not going to let you commit suicide. He had learned his tactics from the hard-nosed Big Red One—and from the North Vietnamese Army—and this experience made him credible to the grunts as he began to tighten up the company. He fired one, young, scared lieutenant. He started operating at night. He organized the zapper squad to muster some esprit de corps.

He screamed, cajoled, consoled, and after awhile it began to pay off. The young grunts seemed proud to realize how good they really could be.

Delta Company became the best.

Whittecar knew his maps, his tactics, and his soldiers. He was respected by his grunts, and the mutual feeling was the cornerstone to their new spirit. He was not a buddy to his men. He loved them like a father, but it was a restrained feeling. He allowed himself to become close to only a very few. To know their personal stories and hopes would have drained him of the ability to push his young draftees into the aggressive mind set needed to prevail against an aggressive enemy. Whittecar was a promoted grunt. His loyalty channelled down to the GIs and he could bullshit easily with them. He could also be icy tough on them. He was brave. He won his second Silver Star during a routine patrol in Hiep Duc. The point man had spotted a hootch in a clearing and Whittecar lay with him in the tall grass along a path, discussing the best way to get to the hut without being spotted. Just then, two Viet Cong appeared on the trail. The point man hollered and sprang up in front of Whittecar. His M16 jammed. Whittecar instantly shoved him down, stepped forward with his AR15 automatic rifle, and chopped down both Vietnamese.

In June, he turned over the company to platoon leader Mekkelsen. In the seven months that Whittecar had commanded Delta Company, they had the highest body count and the lowest casualty rate in the battalion.

Not a single man had been killed.

The first order of business on 18 August was to retrieve Hurst's body. Whittecar huddled with his senior RTO, SP4 Michael Day, and his platoon leaders. He decided to leave a group in position at the French

Hootch while two platoons swept into the tree line, the company headquarters in trace behind them with the last platoon. It was hot and unnerving crossing that field, but there was no firing and the GIs fanned out along the last berm, facing the woods. They found Hurst and zipped him into a body bag. It was then that Whittecar saw the movement: where a sixty-foot field of parched grass rolled into the tree line, he saw something move behind a screen of bamboo. He shouted a warning to his men, then heaved two grenades into the bamboo. There was no response, so he tapped a GI and they pushed forward on their stomachs. Twenty feet from the bamboo, a single shot cracked at them. The grunt took it in the leg, and Whittecar triggered a quick M16 burst into the bamboo. Again, there was only silence.

Whittecar helped the wounded man crawl back behind the berm. Then he deployed Delta Company for the counterattack; one platoon was to remain in place with the CP along the dikes while the other two moved around the tree line from two sides. The maneuver was to be like a horseshoe around the bamboo grove, the open end pointing to their paddy. Whittecar reckoned that whatever the company had bumped into the day before had pulled out, leaving only a delaying force; he hoped to sweep them into that open field in front of his berm. He kept in contact with the two platoon leaders as they slowly pushed through the thick underbrush of the woods. They had nearly closed the horseshoe when heavy automatic weapons fire suddenly erupted.

The platoon leaders screamed on the radio that NVA were suddenly materializing from spider holes amid the vegetation. Casualties were heavy.

It was 1210.

The firing was enough for a battalion, and Whittecar quickly ordered the platoons to pull out. They leapfrogged back through the trees, some firing and some running crouched and dragging the casualties, those dropping behind trees to fire cover for the others. By the time they crawled back into the paddy, the NVA were in the brush on three sides of them. It seemed there were hundreds of North Vietnamese around Delta Company, although none were visible as they seared the paddy with a barrage of AK47s and RPGs.

Whittecar ordered a pullback to the French Hootch.

They leapfrogged again, scrambling over dikes while others laid down suppressive fire. The NVA waited until they were in the middle of the field, then started walking 82mm mortar shells through them.

The paddy was overgrown and deep with dikes for cover; still, it took a dozen more wounded to get back.

Around the French Hootch, there was the semicontrolled chaos of medics rushing among the wounded and grunts rushing into place on the perimeter. The NVA fire had ceased and Whittecar stood beside the cement hootch with his radiomen, requesting fire support and an emergency resupply of ammunition and water. As the first Huey started its approach, a 12.7mm machine gun began pounding, and green tracers burned up from the canopy of the tree line. Then another opened fire, and another, until Whittecar had counted seven separate twelve-seven positions in a circle around his company. He screamed at the Huey pilot to get out, then cut to the 4–31 TOC frequency. He reported his estimate that Delta Company was surrounded by a regiment of 1,200 NVA. At that time, Whittecar had 109 troopers, and that included the 5 KIA and the 21 WIA.

■ There was, indeed, a regiment around Whittecar and his men. The first two days of the battle were the bleakest for 4–31 Infantry as far as their being greatly outnumbered and not knowing what was going on. As the scenario was later pieced together, the NVA attack plan had two parts. The *3d Main Force Regiment, 2d NVA Division* was dug in around Hill 102 in the Song Chang Valley; their mission was to attack LZ West and LZ Center. At the same time, the *1st Main Force Regiment, 2d NVA Division* was dug in around Hills 381 and 441 (of the Nui Chom ridge line). While the base camps were being hit, part of the regiment would destroy the Resettlement Village while the rest formed a block across Route 534. This hard-packed dirt road (called the Old French Road) originated at Highway One on the coast and ran all the way to the Resettlement Village, slicing the Hiep Duc Valley horizontally. This would be a likely avenue of approach for any relief force. Supporting these efforts, U.S. Intelligence also placed various headquarters, sapper, mortar, antiaircraft, signal, and transportation detachments; they estimated a total of 3,000–5,000 NVA troops. It was thought that when D/4–31 bumped into the 3d Regiment on 17 August, and B/4–31 the 1st Regiment on 18 August, they accidentally preempted the NVA attack. All that had not become focused on the second morning of the battle. It was figured that D/4–31 had found the main NVA concentration that had hit LZ West a week before. In Hiep Duc Valley, therefore, it was business as usual.

■ At daybreak on 18 August, Captain Gayler, CO, Bravo Company, 4th Battalion, 31st Infantry, had his men ruck up and begin their march across Hiep Duc Valley towards the mountainous spur, Nui Chom, which formed the valley's northern frontier. Bravo had been in the bush since rotating off LZ security a week before, conducting a generally fruitless search for the NVA battalion which had assaulted their base camp. In that respect, it was similar to Gayler's previous experiences in the war. He'd come in-country in January as the air operations officer and took over the company in April; he held a Bronze Star for the June fight in AK Valley, but most of the company patrols were merely what they called Hot Walks in the Sun.

This did not suit Gayler at all. He'd grown up in the rural town of Mineral Wells, Texas, where his parents owned a mom 'n' pop grocery store. He joined the national guard at seventeen, then joined the fire department after a few disastrous, beer-blasted semesters in college. When Vietnam began heating up, he volunteered for OCS and the Regular Army. Captain Gayler was thirty years old, had thirteen years in the military, and wanted his piece of the Vietnam War.

The evening before, Lieutenant Colonel Henry had radioed him with an impromptu mission: a *chieu hoi,* accompanied by two Vietnamese National policemen, would be choppered to his company to lead them to an NVA rice cache. Supposedly, the cache held enough rice to feed an NVA company for a month. The defector said it was tucked near Hill 381 of Nui Chom. By 1000, when Bravo Company was halfway to the ridge line, battalion radioed them to secure a bush landing zone for the arrival of the chieu hoi. As the Huey banked north after dropping off its passengers, a spot of AK47s snapped at it. They were too far away to go after and Gayler really didn't give it a second thought; there was always a sniper or two scampering around.

The day seemed a repeat of so many others.

The temperature hovered well above 100 degrees and the grunts humped as listlessly as always. A berm cut through the desiccated, rock-hard paddies and they moved single file along it, five yards between each man. They humped full rucks, ammo bandoliers hung from shoulders and around waists, and faces and arms were slick with sweat. Fatigue shirts were stained darkly. Each man's view was the same—a sun-bleached helmet bobbing along above the backpack of the grunt ahead.

The zapper squad was on point, followed by Bravo Two under 1stLt Doug Monroe. Gayler considered Monroe his steadiest platoon leader, who knew his tactics, was firmly in command, and at the same time enjoyed an easygoing rapport with his men.

Company headquarters was behind them. With Captain Gayler were his battalion RTO, company RTO, and senior medic. There was also a forward observer team from 3–82 Artillery—an FO lieutenant, his recon sergeant, and their RTO. Gayler had five Vietnamese with his CP, including his ARVN interpreter whom he did not trust, and his Kit Carson Scout who'd traded his AK47 for an M16 and had outgrown Gayler's initial suspicions. The two National policemen had fatigues, bush hats, and M16 rifles, but no packs; they didn't expect to be staying long. The NVA soldier turned defector walked with them. He looked about thirty, was not tied, and wore some anonymous old fatigues.

Gayler had placed Bravo Three, under Lieutenant Maurel, behind them in the middle of the column. That was mostly to keep them out of trouble. Gayler did not like Maurel; as far as he was concerned, he was an immature young man who harassed his troops, much to the detriment of morale, and who simply did not take the time to do things right, much to the detriment of performance. However, their platoon sergeant, SSgt Walter Sheppard, was sharp. He was a young black man who, like almost every NCO in the company, was a shake 'n' bake who had earned instant stripes at the crash course known as the Fort Benning NCO Academy. Such were the manpower requirements of Vietnam. Sheppard was a draftee but had graduated at the top of his class and was sent to the war as an infantry staff sergeant. He more than measured up, but there was sympathetic talk in the platoon that Sheppard was yet another victim of a young marriage straining hard due to separation.

Bringing up the rear was Bravo One, under Sgt Richard S. Allison, and his platoon sergeant, Sergeant Beaureguard. Allison was a city boy, Beaureguard a country boy; both were solid under fire. Allison was a twenty-year-old, blue-collar hawk. His last year in high school, he'd had horrendous arguments about Vietnam with one of his teachers, a young woman just out of college. He'd ended the debate by enlisting in the U.S. Army and volunteering for the infantry; he'd come in-country in November 68 as one of the replacements after the last battle on Nui Chom. Since then, he'd volunteered for the zapper squad, had been promoted to platoon sergeant, and had just been made acting platoon leader when his lieutenant rotated.

Bravo Company was undermanned, down to seventy-five men.

As they moved through the tree lines near a miniature hamlet below Nui Chom, a little Vietnamese boy ran up to Sergeant Allison's platoon. Their Kit Carson talked to him at length, then caught up with the platoon several hundred meters down the road. The boy had told the scout a large NVA force was up ahead, and Allison immediately grabbed the phone from his RTO. Captain Gayler was not swayed by the information. Negative, he radioed back, we've got a mission. The captain received generally favorable reviews from his grunts, but Allison was a dissenter.

This lifer, Allison thought, is too damn reckless.

The platoon crossed the shallows of the Song Lau River and was moving across the several hundred yards of open paddies to the ville when an AK suddenly cut loose, sending everyone to the ground. Gayler, down the trail with his RTOs, radioed the buck sergeant in charge of the zapper squad, "Sick 'em!" The men were all volunteers and it didn't take long; they spotted the sniper, pinned him down with M16 fire, then crept close enough to pitch a few frags at him. Then the stocky sergeant sauntered back to report a body count of one.

He held up the AK47 for Gayler's inspection.

The company halted in the small ville, which was about a hundred meters square and raised several feet from the surrounding paddies like a brushy island. There was a handful of Vietnamese around the hootches— an old man, some women, a few children. As reward for the kill, Gayler told the zapper squad to secure an LZ in the ville for their evening hot meal and to haul out the rice cache. For totally different reasons, he also told Lieutenant Maurel's platoon to stay behind to secure the area and guard their rucksacks, which everyone was gladly unshouldering.

The company continued along the path up to the foothills, approaching another tiny hamlet. Lieutenant Monroe's point squad spotted two men with AK47s across the paddies and opened fire. The NVA disappeared among the hootches. By the time Gayler moved up, Monroe was down along a dike with one of his squads; they were firing cover for another squad as it maneuvered toward the ville through a tree line. One hootch was already afire from an M79 grenade. In the middle of this firefight, Captain Gayler suddenly received a frantic call from Lieutenant Maurel.

His voice was two octaves higher than normal: he was taking fire from all sides, including automatic weapons, rocket grenades, and mortars, and had heavy casualties.

Gayler had Monroe rein in his attacking squad and, with Sergeant Allison's platoon turned around to be point, they made a fast walk back down the trail. The NVA attack had ebbed back—all the time invisible in the trees and dikes leading up to the hamlet—and Bravo Company was able to reenter without drawing a shot.

Lieutenant Maurel's report was not good.

After Gayler had moved on with Monroe and Allison, the zapper squad set up on one side of the ville. To escape the heat, they strung their poncho liners from bamboo and clustered under this pathetic shade. Some rested; some toyed with their captured AK. All in all, no one was paying attention when expertly camouflaged NVA moved right up to their perimeter. One of the survivors later told of seeing moving bushes a second before the NVA signalled their attack by sending an RPG through their poncho shelter. Two men were killed instantly and two others were wounded as the rest scrambled for weapons, or cover, or both. Then came the Chicoms and a complete ring of AK47 fire. A mortar tube was also employed, dropping accurate preregistered fire on the ville. Maurel and Sheppard kept their heads, got their platoon into a tight three-sixty, and raked the surrounding brush with fire. It was enough to keep the invisible enemy temporarily at bay.

Seven GIs had been killed in the initial assault.

The rest of Bravo Company was taking up positions on the ragged perimeter—and dragging in the bodies from the zapper squad—when the mortar began firing. Then the AKs and Chicoms began all over again. They were coming from all sides and, from what Gayler could discern in the cacophony as he pressed into the dirt, it sounded like an NVA battalion was around them. How had they been able to walk through this circle? The NVA would have been wiser to keep the platoons separated and overrun them in detail; but they had not, so Bravo Company was able to mass its fire. Gayler also got on the horn to request what he later reckoned saved his company from annihilation—Cobra gunship support. Henry answered, "Roger, it's already in route."

The French Hootch became the center of Delta Company's defense. It had a twenty- by thirty-foot cement foundation, four feet of crumbling walls all the way around, no roof, and a battered front porch still overhanging a doorless door frame. The FO and RTOs set up their radios in it and the grunts dug foxholes in a thirty-meter circle around it. The medics treated the casualties there, the wounded lay in a row along an outer wall, the dead were beside them in body bags. After checking the miniature perimeter, Captain Whittecar talked with SP5 Kim Diliberto, his senior medic. He said one of the GIs would die from loss of blood if he were not immediately medevacked; during the ambush in the tree line, a Chicom had nearly blown off his arm at the shoulder. Whittecar was very hesitant to call in a medevac considering the circle of 12.7mm guns, and he walked over to see the man for himself.

The kid was propped against the hootch, his wound still gruesome to look at despite the bloody bandages over it. He looked pale and weak, but in good spirits. Whittecar knelt beside the soldier. "Do you think you can hold on?"

"Hell yes. We're gonna kick their ass like before."

"You got that right."

His face suddenly drained and he mumbled, "I'm not feeling too good." Whittecar reached to his shoulder to balance him, but the GI fell forward onto him. "Medic!" Diliberto was beside him in seconds, but the man was already dead. Whittecar stood there shocked as they put him in a body bag and laid him with the others.

They were outnumbered, outgunned, surrounded. Whittecar had never been in such a situation before, had never felt such dread before.

He always remembered this as his moment of truth.

Whittecar was standing beside the crumbling front porch, talking with Diliberto and several others, when the cracking reports of AK47s suddenly blasted from the edges of their grassy perimeter. Everyone dove to the ground or disappeared into foxholes as Whittecar quickly jumped back up and sprinted into the hootch to join his FO and RTOs. The North Vietnamese were attacking. The GIs returned fire, flattening the grass with M16 and M60 bursts and M79 grenades, while Whittecar and his FO brought in 105mm artillery as close as they dared. At the same time, Whittecar cut to the frequency of his platoon leaders and ordered a counterattack. He didn't want his men sitting in holes dying, perhaps even panicking in their helplessness. Some probably couldn't face that order and stayed in the womb of their foxholes, but other grunts attacked like the NVA, individuals crawling through the elephant grass on their stomachs, M16s in front of them, tossing hand frags up and over the high grass. Few, if any, of the GIs even saw an NVA in the tangle, even though they were within yards of each other at times. But the maneuver shocked or confused the NVA enough that they withdrew to the paddies and surrounding wood lines.

It was only as the firing slacked off that Whittecar noticed Diliberto. He was sprawled outside the French Hootch where they'd been talking, a bullet hole in his temple. He'd been killed instantly in the first burst.

The FO kept the artillery thundering around them, close enough so that U.S. shrapnel whizzed over the heads of the men in the foxholes and bounced inside the perimeter. At the same time, Whittecar talked in the gunship pilots. He described the location of one 12.7mm position in the bamboo grove, and the Huey bore down on it. The gun crew did not fire—perhaps not seeing the gunship, perhaps afraid to pinpoint themselves—but other 12.7mm guns began snapping tracers at it from hundreds of yards away. The pilot punched off a cluster of rockets, then pulled up, the bamboo erupting, shattering in his wake. Whittecar thought he saw an arm spinning up from the explosions.

As the Huey banked around, Whittecar radioed the pilot to clear out for the antiaircraft fire. The gunships cleared the airspace, and he talked in the Phantoms who laid nape in the tree line across the paddy and on suspected mortar locations. The NVA barely fired now, trying to become invisible in the thick greenery. The Phantoms came in Danger Close over the canopy, close enough for the grunts to read the aircraft markings, to see bombs disengaging, to hear the drag fins snap out, to feel the whump of bursting silver napalm canisters. The FO kept up the arty bombardment too, ceasing fire only long enough to allow the gunship and jet passes. Whittecar would line up a Phantom with a target, tell the FO to cease the arty, the napalm would burst, the jet would pull up, and the arty would be turned on again until the next strafing run.

The grunts of Bravo Company meanwhile had formed a tight ring around the hootches of the ville. They hunkered behind boulders or stubby trees in the tall grass and dug foxholes. They M16'd or flung grenades at every noise or rustle in front of them. Few, if any, NVA offered themselves to rifle sights, but they kept crawling closer along the dikes and hedgerows. Chicom stick grenades suddenly bounced next to GIs from out of nowhere. A bush stirred and M79 grenades were pounded into it. RPGs slammed back.

The NVA fired their mortar again. It was close enough for the grunts to hear the pop of the outgoing round and to flatten even more in the dirt. Every round landed inside the ville, jarring the earth under their chests.

There were lulls and two heavy flare-ups.

Captain Gayler was in the center of the perimeter, set up in a tapioca field. The garden had eighteen-inch-deep furrows, and he was pressed flat into one, facing Lieutenant Shortround—his arty observer who earned the nickname because of his short, stocky build—who was also stretched out in the ditch. A map was spread between them. The arty recon sergeant was down in the furrow to one side of them; their RTOs were in the furrow to the other side. Gayler had never been so scared and, most likely, neither had Lieutenant Shortround. But the young FO was a cool head; he tapped the map as if he were discussing the weather, "Now, if I was the dink commander, I'd put my mortar over there. . . ." He was on the radio to the artillery batteries on LZ West and LZ Siberia, walking their bombardment through the trees across the Song Lau.

It silenced the mortar for then.

Cobra gunships of F Troop, 8th Air Cavalry, Americal Division had been scrambled and Gayler directed their fire. Their call sign was Blue Ghosts. The pilots sounded skeptical that hundreds of NVA were around Bravo Company in the broad daylight. They could see none in the thick vegetation, but Gayler wanted their fires within twenty meters of his perimeter. The grunts were pitching smoke grenades to mark themselves.

"Ah, we're sure getting pretty close to you."

"That's affirmative," was Gayler's taciturn reply.

One Cobra made a low run parallel to the line, shattering the hedgerow in front of the grunts with his 40mm chin-turret grenade launcher. His wingman, zipping in next, shouted excitedly, "Four NVA just broke from that bush! You got dinks all over you!"

"Tell me about it!"

It was about then that the Cobras started receiving 12.7mm fire. At 1840, Marine Phantoms began dumping napalm across the river. They also reported antiaircraft fire. Also in the air was Colonel Tackaberry, orbiting in the 196th InfBde C&C; during one of the heavy flare-ups, he cut into Captain Gayler's company net to demand a situation report. Before Gayler could answer the brigade commander—who was considered a spit 'n' polish glory hound by the Polar Bear battalion—Lieutenant

Colonel Henry cut in from his CP, "This unit's in contact. If you want a status report, you call me on my push. Out."

Gayler always had the highest respect for Henry.

The villagers had disappeared into their family bunkers at the first shot. The Vietnamese police hustled their chieu hoi into a bunker also. The ARVN interpreter joined them. The Kit Carson Scout, however, stayed near the company headquarters. For his devotion, he fell dead with an AK47 round through the neck. Another Vietnamese died inside the perimeter. During a lull, a little village girl wandered up to Gayler's group, crying and pointing to her head with bloody hands. The medic pulled her down. She had shrapnel in the base of her skull and died in minutes.

At twilight, a medevac was attempted inside Bravo Company's perimeter. The medics had the most seriously wounded gathered in the garden, and Gayler stood in the middle of it watching the Huey come in while Cobras orbited the ville, pumping out cover fire. He shouted to pop smoke and Sergeant Allison tossed a smoke grenade out. The Huey descended and slowed to a hover. There was the sudden cracking of a machine gun, a blur of green tracers as everyone ducked, the sledgehammer pounding of the chopper taking hits. The cables controlling the rear rotor were severed. Gayler looked up horrified to see the Huey in a wobbly hover ten feet above his head, spinning on its axis. The pilot expertly fought to regain control, eased the ship up over the trees around the garden, then flew away sideways. An hour later, at 1930, a second medevac was attempted. In the dark, Gayler tucked a strobe light into a furrow, then scooted out of the way as the Huey landed right on top of it. He tensed, expecting mortars. The wounded were quickly loaded on; the pilot did a torque check and radioed he could carry one more. An eighth GI was put aboard and the ship pulled out without drawing a shot.

At about 2200, 2dLt James Simms of 3d Platoon, Charlie Company, 4th Battalion, 31st Infantry linked up with Captain Gayler and Bravo Company.

By then, Bravo had ten men dead, twenty wounded.

Charlie Three had been in the bush near the Resettlement Village when the ambush began. Their sister platoons and company commander Murphy helicoptered down from LZ Siberia. They all linked up and NDP'd near Hill 118, popularly known as Million Dollar Hill (denoting the cost of helicopters shot down on the knoll in one day during the campaign to reclaim the valley). From there, under Lieutenant Colonel Henry's direction, Captain Murphy sent Lieutenant Simms's platoon to link up with Bravo and lead them back to their haven. He was reinforced with a squad from Charlie One under a GI named Williams.

It was about a four-kilometer hump to the east, an increasingly nervous march in the dead of a moonless night. The only sound was the scrape of dry grass as they moved, then the muffled exchanges from Bravo's besieged perimeter. When they got close, shell casings from strafing Cobras fell among them, and they noticed they were walking through patches of bloody grass. They filed into Bravo's perimeter during a lull.

Both groups were very glad to see each other.

Captain Gayler and Lieutenant Simms hashed over plans for getting out. Simms's group had crossed the Song Lau and walked up the trail unopposed, which relieved Gayler: the back door might be open! Everyone was in need of rest, but he wanted to get out as soon as possible. His position was untenable, zeroed in. He told Simms that his platoon would be carrying the bodies out. Some of the GIs standing there muttered, "Aw shit, carry your own bodies." Gayler was in no mood for it. "I know your people are tired, lieutenant, but we've been fighting all day, and either your people are going to carry them or *you're* going to have to deal with me in the morning."

It took an hour of confusion in the dark to chop down bamboo poles. The dead were wrapped in ponchos, tied to the poles with GI bootlaces, and shouldered between two to four soldiers. The rucksacks and gear of the casualties were also distributed. PFC Rocky Bleier, an M79 grenadier who had come with the attached squad, saw one corpse laying unnoticed in a ditch. He turned to one of the other GIs from Charlie Company, "C'mon, let's take this guy."

"Hell no, our platoon's got rear security."

"But there's nobody left to take him."

"I don't give a shit. Let him lay there."

Another grunt, however, said he'd help and they lashed the KIA to a bamboo pole. Bleier handed his M79 to another GI. They had just started into the paddy when Bleier's partner slipped off the dike, splashing into the water, the dead man yanked down onto him. He instantly scrambled out from under the stiff corpse and jumped on the berm, looking at Bleier with horror. It was the first time Bleier had seen a dead American, and probably the same for his buddy.

The column moved across the open paddies from the village to the tree lines along the Song Lau. Monroe's platoon was on point, followed by Gayler's headquarters; Maurel's platoon; Allison's platoon; Simms's platoon with the bodies; and, finally, Williams's squad covering the rear. The point squad was cautiously approaching the stream when a USAF prop plane droned to the south on the other side of LZ West, above where Delta Company was also fighting for its life. The plane suddenly started dropping basketball flares, which turned the paddies into shimmering stadiums for miles around. Everyone jumped behind the berms and Captain Gayler radioed Captain Whittecar, asking if he could hold the illumination until he'd crossed the paddy.

"Okay, Hank. Make it fast, though."

The stream was only ankle deep and they moved across it quickly. The last of Maurel's platoon and the point of Allison's were crossing when the thickets to the left abruptly exploded with AK47 fire. Chicoms were flung in. Sergeant Allison instantly dropped flat, triggering his M16 into the black. He could see nothing. Up ahead, everyone had rolled into the brush at the first shot. Gayler nervously noticed a rise about thirty meters off the trail, and could just imagine NVA popping over the crest to fire down on them. GIs around him prepared grenades, but nothing happened. All the firing was at the stream; occasional bursts, shouts, and grenades were tossed back and forth. The firing had halted the entire column. Gayler radioed Allison: "What the hell is going on?"

Allison said they were pinned down and needed illum.

Gayler said no. His men were strung out on the trail with only some brush for concealment, and flares would be like turning spotlights on fish in a barrel. He was anxious to escape the battalion or regiment around them, and told Allison to get his damn platoon across.

Allison said his men were hesitant to cross the open river.

Gayler's reply was a harsh Texas bark, "Sergeant, if I have to come back there myself, I'm going to whip your ass."

Allison did not like officers in general, and Gayler in particular. In a fit of courage born of anger, he unslung his ammunition bandoliers and dropped them and his grenades in front of him. Then he cut loose into the black tangle to his left, screaming at his men to move it. Which they did, jumping five feet down the bank, splashing across, then scrambling up the ten-foot berm on the other side. Allison emptied his M16, pitched a frag, crammed in a fresh mag, kept firing. He suddenly felt a strong thud against his chest—then the Chicom bounced to the ground, rolled over the embankment, and exploded. If he had not been so close to the edge, the grenade would have gone off at his feet. He'd already been wounded once that day; during the mortaring, a piece of shrapnel had pierced two packets of Kool Aid in his pocket and stuck in his chest. It burned but barely bled, and Allison did not report it.

The NVA finally seemed to fade away.

With Sergeant Allison's platoon across, Lieutenant Simms's men followed. First, though, Captain Gayler passed word to leave the bodies in the paddy.* PFC Bleier, coming across with the last squad, retrieved his M79. The men were moving down the embankment when an AK47 sprayed around them. Bleier dropped into a patch of wet, muddy weeds, then propped up and started slamming grenades in return. They exchanged fire for fifteen minutes, then the NVA once again just stopped. The squad got back up, very anxious not to be left behind, and filed slowly and quietly across the stream. They bunched up nervously on the opposite bank: where did everyone go! No one was in sight. The footpath veered to the right and, after a brief, hushed argument, they decided to follow it.

It was pitch black and they trod slowly, tensing up, expecting another ambush. They had little idea where they were. Within five minutes, the pop of a mortar burst the silence, and four rounds crashed right into the crossing site. It had taken the NVA ambushers too long to relay the coordinates to their mortar crew, and they merely shelled empty space. But it sent Williams's group into a headlong run, with Williams himself leading the panicked stampede. They could have easily stumbled into another ambush but, luckily, what they ran into was the back of their own column.

The shooting was sporadic all evening around Delta Company's perimeter, getting concentrated once more around midnight. Whittecar

---

* Major Lee commented, "Lieutenant Colonel Henry and I decided not to sacrifice the live for the dead. We got all the bodies later. The pressure to carry them under any circumstances came from Division and Brigade Headquarters. We said no—it wasn't worth it."

was taking a quick sleep on the cement floor of the French Hootch, head on his helmet, when the first RPG crashed in. It slammed into a tree limb above him, exploding with a rain of hot shrapnel. Whittecar snapped awake. His helmet was shattered, his head nicked, and a long sliver of shrapnel was burning in his leg. He yanked it out and flipped it away, then called in the dark, "Is anybody else hit!"

SP4 Day answered and he crawled quickly to him. The front of the young GI's jungle boot was torn open, a couple toes blown off. A medic tied field bandages around Whittecar's leg and Day's foot; Whittecar asked Day if he could still handle the radios.

"Sure," Day said, "I don't need my feet for that."

Day had been Whittecar's senior RTO during his previous command of the company, and that's why he had picked him. The kid was solid as a rock under fire. So was Whittecar. He had the line open to Major Lee in B-TOC and, after getting the wounded taken care of, he laughed into the radio, "That goddamn guy knocked the helmet right off my head!" AKs and RPGs kept flashing from the thick elephant grass thirty meters from the GI foxholes. The NVA also employed a captured M79. At dusk, Whittecar had ordered his men to dig new holes on the assumption that the NVA had observed all their original positions during the day. The ploy worked; most of the RPGs were slamming around the old, empty holes. Whittecar was on the horn to his platoon and squad leaders: fire only if you've got a target; don't give your positions away unless you have to.

He prayed there would be no panic.

Out on the line, Specialist Ferris crouched in a foxhole with another grunt from the zapper squad. They triggered quick bursts at the muzzle flashes. A Spooky gunship orbited them, a brilliant red line of gatling gun tracers stitching a wall around the perimeter. Chunks of ruptured sod pelted back around Ferris. He'd never been so scared. Around the two of them, it was a dark nightmare, silhouetted by quick flashes and weird shadows. There were movements, bursts of fire, shouts.

"Medic!"

"We need more ammo up here!"

Men screamed in pain. Ferris knew he was going to die. Behind him, he could hear AK rounds ricocheting off the cement hootch.

In the middle of it, something exploded near his hole. Ferris was so scared, it took him a few moments to realize that his back, arms, and legs were burning from fragments. He stayed in place, hands tight around his M16. Nearby, Cocoa hollered that he'd been shot through the hand. He too kept firing. All around the perimeter, very frightened men, some with wounds or concussions from the RPGs, were tight in their foxholes, managing to keep the North Vietnamese back.

There was a lull as the NVA, forever invisible, seemed to ebb back into the elephant grass. That's when Whittecar decided to gamble with a medevac; some of his wounded were near death. He talked one Huey in, lights off, coming in low over the treetops, several GIs flicking on flashlights in the LZ clearing beside the French Hootch. The pilot flipped on his landing lights at the last moment, flashing on the stark scene of flattened elephant grass and helmet tops in holes. He settled in the low brush. Major Lee had ridden the Huey down from LZ West to get a feel for what was going on; ammunition was quickly shoved out, wounded were taken aboard, then the chopper roared out from its hover and disappeared into the blackness.

There had been no NVA fire. Why not? Whittecar reckoned that the NVA were maneuvering into new positions for a renewed assault and didn't want to expose themselves. Which didn't mean, however, that he didn't think those chopper crewmen were among the bravest men on earth.

It started all over again, AKs and RPGs.

Whittecar was too aware of the desperation welling in his chest. There was no doubt in his mind they were going to be overrun and killed. He decided to break up the company, every man on his own to get back to LZ West any way he could find. He almost passed that order, but the wounded gnawed at him. There were still casualties around the hootch who couldn't walk. He couldn't abandon them. Hell with it, he finally resigned himself; we're going to die, but they're going to pay too. It was no small solace to him that he thought his men would fight to the last man.

All night, Whittecar was on the radio to Lee; this was his umbilical cord. Inside the TOC bunker, under fluorescent lights, Lee was urgently working several radios to bring their firepower to bear. He had gotten the USAF Spooky gunship over Delta Company only after much arguing with brigade operations to convince them he was not exaggerating. Once the Spooky came on station, Whittecar took over and brought the minigun fire in a circle around his perimeter, thirty meters out. He joked over the radio to Major Lee as calmly as he could, "I finally got the sonsabitches where I want 'em. They're all around me and they're not going to get away this time!" Lee laughed, as did the CP GIs in the hootch. Which is exactly what Whittecar wanted; keep their spirits up, because it's not going to do these men any good to know they're going to die tonight.

Bravo Company linked up with Charlie Company around three in the morning. Captain Murphy told Captain Gayler to get his exhausted GIs inside the perimeter; his men would handle all the security watches. The grunts spread out in the elephant grass and fell into a comatose sleep. Before passing out himself, Gayler called up his platoon leaders to check that everyone had been accounted for after their long, confused march. Everyone had been.

In the morning, however, Lieutenant Maurel said there'd been a mistake. One of the RTOs, PFC Marion Feaster, a black kid from Florida, was missing. An angry Gayler radioed Lieutenant Colonel Henry to alter his initial report. He'd just gotten off the horn when AK47s cracked from outside the perimeter, and a lone GI came crashing and hollering through the brush, diving into the perimeter as others returned fire.

It was Private Feaster himself.

He reported to Gayler. As it turned out, he'd been coming up the stream bank when the ambush was sprung. He spun back to seek cover in the water, dropping his M16, and the GI ahead of him thought he was dead and grabbed the rifle. Feaster hugged the bank during the fight, finally slipping into an exhausted sleep as the cat 'n' mouse dragged on. He was jolted awake by the mortaring. Armed with only two fragmentation grenades, his ruck, and a radio ruined by shrapnel, he waded down the Song Lau in the general western direction the column had been moving. He came upon two NVA chattering on the bank. Feaster tossed a frag in their laps as he scurried up to the trail. He was walking down the path when AKs suddenly cut loose from behind; apparently, the NVA had let him pass through an ambush, realizing too late that he was not the point man for a bigger catch. Feaster paused long enough to hurl his last grenade at a party of NVA coming after him, then ran back to the stream and moved quietly along it until dawn. Then he returned to the trail and had almost made it back to his unit when he saw a couple of NVA about the same time they saw him.

That was the firing everyone had heard. Feaster, who was built like a black bull, pounded down the trail as fast as he could, bellowing out the battalion's running password, "Polar Bears, Polar Bears, I'm a comin' in, Polar Bears!"

Feaster shook like a leaf as he told his tale.

Gayler smiled, "Well, looks like you're going to have a good story to tell your grandchildren!"

Medevacs were called into Charlie's perimeter for the last twelve of Bravo's seriously wounded. One of those going out was Lieutenant Shortround. His recon sergeant told Gayler that he'd taken a piece of shrapnel in his heel while directing arty from the garden. He hadn't even told Gayler. The sergeant also said that during the night march, the lieutenant was toughing it out but was almost delirious with pain; several times he had to grab his ruck to keep him from passing out on his feet.

Also going out on the medevacs were the National policemen and their chieu hoi. Grunts were mumbling bitterly that that fucking dink had led them into the ambush with his tale of a rice cache. Perhaps, perhaps not, but if Gayler had not put his foot down, they would have executed the NVA on the spot. Some men never quite forgave Gayler for not allowing them their revenge. Their ARVN interpreter also tried to leave on the medevac. Gayler was on the radio with the pilot who said no way, he was already overloaded. The arty recon sergeant was near the Huey. Gayler pointed at the deserter and signalled to keep him back. The sergeant shoved him back three times, but the man kept trying to edge around. Finally, the husky sergeant cold-cocked him, dropping the little ARVN like a sack of oats. The ARVN retreated back to Gayler, screaming that he was going to report the incident.

"Go right ahead."

The survivors of Bravo Company—about 40 percent of the company had been medevacked—were ferried to LZ Siberia aboard two Chinooks.

Delta Company was not in a position to be extracted that morning, but they did not die as Captain Whittecar had feared. At 0700 on 19 August, there was another attack, but this one was less fierce and another barrage of artillery and mortars ended it quickly.

Reinforcements arrived, in the form of Charlie Company, 2d Battalion, 1st Infantry, airmobiled in from the vicinity of Hawk Hill. Battalion had requested reinforcements from brigade, and these were the first to be piecemealed in. They had landed on LZ West on 18 August and Henry conferred with their CO, Capt Rudolph Yap, an Oriental-American. In the morning, they pushed downhill and Delta Company fired a Mad

Minute, a deafening, small-arms barrage designed to keep the NVA down while they hiked in. Whittecar met briefly with Captain Yap, then Charlie Company dug in adjacent to Delta Company, expanding the perimeter around the French Hootch.

Medevacs came in too, landing unopposed in the LZ clearing. Specialist Ferris got his reprieve, climbing aboard a Huey in ripped and bloody jungle fatigues. It was a crowded ship, but only a short flight up to Landing Zone West.

Relief had come, but the battle was not over. From positions around their base camp, LZ Center, the 3d Battalion, 21st Infantry was making a helicopter combat assault into the Song Chang Valley. The CA was hot. Whittecar saw the 3–21 C&C Huey buzzing around the gun positions on Hill 102 to the east. He screamed at his RTOs to tell that ship to clear the hell out. He didn't know 3–21 radio frequencies, so he could only call the 4–31 TOC and tell them to relay the message to the pilots. It was too late. He watched the Huey corkscrew down, a body falling from the open cabin door, then impact in flames behind the tree lines.

Captain Whittecar screamed at no one in particular, "How goddamn stupid can you be! This ain't a sightseeing tour!"

Chapter Eight

Hot CA Into AK Valley

The battle which B/4–31 began in Hiep Duc, better known as Death Valley, became the responsibility of 4–31 Infantry. The battle which D/4–31 began in Song Chang, better known as AK Valley, became the responsibility of 3–21 Infantry. The 3d Battalion, 21st Infantry, its command standard recently passed to LtCol Eli P. Howard, was headquartered on LZ Center (seven kilometers east of LZ West) and was also responsible for LZ East.

The 3d of the 21st Infantry had been making contact since May.

The recent history of the Gimlets, as the battalion called itself, could be traced most actively through C Company. Its commander, Capt Ernie Carrier, was a hard-core Cajun who won his third Silver Star and third Purple Heart during Operation Frederick Hill. The operation began on 12 May 1969, when an NVA regiment overran a South Vietnamese militia outpost in the coastal plains of Tam Ky. The 3d of the 21st Infantry was committed, and Carrier—who'd come in-country as a second lieutenant in November of 67—had not seen worse. On 14 May, Charlie Company was moving across an open rice field toward a tree line pounded by Marine Air when they found themselves in the middle of an NVA battalion. They took withering fire from all sides, including mortar and recoilless rifle rounds; an assault sent them scrambling back. Carrier got the survivors into a hasty perimeter, and there they halted the attack. A medic named Shea ran out four times to drag wounded into their little island; crawling towards a fifth man, he was wounded, then finally shot and killed as he continued his efforts. A GI who was separated from his platoon in the paddy was dragged off as a prisoner. Helicopters carrying ammunition resupply were almost shot out of the sky above Charlie Company; they were driven away. With darkness, artillery and gunship fire shook around the miniature perimeter. Illumination splashed above the company but, in the seconds of darkness between each flare, the NVA scrambled closer with RPGs and grenades. North Vietnamese were gunned down within yards of the perimeter. They pulled out only when the dawn brought reinforcements; they left more than thirty bodies behind.

Charlie Company survived that night because the men had guts; but of the eighty-nine men who started the fight, only thirty-six were unscathed.

PFC Daniel John Shea won the Medal of Honor.

"A few days like this," Carrier wrote home, "and it's looney bin time." But the action had routed the NVA around Tam Ky, and 3–21 rotated its bloodied companies through Chu Lai stand down. By mid-June, they were back in action again, this time closer to home—in and around AK Valley. Bravo 3–21 (Capt Arthur Ballin) took casualties in a bunker complex—from which the NVA evaporated during the night—and the battalion reconnaissance platoon also pulled out of a bunkered area with several wounded. Delta 3–21 (Capt Steve Sendobry) was CA'd in to relieve Echo Recon. Delta called itself Black Death, and Sendobry was a strong commander on his second tour, but they fared no better; when the Gladiator Platoon, under 1stLt Steve Maness, took point, they came under heavy fire. The point was shot in the head and the platoon sergeant at the rear of the column was shot in the leg. Lieutenant Maness crawled forward with two men and managed to throw grenades into several bunkers; Maness got a hand on the point man, but could not pull him back under the fire. The next day, Maness and a squad got the body, but took more casualties in an ambush.

That night, 10–11 June, Delta humped toward LZ East to reinforce for an expected ground assault; the company was still three hours away when the flares began popping above East. The men could see NVA flamethrowers arching through the black. On LZ East, 1st Platoon of Alpha 3–21 and a detachment of artillerymen from B/3–82 were fighting for their lives. At least one bunker was overrun by NVA; when the only officer on the hill was wounded, the Alpha platoon sergeant, SSgt Bill Cruse, took command. For forty-five minutes, he was everywhere along the bunker line, holding the men together.

The NVA pulled back before daylight, leaving twenty-seven bodies in the wire; Colonel Tackaberry choppered in to pin Staff Sergeant Cruse with an impact award of the Silver Star.

LZ Baldy was also penetrated.

Charlie Company—its members almost all green seeds now—stumbled into a bunker complex of its own. The point man fired on some moving bushes—the site of the NVA listening post, Carrier would later realize—and turned up two NVA bodies. They continued towards a hootch on the next hill, and an RPD suddenly opened fire from within it, gunning down the point man and the four grunts behind him. Under cover fire, Captain Carrier crawled forward with several men; one GI got close enough to report that three North Vietnamese were standing over the bodies and kicking each one in the head. The company pulled back to another hill and directed in the air strikes; then Charlie Company worked its way back up the blasted slope. There was nothing there: not the five GIs, nothing left of the NVA except a few shattered bodies and weapons. They did find bunkers on the hill, though, lots of them.

The NVA had done their damage and vanished.

To reinforce 3–21's hunt, elements of 4–31 moved in at the end of June. Delta 4–31 (Captain Mekkelsen) was the first into AK Valley. By this time, the NVA were breaking up into groups of three to five, toting full packs, and hiding what they could not carry. Delta uncovered more than two hundred spider holes and bunkers, connected by a maze of tunnels and trenches, plus rice, ammunition, and enemy documents. Their patrols also crossed paths with some of the evading NVA, and they got credit for twelve kills. Delta eventually secured an LZ for the arrival of Bravo 4–31 (Captain Gayler) and Echo Recon 4–31 (1stLt Barry Brandon); Delta departed on their lift birds.

Bravo took some wounded when they were mortared while crossing an open paddy; on 27 June, Alpha 4–31 (Captain Yates) was CA'd in to reinforce. Alpha unassed their Hueys and began humping off the LZ; almost immediately their point man was killed in an ambush. The company pulled back as Bravo advanced towards an adjacent hill to help direct their supporting air strikes. The men were stopped cold by a barrage of AK47 and RPG fire. The next day, the NVA let Alpha get within twenty feet of their hidden bunkers before dropping the point man with three rounds in the head. Alpha pulled back again as the jets shrieked in. Bravo, meanwhile, pushed uphill again; while most of the men hunkered in the vegetation, some heads down and some returning fire, a foolish few carried the fight to the enemy. They crawled close

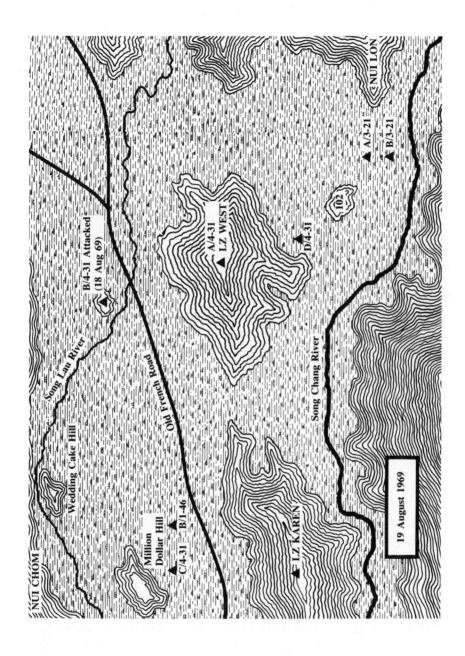

enough to lob grenades into two spider holes, killing the snipers; the rest of the NVA pulled out. The next day, 29 June, the fight was over. On 2 July, Bravo was to be flown to Chu Lai for stand down; Alpha moved out to secure the extract LZ for them, and an NVA command-detonated mine blew away two grunts and wounded two more. On 5 July, Alpha and Echo Recon were also pulled out to Chu Lai to rehab.

The *3d NVA Regiment* had not been pinned.

A frustrating comment on the war of attrition was that the last position Alpha 4–31 secured before lifting out was Hill 102, which in August the NVA were using as a headquarters and an antiaircraft site. The June operation had not cornered the enemy, and by July activity had tapered off. The Polar Bears pulled out and the Gimlets resumed routine patrolling; the battalion commander rotated and the new colonel—Howard—arrived during the lull. At least on the surface, everything seemed secure.

It was 19 August 1969. Captain Carrier was on LZ Center, bags packed, finally going home. His executive officer, 1stLt James V. Gordon, had taken command of Charlie Company. They were rucking up—3d of the 21st Infantry was humping into AK Valley to relieve the pinned-down survivors of Delta 4th of the 31st Infantry. So Carrier was saying good-bye on a hot, frustrating day. The North Vietnamese had quietly slipped back in from the western mountains and resumed their positions in the bunker complexes. They had picked the time and circumstance to come out of the woodwork; this battle was to be on their terms, and their only goal was to stack up American bodies.

■ A Company, 3d Battalion, 21st Infantry, 196th Infantry Brigade, Americal Division, under 1stLt Eugene Shurtz, Jr., was to lead the Gimlets into AK Valley. They were on a hill called the Birthday Cake, so named because it terraced to its low peak, the handiwork of rice farmers long gone. Alpha Company had humped up it the previous day with PFC Thomas G. Goodwin walking point. Halfway along, Lieutenant Shurtz had halted him to show him his map and confirm where they were.

Shurtz was brand new and trying hard.

Goodwin, on the other hand, was twenty-one years old and had been in the bush ten months. He was never exactly clear *why* he was there, but his father had fought in the Battle of the Bulge and his older brother had also done his time. He was from a solid, patriotic family, and when the government asked, he did not think to resist. Actually, Goodwin was a grunt because of a fluke. He dropped a class in junior college, knowing that cancelled his student deferment, but figuring he could slip by to the next semester when he'd resume a full load. Think again. After the draft finally deposited him in Vietnam, he decided what the hell, it was time to see what he was made of. He refused an assignment as the platoon RTO and instead volunteered to walk point. Because of heavy casualties in the recent heavy fighting, he'd even served as acting platoon leader. On the Birthday Cake, Private Goodwin was acting squad leader, first squad, 3d Platoon; of those men, he'd written his parents recently that he had, ". . . a good squad. In fact, it's so good it makes the other squads look sick."

Before Alpha Company departed for AK Valley, the 3–21 C&C landed on their hill. Lieutenant Colonel Howard was there to see Lieutenant Shurtz; A Company was to conduct an airmobile combat assault into the paddies between Hill 102 and the Nui Lon ridge line. The men would be going in with as much ammo as they could carry, but no rucksacks and only two canteens per man; there was no reason to carry C rations. Howard obviously was not expecting a prolonged fight; but as things developed, the Gimlets's piecemeal response to the NVA attack was unwise. The cadre of leadership in their foe, the *3d NVA Regiment,* was most likely unchanged from the battle in June, and their bunker tactics were the same as they had been then and many other times in the past. But it was extremely difficult for the U.S. Army to take advantage of this repetition because the leaders at battalion and company level changed so often.

The C&C also dropped off Ollie Noonan of the Associated Press; he had been covering the 11th Brigade at Duc Pho and had just returned to the Da Nang press center when the action broke. He and his partner, Richard Pyle, were the first reporters on the scene, having choppered up only that morning. Pyle went to LZ West while Noonan went to LZ Center and thumbed a ride aboard the C&C to get to the bush. He was a tall guy with a handlebar mustache and a Boston clip, who was affable to the curious grunts. Men were shouldering ammunition bandoliers and checking rifles as they talked, getting ready. Hueys began orbiting their green hill. Smoke grenades were tossed out.

Alpha Company left the Birthday Cake in intervals.

The first lift was greeted by AK47 fire from the trees as the Huey settled into a sun-blasted paddy in AK Valley. Lieutenant Shurtz disembarked from the second lift. One of the birds was coming out when an RPG shrieked past it; the pilot veered to avoid a possible second shot, the tail rotor smacked into a palm tree, and the Huey did an uncontrolled spin at fifteen feet before crashing to the ground. The crew grabbed their M16s and scrambled aboard another Huey that had just off-loaded its grunts. Shurtz hiked to the abandoned Huey to turn off the engine before it caught fire. He couldn't figure out how, and the engine pumped away until it ran out of fuel at dusk. Before retiring to the cover of a banana tree grove, Shurtz made a point of spinning the radio dials to get them off the frequencies, and he policed up the maps and code books the rattled pilots had left behind.

Coming in on the next lift, Private Goodwin and part of his squad were crowded into a Huey with their new platoon leader, Lieutenant Tynan, and the hitchhiking Noonan. Starting their descent into the LZ, they could see the downed chopper. Noonan leaned past the door gunner, taking photographs, and Goodwin shouted to his new lieutenant over the thump of the rotors, "Boy, is this a hot LZ!"

Lieutenant Tynan just smiled.

Then Tynan hollered back in the vibrating cabin: as soon as they landed, Goodwin was to lay down some cover fire from the edge of the paddy. They dropped in with the door gunners firing into the far brush lines. The skids touched the dry paddy and everyone tumbled out, unable to distinguish NVA fire amid the racket of M60s and jet turbines. Goodwin tagged Donny Anderson and they jogged towards the far end of the paddy. When the Hueys roared out over their heads, they were abruptly aware of the enemy fire.

"Hey, Donny, let's just get out of here!" yelled Goodwin.

They ran back to the brushy banana trees where the company was gathering. The NVA strafing had evaporated as soon as the last chopper had beat it out of the landing zone; the nervous pilots in the final lift had dumped the grunts from a six-foot hover.

Then, with the noonday sun frying them, they began the sweep. It was Goodwin's squad's turn to be on point, and he already had a volunteer point man. A green seed named Mack had recently received a Dear John and commented apathetically that he had nothing to lose; he'd never walked lead before so he joked, "Yeah, I wanna walk point, I'm going to sniff those dinks out!"

Mack took the point.

Anderson walked cover man.

Goodwin was third; the other five were in line behind them.

They started down a trail which ran from the banana trees into an open patch of waist-high brush with tree lines on three sides. No one really knew what was going on, and Lieutenant Tynan said to be careful because friendlies were in the area. That meant that the point man could not just wheel and deal at the slightest noise. That was fatal because—as it was pieced together later—Mack and Anderson walked right up to two North Vietnamese regulars sitting beside their bunker in the parched scrub brush. The NVA wore standard fatigues, web gear, ammunition pouches, and pith helmets. Mack the green seed—who thought the enemy wore black pajamas—probably wondered if they were ARVN. For his hesitation, Mack and Anderson took a burst of AK47 across their chests.

Goodwin threw himself into the brush off the footpath at the first shots. Another AK opened up from the left, putting full auto bursts over him. Goodwin could hear the rounds snapping over his head. When the NVA changed magazines, Goodwin fired back from the prone—single shots—trying to walk his rounds into the tangle from where he could hear the enemy. He screamed for his point men, but there was no answer. He began crawling back. Down the trail he found Randy Grove and Ralph Poe, his only old-timers besides Anderson. One of the green seeds was shot; the other two were passed out from shock or heat exhaustion.

Goodwin, Grove, and Poe got out on their bellies. The rest of the company was still in the banana tree grove, everyone crouched behind cover from all the stray rounds slashing through the foliage. The men were wilted from the heat. Goodwin came up to his knees and waved at a medic, "We've got some dead and wounded, I need you to give us a hand!"

The medic simply shook his head no.

Since the company headquarters medic, a conscientious objector named Doc Peterson, had an excellent reputation, this man was most likely the 1st Platoon medic, another conscientious objector who refused to carry a weapon and made no bones about his reluctance. He was, all in all, a nice, spacey kid who dabbled in oriental religion and culture and who was literally shaking in his jungle boots every minute the company was in the bush. Sometimes this medic did his job and sometimes he hid in a foxhole; there were grunts who wanted to blow his head off.

Goodwin suddenly noticed that everyone, including the officers, was looking at him from behind the trees. He barked at them, "Yeah, we got some real bad shit up there! They ambushed us!"

■ Alpha 3–21 combat assaulted into AK Valley, and Bravo 3–21 was close behind on foot. They'd started out from Hill 352 after a platoon from Charlie 3–21 was brought in to pick up their rucks—Bravo Company was being sent in fast and light. At least one man kept his rucksack, though. PFC Eric R. Shimer, a grenadier in third squad, 3d Platoon, dumped the paraphernalia from it and reshouldered it with only his last can of warm beer, a can of charlie rats, and thirty rounds of ammunition.

Private Shimer was one of the new breed of grunt that came when the rules governing student deferments were changed. He was drafted out of law school at Villanova University. On his helmet cover, he had opted for something "ethnic, esoteric, and double entendre," namely a penned-in Iron Cross with the words *Gott Mit Uns*. Shimer was a conservative, but also a sardonic realist. It was perhaps cynically appropriate that his Purple Heart was the result of what was euphemistically called "friendly fire." A Marine Phantom had accidentally toggled a 750-pound bomb within twenty meters of his squad during the June bunker fight, and Shimer caught a two-centimeter piece of steel in his leg.

Shimer had been in-country five months.

Shimer's platoon, under 1stLt Gordon J. Turpin, had the drag position as they humped down the jungled ridge line and then toward AK Valley to the west. The platoon used the main trail not by choice—it was easily ambushable—but for speed. It was more than five kilometers as the crow flies. No one really knew what was going on, the men were hungry and fatigued, and the sunbake practically finished them. By the time they approached Alpha Company's noisy perimeter, Shimer thought they were a bunch of zombies.

They'd been pushed too hard, too long.

Bravo Company had not had a respite from the field since right after the May battle. Finally, on 6 August, they had been lifted to LZ Center via Hueys, then were loaded on Chinooks bound for Charger Hotel, the brigade's stand-down billets in Chu Lai. They turned in their gear, were issued fresh fatigues, then straggled off in little groups to the Americal PX and the USO. Bad rumors were afloat, all of which the company commander, Capt Ronald V. Cooper, confirmed that night.

Most of the company had gathered, some stoned, some drunk, for the floor show. Captain Cooper came on first, looking very distraught. "I hate to tell you this, but . . ." Stand down was cancelled. Bravo was going back to the bush in the morning.

The grunts burst into shouts and obscenities.

On 7 August, Bravo Three was lifted to LZ East, the rest of Bravo to LZ Center. More wire had been strung since the sapper attacks, and the nightly artillery barrages around the perimeter were close enough to send everyone ducking their own shrapnel. Nerves were clicking.

On the 9th, Bravo airlifted to abandoned LZ Prep.

On the 11th, the men conducted a predawn patrol which found nothing, then spent the rest of the day dismantling the LZ prior to abandoning it again.

On the 12th, the artillery was lifted off by Hooks and the infantry in Hueys. LZ Center had just been mortared and Bravo Company was sent to augment Delta Company on the bunker line. That night they watched flashes light up AK Valley; the concussions came ten seconds later. Marine Air was clearing the way for a group of planes spraying Agent Orange. The fire base mortar crews fired parachute flares all night and, in the light of one, Shimer and his buddy Ski suddenly noticed an NVA strolling through the wire below their bunker. The flare burned out before they could "fire him up." Mortars were employed.

On the 13th, which was Shimer's twenty-third birthday, Bravo got the good news. Stand down had been rescheduled for the 16th. Then to prove how really fragile the grunts' existence was, orders were changed and they humped off Center in a driving rainstorm. Again, they had no idea what was going on. Crossing a swollen stream, Shimer slipped on the rocks and nearly drowned when his pack got up over his head. Halfway to the company's destination, Hill 352, Lieutenant Turpin took out a short patrol to investigate some hootches. He told Shimer to recon by fire; Shimer blasted some of his misery out the barrel of his grenade launcher.

Bravo Company chopped out a mini LZ atop 352, a mortar tube was airlifted to them, and Shimer wrote home, ". . . our position is right under the landing pad, and the hooch comes down when the birds come in. The ants regard my air mattress as a freeway."

On 14 August, Turpin took out a night ambush to the main trail below the ridge. The men dropped their rucks in the company pos, put on war paint, and set in behind a dike. As soon as they got their M60 and claymores in place, everyone promptly passed out from exhaustion. Only Lieutenant Turpin and his RTO stayed awake. As Shimer noted, the platoon leader "could have had us all court-martialled for dereliction of duty, but, being a realist and a decent guy, he just kidded the hell out of us."

At dawn, the men learned the rest of the company had been mortared during the night and some men had been dusted off. There was an NVA regiment around them, somewhere in these jungled ridge lines.

They patrolled and patrolled, but found nothing.

On 17 August, at dusk, Third Herd went on another wild goose chase while the rest of Bravo Company humped to Hill 200. Third Herd had to make a forced march to rejoin the rest of the company and arrived after dark with no time and little energy to set out their trip flares and claymores.

On the 18th, at dawn, the platoon set out to secure a day laager at the base of Hill 434. The platoon took a helicopter resupply there, then higher sent a change of orders. There was talk of a company from 4th of the 31st Infantry being pinned down, and the platoon was to rejoin the company back at Hill 352. They humped across a stream, then got snarled and lost in the thick brush of the ridge line as darkness fell. Turpin told Shimer to fire an M79 illumination round. This pinpointed them to any lurking NVA, but it was a beacon for Captain Cooper to radio them directions. It was brutal going. When they finally broke into a clearing at the top of the ridge line, they had to medevac one man for a suspected heart attack from the heat. They finally dragged into the company pos one hour before midnight.

On 19 August, Bravo Company filed through the river flats of AK Valley as word filtered down the line that Alpha Company had fifteen dust-offs. They'd finally found the NVA, or the NVA had found them; details were never clear among the grunts. Bravo linked up with Alpha on a hillside of cane and elephant grass. The firing was up ahead, invisible through the brush, and a fire crackled and rolled smoke back over their heads. Shimer donned his gas mask, found a spot of shade to sit in, and figured that at least the smoke was concealing them.

From within the banana trees, Lieutenant Shurtz was on the horn with Lieutenant Colonel Howard who was orbiting in his charlie-charlie bird.

The two men did not get along.

It was a matter of style. Howard was a hot-tempered taskmaster. His enthusiasm, or rather what the grunts thought of it, was noted by Private Shimer when they returned to LZ Center after one particularly exhausting patrol. ". . . The first sergeant met us with two garbage cans full of cold beer. We needed that. The new battalion commander, a distinguished looking black man, also met us at the wire. We were required to unload our weapons and salute with a snappy, 'Gimlet, sir!' We did not need that."

Captain Carrier—who was called Outlaw and who gave his men nicknames like the Butcher Platoon—was more in tune with Howard, who was called the Skull because he shaved his head. After Carrier lost five men in the bunker complex, Carrier pushed hard and bumped into two NVA platoons on the run. He gave pursuit with revenge in mind, and stumbled over a gut-shot North Vietnamese soldier. The battalion commander—Howard's predecessor—was overhead in his C&C and radioed Charlie Company to secure an LZ to medevac the wounded prisoner. Carrier argued, "Aw shit, sir, this dink's going to be dead in ten minutes, and we've still got a chance to catch his buddies!" Carrier's Kit Carson Scout ended the argument by shooting the NVA in the head, and Charlie Company continued their hunt. Howard liked such aggressiveness, especially when it racked up the numbers. Lieutenant Shurtz was, by comparison, a husky, crew-cut ROTC graduate from Iowa who—only twelve days in command—came across as an earnest, green kid. His troops liked him, but they had not seen enough of him in combat to respect him.

In what was Shurtz's first real firefight, Alpha Company had just been humping out of the LZ when the point squad was machine-gunned. Lieutenant Tynan sent PFC Goodwin back down the trail with another squad. Randy Grove crawled as close as he dared to that first NVA bunker and kept the NVA's heads down with his M16 while Goodwin fired his M16 from a crouch and hollered directions. The rest of the men began dragging the wounded and the heat casualties back down the path.

A machine gun squad was fed in to help them. It was under PFC Robert Kruch, and if Goodwin thought his squad was the best in the company, Kruch thought his might be the worst. Kruch—who was drafted during his final term in college, and who was antiwar but curious—had been in the bush all of three weeks. He was in charge of five even newer men only because the real squad leader had, in his opinion, shammed his way out; he was a short-timer who, sensing what was about to happen, claimed to be sick. He had been medevacked the day before.

Kruch's squad had been in the last helo lift; in the confusion generated by the downed helicopter—it was impossible to determine the source of enemy fire in the racket—he and his two riflemen jumped behind a dike and became separated from their machine gun team. They finally scrambled into the banana trees, then hustled down the trail to help get the casualties back. They found their gun team holed up in a cluster of trees, the machine gunner firing his M60 into the green tangle. There was a shout to pull back. The machine gunner—who had previously bragged about being an enforcer in a Chicago street gang—was visibly shaken. As they got up to go, he grabbed the M60 barrel and burned his hand. Back at the LZ, he told Kruch he had to see a medic. Kruch never saw him again.

Mack and Anderson were lying on the trail, and the grunts clustered around them. Kruch knew Mack; he was from a different platoon, but when you're new and scared shitless you latch onto buddies. Mack reminded him of one of his younger brothers. The kid's chest was blown open; you could see the heart beating. A medic crouched beside him, "C'mon, man, hang on, a chopper's coming!" Mack turned ashen very quickly, then just stopped breathing. Kruch vomitted into the brush along the footpath.

Captain Carrier was on the chopper pad at LZ Center when the medevacs and battalion command ship landed. Among those lifted out of Alpha Company's perimeter were four heat casualties. They lay like statues in the LZ. Lieutenant Colonel Howard eyed them suspiciously; Alpha had flown into the valley, but Bravo, which had humped in, didn't have any heat medevacs. The battalion had an unscientific method to sort out malingerers: a dousing of ice water on a genuine heat casualty would have no effect, but a faker couldn't help but flinch.

With satisfaction, Carrier watched as Howard had a bucket of water fetched and poured it across the men himself. They jerked painfully. All four of the malingerers were black, and Howard was black, and he turned on them with contemptuous wrath. The impression one got from Lieutenant Colonel Howard—who had fought in Korea when the military was barely desegregated—was that he was very sensitive about and proud of his race. He wanted no one to think they couldn't hack it.

"Get ready, we're going back in!"

The four were up now, three of them tight-lipped, one arguing back until he decided it was best to shut the hell up. Howard looked to be on the verge of unholstering his .45 and shooting the coward.

Meanwhile, Howard's RTO edged over to Captain Carrier. He'd just recently been sent to battalion from Charlie Company, and he hoped to find some consolation with his former commander. He was a stocky, sharp kid named Richard Doria, and he was horror stricken. "My God, we can't go back in there! This colonel thinks he's King Kong, but the dinks got a ring of .51-cals. Ask the helicopter crew . . ."

"I ain't asking the pilots nothing!"

Carrier was Airborne Ranger and he did not like that kind of talk, but Doria was not going to let it die. "If they weren't black," he pressed, "we wouldn't be going back in. He just doesn't want the guys to think he lets the blacks welch."

"If you don't go, there's no doubt you're going to jail," threatened Carrier.

Doria had been Carrier's RTO during the nightmare in May; he had served ably and, after much time in the bush, everyone was glad when he was selected as battalion radioman. It got him out of the grunts. Carrier finally relented and went to the colonel. But Howard was adamant: he was going to put those shirkers where they belonged! Carrier put his arm over Doria's shoulder, "You've done this before. We've been on CAs under fire. You can do it again. I've been scared, I've been so afraid I've cried on the radio. But you gotta do the job." Doria said nothing. He just resigned himself and climbed back aboard the command helo, but his face was a mask Carrier had seen before. The man was seeing his own death. The Huey rose from the helo pad and dipped into the valley. From the bunker line on LZ Center, Captain Carrier saw what happened next.

As the 3–21 C&C bore in towards Alpha Company, Colonel Tackaberry was in the 196th InfBde C&C, orbiting one aerial tier above battalion's airspace. Tackaberry monitored the radio and heard Shurtz request Howard to take out their civilian photographer because he did not want to spend the night in the valley. Tackaberry broke in on the transmission and said he could pick up the man since he was returning to LZ Baldy for the nightly briefing. Howard said no problem, he was going in anyway.

Howard radioed Shurtz and his RTO, SP4 Chuck Hurley, "Zulu Alpha Niner, I'm inbound into your position with replacements."

Shurtz and Hurley guided in the battalion commander. The NVA were coming out of the woodwork all over the valley, but seemed mostly concentrated to the west near Hill 102 and south along the Song Chang. The C&C should come in from the east, from along Nui Lon ridge; land in the paddy adjacent to the tree grove; then pivot one-eighty and go back the way they'd come. That's exactly what the pilot did, pausing long enough to kick out the four malingerers and take Noonan aboard.

Then the C&C hopped over to Bravo Company; they were set up in a thick plot of elephant grass and trees south of Alpha Company and closer to the river. Captain Cooper and his RTO, SP4 Robert Munson, were with their FO, Sgt Bass, and his RTO, PFC Roland Lasso. Howard came on the radio to request landing directions. Things were chaotic now and—as Private Lasso recounted it—the first landing attempt was waved off as enemy fire suddenly cracked at the descending helicopter. Howard said he was going to give it another try. Cooper argued with him on the radio, "This area is too hot! I'm not going to have one of my men shot off a paddy dike trying to guide you in! If you're still coming in, you're on your own!"

A second attempt was aborted under fire.

The C&C finally banked away, but then darted towards Hill 102. It buzzed low, and Howard and his sergeant major were knocked out the open cabin doors as the chopper was hit by 12.7mm fire or an RPG. The Huey nosed towards the valley floor as the fuel tanks ignited, and it was a ball of fire and coming apart even before impact. Howard did not seem the kind of man who believed in premonitions, but something odd was remembered later by his battalion staff. A young ocelot had been caught on LZ Center; it was nicknamed Skates Two, which was Howard's radio call sign. The night before the colonel's death, the ocelot had escaped from its cage and been killed by the pet dogs of the headquarters company.

Colonel Tackaberry, flying back to LZ Baldy as dusk approached, had been monitoring the battalion net. Howard was talking, but he suddenly blurted, "Oh!" as though he'd been punched in the chest. An excited voice came through the static hiss, "Looks like they've been hit!" Tackaberry told his pilot to turn around and, in ten minutes, they were over the crash site. There was a smoky imprint on the vegetation, the tail section was still intact, parts were strewn about, the rest was melted magnesium. There were no signs of survivors. Until the bodies were recovered, the U.S. Army would carry those aboard as Missing In Action:

LtCol Eli P. Howard
WO1 Johns D. Plummer
WO1 Gerald L. Silverstein
SgtMaj Franklin D. Rowell
SP4 Richard A. Doria
PFC Stephen L. Martino
PFC Stewart J. Lavigne
Mr. Oliver E. Noonan

Lieutenant Shurtz did not see the crash. He had watched the Huey crest the hill, wondering why the colonel was going the wrong way. Then he walked over to his platoon leaders. 2dLt David Teeple, Alpha One, was new. 1stLt Dan Kirchgesler, Alpha Two, was the most experienced officer there. 2dLt Bob Tynan, Alpha Three, was also new but learning fast. They'd been monitoring the battalion net, and one of them commented to Shurtz, "The C&C is down."

"Yeah, I know, he just dropped off four guys."

"No, they've been shot down."

"What!"

"The colonel apparently spotted a .51 on the ridge and went down to take a look."

The 3d of the 21st Infantry had gone in expecting to clear up a spot of trouble, but had walked into a regiment. The confusion started there and was capped when the battalion commander was suddenly blasted out of the sky. That night in the Song Chang Valley was a mess, hard to piece together; but a picture—probably flawed in parts—emerged. Bravo Company had been ordered to secure the crash site. The order was issued either by Maj Richard Waite, BnXO, or Maj Richard Smith, BnS-3, but they should not be labelled incompetent. Their place was properly in the TOC bunker on LZ Center, but with the command ship gone so were their eyes. They could not gauge the true field picture, which was that the wreck was well inside enemy lines.

Captain Cooper gave the mission to 3d Platoon.

Lieutenant Turpin, Bravo Three, resisted the order. Turpin was no timid college draftee but an OCS mustang lifer considered a bit crazy by his grunts because he loved the bush. He'd previously been a sergeant first class in the special forces. He was aggressive but also realistic, and he argued that, with darkness falling, it was useless to risk ambush to recover a cabinful of corpses.

Cooper agreed and radioed LZ Center to respectfully decline the mission; to listen to another version, the order was pressed and Cooper snapped, "If you want it so bad, major, you walk point!"

Captain Cooper may have said that; he was a hard man to define. The captain he replaced was a stocky supply type who loved his creature comforts, hated to hump, and didn't seem to be looking for a fight. When Cooper, who was tall and lean, took over after the June bunker fight, he kept resupply to a minimum and kept the company moving hard. He was looking for the enemy. He was respected throughout the Gimlets. Even Captain Carrier noted, ". . . He was the best thing to hit the battalion since me. He looked out for his men and showed a lot of command presence." But he was no lifer. He was a young man who was easy to talk to, and who flashed the peace sign and seemed very plugged into the bitterness of his grunts. Sometimes at night, after hacking out a spot in the bush, some guys would pass a joint to mellow down from the day's hump. Captain Cooper seemed the kind who would, in a moment of weary comradeship, say fuck it, and take a hit. There was talk to that effect; others thought that was bullshit.

A journalist who joined Bravo Company in the bush two weeks later caught the flavor when he recounted conversations in the company headquarters at dusk:

"Someday we're going to get together and all of us are going to say we aren't going. The only thing that is stopping us now is Long Binh Jail, but if we all stick together, they can't lock us all up."

"Right on," said another. . . .

Captain Cooper came over and joined the circle. "Hiya Coop," said one of the men. Munson, the radio man, took a boxing stance and pretended to hit the captain, "You wanna take a picture of us kicking the shit out of the captain?"

Cooper sat down and we continued talking. "He knows what it's like out here, not those generals and colonels with their grid maps and grease pencils," said Munson. "There are no lifers out here."

Like them, Cooper was in the Army because he had no choice, and like them he had no love for the war. He didn't care about "body count" or about "making major." All he wanted was to get as many people out alive as he could.

Bravo Company did not move from their night defensive position, but it was not a quiet night. The North Vietnamese were up and moving with the darkness and, from within the center of the company, the Bravo CP worked with B/3–82 Artillery on LZ Center. The shells slammed into suspected targets around the grunts; most of them simply ignored it. Claymores and trip flares were in place. PFC Shimer noted, "I discovered I could sleep through any commotion as long as it did not affect me or my defensive sector. But as soon as anything happened on my part of the line, I was instantly awake and taking appropriate action. This honing of the nervous system took over ten years to wear off."

■ It was almost midnight before the North Vietnamese attacked again the French Hootch and the joint perimeter of Delta 4–31 and Charlie 2–1. Movement was heard all around the circle. Then came the crashing of RPGs and AK47s, the eruption of return fire, and the lull to sporadic shooting. Fifteen men were wounded, most of them from Charlie Company. Several grunts from Charlie carried one of their wounded buddies to the medics in the French Hootch. When they checked on him, one grunt mumbled, "Aw hell, he's dead." Captain Whittecar couldn't believe it. There wasn't a mark on the kid. He started mouth to mouth, then banged the man's chest until he could hear a heartbeat. In a couple of minutes it stopped again, and Whittecar put his hand under the GI's head to give him artificial respiration again. The back of his skull was mashed, blown away. Whittecar let him drop. Only later would he reflect on how cruel his reaction had been: Goddammit, I haven't got time to waste on a dead man!

Spooky was on station again, miniguns funnelling thousands of rounds a minute around the perimeter. Whittecar's only strobe light had been damaged by an RPG, so he had to constantly hold the on-switch. The French Hootch was in the center of the perimeter, and Whittecar lay on his back in the center of the floor. He held the strobe across his chest, had the radio beside him, and told the gunship pilot to hit everything thirty yards outside the light. RPGs slammed against trees and branches, raining down shrapnel. More than one RPG sprayed inside the hootch, kicking up gravel and dust, while the GIs pressed against the inside walls, hands over their faces. Whittecar, stretched across the floor with his strobe and radio, was amazed that he was only scratched in the explosions.

They went on all night.

■ Alpha Company 3–21 was probed. For Private Kruch it was a long night of blacking out, then coming to an adrenaline high at every noise in the dark. His squad was on the side of the line facing the paddies. In the far tree line, things seemed to be moving, but when flares popped there was only stillness in the harsh shadows. The man with the M60 fired—giving away his position just as the NVA probers wanted—but the antique weapon kept jamming.

On Private Goodwin's side of the line, the men had dug shallow holes among the banana trees. A hootch sat in a clearing and the shrill screams of an arguing Vietnamese woman echoed from it. The voices of her antagonists could not be heard, but Goodwin instinctively thought he knew what was happening: the NVA were forcing her boy to walk at them to trip a flare or claymore. An AK shot suddenly rang out and the woman stopped shouting. A few minutes later, the men heard footsteps approaching. Randy Grove pulled a hand frag from his web gear, and Goodwin whispered not to pop the spoon before throwing it. That way the kid would hear the midair pop and beat it. That's what they did, and the figure scampered away.

Thirty minutes later, there was a sudden, earsplitting crash outside the perimeter. A grunt bellowed, "Incoming, incoming, incoming!" Goodwin thought it was really a damaged tree that the NVA had shoved down to snap trip-flare and claymore wires, and he hollered, "No, man, that's an incoming tree!" The tension was released in a burst of laughter down the line. Someone threw a frag towards the shadows.

Two hours later, the NVA dropped mortars around them, and at daylight, they discovered the downed Huey had been stripped of all salvageable gear.

Chapter Nine
Body Bags

Lieutenant Turpin of Bravo Company 3d of the 21st Infantry had the point on 20 August. At 0700 he passed word to his men to stay in their holes since artillery fire began pounding to the west. Hill 102 was in the process of turning from green to brown. Mild vibrations rolled back under the grunts. The arty stopped. Marine Phantoms rolled in.

Then Third Herd moved out with third squad on point.

Turpin trusted the third squad. Three weeks earlier, several Vietnamese had been spotted on a patrol and Turpin had radioed Cooper to volunteer his platoon to investigate. The men had crawled along terraced dikes to within thirty meters of a hootch in a lower section; a GI spotted two armed dinks. Turpin positioned Shimer and another grenadier on the trail to cover their attack, then he crept forward with Bob Boyd and Ray Wilcox. The two grunts rushed the hootch, flushing three NVA, and Lieutenant Turpin squared his M16 sights on them. He killed one Vietnamese and wounded another who managed to limp away with the third man. Shimer came up with the rest of the platoon and fired his M79 into suspected escape routes, but it was all over. Turpin summed up the action by recommending Boyd for a Bronze Star and commenting, "He's the ballsiest guy I've ever known."

In AK Valley, the NVA were ready. That's why the grunts were spitting out bitter comments the second morning of the battle. Bravo Company had a strict policy of rotating platoons, squads, and even individuals on point. Third Herd had been in the drag position during the previous day's hump, which meant they had at least another day before they were supposed to be moved to the front. They're screwing us, Shimer thought. It was because they were reliable. A lot of guys wouldn't even raise their heads to return fire, but that was not a problem in his squad. The men were not at all happy with their jobs, but they accepted the reality of what they had to do to survive. When Shimer had first joined them, they had said they had only two rules. They never left a wounded man behind and, if someone got killed because you decided to get stoned in the bush, well, you'd get a body bag too.

Lieutenant Turpin went to another squad first to take the point. They refused. It was not their turn.

Turpin walked up to Sgt Lowry Cuthbert, third squad leader, who argued and complained but then told his men to saddle up. They too argued and complained, but followed orders and moved out single file through brush. They were spaced out with a point man, cover man, Shimer with the M79, and Cuthbert leading the other three GIs of the squad. The rest of Bravo Company followed single file. Two hundred meters out, the thick vegetation gave way to a scrubby clearing around an old hootch. Sergeant Cuthbert got them on a hasty skirmish line but, as they were about to cross, an M79 popped over their heads and exploded to their front. Cuthbert shouted back to Turpin to stop the platoon's firing. Shimer stood hunched with his buddy Wilcox, pissed that they were exposed and wanting either to press on or to pull back into the trees. He scanned the front for targets, which was proper; however, stopped and exposed, he should have been kneeling or at the prone. But he was too fatigued to get down if they were going to be moving soon, and his mind was working too slowly. The grenadiers in Bravo Company carried their M79s with the breeches open, so they wouldn't have accidental discharges; anyway, no one would fire over a full platoon. The grenade must have been fired by an NVA. Shimer should have realized that. He should have been flat in the grass. But none of it really registered in his numbed brain.

For that, Shimer became Bravo's first casualty.

What sounded like an M16 suddenly fired from ten feet behind him. Shimer was kicked in the back, face first into the grass, his half-empty rucksack on his head. There was no initial pain, but instant realization that he'd been hit badly. One round had drilled through his right arm, blowing out bicep and tricep, shattering bone. It hit his ribcage and tumbled horizontally like a ripsaw across his chest. It left a bloody furrow, hit his breastbone, sent fragments into his bronchial tubes, then punched out the left side of his chest. Shimer could sense all that had happened. He could also feel the blood dripping into his lungs and he knew that could kill him.

But his lungs were filling up slowly. He realized that if he stayed calm, he would live. That's what he concentrated on.

There had been only one burst of enemy fire.

Everyone had ducked flat, then rushed into position. Some ran to Shimer. Someone got his pack off and rolled him over. Gary Knoll, the platoon medic, was quickly there; he looked like he was going to vomit as he stared down at Shimer, but then quickly went to work. There were shouts that Wilcox had killed the dink in the spider hole. Sporadic shots began cracking past them and everyone got down except Lieutenant Turpin—who always led by example—and his RTO. Turpin looked down at Shimer, called for a dust-off, and told the pilot to be quick, "He don't look good. He's gonna die."

They rolled Shimer into a poncho, and George Beason and Ski, from another squad, hoisted him and started back. They passed the rest of Bravo Company, which was still filing forward through the trees.

Withering fire suddenly burst from the front and flanks.

They set Shimer down at the night pos and Beason crouched with him. The morning cool had burned off and Beason pulled out his canteen for Shimer as the air turned hot and hazy. Beason kept him from passing out. Other wounded were being dragged back. Hueys were circling but not landing until all the casualties had been gathered in one place.

The North Vietnamese had waited until most of Bravo Company had filed unaware into their bunker complex; then they commenced their horseshoe ambush. Bravo was strung out and pinned down. As usual, only a handful were doing the actual fighting. Many of those on point couldn't or wouldn't return fire for all the rounds snapping above their prone bodies. The men at the rear of the column were head down in the bushes, unable to fire for fear of hitting comrades ahead of them in the tangle. The fight quickly disintegrated into mass confusion. From his CP, Captain Cooper ordered a pullback to allow firepower to be employed.

From his CP, Lieutenant Shurtz moved men to protect Bravo's flank and to secure a medevac landing zone. Some of his men volunteered to crawl into the buzz saw to help drag Bravo's casualties back.

Bravo Company finally inched back into the foxholes of their night position, and Captain Cooper stayed on the horn shouting for air strikes.

Before the Phantoms came on station, one or two medevacs were able to come in for the most seriously wounded. Private Shimer was going into shock; his lungs were heavy with blood and his breath was labored, but he lay there, concentrating on the simple act of breathing. The unarmed medevac descended, a big red cross on its front, and Shimer's buddy Beason shouted for assistance. Several GIs grabbed Shimer by his arms and legs and heaved him aboard the first Huey as soon as its skids settled in the grass. Fire cracked over the landing zone. Shimer was first aboard, flat on his back on the floor. Others were quickly shoved beside him; then there was the sensation of lifting off. Just then, Shimer felt a whip of heat as a round passed his face, and he saw the pilot jerk in his seat as he was nicked.

Phantoms rolled in after the medevacs.

Bravo Three had taken the brunt of the ambush and PFC Richard Senske, a sharp OCS dropout and acting platoon sergeant, had assumed command. From their point squad, only Lowry Cuthbert, Bob Boyd, and Frank Juarez crawled out physically unscathed. Rick Shimer and Lupe Tobias were wounded.

Ray Wilcox was killed.

Joe Paparello was killed.

Milton Mendoza, a medic who ran up from another platoon, was also killed. All together, Bravo Company lost five dead and twenty-four wounded. Alpha Company also took casualties helping get these men back: three volunteers themselves from PFC Goodwin's squad—Ralph Poe and two green seeds, Harry and Diaz—were wounded.

Lieutenant Turpin was also shot.

The last medevac had sailed in and out under fire, and the jets were pounding in when Turpin was dragged into Alpha Company's LZ perimeter with a sucking chest wound. While Cooper directed the air strikes, Shurtz got on the radio to B-TOC to request another medevac. He told the major on LZ Center that the jets were running north-to-south on the NVA bunkers to their front, and a medevac might land behind them in the paddy to the east. The wounded lieutenant was lying twenty-five feet from Shurtz and his RTO, under morphine and tended to by Doc Peterson.

The medevac was refused as too dangerous.

Lieutenant Turpin—Shurtz didn't know who he was at the time—died in the dirt as the Phantoms dropped delay-fused bombs on the bunker complex.

Bravo died that day, and Alpha melted.

Several grunts came up to Shurtz, jerking the frightened medic along by his collar. One of them spat, "This guy was hiding in a foxhole with his hands over his ears! Keep him with you 'cause if he comes near us, we're liable to blow him away!" The medic was mentally a million miles away. He wasn't the only one. Private Goodwin had settled behind a banana tree; at each Phantom pass, the NVA turned their weapons skyward and he rolled behind the tree as bomb fragments slashed the surrounding brush. No resupply choppers could get through this crossfire, and Goodwin was down to half a canteen and a single bandolier of rifle ammunition. Most of the green seeds were completely out of water: Goodwin wouldn't share his when they asked, but he did suggest they use their machetes to get into the banana trees and chew the tart but moist meat. Others were going a little crazy in the sunbake. They licked sweat from their arms, which only made them retch. Some stripped bark from the trees to eat. Everyone was almost out of food.

Finally, a water detail was organized; on Shurtz's map, a well was indicated to the east along the route Bravo Company had humped in on the day before. The detail set out and was gone too long. Shurtz was extremely worried, until the GIs finally came back and reported that NVA were refilling canteens from the well when they got there. They laid low and snuck up to the well after the enemy moved on. As if to confirm that the North Vietnamese were everywhere in AK Valley, as A and B/3–21 shored up their perimeter, a platoon from C/3–21 was CA'd behind them atop Nui Lon and almost immediately came under mortar fire.

■ While B/3–21 was being mauled, D/4–31 to the west—three days under fire, and Captain Whittecar, two days back in command—finally got their respite. Helicopters were able to shuttle in resupplies of food, water, and ammunition and take out the last of the wounded. By that time, the medics in Delta Company were using fatigue shirts for bandages. The dead went out last in body bags. One Huey took fire ascending LZ West's mountain, banked sharply, and a body fell out and crashed through the jungle canopy. He was later located.

Then came Delta's first quiet night. At 0500, however, a trip flare burst outside the perimeter and M16s chopped at the grass until 81mm mortar fire was directed in. At 0630, several RPGs were fired, but they exploded short of the ring of foxholes. Five minutes later, Charlie

Company's side of the perimeter came under heavy fire. It was returned. At 0700, the Blue Ghost Cobras came on station, pumping rockets and miniguns around the perimeter amid a crossfire of 12.7mm and AK47 tracers. It was enough to quiet the NVA, and at 0800 on 21 August, Delta Company, 4th Battalion, 31st Infantry, left the Song Chang Valley. The Cobras fired cover as the Hueys shuttled the GIs up to LZ West.

Whittecar and his command group were on the last chopper out; it was no less than a great relief. It was also the end of Whittecar's command; within days, he was medevacked to Chu Lai with infected wounds.

In the aid station on West, Doc Kinman probed Whittecar's leg for more shrapnel, but there was none and he began to bandage it. Whittecar sat there, trying to define his emotions. GIs from Delta, also in the aid station, looked at Whittecar and he looked at them. The pride and relief were palpable. They've given their all, and so have I, thought Whittecar. He was proud, sad, exhausted from three sleepless nights, almost overcome by his emotions. There was talk of a Distinguished Service Cross and he thought, goddamn, I did it. The next moment he doubted himself. The two GIs closest to him were gone—the medic with a bullet in his head, the radioman with a mangled foot. Seven of his men were dead; almost everyone was wounded. Could I have done something differently? he asked himself. One grunt came to him privately, "I wanted to thank you for coming down. I know you didn't have to, but I wouldn't be alive now if you hadn't." That meant a great deal to Whittecar, but it did not erase all of his hauntings.

■ The night of 20–21 August was a long one for Alpha Company. Some men with minor wounds had not been evacuated, and their occasional groans during the night were bad for morale; everyone realized there was no guaranty of a medevac if they were hit. Lieutenant Shurtz and Doc Peterson sat bleary-eyed in the grass, filling out medevac slips for the casualties and radioing them in on a secure net with scrambler. Battalion radioed back that one of the men reported evacuated with wounds could not be found in any hospital. As they pieced it together, the missing man had been hit while helping get Bravo's wounded and, although this was reported to Shurtz who then filled out a medevac slip, in the noise and confusion of the fight, the man had not been dragged back. His body was recovered in the morning; reportedly, he had an old bullet wound in his leg and a fresh one in his head. His body and the body of the dead lieutenant were zipped into body bags, and Lieutenant Tynan detailed Private Goodwin's squad to carry them as they saddled up that morning. Goodwin objected that they needed to maintain twenty paces between each man on the march, and a six-man cluster dragging a body bag was too dangerous. The platoon leader reconsidered in their favor and they left the two bodies hidden among some trees in the LZ, to be recovered after the battle.

The previous day, LtCol Robert C. Bacon, who had served as an ARVN advisor his first tour, was helicoptered from his new staff position at Chu Lai to assume command of the Gimlets. The battle between the 3d Battalion, 21st Infantry and the *3d NVA Regiment* centered on pushing through to the C&C crash site to recover the bodies. Few grunts appreciated such reasoning—dying for the dead—and morale was sagging.

On 21 August, A Company took the point.

Machine gun teams moved across the paddy and secured the tree line without incident; then the rest of Alpha Company advanced from the banana grove. From there, they humped over one of the Nui Lon fingers with 2d Platoon leading the way; its commander, Lieutenant Kirchgesler, had told Lieutenant Shurtz that, as the most experienced officer there, he did not resent taking point consistently.

Lieutenant Teeple was in the middle.

Lieutenant Tynan brought up the rear of the column.

At the grunt level, these maneuvers were not seen in ordered terms. There was no rationale. The platoon had not been resupplied in two days, and had to function on a few sips of hot canteen water a day and the few C rations they'd had the foresight to jam into their claymore pouches before being CA'd in. Ammunition was precariously low. Captain Carrier noted what was beating them the most:

I remember standing on LZ Center thinking that this had to be the hottest I have ever seen it up this high. The windsock moved only when a bird flew in. I wish I could convey just how miserably hot it was. Ever stood in the thick woods in the summer and had your cigarette smoke float straight upward. Couple that with swinging a machete in briars and brush that take you thirty minutes to move thirty feet.

The elements had gotten the best of Private Kruch, for one, and he trudged along under bandoliers of M16 and M60 ammunition, hands wrapped around a battered and unreliable M16 rifle. He was half-delirious from an empty stomach and the heavy, stale air trapped amid the vinery of the windless valley floor; and he was completely terrified by the invisible enemy. Oh God, what a mess, we know there's another ambush waiting! What are we doing! he kept thinking. The platoon crested a low hill. All Kruch could hear was a ringing in his ears, and the hair on the back of his neck seemed to stand up. NVA fire erupted from nowhere. The platoon was in a network of spider holes and bunkers covered with banana leaves and indistinguishable from the rest of the landscape. The return fire seemed only to chop weeds. Several men had been hit—one was screaming bloody murder that he was shot in the hip, couldn't move, the dinks were right next to him!—and, as always, Lieutenant Kirchgesler started towards the hottest spot.

The lieutenant was shot dead.

Kruch and his squad had scrambled into a furrow off the path and were returning fire. AK47 rounds suddenly snapped from the rear. Kruch froze as dirt kicked up a yard away; then he dropped into the ditch and shoved his M16 back up, madly squeezing the trigger. The NVA seemed to be everywhere!

Lieutenant Shurtz was down in the crossfire with Specialist Hurley, his senior RTO; it seemed impossible to get Kirchgesler's body back without sacrificing more lives. Shurtz radioed the point platoon to leave the body and pull back under cover of air strikes and artillery, an order for which he never quite forgave himself but he could think of no other alternative. The rest of Alpha Company was strung out behind the point of contact, having flopped into the vegetation along the trail. They lay there unmoving, unable to fire, ducking even lower as stray bursts clipped foliage overhead. Lieutenant Tynan and Private Goodwin lay beside one another, trying to figure out what was going on. They could hear two NVA machine guns and sporadic AK47 fire. Word came to send men back to secure an LZ for the medevacs, so Goodwin and Grove, the last men in their squad, set out with several others. They found a burnt-out clearing about fifty meters back; it was an old potato field on the opposite side of the terraced hill from the NVA bunkers. Goodwin commented that they'd found their landing zone, and at that moment the first mortar round crashed into them. Over the noise of the firefight, Goodwin hadn't heard the whistling descent, but the sudden explosion sent him into a frantic run for boulders forty yards away. Several more rounds thumped in, but Goodwin and Grove made it safely to cover.

Then Goodwin realized that, although he was still gripping his M16 in his right hand, his sleeve was soaking with blood. His hand was numb. Grove had caught some shrapnel too, but they were still on their feet and they headed back towards their platoon.

The rest of Alpha Company was pulling back to that potato field. A medevac with gunship escort tried to hover-land against the slope of overgrown terraces. The Huey glided into a hover and Kruch and another GI hefted a wounded soldier above them. They gave a final heave and got the man aboard. Kruch collapsed with a wrenched back.

Goodwin and Grove also boarded, and Goodwin's biggest worry was that they'd be shot down as soon as they cleared the trees. Medevacs had no door gunners and the medic had taken away his M16. He heard the AK47s as they pulled up, but in seconds they were high and dry.

A good amount of ammunition, charlie rats, and water blivets had been shoved out the cabin door before the Huey banked away. Those items were more precious than gold, and it must have been a mob scene because the only thing left for Kruch and his squad was a can of peaches. They angrily split it; then the company dug in around the potato patch, expecting to be mortared, praying they wouldn't be overrun. Gunships orbited them and illumination was fired when night fell, but there was no attack. The only reason the NVA don't attack, Kruch thought, is because they don't know how exhausted and undermanned— and green—we are. He did, however, hear Vietnamese voices only a hundred feet from their ring of holes; he crawled back to the company headquarters to report it. He noted with disgust that ". . . some of the officers had two or three full canteens, and I found empty C cans and everyone asleep."

■ By dawn the next day, 22 August 1969, A Company, 3d Battalion, 21st Infantry existed mostly on paper; but they had really died on 4 August.

Even then, they were not all they could have been. The former company commander, Capt Dennis Chudoba, USMA class of 1965 and veteran of a 1966–67 tour with the Gimlets, was a decent enough guy but he did not have the aggressive nature required of a combat leader. If a squad was suspected of faking an ambush, or if Search & Destroy became search & evade, nothing was really done about it. This problem was most severe in 3d Platoon, which had been without an officer for too long. 2d Platoon was lucky to have had Lieutenant Kirchgesler. 1st Platoon had 1stLt Harvey Browne, who joined them after four months with division surveillance, and Staff Sergeant Cruse, who had risen from private to staff sergeant in his eighteen months with the company; they tried to convince their reluctant draftees that the only way to go home alive was to find the NVA first and kill them.

The beginning of the end for Alpha Company came on 3 August, when they and Echo Recon were lifted to Chu Lai for stand down. There was some animosity between those infantrymen and the reconnaissance troopers. The story was that their ineptitude in okaying an LZ actually covered by the enemy had resulted in the death of a popular Alpha short-timer. Whatever the truth of that, when a Filipino band started a shrill Beatles' imitation during the floor show that night, the place suddenly erupted in a chair-throwing, fist-swinging donnybrook between Alpha GIs and Echo GIs. As punishment, Lieutenant Colonel Howard cancelled stand down and assembled Alpha Company at the Chu Lai helipad the next morning. Lieutenant Browne thought the punishment was a complete bust. Everyone expected to be sent to LZ Center, so some grunts had cases of soda strapped to their rucksacks. Others were still blitzed from the previous night. Still others were missing; they were at the beach and hadn't gotten the word. They were hustled aboard a Chinook—then got word in flight that they were to make a combat assault. No one knew what was going on. They CA'd into a paddy secured by some headquarters personnel. Browne's platoon was first in; as they came off the Hooks, the battalion operations officer grabbed GIs and rushed them into defensive positions. Kirchgesler's platoon came in next, and the grunts suddenly realized they'd been landed next to an NVA company. Figures with AK47s and RPGs could be seen moving away through the trees.

Kirchgesler moved after them and, within fifteen minutes of disembarking, Alpha Company was in contact. Browne was sent to outflank the firefight. He got his grunts on line and asked them their names. They were almost all replacements out of the Americal Combat Center and handed to him just an hour before at the Chu Lai helipad! He was thinking with a weariness that did not allow irony, "Oh well, here's another goatfuck." They got into a tree line. The contact sounded to be a few tree lines away, so Browne crawled fifteen meters into the grassy paddy ahead, then got up to appraise the area. An AK47 instantly punched him down. The bullet drilled through his left forearm and through an M16 magazine in the bandolier across his chest, then thankfully stopped halfway into a green army note pad in his pocket. His spacey but occasionally valiant medic, Doc Sanders, quickly crawled out to him, grabbed his shoulder harness, and dragged him on his back as he pedalled with his feet. The operation sort of fizzled out as he was loaded on Lieutenant Colonel Howard's C&C for medevac; in the meantime, the NVA unit melted into the vegetation.

Lieutenant Browne was given a Silver Star and Purple Heart, and he was medevacked to the United States.

Staff Sergeant Cruse rotated in days.

Captain Chudoba departed.

Chudoba and Howard mixed about as well as oil and water, and the confusion of the 4 August contact further deteriorated the battalion commander's view towards this cautious, thin, bespectacled subordinate. On 6 August, Alpha's night perimeter took fire; Chudoba wanted massive artillery, but Howard thought he was exaggerating and shouted at him to get his ass to the point of contact and determine exactly what was going on. In the morning, Lieutenant Shurtz—recently choppered to LZ Center as a replacement—was told to ruck up. He was the new commander. "What, did Chudoba get wounded?" asked Shurtz. "No, the colonel fired him." A Huey lifted Shurtz down to Alpha's bush position, and he disembarked from one side as Captain Chudoba boarded from the other.

Shurtz walked up to his headquarters group. The senior RTO introduced them, "I'm Chuck. This is Doc Peterson." He pointed to their lieutenant from the Field Artillery. "This is the FO, Al. What should we call you?"

"Well you've got two choices. It's 'Lieutenant Shurtz' or 'Sir.' "

Their jaws dropped.

The company seemed lax, and this was a first step to bring back old-fashioned discipline. Shurtz was Regular Army, a distinguished military graduate of his ROTC class and Ranger-qualified, a man who intended to follow in the footsteps of his father, a career lieutenant colonel. But his first operation with Alpha Company was not a textbook affair, and the realities of the bush began to stun him. The company kept pushing for the NVA column, but the only contact they made was with snipers. They swept towards each one, only to find farm villages each time, complete with Vietnamese going innocently about their chores. Per training, Shurtz had the males of military age rounded up—the village children, meanwhile, were peddling plastic baggies of marijuana—and choppered out. The results were negligible and the colonel finally choppered in to administer a pep talk and ass-chewing. The colonel was in his best form.

"What's your company nickname, lieutenant?"

"Alpha Annihilators, sir," Shurtz answered.

"Do you know the definition of Annihilator? It's not going to do any good to send these people in for interrogation, so they can come right back out here and shoot at you again." The colonel raised his voice. He didn't want any prisoners. He wanted body count!

Shurtz couldn't quite believe what he was hearing.

The battalion commander promised the men hot pizza for kills and, getting none, it was as if they made the colonel's shit list. Their resupply became sporadic, as if they were being punished.

It was all flaky.

Then came the battle in AK Valley when Alpha Company's only experienced officer, Lieutenant Kirchgesler, was killed. That left Lieutenants Shurtz, Tynan, and Teeple as the untested leaders of a company with too many untested soldiers. Forty percent were green seeds, and they were simply not prepared for this battle.

■ On 22 August, it was Lieutenant Teeple's turn to lead the way back to the bunkers, where they were promptly hit in the crossfire again. Sgt Derwin Pitts—a tall, thin country boy and a good squad leader—was killed going for Kirchgesler's body. PFC Ray Barker—a married kid who'd been drafted after college and who wanted nothing to do with Vietnam—was shot in the head going for Pitts's body.

The crossfire was withering, and the platoon fell back towards the potato patch, dragging Barker's body and four wounded.

Pitts was left near Kirchgesler.

PFC Kruch, for one, was sitting in a dazed heap, unable and unwilling to move again. From the day he'd arrived, things had stopped making sense. He was one of the new draftees and all he knew were the ragged, last three weeks of Alpha Company's history. The grunts were mostly new guys, not sure if they were doing anything right, unbonded yet; they were just targets for an experienced enemy. The only resolution

Kruch made was that he wasn't going to die for some stupid officer sitting in the TOC bunker. So, when one of the new lieutenants ran up and said they were going back again for the bodies, he argued that it was suicide. The lieutenant looked scared too, but orders were orders and he pointed his .45 pistol at him; Kruch brought his M16 to the lieutenant's chest and said he wasn't going anywhere. The squad was not budging and no one really was going to shoot the other; the lieutenant finally holstered his weapon.

Word was passed to pull back to Nui Lon, and what ammunition they could not carry was buried in the potato patch. The grunts were punch-drunk from the sun and their march fell apart into disorganized bands; Kruch was terrified they might get separated from the rest of the company. The North Vietnamese were following them on the trail, keeping their distance but watching the entire time. Kruch could hear them talking.

Delta 4–31—which had the best reputation in the battalion—had pulled out the previous morning and by that afternoon Alpha 4–31—which had the worst reputation—had humped down from LZ West to assume their positions. Alpha Company had been pulling LZ security since the battle began. They snaked down the trail in a heavily burdened column, with full rucks and full loads of ammunition, and finally married up with Charlie 2–1 in the late afternoon. The brush around the French Hootch had absorbed most of the shell and smoke of the last four days; the only sign to the newcomers of the ferociousness of the battle were the treetops.

Many were splintered from RPGs. Everyone made a point of digging deep foxholes. That night, the NVA dropped in fifteen mortar rounds.

The morning of 22 August, Alpha Company moved out.

Alpha 4–31 and Charlie 2–1 hiked towards Hill 102 through shimmering, hot paddies; muffled explosions drifted back to them as air and arty once again clawed at the trees on the targeted hill. Alpha Two, under 2dLt Stephen Moore, was on point. About a hundred meters into the hump, a tree line intersected their dike. Lieutenant Moore sent one squad around one side of it, while he and his platoon sergeant went around the other with SP4 Al Holtzman's squad. The point man, SP4 Robert Jeans, hiked the last berm into the woods. Lieutenant Moore was up near him when the North Vietnamese killed him at perhaps ten feet with an M79 to the chest. An RPD and several AK47s opened fire too. Prune Jeans dove for cover and ended up in a shallow depression only yards from the NVA holes; he couldn't even lift his head in the crossfire.

Behind him, the rest of the squad was scattering behind dikes, all except one big, dumb kid who spun around and started running back. The NVA shot him off the dike.

In moments, the North Vietnamese had killed four men from the lead platoon and wounded four more. The rest were pinned down. Specialist Holtzman figured there was only an NVA squad dug in among those trees; the difference, he thought, was that they had their shit together and we didn't. The NVA were between the two squads, so they couldn't fire indiscriminately into the trees. Most of his squad had picked a piece of dike anyway, and were pressed firmly against it, heads down. Holtzman hollered at a GI near him to get his ass up and return fire. "No way," he screamed back. "I'm not stickin' my head up to get blown away!"

Assholes! It was an inexperienced company, Holtzman reckoned, with only a handful you could really count on; the rest wanted to go home alive any way they could.

The platoon sergeant shouted to him to fire cover for Prune to get back. From where Holtzman was, Prune was about a hundred feet ahead, only ten yards from the berm from which the NVA were firing. He hollered to him; Prune called back that he was okay but could not move. Holtzman stuck his head up long enough to blast a LAW rocket into the trees and fire his M16 over Prune's head. It produced a lot of noise and dust, but the NVA were still invisible and still firing; Prune was simply stuck.

Coming up from behind, Captain Mantell placed the other two platoons so that their firepower would allow Alpha Two to pull back. As the company separated, more NVA emerged from the tree lines. The lead squad of Alpha One almost immediately came under fire and radioed their platoon leader, First Sergeant Price, that they were pinned down. At the same time, Price received another call from Sergeant Causey, the platoon sergeant, who was with their rear squad: he had seen two NVA walk into the French Hootch area they'd just vacated. Top Price called back the point squad and sent back an M60 team to cover their rear. He also got on the horn to the artillery battery on LZ West; the barrage to their front allowed the platoon to move undetected from their paddy up onto a brushy finger of land that overlooked the ambushed paddy. From there, they could see 3d Platoon moving into position along the dikes to help 2d Platoon get back. Top Price, crouched on the forested finger with binoculars, was on the radio with Captain Mantell; both agreed that an assault would be suicide. Therefore, their concern was to get back the stranded men. Under 3d Platoon's cover fire, 2d had been able to crawl back, dragging three of their wounded and two bodies. Two KIAs were still in the paddy.

So were Prune and a medic shot in the jaw.

It was a hot, dangerous day and the grunts were glad to slump among the trees on the ridge, out of harm's way. Top Price asked for a volunteer; he needed someone to fire LAWs down onto the bunkers so the two men could get back to their lines.

Specialist Parsons stepped forward. He was a draftee who'd been introduced to marijuana in Vietnam and who was just doing his time; but he couldn't stomach the thought of another grunt lying out there.

Price asked how many times he'd fired a LAW.

"Once," Parsons answered, "back in basic."

That was not very inspiring, but Price thought the kid looked sincere, so they collected all the rockets in the platoon and moved to the edge of the woods. Tom and Shorty accompanied them with the M60, as did a 2d Platoon GI who'd been sent to point out the exact locations of the NVA bunkers. The GI looked scared and pissed, Parsons thought, but also anxious to help out his buddies.

Parsons and his guide positioned themselves behind a banana tree at the edge of the high ground. It was a clear shot down, maybe fifty yards from the bunkers, but Parsons was extremely anxious: he could see a GI huddled in a depression only yards from the North Vietnamese. The man seemed to be moving, but Parsons found it hard to tell through the shimmering heat and the sweat pouring down his face. There seemed to be invisible steam in the brush around them. Parsons prepared the first LAW, then remembered about back-blast from basic training and glanced behind himself. Two grunts were standing there. He hollered at them to get out of the way. He shouldered the rocket, sighted in on where his partner was pointing, and squeezed off the shot. It exploded near the earthen berm. Parsons could barely make out an NVA squeezing from a spider hole; he scrambled on all fours through some elephant grass and seemed to disappear when he reached the berm. Was it a tunnel? Parsons wondered. He fired another LAW at where the man had vanished and it blew up from within the berm, sending debris whizzing. He was feeling more confident, and his guide was excited. "Blow 'em out! See that red banana leaf, that's where they are!"

Shorty was firing the M60 across the paddy, but the red tracers snapped about ten feet above the embankment. Parsons thought Shorty was a cocky bastard, and screamed at him to bring his fire down. At the same time, a medevac descended behind them. Two Huey gunships bore in ahead of it, door gunners firing cover with their sixties. They managed to strafe both the finger and the bunkers, luckily hitting no GIs and probably no NVA either. Top Price hollered in his radio at them.

Behind them, the medevac clattered in under fire.

The platoon had passed up numerous LAWs and Parsons stayed in place, slamming them down. With each explosion, pieces of the earthen spider holes and bunkers were ruptured, exposing their form. The NVA were dug in among the roots of bamboo trees, with a tunnel dug to the berm behind them. A couple of NVA were still firing from undiscovered holes; at least Parsons could hear the reports of their AKs, although he could see no one and heard no passing rounds. Both M60s were firing by now, raising dust around the berm. Others fired M79s into the elephant grass around it.

But Prune and the medic were still pinned.

Captain Mantell finally passed the word to retire to the tree line behind them. The two men were still stuck in the paddy, but it would be unwise for the rest of the platoon to spend the night in this maze of NVA bunkers. So they broke faith with two of their own and began digging in amid the trees, expecting a ground assault. They were still digging when Prune Jeans stumbled into their perimeter. He said the NVA had picked up and left with the darkness, and he had just walked out of the paddy. The wounded medic followed him out. They'd been pinned down half the day and looked it, but Parsons almost cried with relief when he saw them. In a letter of recommendation for Parsons, First Sergeant Price described it this way: ". . . the last 2 men were recovered alive and well. The first thing they asked was who fired the L.A.W.'s. I called Spec 4 Parsons over and they both hugged and slapped him on the back for saving their lives. They were both the happiest people I have ever seen. They had lain under the guns of the N.V.A. for 12 hours in an open paddie in the blistering sun with tracers and rockets passing over their heads. A few days later, upon our return to

LZ West, I recommended Spec 4 Parsons for the Bronze Star with 'V' for valor.''

As Alpha 3–21 humped up the bald, cratered knoll on Nui Lon, which was secured by a platoon from Charlie 3–21, they suffered several heat casualties. Guides from Charlie Company led Alpha Company through their trip flares and claymore mines, then set them into position on the perimeter. It was taking forever and men were bunching up; as Private Kruch's squad finally straggled into the lines at dusk, he noticed Lieutenant Shurtz standing there with a glazed look, as though he couldn't believe what was going on. Kruch did not dislike the company commander; he just thought Shurtz seemed to be swallowed up by events.

Kruch screamed at the GIs to spread out. The sun was beating down and he was boiling mad over the resupply and the every-man-for-himself attitude gripping the survivors. He picked up an empty canteen cup laying in the dirt, then threw it down, cursing, "This is the stupidest goddamn place to be!" He bent down to pick it up again when the first mortar round hit. It all happened in a sudden burst of noise and motion, but Kruch saw it in freeze-framed clarity. He was bent over. Then came a sudden, slow-motion eruption of rocks and dirt, bowling over a GI in his squad who was opening a can of charlie rats. The GI standing beside Kruch, who'd joined the squad ten days earlier, was blown onto him, the explosion engulfing Kruch in that instant like a baseball bat against his head.

Kruch was blasted into an old crater, the new kid landing on him. Kruch couldn't breath, he couldn't move, he couldn't get the kid off him. He felt two more rounds exploding. GIs were screaming. Then it was quiet and Kruch realized he was numb. No pain. Grunts clambered down into the hole and hauled him up. He reached back and his hand slipped into a hole the size of a grapefruit blown out of his lower back. That chunk of shrapnel had destroyed his kidney. He'd also been ripped by fragments in his butt, lower back, and legs.

Four men had been hit, and they were dragged to a level spot on the ridge as medevacs were called.

Kruch lay flat on his back in the dirt. He could see another man from his squad sitting there with light shrapnel wounds. The kid had taken the brunt of the explosion, inadvertently saving Kruch. He was dead. The fourth GI, the man kneeling with the C rations, lay beside him. His face was hamburger, but air gurgled in his throat and he seemed coherent. A grunt crouched beside the man, trying to keep him out of shock. "You're going to be okay, just hang in there."

A medevac was orbiting the peak in twenty minutes.

A smoke grenade was tossed out and the Huey began descending. Then came the whine of incoming mortar rounds. The GIs around the wounded dove for cover. Kruch was lying in the open, unable to move as the second salvo crashed in, but he was not worried. All he felt was a wonderful release of tension that it was all over, that he was getting out. He couldn't even imagine that he could be hurt again or killed.

Cobras came in, clearing their guns around the hill, and the Huey darted in. Grunts grabbed Kruch by his arms and legs and hefted him into the cabin. The GI with the mashed face was shoved in beside him and, in seconds, they were lifting off, the metal floor vibrating fiercely under their backs. Then the pain began, and the medevac medic gave Kruch a shot of morphine. The GI beside him stopped his gurgling, labored breathing. Kruch watched as the medic quickly moved to his side and slid a plastic trachea tube down his throat.

In the joint perimeter of A and C/3–21 atop Nui Lon, Lieutenant Shurtz sat with his artillery lieutenant and his two surviving platoon lieutenants. The platoon leaders were frustrated, and commented that what they were doing was stupid and suicidal. The conversation drifted into an angry search for reasons why any of them were even in Vietnam. Shurtz couldn't believe what he was hearing; it was like some leftist bullshit on a college campus. By the standards of 1969, Shurtz was either a superpatriot or a cornball; they had to follow orders, he countered, and don't you think you owe it to the nation to serve here, perhaps even die here?

"That would be the biggest waste," one of the platoon leaders said bitterly; Shurtz finally understood how culturally isolated he was from his young grunts and officers.

He was alone in many ways.

Sometime during the hours of darkness, an NVA 60mm mortar tube began lobbing rounds onto their hilltop. Chicoms and M79 grenades started exploding too. Lieutenant Shurtz had not had time to dig a foxhole and had not ordered anyone to do it for him; he ended up on his back in a one-foot sleeping trench with a radio to each ear. One was to his platoon leaders, who had their men returning fire; the other was to battalion, which got a Spooky on station. Most of the Chicoms thrown into their circle were duds, but the captured M79 rounds exploded against boulders and sent fragments whizzing through the darkness. Two GIs were wounded, but when the miniguns started screaming from above, the NVA fell back downhill. Alpha Company found their blood trails at dawn.

■ On 22 August, Private First Class Shimer awoke in a hospital in Da Nang and watched the Armed Forces Vietnam News on television. He recounted later: "There was this clean, well-trimmed, well-fed SP5 in a freshly starched uniform, looking square at the camera and, with a straight face, saying, '. . . and there was light contact reported throughout the Eye Corps area.'"

Chapter Ten

I Am Sorry, Sir, But My Men Refused To Go

23 August 1969. Lieutenant Colonel Bacon had four companies of Task Force 3–21 in position for the final assault on Hill 102 itself. An initial move up the west slope was met by heavy fire; most of the NVA had suddenly disappeared from the bunker maze around the knoll, but at least a few were still in place. The infantrymen were pulled back and another barrage of air, arty, and napalm was turned on. Sometime after noon, a second advance was attempted, this time up the northern slope. The only resistance was four mortar rounds dropped in from another position, wounding six; then Hill 102 was captured.

Alpha 4–31 were among the last up the hill. When they got into position for the advance, it was not altogether clear that the hill was deserted by the enemy. Specialist 4 Parsons, for one, was on edge. He hadn't had a cigarette in days and was almost shaking with a nicotine fit. No one had any smokes left, but a pair of Texas infantrymen did offer him a chaw of Red Man tobacco. Parsons took a big helping. He was a city kid, and the boys from Texas forgot to tell him not to swallow. As Alpha Company rucked up and started trudging uphill through the upturned earth and shattered trees, Parsons barely limped along. The sun was scorching on the denuded hill and he was reeling, vomitting tobacco every few steps. For the rest, it was a rather pleasant hike. No crossfires materialized and the grunts started carrying their M16s like tramp sticks and joking with relief.

The crest was a hot, barren dustbowl. Alpha Company secured an LZ for the resupply ships and the GIs, now helmetless and stripped to the waist, took turns guiding in the Hueys. Parsons took his turn at dusk. He directed one ship to a low hover, a couple feet over broken tree stumps, and an entourage of war correspondents disembarked from the skids. They had Asian cameramen and were suited up in a mixture of green fatigues and khaki safari gear; he heard one or two grousing that they could have twisted their ankles jumping like that. Parsons didn't know whether to get mad or laugh.

The capture of Hill 102 was the unglamorous end to a dirty, little fight which had not shown the best the U.S. Army had to offer. All the men found were empty bunkers and some foxholes still intact from when GIs had encamped on this hill during the June fight. No body count, no captured gear. Just a hill of dirt.

The *3d NVA Regiment* had vanished during the night.

Alpha Company dug in atop Hill 102; it was sometime after dark that Parsons saw a senior officer—he thought it was Bacon—and several other officers talking with the reporters about the next day's plans to recover the bodies at the helo crash site. Several of the correspondents were smoking, as was Parsons's company commander, the red ember tips a beacon to the enemy. The captain was considered an intolerable lifer and there was some bitter talk of him catching a bullet in the back the next time they made contact. It was with some relish that Parsons strode up and plucked the cigarettes away, snapping, "If you're going to smoke on this hill, you're either going to do it in a hole or not smoke at all." The reporters looked angry and the captain was burning. Parsons thought he probably would have been court-martialled if the colonel had not been a nonsmoker. The colonel said, "Soldier, you're right. We're sorry. They didn't realize what they were doing."

The morning sun brought a surprise. When they'd dug in at dusk, Shorty had struck his shovel against a rock which, it turned out, was really a dud U.S. artillery round. Parsons and his M60 crew sat in the upturned earth, sweating under the scant shade of a rigged poncho hootch. The rest of the platoon humped downhill on a recon patrol. Someone on the hill had a radio and they passed the hot afternoon listening to the Cubs and Astros ball game.

Besides unloading food and water, the morning resupply bird on 24 August—Black Sunday—also dropped SP4 John Curtis into Alpha Company's perimeter atop Nui Lon. Curtis, a wiry nineteen year old with *Peace* printed across his helmet cover, was returning from R and R. The first he heard about the battle was when he was checking in with the 3–21 Rear in Chu Lai. A couple of guys there knew he was a short-timer and a point man and encouraged him to ghost around Chu Lai until things cooled down. One buddy told him point-blank, "If you go out, you'll die."

Curtis caught the flight to LZ Center because he felt he had to. It was not because he had any love for the Green Machine or because he really cared who won the latest fight in AK Valley, but because his squad was family.

And they needed help.

Alpha Company could have used Curtis, who was a squad leader in 3d Platoon. He came in-country in November 68; in March 69, when his platoon was ambushed, he had dragged two wounded men back to where the medics could get up to them, then had crawled forward with a radio and directed artillery into the enemy tree line. Shortly thereafter, a Silver Star was pinned to his weathered fatigues.

Curtis had basically been running the platoon in the long interim between the departure of their last lieutenant and the arrival of Lieutenant Tynan. He led because he had a strong personality, not because his background was in any way uncommon. His father was a construction worker in Tennessee. Curtis had enlisted right after high school since ". . . I knew I was going to get nailed anyway." In the bush, he knew what he was doing; in the rear, he smoked and drank his brains out. Almost everyone in his platoon at least tried grass on stand downs. Curtis knew of no other way to escape, if just for awhile. To him, it was all a waste. He'd come to the military apolitical, but had become increasingly frustrated with the way things were in the field. He always felt they could have won if they'd really tried, but with the restrictions and walking-in-circles operations, the only real goal was to survive, and to take care of your buddies.

Those were abstract thoughts. When Curtis disembarked from the Huey, the only thing that registered was shock. Tom Goodwin, whom Curtis considered a nice, mellow guy, was gone; in fact, his entire squad was gone. In his own squad, only Jay Curtis and Steve Niebuhr, plus a couple green seeds, were left.

Alpha Company, which had come to AK Valley with ninety-five men, had fifty-two left. Eight GIs had been killed.

They didn't know if they'd killed a single NVA.

They hadn't seen any.

Curtis rejoined his squad the same time their platoon was ordered to take point for the next attack against the bunkers at the base of the ridge. Intelligence suspected the bunkers were empty; the primary mission was to recover the bodies of Lieutenant Kirchgesler and Sergeant Pitts. As the order was passed, Jay and Steve were talking frantically with Curtis. They said they *couldn't* go back without reinforcements, that it was suicide.

Those guys are *done,* Curtis thought.

Jay and Steve said they'd been talking it over and thought it best to stick together and demand to see the inspector general. They wanted Curtis to tell the company commander. He balked—he didn't even know Lieutenant Shurtz—but they pressed it and he agreed on faith in their judgment of the situation.

They did not move out as directed, and Lieutenant Shurtz finally walked up to ask what the delay was. Curtis detailed their complaints; he was backed up by Jay, Steve, and Doc Sanders. They wanted a helicopter to explain their need for reinforcements to the IG before any more attacks were made. Shurtz tried to persuade them to get moving. Curtis thought the lieutenant was stunned by what was going on, and he was right; the man had not commanded the company long enough to understand his grunts or to earn their total allegiance. In officer training, it was understood that the men would simply obey orders. But in real life, his men were hassling and questioning. Shurtz was unsure how to proceed; his two platoon lieutenants were only repeating the complaints of their grunts and saying they couldn't see ordering their men back into those bunkers.

Shurtz finally radioed the colonel. Lieutenant Colonel Bacon was on the ground with Bravo Company—evacuating the bodies from the burnt Huey to Graves Registration on Hawk Hill—when Lieutenant Shurtz came over the receiver. "I am sorry, sir, but my men refused to go. We cannot move out."

"Repeat that please," Bacon said calmly. He was an icy West Pointer from a family of career militarymen. "Have you told them what it means to disobey orders under fire?"

"I think they understood. But some of them simply had enough—they are broken. There are boys here who have only ninety days left in Vietnam. They want to go home in one piece. The situation is psychic."

"Are you talking about enlisted men, or are the NCOs also involved?"

"That's the difficulty here. We've got a leadership problem. Most of our squad and platoon leaders have been killed or wounded."

"Go talk to them again," Bacon counselled, "and tell them that to the best of our knowledge the bunkers are empty. The enemy has withdrawn. The mission of A Company today is to recover their dead. They have no reason to be afraid. Please take a handcount of how many really do not want to go.''

"They won't go, colonel, and I did not ask for the handcount because I am afraid that they will all stick together even though some might prefer to go.''

The picture was that only a handful of short-timers was actually refusing, but the rest of the company had more confidence in their combat experience than that of the new lieutenant. They were frozen, waiting to see which way it would go. Lieutenant Colonel Bacon, if not angry, was at least frustrated. Rational discussions do not always get the job done; before getting on the radio and making the refusal official, the company commander should have simply told the dissidents that they would be taken out for court-martial, then turned to the rest of the men and led them into action. But Lieutenant Shurtz did not have that type of leadership experience; he'd been in the bush only seventeen days. Bacon finally radioed his TOC on LZ Center and instructed Major Waite, BnXO, and SFC Okey Blankenship, BSM, to helicopter down to A Company and get them moving again with ''. . . a pep talk and a kick in the butt.''

That might have been unnecessary; before the arrival of the 3–21 C&C, Lieutenant Shurtz had gone to Specialist Curtis one more time. He made it a direct order and, as far as Curtis was concerned, that was the end of it. He did not consider himself a mutineer, so when the man with the silver bar finally gave him no other choice, he—and the rest of Alpha Company—reluctantly, angrily started moving. Then the C&C landed on the sun-bleached hill, and the grunts sat back in the elephant grass as Waite and Blankenship disembarked. One of the men was crying, and the balking started all over again. Major Waite went to Curtis and asked what the problem was. He sketched out the horrors the company had been through and Waite, considered to be a very good officer, listened patiently. That was one approach. Sergeant First Class Blankenship, meanwhile, was proceeding along a different track. He was sarcastic and ridiculed the men. He made up a story that another company was still on the move with only fifteen men left.

"Why did they do it," Jay asked, unmoved.

Blankenship sneered, "Maybe they've got something a little more than what you've got.''

"Don't call us cowards, we are not cowards," Jay exploded, running up with balled fists. Who is this turd, Curtis thought; he'd never seen the sergeant before and thought he must be some pompous REMF lifer just arrived in-country.

In fact, Sergeant First Class Blankenship was on his third tour and held a Bronze Star and two Purple Hearts. He hailed from the coal-mining country of Panther, West Virginia, the eldest of eight children to Mose and Wadie Blankenship. He was a hot-tempered, high school dropout, divorced three times. He was a big man, over six feet and two hundred pounds, a hard-core soldier. He'd been made the battalion sergeant major after the command ship was shot down; before that, he'd been serving as battalion operations sergeant. That was a TOC job and he was not as lean as when he'd been in the bush. In fact, when he was rucking up on LZ Center to go out to Alpha Company, Captain Carrier jokingly gave him some salt tablets for the heat. Blankenship laughed back, "You know, I might need these!"

But the men of the Gimlets were especially resentful of their superiors, and bitter that they were chronically short of new weapons and supplies. Platoons were rarely, if ever, at full strength. Many men saw themselves as pawns for someone else to make full-bull colonel. It was this lack of trust which fostered the hostility towards Sergeant Major Blankenship. It also helped spark the refusal to begin with. Perhaps what the leadership lacked was not tactical competence but personality, noted a company commander in the 196th Brigade:

Mostly the problem of command was a lack of understanding on the part of field grade officers of the changes that had come in the civilian world which the troops brought with them when they entered the Army. The new breed of enlisted men demanded a more personal approach from all levels of command. Captains were no longer the remote company commanders they had been in some other wars. In Vietnam the company commander's headquarters were what he could carry on his back and the radios of the men around him. Orders from battalion and brigade came over the radio and were overheard by many of the troops. The captain could no longer pretend that it was his order that the hill be assaulted, the men had already heard the colonel tell the captain to "take the hill." Problem was, as the men saw it, the colonel wasn't out there to lead the charge. He was safely back on the firebase issuing orders from the heavily protected TOC bunker. Most of these enlisted guys were between the ages of eighteen and twenty-one. They were totally unschooled in the military arts regarding the proper locations of various headquarters in order to maintain the optimum tactical coordination. All they knew was that the man ordering them to their deaths wasn't out there taking the same chances with them. Nor was he there to explain why such and such a hill was worth taking—especially when they'd already taken it twice before and walked away from it as soon as the battle was over.

Major Waite lent a sympathetic ear and Sergeant Blankenship pricked at the grunts' manhood; then they both said it was time to move out. By then, the rest of Alpha Company had rucked up again and gotten back in file formation; the cluster on the LZ broke up and Curtis's group rejoined them. They began humping downhill towards the bunkers. The NVA really had pulled out, and the only things to be found were the bodies of Lieutenant Kirchgesler and Sergeant Pitts. The sun had done horrible things to them. They pushed them into body bags—those rubberized, green, canvas sacks with a long zipper and carrying handles— then carried them to a clearing and called a medevac.

The next morning, Lieutenant Colonel Bacon took his C&C over to Alpha's position with Capt Bernhard F. Wolpers aboard. There were no charges to be made against anyone involved, but Bacon relieved Shurtz; Captain Wolpers—a tough soldier with a thick, German accent— was placed in command. Bacon was a real pro and this was one of his steps to get a worn-out battalion back on its feet.

Lieutenant Shurtz was shattered. When Bacon took over the Gimlets, Shurtz had thought, finally here's someone who's calm and rational that I can work with—and the first thing he does is fire me!

There were tears in his eyes.

Shurtz was removed on 25 August and Alpha Company stayed in AK Valley making no contact until 31 August. They humped back to LZ Center for their turn on bunker watch. A throng of journalists was waiting for them; it was the first time the grunts knew that the conversation between Bacon and Shurtz had been taken down by some reporters who happened to overhear it at LZ Center, and it was making headlines around the world as the first recorded combat refusal of the war. Many of the stories on Alpha Company referred to the "grunt revolt," with unsettling connotations of a militant underground. Never mind that similar incidents had occurred numerous times during glory days of WWII and Korea. Only a few understood that the young men in Alpha were simply soldiers in a company that had seen one battle too many. One of the reporters was James Sterba; after noting that Army policy was that a man who reenlisted would be taken out of the infantry, and that the Americal sent a reenlistment NCO to every fire base every two weeks, he commented:

> On a sizzling hot day in August, it was less than ironic, then, when a helicopter touched down on Landing Zone Center . . . and dropped off a reenlistment sergeant. That was the day that a ragged, demoralized, exhausted company—Alpha, Third Battalion, 21st Infantry, Americal Division—trudged up the hill from a week of hell in the valley below with only half the men it had started with. World-famous Company A, the one that had refused, for an hour, to go to war, was being given the opportunity by the United States Army to re-enlist, to serve for three more years, but not "out there." By the end of the day, the re-enlistment sergeant's results, remarked one officer, had been "outstanding."

Lieutenant Shurtz, meanwhile, was being shuffled away. Most agreed his downfall had been born of inexperience, not a lack of courage, and that he'd been made a scapegoat. To his superiors, he had waffled when he should have charged—and he had embarrassed the division in front of a hostile press. For this, he was reassigned as assistant brigade personnel administrative officer on LZ Baldy, then promoted to captain and sent to Chu Lai to complete his tour as the brigade stand down officer.

Two days after securing Hill 102, Alpha 4–31 abandoned it, just as they had done when they took it the first time in July. Two days after that, they got word that they were moving back to LZ West, from where they would CA into Hiep Duc. The action on that side of the ridge was still fierce and SP4 Parsons jotted in his pocket diary, "We're going over to Hiep Duc Valley tomorrow. Looks like Ass kicking Alpha has too go clean up there own AO now. Boo Coo Dinks over there."

PART ■ ■ ■
Death Valley

Chapter Eleven

Surrounded

Charlie 4–31, which had gone into the Hiep Duc Valley to support Bravo 4–31, was itself supported on the afternoon of 19 August 1969 by the arrival of Bravo Company, 1st Battalion, 46th Infantry (recently assigned to the 196th Brigade after having come in-country with the 198th Brigade). They normally operated to the south out of LZ Professional, but had deployed to an ARVN compound outside Tam Ky five days earlier. When Bravo Company was opconned to the Polar Bears this afternoon, word at the grunt level was sparse; all they knew was that another company in another battalion of the Americal had been ambushed and they were going in to recover the dead.

Bravo had about two hours to ruck up before a single Chinook arrived to ferry them, a platoon at a time, to ARVN LZ Karen. The airlift was completed by 1300 and the grunts spent another hour sitting in the direct boil atop the dusty, bald LZ. It was then, after the company commander got maps of the new AO and tuned his radio to the 4–31 frequencies, that they moved out. They were to hump northeast off the LZ and link up with Charlie 4–31 below Million Dollar Hill. The company commander, Capt Alva R. King, assigned the lead to the platoon under 2dLt James T. Baird and Sgt Charles E. Brown, who in turn gave the point to Sgt Greg Lynch's squad.

Which is how PFC Calvin Tam ended up walking point.

Tam was the son of Chinese immigrants who'd settled in San Francisco, but that was about the only thing that distinguished him from his comrades. Like them, he even referred to the NVA and VC as "gooks," it being a matter of good guys-bad guys, not a racial issue.

He was a typical GI in a typical company of the Americal Division and, like almost all of them, he was a draftee. He was twenty-one years old.

The draft notice had come when he was floundering in junior college and feeling pressure from his father, a successful chiropractor, to do something with his life. He felt naive and mixed up, not ready to cement his future to a job; since he was vaguely supportive of the war, the Army seemed to offer a break, a chance to reorient himself. If anything, though, the Army and Vietnam only added to Tam's adolescent confusion. He expected some sense of mission to be stressed, but the mentality in basic and advanced infantry training was much different. There was no talk of victory. Everything was geared to staying alive. Do your 365, survive, then put it behind you. No goals, no causes, no reasons. It was not very inspiring.

The attitude was magnified with each step closer to Vietnam. On his first day with Bravo Company in June of 69, Tam hopped off a resupply chopper with fourteen other green seeds in the middle of nowhere, and saw his platoon-to-be coming in from patrol. The grunts were talking about having spotted two VC in a valley and watching them walk off; the gist of the conversation was that it was too hot to be shot at. The next morning, Tam went on his first combat patrol. His squad humped off the company hill, walked several hundred yards into the brush, then flaked out under two, big, shade trees. Most took naps. This is weird, he thought, not sure what to say or do, not sure if he should relax or be paranoid. He heard his squad leader radio in phoney patrol positions; then, after two hours of rest, they hiked back to the company, mission accomplished.

It was a fragmented company, Tam thought. Comradeship seemed to extend only among certain groups—blacks, hispanics, or GIs who'd come in-country together. Just a bunch of guys thrown together. They weren't good, but they weren't bad; Tam could never completely decipher it. Considering that they were citizen-soldiers with only a few months of experience, they held their own against hardened peasants who'd been fighting for years. Each platoon had a few grunts who did more than their share. But others could be counted on to do no more than duck into a ditch if anything bad happened. Most seemed to sway in the middle, their performance gauged by the mood of the moment or how sharp the lieutenant was that day.

Lieutenant Baird should have been great. He was a West Point Airborne Ranger, an intellect with glasses and an urbane manner (he even subscribed to *National Geographic* in the bush). He seemed out to prove himself, and on some days he was a pro. Other days were different. During Baird's first week in the bush, which would have been Tam's third, an M60 gunner stepped on a booby trap which killed him and wounded the soldiers ahead and behind him. Talk was that the lieutenant was stunned into inaction, and several old-timers had to step in and get security out and the medevac in. Tam had been rattled too, and he thought, maybe I'm expecting too much of this man just because he has a bar on his collar. He just didn't know. Tam was so pissed off about having been sent to Vietnam, while most of his buddies were still in college having a good time, that rational thought shut down. Baird had chewed his ass out the few times he walked point, so he was mad. But when he thought about it, he probably did deserve what he got and he was embarrassed that he could act like such a young smart ass.

He didn't like Lieutenant Baird, but the man was only doing his best to keep them alive. Tam never felt that charitable in the middle of a hot rice paddy and—like most grunts—his selfish anger also picked on the common, human frailties of his platoon sergeant and squad leader. Sergeant Brown was a little guy—five-five—who kidded Tam, who was five-four, that he was glad someone shorter than he had finally come in. Brown was an old-timer who did his job well, but sometimes it looked like he was just guessing. They were all young draftees, trying to rise to the occasion and wishing they were back home the whole time. Amateurs.

By 1969, there were few professionals left to form the group backbone in the rifle companies.

Most were dead or had already done their time.

Whatever core of professionalism there was in Bravo Company came from Captain King. He was considered competent, concerned, and, to all the draftees' relief, not overly aggressive. He knew his job and, in a low-key manner, he simply did it. The old-timers told Tam that the previous CO had been an incompetent, and the first sergeant such an intolerable lifer that someone had taken a shot at him during a firefight. Now King was in charge, and a staff sergeant had been assigned as the field first. All of which was good for Bravo Company, considering the situation in Hiep Duc Valley. But things were never perfect; the company had not made a solid contact since May, and many of the men were new and untested.

Hiep Duc was to be their first taste of combat.

The day was hotter than most, well over 100 degrees, as Tam discovered as he walked point. There were no clouds, little shade, and everyone was quickly soaked under full packs and ammunition. Tam walked lead through the Resettlement Village—its tin roofs shimmering among the trees—then the squad leader rotated points. They seemed to walk forever through the sweltering paddies.

Finally, Captain King called a rest break, then another. They were saddling up from the second stop, putting helmets and rucks back on, when the radio crackled. The platoon RTO had a squawk box secured to the back of his radio and Tam stood close enough to listen. A lieutenant from another platoon was reporting a heat casualty to Captain King and requesting a medevac. King asked who it was. The lieutenant mentioned the GI's name and everyone instantly recognized it. He was a shammer, considered a sorry case by most of the grunts. He'd been in the hospital when Tam joined the company: on a patrol, his M16 had suddenly discharged, putting a round between his toes. There was no way to prove he'd done it on purpose and, although the wound was minor, it won the GI a vacation in the rear.

Captain King paused for a moment when he heard the name, then said, "We can't wait for a medevac. Put this guy in the shade, make sure he's got salt tablets and water, and leave him."

Tam walked behind the RTO as they got moving again and, fifteen minutes into the hump, the lieutenant came on the net again. He reported that the heat-stroke victim had made a miraculous recovery and had rejoined the platoon. There was a spatter of weary, spiteful laughter among the grunts. It had been fairly easy for the malingerer to catch up with the company because they were taking it slowly. A dog handler and his German shepherd had joined Bravo on LZ Karen, and they led the way. The dog alerted several times to things unseen in the brush, but nothing came of it. The heat was draining the dog too and more than once the column had to stop while the handler gave him water and rested him in the shade.

There was no sign of the NVA.

Charlie 4–31, after helping in the evacuation of Bravo 4–31 that morning, shoved off that afternoon to link up with Bravo 1–46. They humped single file through the thigh-high mud of a paddy; they suddenly froze when the point man spotted a lone hootch at the far end of the field. The men fanned out on line, a company's worth of weapons sighted on the hut; then the platoon leaders coordinated over the radio, ". . . three, two, one. Fire!"

The sudden eruption reminded Private Bleier of the firepower show staged to bolster the men on the last day of AIT. The hootch shuddered, pieces of it cartwheeled off, the thatch roof caught on fire. The tree beside it was splintered and fell over. After several minutes, the firing petered out and a shrill scream could be heard from within the smoking rubble. A woman climbed out of the family bunker. Behind her came another woman, two men, and several children. Charlie Company hiked forward; the villagers screamed and cried at them at the top of their lungs. One woman stood toe-to-toe with a platoon leader, shrieking up at him as the lieutenant tried to apologize in stumbling Vietnamese. The grunts sort of looked at their feet. We're still too jumpy from last night's ambush, Bleier thought.

Charlie Company kept moving. Civilians who got caught in the crossfire were on their own after the damage was done.

Charlie 4–31 finally linked up with Bravo 1–46 on a hillside, and they set up for the night. Bravo had gotten there first and the grunts of Charlie were bitching, as grunts always do, that "them damn dudes took all the good sleeping positions." Bleier wrote, "Only a section of jungle, briars and elephant grass, was left for us, so our platoon walked shoulder to shoulder, trampling it into a makeshift mattress. I fell asleep next to a tree, with one of its roots jabbing me in the back." Morning was not much better when Bleier found the tree—and himself—crawling with ants. ". . . They were little red ants, the ones we called 'piss ants.' They were acrobats. Just before biting, they'd stick their hind legs in the air, balancing on their front legs and head. They barely pinched the skin, not hard enough to hurt, just hard enough to piss you off. . . . I was plenty pissed off."

It was the morning of 20 August 1969.

Charlie 4–31 and Bravo 1–46, the only U.S. units in Hiep Duc Valley, had spent the night near Million Dollar Hill. Their mission at daylight was to recover and evacuate the dead left behind by Bravo 4–31.

Captain King's company began moving into position around 0700, moving forward along the general path on which Captain Murphy's company had retired the day before. Which is why they came across the hootch that had been used as nervous target practice. The villagers had learned their lesson, and this time they stood before the remains of their home in full view of the passing column. Private Tam noticed that the old people were glaring at them with unbridled anger. Way out, he thought; a whole company of grunts armed to the teeth and these old gooks aren't afraid to let us know they're pissed. He reckoned they were Viet Cong sympathizers. They probably were but he didn't know about yesterday's case of mistaken identity.

B and C Companies were humping through an area that the official report would later designate as the Center of Mass of the *1st NVA Regiment*. At the time, the size of the enemy force was not known. If it had been, B and C Companies would not have separated into platoons. Captain Murphy travelled with Charlie One, which was assigned to recover the bodies and take them to a field landing zone for extraction. Charlie Two was to drop back in reserve to Million Dollar Hill, and Charlie Three was to assist Bravo Company in securing the LZ. Captain King stayed with Bravo Two atop a small hill, while his other two platoons moved into the paddied flatlands.

It was Lieutenant Baird's platoon which was deployed in a circle around King and his radios and all the company's rucksacks. Intelligence may not have yet confirmed the presence of a North Vietnamese regiment, but the grunts felt it. The men were tense, especially the old-timers. Tam, a nervous new guy, could hear the mumbles. "This is it, we're gonna get hit. The gooks know we're gonna come back for the bodies. For sure we're gonna get ambushed."

Captain Murphy's group was moving northeast towards Hill 381 and was about halfway there from Million Dollar Hill when they stopped for a five-minute break. They'd been humping through the paddies along a raised path hemmed in by thick brush, and they rested in a shady grove the path entered. A deep drainage ditch ran along the trail and the trees made it appear like an oasis in the dead paddies.

Charlie One got moving again down the berm. Murphy counselled them, "Be careful. We'll be in open territory. Stay about eight yards apart."

There were twenty-five GIs in the platoon.

Private Bleier was eighth man back in the platoon file. It was another raging hot day; sweat stung down his face from under his helmet, and he looked and felt like a pack horse. He toted an M79 grenade launcher, which hung from a strap around his neck with an o.d. green towel tucked under it. His rucksack weighed about fifty pounds and that weight was doubled by the sixty M79 grenades he humped. Half were in a bag secured at the top of his ruck; the rest were in another bag hung

across his chest. Five canteens hung beneath the ruck. Many of the
grunts also tied cloth bands around their legs, just below the knee, to
keep leeches from slinking up to their crotches.

A GI named Dave was behind Bleier. Behind Dave were his best
buddies—Doc, the platoon medic, and Hawaii, a new guy. Hawaii was
nineteen, drafted, and had only six months left in the Green Machine
when they sent him to Vietnam. Nevertheless, he was a bright kid. His
fiancee wrote him daily, and he beamed at the letters. That's probably
why Bleier liked him; too many others in the company were overly
sullen about their fate.

The platoon had hiked into an open paddy when the point man
suddenly shouted, "Gook, gook!" He triggered a couple of hasty shots,
then began jogging down the path after the figure. The platoon followed.

Then came the cracking report of an RPD machine gun.

Bleier instantly jumped to his left, off the berm and into the dry
paddy. He rolled onto his back to release his pack suspenders, but the
easy-snaps wouldn't budge. He finally slid his arms out, then shoved
forward on his stomach, cradling his grenade launcher and ammunition.
It was twenty yards to the next dike. He peeked over. Twenty yards
farther ahead, the four men in the lead were pressed flat behind a dike.
It was only two feet high, and twenty yards beyond it was a wooded
knoll. The NVA were firing from within its thickets.

Bleier could see the brush twitch when the RPD fired.

He rolled onto his side, snapped the M79 open, and dropped a fat
round in. Just as he propped himself up to fire, he heard Dave shout
his name and felt a dull thud against his left thigh. He thought Dave
had tossed a pebble to get his attention, but then it stung. Blood was
soaking his fatigue trousers from two neat holes, one in front and one
in the rear. The round had sheared four inches across his thigh, leaving
an inch-deep furrow that gushed red.

"Dave, I'm hit!"

Bleier had moved away from his pack, so Dave dug into his own
and tossed him a bandage. Bleier wrapped it around his leg, then looked
around; almost everyone else had jumped to the right side of the pathway
berm. In a fright, he punched a few grenades at the knoll, then scooted
back to his pack. To his left was a hedgerow ten feet high, and he
crawled for it. From the cover, he saw an RPD burst splatter across
his rucksack ten feet back. Dave was behind a boulder fifteen yards
behind him. "Rock, you okay, you okay?"

"Yeah, yeah, I'm okay!"

"I'll tell Hawaii to send word that you've been hit!"

"Okay, okay, get a medic up here!"

Dave hollered for Hawaii over the automatic weapons fire. No answer, no movement. He looked back. Hawaii was face down in the paddy. "Rock, I think Hawaii's been hit!"

Bleier was frantic, "Hawaii, Hawaii!"

Doc crawled to the slumped man, then shouted, "Hawaii got it, he's dead!" Bleier could only look down and ask the Lord to take care of him.

What was agonizing and chaotic up front channelized back to Captain Murphy in the tree line. There it was calm. Murphy stood in the ditch with his RTOs, on the blue-leg net to the lieutenant commanding Charlie One. He got the coordinates, then hollered to his FO, 2dLt William P. Wilson, to crank up the artillery. Wilson sat along the edge of the ravine with his recon sergeant and radioman, and pulled his map and phonetic code book from his trouser side pocket. He got on the red-leg net and, in short order, the 105mm artillery pieces on LZ Siberia were raising dust around the enemy knoll. The platoon leader radioed back adjustments, which Wilson relayed.

The NVA must have had solid spider holes, because the arty did not diminish their fire. Charlie One was pinned down in the open with casualties, their response broken down into private, little wars.

Doc was calling to Bleier, "How do you feel?"

"I think I'm okay."

"You think you'll be able to walk?"

"I don't know, I've never been shot before."

Bleier lay immobile behind the visual cover of his tangly brush line. He was parched, exhausted, his mind working slowly. Should I get my pack? No, I don't know how fast I can move. They'll probably see me. This hedgerow isn't much protection. That was a terrifying thought. Only Dave and Doc were near him; the rest had worked their way to the right of the path. They had to keep the NVA down long enough to get the point men and their wounded, and the lieutenant was hollering for the grenade launcher.

Dave answered, "Bleier's got it, but he's hit!"

"Well, you get it from him!"

"I can't, I can't reach him. There's too much open space!"

"Well, we gotta get some grenades on that machine gun, until we can get our own machine gun set up!"

Bleier could not see the knoll from his position, but Dave to his right-rear could see just past the edge of the hedgerow. Bleier lobbed rounds over the brush, Dave hollered directions, and the fourth M79 grenade exploded in the general vicinity. He kept blasting rounds up and over, emptying his bags, but it had little effect. The NVA kept scything the torrid air. Bleier sank to the ground, the M79 empty beside him. The sun withered him; his leg wound burned under the bandage. He could hear Vietnamese chattering in the brush; over the squawk box of an abandoned radio he could hear the lieutenant calling the captain, "Christ, they're all around us. There's no place to hide. There's no cover over here. They're everywhere."

A GI was raging on the other side of the path. His buddy had just taken a burst in the stomach. Up ahead, the four point men were clawing into the sunbaked paddy, trying to get lower under the machine gun fire. One was screaming, "Jesus, they're moving, I see 'em! Get that fucking machine gun set up!"

Oh God, Bleier thought, they're gonna overrun us.

He gripped a wooden cross that his counsellor at Notre Dame, a priest who'd been in WWII, had given him. Bleier was from Appleton, Wisconsin, the son of a salt-of-the-earth Irish Catholic tavern keeper. He stared at the cloudless sky, the sun like a blowtorch against his face, and he prayed. He prayed more fervently than he ever had. "Dear Lord, get me out of here if You can. I'm not going to bullshit You. I'd like to say that if You get me out of here alive, I'll dedicate my life to You and become a priest. I can't do that. . . ." What he did promise was to take life as it came if he survived.

Five minutes later, Bleier got his answer. Doc had bellied up to the boulder with Dave, then shouted to the hedgerow, "Rock, you and I are getting out of here!" Doc stepped out from behind the rock—and instantly screamed and doubled up. A bullet had split his thumb open, but he tried again. This time he made it. Bleier bandaged his hand, then Doc insisted, "Let's get out of here." The medic did not have a weapon—many of the medics in the brigade were conscientious objectors, and he may have been one—and Bleier left his empty M79 in the paddy. They were helpless as they crawled down the hedgerow to the left edge of the paddy. They made a beeline for the CP, pushing straight through thickets and elephant grass up to the last clearing. The medic went first, Bleier hobbled after him, and in the trees they found Captain Murphy and the company headquarters.

"How you feeling, Rock," the captain asked.

"Fine, sir."

"Do you think you can hang on for a while?"

Bleier nodded.

"Well, good. I think you're lucky. It looks like you've got a million dollar wound there. It'll get you out of the field for a month or so, then you might have to come back." That sounded great. Bleier drained a quart canteen in twenty seconds, then bummed a cigarette to celebrate. He'd never felt so relieved; he was back with the captain which was like, he figured, being back in the womb.

Twenty minutes later, the rest of the platoon made it back in a low-crawling row. By the time they got out, the NVA were firing on them from three sides and Blue Ghost Cobras provided cover. They brought out their five wounded, but left their three dead. Most also left their rucksacks and the LAW rockets secured to them. The rucks must have been like little treasure chests to the NVA emerging from the brush. If they opened Bleier's rucksack, they would have found a hammock, air mattress, poncho liner, mosquito netting, socks, sandals, cans of fruit and soda, dehydrated LRRP rations, iodine pills, calamine lotion, and a camera.

According to the battalion journal, Charlie One had been ambushed at 1020 and had pulled back to the CP by 1344.

At 1510, the firing resumed.

The NVA had followed the platoon's retreat and crawled into the fringes of the tree line. There was a smattering of AK47 fire across the path where the platoon was hunkered down. Then came the Chicom grenades. The NVA were that close, although invisible. Lieutenant Wilson was crouched at the edge of the ravine when he saw the grenade come out of nowhere. It landed at the edge of the ditch and he instantly shoved his face into the dirt. An ear-popping explosion left his RTO temporarily rattled; Wilson shoved his M16 up and squeezed the trigger.

He flashed to the training NCO at Chu Lai. They had laughed when he said that many a time they would shove their faces down, raise their M16s over their heads, and fire blind. That's just what he was doing now on terrified instinct.

When the attack began, Captain Murphy was on his stomach, three radios around him. He was working all three at the same time, propped on his elbows and peering over the brush with his binoculars. Rocky

Bleier sat on the pathway six feet to his right. Tommy Brown was sitting right behind him. Then came a pop!—the sound of a detonation string being pulled from the stick handle of a Chicom. Murphy bellowed, "Grenade!" and ducked his head into his arms. Bleier rolled flat on the trail as Brown hurdled over him trying to escape the grenade which had almost landed in his lap. Boom! Bleier woke up, ears ringing. He looked around. A two-foot hole was blown into the dirt where he'd been sitting. Brown was sprawled a few yards away, his trouser legs shredded with shrapnel, moaning loudly. Bleier's fuzziness wore off; he realized he was unscathed. He could also hear the AK fire snapping over his head. He had no weapon, no idea what was going on, and could only squeeze into the dirt, head down under the cacophony.

It was five minutes before he could look up; when he did he glanced up at another Chicom coming right down on them. It landed on Murphy's back, bounced off, deflected towards Bleier. It was top-heavy on its stick handle, bouncing crazily, and it landed at his feet. It was an instantaneous decision, jump back or jump over it, and he crouched to spring forward just as it exploded. The next thing he knew, Murphy was pushing him off, rolling him onto his back with a shove. Bleier stared uncomprehending at Murphy, who was barely out of his daze, groaning, the inside of his legs saturated with red-hot shrapnel.

Bleier looked at his own legs. The right one was quivering uncontrollably. It scared him and he grabbed at it, suddenly feeling his blood-soaked trousers and the stab of pain in his right foot. His trousers were ripped from dozens of fragment holes, but it was his foot that was throbbing. One toe was shattered, the skin ripped open.

The platoon medic was wounded so Doc Smith, the headquarters medic, had his hands full. He crouched beside Bleier and used his long surgical scissors to cut off his jungle boot; he tied gauze around his foot and said, "That's all I can do for you right now." Others dragged a dazed Captain Murphy into the safety of the ditch. Bleier lay where he'd been wounded and watched as Doc Smith ". . . low crawled away like an alligator down the pathway."

The unwounded returned fire as fast as they could.

2d Platoon of Charlie 4–31 humped off Million Dollar Hill to reach Captain Murphy's besieged group. As soon as they reached a clearing at the base of the hill, the NVA dropped mortars on them. They fell back to medevac their casualties. 3d Platoon also tried to move in, but were caught in a firefight of their own. Lieutenant Simms, the platoon leader, was considered the best one in the company. (During a later fight on Banana Tree Hill, Lieutenant Wilson saw Lieutenant Simms walk up to a hole where two replacements had thrown themselves when the bullets started flying. Under fire, Simms stood at the rim of the hole, pointed his AR15 at the trembling kids, and said, "You either come out on your own, or we'll have somebody drag you out." They scrambled out and joined the firing line.)

Today, even 3d Platoon couldn't break through.

A pair of Blue Ghost Cobras did, however, get above 1st Platoon. Bleier was lying among the three abandoned radios of the company headquarters when a pilot came on, "Pop smoke, pop smoke, mark your position." No one had any smoke grenades; they'd been on their rucks which the NVA now had.

"Well, what are your coordinates?"

From above the tree line, neither U.S. nor NVA soldiers were visible. Bleier concentrated through his pain; had he heard the captain mention the map coordinates? He couldn't remember. The situation seemed hopeless!

A GI finally calculated their azimuth with a compass and range finder; it was relayed to the pilots along with instructions to strafe the open paddy to destroy the packs and LAWs, and to strafe only ten yards into the edge of the woods. That's where the NVA had crawled. The grunts were deeper into the tree line island. The first Cobra probably did some damage to the NVA, but he also fired a 2.75-inch rocket into the platoon's farthest hole. Lieutenant Wilson was crouched along the ravine when a skinny, red-headed Tennessean ran back. He was miraculously unscathed, but the M60 in his hands was totalled, and he was screaming bloody murder about gunship pilots. The friendly fire had killed one rifleman and gravely wounded the platoon's last grenadier with shrapnel.

This mess of a firefight was Lieutenant Wilson's first. In the weeks before, he'd seemed to be the caricature of the green second lieutenant: skinny as a rail, thick glasses, his fingers and arms bandaged by Doc Smith from all his elephant grass cuts. He was walking on glass his first operation; if a leaf dropped from a banana tree, he nervously pumped an M16 burst into it.

Wilson was a pleasant North Carolina Baptist who simply did not have the warrior's streak in him. He had enlisted for Artillery OCS after college to avoid the potluck of the draft, and had landed at the 90th Replacement Battalion, Bien Hoa, in the third week of June 1969. He toted his duffel bag through in-processing, rolling sweat, miserable and excited, amazed that such a place really existed. What am I doing here? he wondered. At the O Club, he ran into one of his OCS instructors, a gung ho captain also just arrived for his first tour. He was insisting on duty with the 1st Air Cavalry Division and wanted Wilson to join him.

Wilson begged off. He wasn't looking for such trouble. So it was, on his second morning, he was put on a transport plane to Chu Lai. He and the others were driven in jeeps from the airfield to the Americal Division Combat Center. It was a beautiful area; blinding white sand and an inviting ocean view. Wilson hated the concertina wire and guard towers dotting the beach. It was like a ruined paradise. Introduction classes were conducted on bleachers built into the sandy hills with awnings over them. One class was on marijuana. The instructor NCO said it was very prevalent and he passed a lit butt through the circle of officers, telling them to smell it and sample it if they wished, so they would recognize when one of their men was stoned. It was the first and last time Wilson saw marijuana and he wanted nothing to do with it. The mine and booby trap class was the most interesting. The sergeant started it off in a colorful manner, tossing a defused grenade into the bleachers, then laughing as everyone ate sand. He took them down a path in a jungled training compound. An E-tool was stuck in the middle of it, and the sergeant sounded as though he were counting cadence. "Okay, gentlemen, now it's decision time. What do you do? Go around it, move it . . . ?" Smoke grenades were rigged as booby traps and it was scary and fun.

After the two-week course, Wilson was sent to Fat City, the Division Artillery compound in Chu Lai. It was indeed fat living. The next day, he reported with three others to the air-conditioned office of the DivArty commander, a bird colonel. He gave them their marching orders alphabetically and Wilson fretted; the last one's always the worst. The first two officers were assigned to batteries in Chu Lai; the third got an aerial observer job; and Lieutenant Wilson—oh no, he thought, the shit's going to hit the fan—you're going to Charlie Battery, 3d Battalion, 82d Field Artillery. The next morning, Wilson caught a Loach to LZ Baldy. He wasn't really aware of the change in atmosphere until he noticed the

Cobra escorting them. He took a photo of it through the window. They landed on the base camp LZ and he hopped from the Loach, feeling like a duck out of water—helmet cover and fatigues unsoiled, jungle boots shiny black and green, his bag in one hand, an unloaded M16 in the other.

Wilson spent two nights at the 3–82 Rear on Baldy, then hitched a ride aboard the 4–31 C&C Huey to LZ Siberia. The hill was very spartan. Wilson met the battery commander, executive officer, and first sergeant, and got a slap on the back, a welcome to Vietnam, and a walking tour of the hill. Within a day, he was choppered over to LZ West where Charlie 4–31 was pulling its week of palace guard. Wilson was their new forward observer. In the TOC bunker, he met Captain Murphy. They shook hands, then Murphy hefted a radio and said, "Let's do some shooting." From the bunker line, Wilson could just make out the intended practice target—an abandoned, demolished collection of hootches. He checked his map and read the coordinates to his battery on Siberia; the first round landed halfway up the slope of West. Murphy said nothing for a moment, then very calmly, "Lieutenant, you gotta remember. The French made this map. We didn't. It's not accurate. What you see and the coordinates they appear to be on are not where it really is." Wilson adjusted the fire by sight and hit the huts. Murphy said, "Cancel the fire mission. Let's go get some chow."

That's how Wilson thought of Murphy: friendly, businesslike, intense. He was on his second tour, which gave Wilson much confidence. He needed that because when Charlie Company finally took to the bush off LZ West, Wilson was a walking bundle of nerves. They patrolled Banana Tree Hill and, although the grunts seemed casual about the place, Wilson envisioned snipers behind every tree. He nervously vomitted his meals at night. Murphy was not a pal to anybody, but he was an officer who took care of his men. He talked with Wilson in their poncho hootch at night; he mixed him a canteen of Kool Aid to calm his stomach.

After a while, Wilson's trauma wore off. In his six weeks with the company, he'd made one contact—a couple of snipers who took off as soon as he called in the arty. His knees were weak, but he'd done his job. After a while, it didn't seem so bad. The days were long and hot, but the evening resupply bird brought in heated food in mermite cans and Cokes and beers on ice. They had the Arsenal of Democracy backing them up, and the enemy wanted only to avoid them.

It was confidence born of ignorance.

They had walked into this, but what it was he had no idea. The NVA were all around them. They were standing up to gunships and artillery, and Captain Murphy—the heart and soul of the company— was semiconscious in a ditch. He was groaning loudly. It annoyed Wilson, chilled him, unnerved him, made him wonder what the hell was going on.

Wilson felt very alone. No one seemed to be in control. Men just hunkered down behind some cover, glancing around between bursts to make sure there was still another GI on either side of them. Wilson and crew were on their stomachs in the drainage ditch. The raised path ran across their front, and they could see beyond it about six feet into the brush. The wall of vegetation extended perhaps another fifteen yards to the paddies. That's where the NVA were, behind the last dike and crawling into the trees. They stayed low, pinning the grunts with AK47 fire. Lots of it.

Wilson could see the brushy wall flicker.

He'd drop down and, as soon as the enemy stopped firing, he'd raise his M16 over his helmet and pull the trigger.

He and his RTO were glued to each other, the line open to LZ Siberia to bring the 105mm shells within thirty meters of their perimeter. It was hairy; Wilson would scream, "Danger Close, Danger Close!" and concussions slammed under their chests as they ducked. Shrapnel oscillated overhead. Tree branches and clods of dirt crashed down. The Cobras darted in between artillery salvos. The North Vietnamese kept firing; they survived because they were daring, crawling into that insulation space around the U.S. perimeter. They were hidden there among the trees.

The company Kit Carson Scout scrambled to Wilson's group. His name was Nguyen Van Ly, but he was better known as Twenty, and he had a good reputation. He had been an NVA and he knew of their low-crawling tactics. He rushed from side to side in the loose circle, firing his M16 and throwing grenades. He pitched one a mere fifteen feet in front of them, and everyone ducked as the explosion kicked their brains and sent frags whizzing through the brush around them. As soon as it went off, Twenty jumped up, emptying his rifle at what to an untrained eye was nothing. During a lull, Wilson tried to raise B-TOC on LZ West. The NVA were jamming the primary frequency. He switched to the secondary and, when the TOC answered, he burst into an excited, profane dialogue to let the world know they were still out there and needed help right now!

Lieutenant Colonel Henry came on the line, "This is Cave Man One. Calm down. What exactly is Captain Murphy's status?"

"Murphy's been hit in the legs. I can't get to him, I'm too busy where I am. When are we going to get some help!"

"Help is all around you. It's just a matter of time before it gets to you. So relax and take care of your situation."

What the hell is that supposed to mean!

Captain Murphy's first tour was cut short when he was wounded. He thought he was going to end his second tour by getting killed. The company had started this patrol with thirty-three men; now six were dead and twenty-one wounded. That left six unscathed and, judging from the amount of fire their little circle was taking, there were no fewer than a hundred NVA around them. He looked at his grunts and thought he was seeing men about to die. There was no stopping it. Murphy called Twenty to his side. He gave him the headquarters PRC77 radio and said, "If they make an assault, we won't be able to hold them. When that happens, I want you to get away. Take this radio and put it in the hands of an American officer. Do not give it to anyone else. If it looks like you're in danger of being killed, destroy it."

When Wilson crawled down into the ditch to check on the captain during a lull, he found Murphy propped up, legs bandaged. Murphy took his radio code book from his baggy trouser pocket and began tearing each page from its staples and burning them one at a time with his cigarette lighter. He looked at Wilson, "You might as well burn yours too." Wilson didn't.

He didn't want to accept what was happening.

Bleier saw Murphy call over the platoon lieutenant. "Make sure each man has his weapon and all his ammo within reach. I want you to take every man who's able to hold a rifle, and prop him up against a rock or tree stump. We're going to need everything we've got."

Chapter Twelve
Running

Captain Murphy was a good officer, and the inexperienced, terrified grunts around him were, indeed, giving it everything they had. They could not see the NVA for all the vegetation, but the enemy's view of them was not clear either; they were raising a hell of a racket with all their firing, and the NVA wouldn't have been able to guess that only six of the men facing them were not bleeding.

Private Bleier, with two bandaged legs, crawled off to their left flank with an M16 he found in the dirt. Very few GIs were on that side and he figured he'd have to help. He lay behind a thin tree and fingered the M16, wondering how accurate he could be with it. He hadn't fired one for real since AIT. The biggest problem over there was not the NVA, but a brush fire started by the gunship rockets. Smoke rolled over them and Bleier had a panicked thought: if the flames sweep in, I can't walk and, between the fire and the shooting, the guys would probably take off without thinking about me.

Nevertheless, he stayed in position. Most of the men in the miniature perimeter were similarly steeling themselves. The attitude was to go down fighting.

But the final assault never came.

Sometime after 1700, the enemy fire tapered off, then stopped completely. Everyone warily stayed in position, wondering what was happening. As it turned out, the NVA had pulled out of the wood line and moved back across the paddies to their entrenched positions. Charlie One had been theirs for the taking, but they had not finished the job. Why not? Murphy speculated that they had killed or wounded the NVA commander. Perhaps the massed firepower had inflicted too many casualties, although the retiring NVA dragged with them however few or many bodies there were.

3d Platoon walked in without being fired upon, and Bleier heard a sergeant say, "All right, let's get the fuck out of here."

He closed his eyes and praised God.

A GI ran up and dropped to his knees beside him, talking excitedly, "Rock, Rock, we heard you were dead!"

"No, I'm not, but what do you say we get my ass out of here?"

It was getting dark as the two platoons from Charlie 4–31 made plans to rendezvous with Bravo 1–46. Captain King had come as close as possible; now Captain Murphy had to complete the link up. 3d Platoon was exhausted from a fight of their own; there weren't enough men to carry all the gear and wounded, so they destroyed two M60s and some other equipment. Captain Murphy was the first wounded man carried out in a poncho. Bleier was next, four grunts from 3d Platoon trudging along with him. It was an ordeal; every time they put him down to rest, they pleaded, "Rock, can't you walk. . . ? Let us drag you by your shoulders." Bleier had to beg them to carry him, but after several hundred meters the plastic poncho ripped open. Two of the grunts got him between them, arms over shoulders, and they kept limping along. Bleier put his weight on his "good" leg—the one with the thigh wound— but after perhaps a kilometer, he collapsed. His shoulders just gave out and he moaned, "I can't go any farther this way."

That's when a grunt in the column stepped up and said he'd carry him fireman style. Bleier later wrote:

I never knew his name, and I don't think he ever knew mine. I didn't know anything but nicknames for most of the guys. But the Army had a beautiful way of making names seem unimportant, and race, and color, and creed, and social status. We never looked for any of that in each other. The Army is a great equalizer. I was white, this guy was black. We had travelled thousands of miles to meet in a jungle. After this night, I would never see him again. We both knew that. Yet here he was, offering to pick me up bodily and help save my life. That's a special kind of love.

Lieutenant Wilson was near the front of Charlie Company's column. By the time the re-act had arrived, he was out of grenades and into his second and last M16 bandolier. He also carried 250 spare rounds in his rucksack, but he'd fired all that and passed out the rest to the grunts around him in the ditch. The dog handler from Bravo Company met them along the path and led them back to where Bravo had reorganized. Every fifty feet, the German shepherd would alert to things in the tree lines, and the handler would have to break him from his point and keep moving. The NVA are there all right, Wilson thought, but if we don't mess with them, they don't look like they're going to mess with us anymore tonight.

The columns were getting strung out.

By the time Captain King and Lieutenant Baird's platoon had linked up with the rest of Bravo Company, it was dark. They reorganized along a path in the pitch-black. Private Tam and a buddy named Steve Larado were the last men in their platoon file. They whispered with the point men of the next platoon about what had gone on, until one of them suddenly said, "Hey, man, I think your platoon just took off."

Tam turned around. No one was in sight.

They started down the trail, Tam in front, Larado a bit behind, growing more and more apprehensive when they realized their platoon was not just a few steps ahead. It was dark and the brush was higher than their heads on both sides of the path. Tam's heart was beating furiously, hands clenched around his M16, expecting the worst. They walked slowly and softly, whispering into the black void, "Hey, hey, 2d Platoon." There was no answer. About eighty yards into their terrified march, the trail forked. For no real reason, they took the left fork. They had crept about forty more yards when the path entered a clearing. They crouched in the bushes at the edge, ears straining until, hearing nothing, they decided to double back.

A squad leader stood invisible back at the fork, hissing in the dark, "Tam. Larado. Where are you guys?"

"Yeah, we're right here."

The squad leader whispered harshly, "What the hell's the matter with you? You want to die or something?"

He led them about fifty yards up the right fork to where Bravo 1–46 had collected the dead of Charlie 4–31; they were wrapped in ponchos and tied with GI bootlaces to bamboo poles. All you could see were the jungle boots. Chilling. The men were scared, weary, depressed, their emotions amplified when Charlie Company linked up with them. Actually, they simply straggled past them on the trail to take the lead, and Bravo Company became the tail. A touch of panic was beginning to affect each of them. American soldiers were not trained to operate at night. The darkness belonged to the enemy, and the GIs were scared shitless.

Bravo and Charlie Companies were humping for Million Dollar Hill which, because the battalion was spread so thinly in two valleys, was defended only by Major Lee and three young soldiers. Two of the GIs were from Charlie Company; the third was an anonymous enlisted guy who Lee had grabbed at LZ West. The GI was not very inspired by the mission and sat down on the helipad, mumbling, "I'm not going out there." Major Lee had to drag him physically onto the C&C Huey.

They were all alone on that hill in the middle of the night. Lee had them sitting at the four compass points, and he counselled them: "Don't yell, don't even talk, don't fire at the boogyman, only shoot if you've got something in your sights." As the night dragged on, though, he became nervous about his partners. He was afraid they might fire at nothing and give away their position or, worse yet, gun down the point men of Charlie Company as they approached. He finally took their M16s away, laid them in a pile with his own rifle, and sat down with the radio to lead Charlie Company to the hill.

They finally appeared out of the darkness.

Rocky Bleier, riding on the shoulders of the black soldier, must have thought the night was never going to end. He was in his own private torture. Each time his torn legs caught on bushes and vines, he jerked like a cattle prod had been jammed into his wounds, and the GI carrying him was knocked off balance. It was a struggle for him, too, lugging Bleier's big frame, and Bleier, pressing on his back to relieve the pressure on his stomach, pushing into the rescuer's shoulder. Every thirty yards they had to stop while the grunt laid Bleier in the grass and tried to catch his breath. Every time they stopped, two or three GIs in the column passed them in the dark. They kept pushing, but fell farther and farther behind, until Bleier collapsed onto the side of the road. He was completely drained; his eyes were brimming with tears. He looked up at his rescuer, mumbling, "I can't go this way anymore. Get me a stretcher. It's not that much farther."

The GI stopped a 3d Platoon RTO and the man radioed ahead to the medevacs coming in. Then he continued on. He was the last man in their column.

The pain became too much for Bleier to bear, each heartbeat thumping through his right foot. He lay there, crying and gritting his teeth, ripping up clumps of grass with his hands. His buddy held onto him, and Bleier squeezed him tighter with each surge of pain. He held Bleier's hand, soothing him, "It's all right. You're okay. We're going to get there."

Bleier was sobbing. "We are so *alone*."

Time was meaningless, so he didn't know how long it took for the four men to stumble down with a poncho liner. They were exhausted too, and couldn't muster the strength to lift him. So they dragged him the last several hundred yards, bouncing over rocks and debris, Bleier's legs crashing together inside the poncho. The medevac landed atop the hill, and a narrow rocky path led up to it. They shouldered their way through the brush hemming in the path, stumbling, losing their grip, Bleier rolling down the hill and screaming into the night sky. They finally got him to the crest and sank to their knees. Bleier looked up at the helicopter blades thumping above him. "Thank you, Lord."

The Huey lifted off without him; it was already full. It had taken Bleier six hours to reach the bush LZ, but now he had to wait another two hours for the next medevac. A medic gave him a shot of morphine, but it did no good. The drug was washed from his system by shock, confusion, pain, and fear. "I gotta get another shot!"

"No, I can't do that," the medic said.

Bleier raged with all the patience of a man whose foot was being held in a fire. "Why not? I'm in pain. Do something!"

"It might knock you out, or disguise the seriousness of your wounds. The doctors at the aid station will want to know where it hurts."

"I don't give a shit. Now give me another fucking shot!"

"No."

"Well, then get the fuck out of here!"

Bravo 1st of the 46th Infantry got moving again after Charlie 4th of the 31st Infantry passed through. There were four men to a body, carrying and dragging the bamboo litters across the ground. The bodies were heavy and the exhausted men traded every fifteen minutes. After his turn, PFC Calvin Tam walked along, feeling very alone in the moonless night. He was slung with six M16s for men hefting the litters. His mind was blurred with weariness, numbed with fear. When are the gooks going to sneak up and hit us? Where are they? He pictured them lying in the brush, eating rice and sleeping, satisfied with the day's catch. Lucky us. Maybe they're out of ammunition. Tam kept plodding.

The column started getting strung out along the trail. Tam noticed exhausted grunts sprawled in the thickets along the side, trying to get a few minutes rest before resuming the march. One GI had cracked, or was at least putting on a good show to get out. Tam passed him on the trail. He was a short, fat guy who, during his two weeks with the company, had complained constantly and loudly that since he was an 11 Charlie mortarman he should not have been assigned as an 11 Bravo infantryman. His grousing had won him the promise that the first opening among the mortar crews on LZ Professional would go to him.

The man was wide-eyed and babbling. A squad leader told him to shut up and, when that didn't work, began slapping him.

Tam forced himself on, concentrating on the pack bobbing ahead of him in the dark. He'd never been so tired and scared. Keep going, don't panic. Be a good soldier, don't feel sorry for yourself.

Keep going!

They caught up with Charlie Company near Million Dollar Hill. Tam sank into the elephant grass, his brain whirling unfocussed. He was dimly aware of a prop plane buzzing overhead. A flare was dropped from it and night was suddenly day. Tam and everyone around him instantly jumped off the trail, rolling into the underbrush to escape the exposure of the glare. Twenty minutes later, they heard a single Huey bore in. It landed about a hundred yards away, on the crest of the hill.

It was 0200; this was the third and last medevac of the night. It was handled quickly, frantically before the NVA had a chance to open fire on the thumping rotors. Private Bleier was lifted inside the cabin and Captain Murphy came on next, the last one on. Bleier described the evacuation:

> . . . Murphy almost fell out as we were taking off. The bottom third of his legs dangled outside the doorway. I held him by the shirt, but there was no room to pull him farther inside. The aircraft was jammed wall-to-wall. My admiration for Murphy at that moment was total. He had gotten to Million Dollar Hill about ten o'clock, and could have gone on the first medevac run. But he waited four hours while the rest of us straggled back, insisting that he be the last man evacuated. Now he was flying to the aid station with his shrapnel wounds exposed to the violent force of the cold winds. His legs banged against each other and against the helicopter door, buffeted by the air currents. The pain registered in his face was inhuman.

Bleier's agony was overwhelming too. He could not believe the pain, the fire ripping at a million raw nerve endings, pulsing, consuming him. He faded in and out, thinking who *am* I, who is this happening to? It was a ten-minute flight to the 23d Medical Company, Americal, on LZ Baldy. The medics gave him the once-over in the med bunker, which meant clean bandages and, finally, a second shot of morphine. That did the trick. When they hefted his litter into the next chopper, he was feeling calm and drowsy, marvelling at the brilliance of the moon and stars from the cabin door.

By 0500, Bleier was being rolled into the 95th Evacuation Hospital, Da Nang. After he was admitted, a man approached him and said he was to store his personal belongings. All Bleier had was the wooden cross given to him by the priest; it had gotten him through WWII and, as far as Bleier was concerned, it had gotten him through Vietnam. Ten minutes later, a female Red Cross volunteer came to collect his things. She sighed at his story of having given the man his wooden cross; happened all the time, she said. Simply put, unknown persons were robbing wounded soldiers coming into the hospital. The combat infantrymen in Vietnam had a harsh acronym for support soldiers, too widely applied, but sometimes very appropriate: REMF. Rear Echelon Mother Fucker.

Bleier's gurney was wheeled into a waiting room. Captain Murphy and the wounded survivors of his platoon were there. An orderly shaved his stubble but agreed to leave his handlebar mustache, the symbol of the draftee grunt. By 0600, Bleier was in surgery. He was put under and the Army doctors used scalpels to scrape away the skin burned by the sulfur-coated shrapnel. Then they removed the fragments from his feet and legs—there were more than a hundred pieces.

Fifteen minutes after the last medevac off Million Dollar Hill, Bravo Company was moving again. They walked back into the paddies atop a dike. It was dark. Private Tam fell, tumbling four feet down into the dry paddy. Not a bad fall, but when he stood up, pain shot through his right leg. He crawled back up under his pack and gear, figuring it was just a bad sprain, and kept humping, actually limping down the trail. The pain got worse. Tam faded into numb exhaustion, then sharp pain; each step was a jolt of electricity. They seemed to go forever. Tam didn't know what to do but keep walking. It wasn't until after 0400 that word was passed to drop the bodies. They moved on to a clearing beside the trail, where they collapsed into a loose perimeter with part of Charlie Company. Tam took off his pack and helmet, lay in the grass, and fell instantly asleep, no idea if anybody was on guard, no idea what was going on.

He slept three hours. At 0700 on 21 August, Tam groggily awoke. He noticed the closest GI was thirty feet away. "Hey, where's 2d Platoon!" A guy from another platoon said the CO had sent them back down the trail to see if they'd been followed. Tam noticed a GI from Charlie Company. The man sat in the grass, knees pulled up, head on them; he was mumbling to himself, "I can't take this shit anymore, I just can't take this shit anymore."

It made Tam suddenly very grateful that he'd missed the ambush and, at the same time, uneasy with guilt that he hadn't done his part.

The Bravo recon had not been out long; Tam was just getting his spoon into the C ration breakfast he'd heated up when there was a smattering of shots down the trail. It sounded about a hundred yards away; everyone scrambled for rifles and gear. Within minutes, the platoon ran back down the path, hollering, "Gooks, gooks, get out of here!" No one seemed to be giving orders, and they were swept up in the rush. Tam quickly shouldered his ruck and limped along with them, confused and still starving, wondering if this was how they were supposed to behave. It made sense to get away from such an overpowering enemy force, but this was some kind of mob scene. We're just asking to get ambushed!

Around noon, rumors rippled down the column that they were heading back to Million Dollar Hill, where they would stop. At least they had an objective. Bravo Company was unfamiliar with the local nicknames, and a grunt near Tam mumbled, "Why do they call it Million Dollar Mountain?"

"It's worth a million dollars when you get there," someone ventured. "It's like a safe place."

By the time Tam limped up to the base of the hill, there were already knots of GIs sprawled in the shade of the trees. He thankfully plopped down under a patch of shade too, and noticed a grunt leaning-sitting on the hillside several yards away. He had glasses, lieutenant bars, a bandolier of M60 ammunition over his shoulder; he was gone, drenched in sweat and staring like a zombie. Tam finally forced himself to stand and started climbing the wide trail that wound up the gradual incline of Million Dollar Hill. He couldn't make it. A buddy named Johnny Reno came by and put an arm around his shoulder. Tam was a small guy and Johnny wasn't much taller, but he kept tugging him along. Tam, at the end of his physical and emotional strength, gritted his teeth and started crying, "Hey, thanks, John, thanks, man, I'll pay ya back."

"Hey, don't sweat it."

It took thirty minutes to struggle to the crest. The grunts were moving like zombies, rigging ponchos in the brush to escape the pounding sun, collapsing in catatonic sleep, mumbling desperate rumors that they were going to be choppered out. Tam noticed one GI at Captain King's elbow saying he had to get back to LZ Professional to see the reenlistment NCO about getting out of the bush. Down in the valley, they could see Marine Phantoms coming in.

Tam sat down, staring off into space. He vaguely noticed Captain King and a medic standing in front of him. The medic was talking, ". . . Tam's been limping all day and night. I think we better get him out of here. . . ." He suddenly realized they were talking about him. King said, "All right, let's do it," and continued on his business. The medic knelt beside Tam, filled out a medevac slip, tied it to his buttonhole, and told him to get aboard the medevac coming in. Tam was stunned, feeling almost like a deserter. The Huey dropped them off at an LZ and, an hour later, Tam was put on a ship for Chu Lai. He ended up in a large tent equipped with operating tables. Medics cut off his boot, took X rays, and much to his surprise, declared he'd suffered a simple break of the fibula bone. He was fixed with a plastic splint and helo'd to Da Nang, where a cast was put on his leg. The next day, he was helo'd out, this time to the 6th Convalescent Hospital, Cam Ranh Bay. Tam's bizarre odyssey from a battle he had missed did not end there. As part of the Summer Offensive, the NVA had begun launching terrorist rocket attacks on hospitals. Tam lasted two weeks and one raid before the decision was made to further evacuate patients who couldn't run quickly to the bunkers. He ended up in Japan, from where he expected eventually to rejoin his platoon. Instead, his ward was cleared out to make room for a surge of casualties and he was flown to an Army hospital in the United States. When he was discharged from there, Tam was cut orders for duty in the Panama Canal Zone.

Chapter Thirteen
Enter The Marines

In the late morning of 21 August 1969, LtCol Marvin H. Lugger, CO, 2/7 Marines, met with Colonel Codispoti at the new regimental headquarters on LZ Baldy. Codispoti informed Lugger that the Army was in heavy contact in the Hiep Duc Valley and had requested a Marine element to move in and relieve some of the pressure. He himself seemed indifferent to the request and told Lugger to handle the situation as he saw fit. Lugger jumped at the opportunity. With almost four months in command and a new post waiting in two weeks, he had yet to take his battalion to the field for a full-fledged combat operation. Prior to this, they'd been in the Da Nang Rocket Belt.

Lugger was briefed by the S-3, 196th InfBde, who said that they needed any troops the Marines could spare and they needed them right away. Lugger decided to march south past the eastern tip of Nui Chom from his battalion base camp on LZ Ross. Once in the valley, the Marine block would face west, separated by three or four kilometers from the Army units moving towards them. The tip of Nui Chom rose to form Hill 441, and just west of that was Hill 381; the Army said the command posts of the NVA units they were engaging in the flatlands were probably dug in around those peaks.

Lugger radioed his CP to have F Company (1stLt D. C. Ehrsam) and G Company (1stLt J. P. Larrison) put on standby at LZ Ross. Golf Company was still coming in from patrol, and Fox was just starting down the road to take their place. Lugger helicoptered back; organized a jump CP including his S-3, Maj Mel Horowitz, and his BSM, SgtMaj Henry Black; and by 1400 the column was moving. They followed

Route 535 for seven kilometers with Fox in the lead, the CP in the center, and Golf bringing up the rear. It was well over 100 degrees and the road south was dotted with heat casualties: Marines lay naked on ponchos in the roadside weeds, unconscious and pale, corpsmen and buddies pouring canteens over them. To hide their intent, the column left the road and marched near OP Lion in Happy Valley; by dusk, they had set up night positions due east of Hill 441.

In the morning, Fox humped up the northeast slope. From the crest was a sweeping view of the valley's terraced rice paddies blanketed by bright green elephant grass. Golf and the CP came around the other way into the valley itself. Major Lee, S-3, 4–31 Infantry, helicoptered into the 2/7 CP to confer with Lugger. The new mission was to push one kilometer west from Hill 441 to the paddies below 381; hopefully, this would exert enough pressure on the NVA rear to force them to lessen their attacks on the Polar Bears.

Helicopter resupply came in, including precious water blivets from the Army, and by dusk, 2/7 Marines had advanced to their new blocking

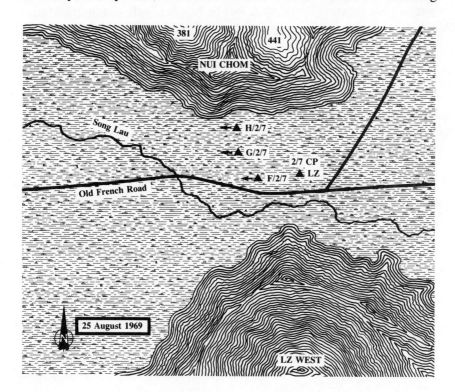

positions. Golf was on the right flank in the shadow of Hill 381. The CP was in the center, along the Song Lau River, which cut the valley lengthwise. F Company was deployed around the CP. There had been no contact, but the sun could kill, and there were numerous priority and emergency medevacs for heat exhaustion patients. Some Marines began shit-canning their gear.

That night, the Marines made their first contact in the Hiep Duc Valley. Around 2100, an ambush team opened fire on an NVA party which appeared to be scouting their lines; the team found two dead North Vietnamese.

The next afternoon, Colonel Codispoti helicoptered into the 2/7 Command Post. Lugger had assumed command of his battalion on 28 April, Codispoti his regiment on 9 July, and in the following weeks their relationship had deteriorated. It was almost inevitable. Codispoti was a New York City Italian. Lugger was a short, slightly built man, very intelligent, but also sensitive and pensive. His parents were both Jewish immigrants from eastern Europe. He had originally been impressed by Codispoti's dynamic and down-to-earth style, but he became increasingly infuriated by his loudly overbearing manner. Codispoti was something of a legend as "a crazy son of a bitch," a phrase both his admirers and detractors used with different inflections. Lugger thought him a tyrant whose decisions were ruled by emotionalism—if he didn't like you, you could do nothing right. The colonel's dislike of Lugger seemed to affect his attitude towards the entire battalion; while Codispoti was seen by 1/7 as a positive leader, at the grunt level in 2/7 he was a remote hard-ass who didn't care about them.

Codispoti thought Lugger indecisive, thus ineffective.

Their uneasy alliance contributed to what occurred during the battle and to Codispoti's eventual decision to relieve Lugger. Lugger, defending himself against what he considered to be an undeserved attack, noted in his watered-down rebuttal:

. . . he was hostile, impatient, and provocative without cause. On two occasions, at my request, we had confidential and honest conversations at which I addressed the question of his attitude toward me, and his evaluation of my performance. At the end of these meetings I had the feeling that there was a better understanding between senior and subordinate. My feelings of confidence were reinforced when on 21 August he gave me his authority to conduct such operations as I deemed appropriate in support of the adjacent Army unit. I felt I had rewarded his confidence when on 23 August he visited my CP in the field. At that time he was filled with praise for my Battalion. I remember with vividness him saying, "You're doing a wonderful job! The Army is delighted over the way you've moved so swiftly. You've taken a lot of pressure off of them."

Just prior to Codispoti's visit, Lugger had been radioed by Colonel Tackaberry, CO, 196th Brigade; he wanted 2/7 to push west. Since this was contrary to his previous blocking mission, Lugger waited until Codispoti's arrival to confirm it. Lugger was to advance the next morning but, in the meantime, G Company was to continue reconning the flanks to gauge the extent of the NVA infiltration.

1stLt Jack Larrison—a stocky, hard-drinking, level-headed young man—had taken command of Golf Company on LZ Ross the day of the move into Hiep Duc. Lugger liked him and, when Golf's captain rotated that day, Lugger moved Larrison in from his slot as the S-5 civil affairs officer. On his third day in command, 23 August, Larrison was directed to recon a thickly vegetated knoll near the base of Hill 381.

2dLt John Pickett, Golf Two, was given the job.

Pickett moved up one side with Sgt William Adams's squad. The platoon sergeant, SSgt Alfred Clements, went up another way with Cpl Randall Black's squad. It was windless and blisteringly hot under helmets and flak jackets; the elephant grass was above their heads at times and it was slow going, the razored edges cutting hands and arms, sweat stinging in the slices and pouring down faces. It was impossible to see more than a few yards into the tangle.

Then the NVA hit them.

There was little to do but squeeze down into the grass as RPDs and AK47s jackhammered from some invisible spider holes.

Lieutenant Pickett radioed Staff Sergeant Clements to bring his squad across, and they got moving with Corporal Black on point. They pushed uphill through the thick brush, then shouldered their way into a small clearing near the crest. Another NVA opened fire. Black reacted before he could think, rolling away, but the man behind him was a second slower. His name was Gerald and the AK burst across his chest killed him instantly. Corporal Black lobbed three grenades towards the invisible sniper; behind him, the rest of the squad huddled low in the grass, gripped by the terror of being impotent in a sourceless crossfire. It was so hot and they were so tired, the grunts seemed almost willing to lie down and accept death rather than move anymore.

Lieutenant Pickett, immobile under his own crossfire, radioed the squad to inch back down the hill.

Black responded that he had a dead Marine up front.

It seemed impossible to retrieve the body without getting someone else killed, and Pickett was adamant about pulling back.

The platoon reorganized at the base of the hill, and Sergeant Adams and Corporal Black volunteered to take a fire team back to recover their dead. Halfway up the slope, the assault began all over again. Two AKs starting firing and, in a mad moment, Adams dropped his helmet and flak jacket and dashed within yards of the spider holes. He pumped his M16 into the brush at point-blank range until one AK was silenced, then scrambled to a boulder five feet from the second hole. He emptied his rifle at it. The AK47 stopped shooting. Adams moved forward and a North Vietnamese fired from the spider hole, killing Sergeant Adams at four feet.

The hill was covered with snipers, at least eight of them, and 2d Platoon retreated again, leaving Gerald and Adams where they fell.

For four hours, company commander Larrison called in air and arty, doing it personally because his air radioman had passed out from the heat. While bombs and napalm scorched the knoll and the grunts nervously waited, the corpsmen treated the casualties at the base of the ridge. Many men had severe heat exhaustion brought on by the 120 degree temperature and the lack of food and water (they had left LZ Ross with only a two-day supply of C rats). And three men had been carried down from the firefight in shock; Golf had not seen solid contact in a long time.

By the time the bombardment ended, the knoll was an ugly brown scar on the lush ridge line. It seemed no one could have survived, and 1st Platoon, under 2dLt Bob Page, moved out. One squad under Sergeant Ferguson was to secure a shattered tree line overlooking the bodies, then provide cover fire while a second squad under Cpl Travis Skaggs retrieved the dead. The platoon moved out as soon as the firing lifted, sweeping uphill through the ash of napalmed elephant grass. Ferguson's squad secured the trees and—unbelievably—the snipers opened fire again. Two men went down with bullets in their legs. Sergeant Ferguson kept his squad firing, and Corporal Skaggs and his squad moved towards the bodies on the crest. More sniper fire erupted, the first burst killing

Private Cunningham and a blistering crossfire sending the rest down, faces in the ash dust, coughing, pressing down under the scythe, baking under the sun. Some men returned fire and an M79 grenadier was able to slam a round into one of the dugouts, silencing one North Vietnamese.

The rest of the NVA were dug in and invisible.

Lieutenant Larrison ordered the men back down, and Golf Company humped up to a second ridge line foothill eighty meters from their target. Larrison stayed on the one-four net, calling in the firepower. Artillery pounded the backside of the knoll as a block to any retreat, while jets shrieked across the slope facing Golf, tumbling more bombs and napalm canisters into what little greenery remained. Medevacs added to the noise. Lieutenant Page's platoon sergeant went out with ash in his lungs. Corporal Skaggs saw the corpsmen frantically giving mouth to mouth and heart massage to a kid in shock who stopped breathing. They kept him alive and, as they hustled him up the back ramp of the Sea Knight, he was like a piece of lumber in their hands.

Even those not in shock or unconscious from the heat were ready to throw in the towel. They were almost out of ammunition, food, and water. The heat was unbearable. The snipers seemed invincible. Men found a spot in the grass and just lay there. Staff Sergeant Clements, an Old Corps lifer with a southern drawl, surveyed his platoon. He was not pleased; the men looked like they couldn't move, like they'd be glad to sit this one out. Hotel Company was humping past then, having come in as the re-act to retrieve the bodies. Some of the Hotel grunts nonchalantly shouted that old Golf could go back now and guard "the pilots," meaning the battalion command post. As Golf watched Hotel heading towards the knoll, they couldn't help but think, almost vindictively: you'll find out.

From his CP along the valley stream, Lieutenant Colonel Lugger had watched Golf Company's aborted efforts to secure the knoll. He radioed regiment to have another company released from the LZ Ross AO; permission was received and, at 1300, 1stLt P. E. Vannoy, CO, H/2/7, was alerted to prepare for a helo lift. By no means was Lugger's opinion unanimous, but he himself did not trust Vannoy; he thought him too unaggressive.

Hotel Company was spread out around LZ Ross in platoon observation posts when the Sea Knights began shuttling them into a bush LZ secured

by F/2/7 in the Hiep Duc Valley. The air strikes were still pounding
Nui Chom as Lugger quickly briefed Vannoy about recovering the casualties, then finally seizing and holding the knoll. Vannoy huddled with
his platoon leaders and asked for a volunteer to get the bodies.

2dLt William T. Brennon, Hotel Three, spoke up.

By 1700, three hours after the first wave of Hotel had been airlifted
in, they had humped north and linked up with Golf. Lieutenant Brennon—
who was considered a good head by his grunts—asked for volunteers
to go up with him.

LCpl Ralph Bruno Sirianni said he'd go.

What prompted him was a subtle sense of duty. Sirianni wasn't a
believer, but his street buddies had always trusted him to cover their
backs when something went down. He'd grown up in the Italian section
of Buffalo, New York, the son of immigrants. His father died when
Ralph was two and his mother, who barely spoke English, worked three
jobs to support him and his older brother. Sirianni grew up in the streets
and, by the time he was fourteen, he ran with a gang that crossed
paths with the police. He ended up in reform school for eighteen months;
afterwards, he forced himself through high school. But he didn't stay
out of trouble and the judge finally gave him the choice of jail or the
service. He checked with the Army, Navy, and Air Force but they all
turned him down because of his juvenile record. The Marine Corps
was much more amiable and he was glad; he wanted to be with the
best.

In June 1969, Sirianni joined Hotel Company in their Dai La canton-
ment. It was a whole different Marine Corps out there. The first thing
the guys in his squad told him was to forget boot camp, that they weren't
fighting to take some objective but to survive. In that larger sense,
Sirianni thought, morale was a disaster. The people back home don't
want us here, he figured, we don't want to be here, and the Vietnamese
don't care. To him, the grunts were just cannon fodder for the lifers to
build their paper records and the arms manufacturers to build their for-
tunes. He couldn't believe they were considered so expendable as to
be sent through the rice paddies like bait. Sirianni regarded the NVA
much like the cavalryman did the Apaches: ruthless and skilled, always
watching, always waiting for the opportunity to hit and run. One rare
occasion, Sirianni's platoon captured a North Vietnamese regular, a lean,
tough kid with modern gear and weapons. He wore a green rain jacket.
Sirianni stood toe to toe with him, staring with hate and fear and satisfaction; and the NVA glared right back at him.

Sometimes, Sirianni's squad would sandbag their patrols. They could find no reason to tread through booby-trapped paddies in the dead of night, looking for people who probably weren't there. So they'd leave the perimeter, find a spot of cover, and radio in fake checkpoints. In the battalion compound, they dropped out. Lots of rock, some marijuana. But, like it or not, Sirianni mostly had to keep in step with the way things were programmed. In that smaller sense, morale was high. The grunts took care of each other. It was a matter of honor. When he was in high school, Sirianni was always in trouble with one particular teacher, a former Marine; when he enlisted, the man had told him, "When you get under fire for the first time, you're going to freeze." In his first firefight, two or three snipers temporarily pinned down his squad and Sirianni ducked behind a small boulder. His foot slipped out, a round kicked up dirt near it, and he yanked it back, terrified. Then his mind flashed to that insult and he thought, I can't go through my life giving him the satisfaction. He forced himself up to return fire. Before his tour was over, Sirianni made sergeant and was decorated for valor.

Lance Corporal Sirianni, who was twenty and known as Tripper, volunteered to retrieve the bodies—he'd known Cunningham from ITR. Sirianni's squad leader, Corporal Beckler—skinny, blond, and quiet— looked at him, then to T. J., a taciturn Mexican. They said they'd go too. Two frazzled looking guys from Golf Company led them up, pointed towards the bodies, then slinked back down the hill. The three volunteers crept up to the crest of the knoll while Lieutenant Brennon and his radioman crouched on the slope directing the automatic cover fire. Sirianni glanced over the crest. He could see one of the dead Marines sprawled in the ash a few yards away, mangled by the prep bombardment.

He started over but an AK47 suddenly opened fire, sending him back. Someone yelled, "Chicom!" and, being new, he hesitated a second. Beckler or T. J. shoved him down from behind and his face was in the dirt when the grenade exploded. Sirianni caught a fragment across the knee, a bloodless scratch, and the other two were similarly nicked. They shoved up their M16s to return fire while Lieutenant Brennon urgently shouted into the radio trying to shift Golf Company's cover fire. It was almost hitting them. There was no response. More Chicoms bounced in.

Brennon finally hollered to pull back.

The retreat left a bitter taste in everyone's mouth—the Marine Corps does not abandon their dead—but what remained of Adams, Gerald, and Cunningham lay with the North Vietnamese all night.

Colonel Codispoti was with Lieutenant Colonel Lugger when the decision was made to break contact and blast the hill again with air power. The jets tumbled more bombs onto the knoll and, as the vibrations rolled back under their feet, Lugger glanced at Codispoti. Lugger was suddenly aware that his regimental commander was viewing these proceedings with a disapproving grimace. But Codispoti said nothing. Lugger was silently frustrated, thinking, well, what does he suggest I do; if we keep running up the hill without supporting arms, we'll just take more casualties! Codispoti was probably thinking of Dowd, for whom he had approved a posthumous Navy Cross, and his battalion's classic use of fire and maneuver. In comparison, Lugger did not measure up. When Codispoti reviewed Lugger's performance in the current action and that which would quickly follow, his words were damning, "As a matter of practice during this battle period, elements of his battalion pulled back immediately upon being hit with enemy small arms fire. . . . Guidance, direction, exhortation and positive orders were given over the radio and at daily personal visits by me to this officer to have his units press forward with fire and maneuver on being subjected to enemy small arms fire, but to no avail."*

Golf and Hotel Companies set their night perimeters along the terraced dikes at the base of the enemy knoll. Sirianni nestled against a berm. NVA on the knoll screamed down, "Marines, tomorrow you die!"

Grunts screamed back, "Fuck off!"

Sirianni, a tough-looking kid with glasses, a tattoo, and thick muscles, was shaking. He didn't smoke but finally got a Pall Mall from his buddy, cupped it in his hands in the dark, and smoked the hell out of it. It calmed him down. He finally fell asleep.

He awoke the next morning to the rumble of Phantoms flashing in on the knoll ahead. Dirt clods flew back at them. He lay there, miserably hot and hungry, then he stopped sweating and things got foggy. The next thing he knew he was waking up in a dark, vibrating helicopter. The crew chief was bending down to talk with him. It was heat exhaustion

---

* A copy of this fitness report was provided to the author by Lugger himself, despite the negative light he knew it would cast upon him.

and Sirianni ended up at 1st Med. The place was already abuzz with casualties and he stared stunned at one Marine; the man himself was staring with numb horror at his shredded leg, which had been blown off six inches above the knee.

At 0500 on 24 August, NVA crept up to Golf Company's perimeter. They tossed Chicom stick grenades over the dikes, then quickly faded back into the dark brush as the grunts responded with M79 and fragmentation grenades. One Marine was killed in the brief, blind melee.

With daylight, the company prepared to attack the knoll again.

The firepower was turned back on for several hours to strip away the last of the vegetation concealing the snipers. H Battery, 3/11 Marines on LZ Ross sent 155mm artillery shells whistling in; Phantoms and Cobras finished the show. Then the grunts began their uphill sweep. The scorching sun was made even more unbearable now that the knoll was bald. They led their attack with M79 CS rounds, but the NVA had pulled out, leaving only one or two men as a rear guard. Corporal Skaggs's squad took some fire but his point man—a young grunt with an Italian name—lobbed a frag into the spider hole. An NVA with an SKS carbine scrambled out, and the point man cut him down. Along the denuded slope, Golf Company found results of their firepower: two NVA roasted to death from napalm in a spider hole, still clutching their AK47s, and pieces of bodies scattered in the upturned earth. They also found the remains of the three Marines who'd died for this hunk of dirt, and carried them down to be evacuated.

Meanwhile, Hotel Company was also assaulting but from a different angle. It was their job to secure the top of the knoll, and Lieutenant Brennon led his platoon up in a basic on-line assault. Cobra gunships pumped in their ordnance ten meters ahead of the platoon while AK fire cracked from farther up the ridge. The grunts ran up as fast as they could under their gear, propelled by adrenaline and fear; when they'd secured the top—without casualties—many simply passed out under the noonday sun. The rest of Hotel hiked up after them, unopposed, and dug in on the bald crest.

Resupply helicopters began coming in, but the NVA opened fire on them from the tree lines in the lowland paddies to the west. Air strikes were called in, but the NVA were dug in deeply and a spotter pilot from the 1st Marine Air Wing was wounded in his cockpit seat.

Meanwhile, 2/7 remained in place and rested.

That night, it was back to business. At dusk, LCpl Rolf Parr, a squad leader in Fox Company, took out two men as the platoon listening post. The battalion had a lot of problem children, but Parr was not one of them; he was a twenty-year-old Indiana farm boy who soldiered along, rather uncomplaining, even though he had an NVA bullet lodged in a bone in his foot. It was a souvenir from Operation Oklahoma Hills. Parr's LP team walked two hundred yards outside their perimeter, set a claymore along a dike, then dropped back fifty yards to set in for the night behind another dike. It was around midnight when the new guy on the team whispered he had movement. He pointed and Parr stared at what appeared to be four posts on the dike a hundred yards ahead. Parr figured the foggy night was playing tricks on the kid's imagination, but then one of the posts moved. An M60 on the perimeter suddenly opened fire and red tracers snapped past the LP. The silhouettes on the dike instantly disappeared. Parr was more surprised than angry with the jumpy machine gunner: he's not supposed to do that with us out here! One of the NVA suddenly reappeared, running in a crouch along the dike towards the team's claymore. Parr tossed the firing handle to the third grunt. They let the NVA get within thirty meters of the mine, then Parr opened fire with his M16. The new guy cut loose too, and Parr shouted at the third Marine to blow the claymore. The figure disappeared in the blast and tracers.

The firing had given away their position and Parr radioed for permission to return to the lines. For reasons not explained to him, permission was denied; it was one long, sleepless night, which turned out to be without further incident. At sunrise, the team heard a single shot from the paddies. Parr's squad found the dead NVA where the claymore had levelled him. The man's legs were shattered, bloody tourniquets around them, and his AK47 was locked in his hands, barrel under the chin. He had—it appeared—killed himself at dawn when he realized no one was coming to rescue him. Hard-core. Documents on the body indicated he had been a lieutenant.

Chapter Fourteen

Counterattack

On 22 August 1969, in Hiep Duc, PFC Michael Kosteczko of B Company, 2d Battalion, 1st Infantry Regiment, came under enemy fire for the first time. This was not his baptism of fire; that had been provided some days earlier courtesy of a U.S. cavalry troop.

Kosteczko had been with the company a week.

He had been born in France, the son of Ukrainian immigrants who continued their migration to Chicago when he was twelve. They were factory workers intent on keeping their only child out of the mills, and they made sure he got to college. He graduated in 1968 with a business degree and, almost immediately, a draft ticket to Vietnam. His mother cried, and he wrote their senator and petitioned his draft board. It did no good, but it was the only legal option he could accept. His girl friend wanted to go to Canada and get married. It was tempting, but he couldn't. When his family first came to this country, they had nothing; now they owned their own home. Kosteczko always remembered that.

Vietnam meant nothing to him, but America did.

He didn't tell his parents when he was ordered to Vietnam, and they didn't know until he got back. Because they barely understood English and because the acronyms of the Army APO mailing system were vague, it was easy to make them believe he was in Korea.

Kosteczko lasted five months in the bush. On 13 December his best buddy, Soupy Campbell, took his place on the trail. Soupy carried an M79; the lieutenant wanted him behind the point, and Frenchy Kosteczko next with an M16 in case of ambush. A few minutes after trading places, a booby trap cleaned Soupy off the path. KIA. Kosteczko became fatalistic to the point of being careless. On Christmas Eve, the company commander sent him to Hawk Hill to finish his tour working in the ammunition dump. Kosteczko finally came home with his Bronze Star, but in the same funk. The nightmares were the worst part; he tried to forget by locking himself in his bedroom in his parent's home, lights out, shades down. Every day was the same: he got drunk alone in the dark and tried to forget as the rock music screamed.

When Kosteczko had first joined Bravo Company on Hawk Hill, he was just like all the other new guys—nervous and green. He rolled through the gate in the back of a truck with Soupy Campbell, fresh from the Americal Combat Center, their new fatigues covered with road dust. That was right after the sapper attack on Hawk Hill and everyone was talking about it; they said the NVA had gotten through the wire, past the bunkers, and weren't stopped until they crossed the camp road and the cav tanks and tracks chopped them down. Dawn had brought the Cobra gunships that hosed their miniguns into the retreating enemy. North Vietnamese bodies were still being policed up. Chicom stick grenades littered the perimeter road.

Kosteczko had spent his first week with Bravo on Hawk Hill. They filled sandbags and strung new wire. They smoked grass and paid the high-class whores five dollars a lay; the local girls would do it for a pack of cigarettes or a bar of soap. They tossed C rations to Vietnamese who begged along the perimeter wire. Some GIs threw the cans hard and aimed for their heads. They finally humped to the bush and by dusk were spread along a hillside. Kosteczko was asleep on his air mattress when he suddenly awoke to the whine of ricochets and the blipping of tracers, and he squeezed down, eyes tight, scared shitless. It turned out the strafing had been courtesy of F Troop, 17th Armored Cavalry, Americal, and the Mad Minute from their night defensive perimeter.

On 20 August, Bravo 2–1 was flown to ARVN LZ Karen.

On the 21st, they humped to Million Dollar Hill and secured it while the survivors of Charlie 4–31 and Bravo 1–46 staggered in.

On the 22d, Bravo 2–1, commanded by Capt Dwight D. Sypolt, led the first counterattack from Million Dollar Hill. Artillery rolled ahead of them as they pushed east, forming the sweep to 2/7 Marines' blocking positions.

By noon, Private Kosteczko's platoon took a break from the heat of the paddy beneath the trees of a little knoll. Several GIs set out to find water and were at the base of another hillock fifty yards ahead when a fierce eruption of AK47 fire suddenly cut loose from it. Kosteczko made a panicked scramble for cover, finally tumbling into a natural trench facing the hillock where the others had rushed. No one was firing back: the water detail was somewhere in the bushes from which the NVA were shooting. The GIs finally crawled back, minus one. They said the NVA had ambushed them from the top of the hill, and one GI had made a run for it. An AK round had hit the LAW hanging across his back, and they'd left his body. GIs were firing back, rising up to squeeze off full auto bursts, flopping back to reload. Kosteczko was not firing. He hugged dirt, confused, bug-eyed with fear.

Someone was asking for volunteers to get the body, and Kosteczko saw two black GIs run up. It surprised him; in base camp, the blacks looked out only for their own. The volunteers clambered forward into the brush. They came back without the body, but one black was dragging the other brother. He'd been shot in the stomach. Another GI sat in the ravine, shot in the knee. Kosteczko felt sick. A medevac landed for the twelve wounded men; then Bravo Company broke contact and pulled back to Million Dollar Hill. By the time Kosteczko's squad pulled back, the scene was getting chaotic. The GIs scrambled from the ravine and hit the trail at a jog, firing into the underbrush to discourage pursuit. Kosteczko was the last in line, panting hard on the run, his M16 locked and loaded, full auto, his finger on the trigger. He was so scared he might get left behind, he kept running into the guy ahead of him—his buddy Foxhole—who was saying, "Watch it, man, before you trip and shoot me in the ass!"

■ "Hiep Duc village is one of those strange little nowhere places that suddenly finds itself in the limelight of the war," wrote an Army correspondent in *Stars and Stripes*.

The village doesn't even rate a dot on most maps. It has dirt streets, houses with tin roofs, and about 4,000 inhabitants. But Hiep Duc, important mostly as a symbol, has become one of the year's bloodiest battles. To the allies, who have promised to protect it, Hiep Duc is a test of the seriousness of their intent. To the North Vietnamese, who have promised to destroy it, Hiep Duc is a measure of their ability to discredit the critical pacification program.

The correspondent's comments explained why Task Force 4–31 and 2/7 Marines were fighting on the valley floor. How they were fighting was something else.

On 20 August, Major Lee had helicoptered to Million Dollar Hill to establish a forward command post. On the 21st, he had flown briefly to LZ Baldy to request the commander of the 7th Marines to send in reinforcements; then he had briefed the battalion commander given that mission. On the 22d, after two sleepless nights and after having been on the receiving end of a good amount of sniper fire, Lee helicoptered back to LZ West. Disembarking, he met LtCol Cecil Henry, BnCO, who was going in to take his place at the Forward CP. At the same time, one of the assistant division commanders, a brigadier general, helicoptered in. He wanted a briefing complete with pins on a map, but Henry tried to beg off. "Major Lee's been out for three days, and I'm going out now. We haven't got time for formality, only a quick run down." The ADC was insistent, so they retired to the TOC bunker. Major Lee, giving the briefing, suddenly started crying. He did not know why. He felt nothing but a numb void; the emotions and frustrations were buried deeply. Henry interrupted, "General, I'd appreciate it if you could leave for a bit. We'll brief you when we have time." The ADC refused, and Colonel Henry exploded, "General, get off this hill now! And if you don't like that, relieve me!"

As the ADC climbed back into his helicopter, he spat, "I'll get you!" There were no repercussions from this ugly incident, which was obviously a personality clash in a highly charged situation. The brigadier's lethargy, however exaggerated, nonetheless stemmed from the mood at division. Henry, who thought they were up against two regiments and perhaps a division in the Hiep Duc Valley, could not convince Major General Ramsey or Colonel Tackaberry of his hunch. At least not initially. He based his estimate on the numerous contacts and the number of crew-served weapons the enemy had, especially 12.7mm guns and 120mm mortars, which were usually reserved for NVA regiments. Also, a note in the battalion journal for 22 August read, "Monitored enemy radio transmissions indicated that a large amount of supplies were being shipped from the north to support two regimental size units."

Although this was the only major action in the Americal TAOR at the time, General Ramsey was not willing to commit full force to it. The general, who had been wounded five times as a young officer in Europe, could be seen on a daily basis at the forward fire bases of his battalions wearing a green baseball cap with two black stars on the front; even the Americal Division's most mean-spirited critic, Seymour Hersh, described Ramsey as "an honest, forthright officer . . . a believer in the system and the soldier." Manpower played a key factor in Ramsey's cautious approach to Hiep Duc. It was always a myth of the Vietnam War that U.S. infantrymen outnumbered NVA infantrymen in actual ground battles. Although the U.S. had a half-million men in the war zone, there were only approximately 80,000 infantrymen in the bush. It was the NVA who could hide in the wilderness, then mass and strike as it benefitted them. A diversionary attack in one area, which drew U.S. reinforcements like a magnet, could leave vulnerable gaps elsewhere.

That was General Ramsey's very real worry.

Major Lee got into shouting matches with brigade staff officers over this lack of support. Colonel Henry kept his bitterness in check because he could appreciate those concerns, but he still thought it was a hell of a way to fight a battle. He requested from a visiting ADC that a troop of tanks from 1–1 Cav be dispatched to help his infantrymen blast out the entrenched enemy. His request was denied on the spot. He wanted another battalion rushed in, but his requests for reinforcements were met piecemeal, one company at a time. No units were committed to destroy, or at least harass, the NVA rear in the Nui Chom ridge line.

Both LZ West and LZ Siberia were subjected to shellings (casualties included Captain Kinman, battalion surgeon on West, hit by mortar shrapnel; and Capt Joel Thomason, artillery commander on Siberia, hit by recoilless rifle shrapnel). Resupply was precarious due to AAA fire, so Henry put LZ West on the bottom of the priority list to ensure that the field companies got the most. From 18 to 28 August, there was no shaving or bathing on the LZ. The mess hall was closed and the support personnel made due with C rations. Medical supplies were low. Those with minor wounds or heat stroke were flown to the battalion aid station; the rest were medevacked directly to LZ Baldy (23d Medical Company) and from there to Chu Lai (27th Surgical Hospital) or Da Nang (95th Evacuation Hospital).

In the valley, 4–31 was spread thinly—of twelve medics in the first three companies committed, one was killed and seven were wounded—and worn out—in three days.

The U.S. Command never completely deciphered the intentions of the NVA in Hiep Duc Valley. One North Vietnamese prisoner provided an explanation which seemed plausible in its simplicity: the NVA had originally intended to destroy the Resettlement Village, but when that plan was blocked, their new directive was to inflict as many casualties as possible until ordered to withdraw.

The terrain suited such a scheme. From their positions on Nui Chom, the NVA commanders and forward observers kept the Army and Marine units under constant visual observation. The NVA troops in the valley were dug in, too. They were not attacking anymore; they sat invisible in the shade of the tree lines in squad- and platoon-sized groups, and watched their enemy come searching for them across the open paddies.

When the Americans came close enough, the NVA killed them.

During this battle, 4–31 still had to commit two companies to the defense of LZs West and Siberia, plus the Resettlement Village, leaving a mixed bag of attached companies to shoulder much of the combat. These troops were generally inexperienced and unfamiliar with the terrain. The battalion journal commented:

Training in the small unit tactics of fire and maneuver, and fire and movement needs to be stressed. Even though this battalion has consistently stressed these basics, it was learned from this action, that units cannot be over-trained; and not until the basics become automatic reactions, do units even begin to be proficient. Individual soldiers seem to believe that this war is drastically different from past conflicts. This is true in some technical aspects, but the small unit tactics have not changed in the slightest.

23 August. At 0640, B/2–1 and B/1–46 moved east again from their spot of poncho shelters around Million Dollar Hill, while Colonel Henry remained at his Forward CP with C/4–31 as reserve and the Echo Mortar Platoon 4–31 (2dLt Charles Allen) dug in near his radios. At 0715, thirty rounds of 82mm mortar fire thumped into the CP; Henry scooted into an old shell crater, but not before fragments burned into his hand and the left side of his face. Echo Mortars pumped 81mm fire in return as a Huey took Henry and three other slightly wounded GIs to LZ West (Henry was back on Million Dollar Hill before dusk). At

1400, Bravo 1–46 made contact with what appeared to be a platoon of NVA; their barrage of AK47 and RPG fire halted Bravo, and they broke contact before dusk in order to evacuate their two wounded and make it back to the CP before nightfall.

Bravo 2d of the 1st Infantry ran into a similar situation. Kosteczko was huddled in the same area as the day before and, once again, the NVA on the knoll had the GIs pinned. A sergeant, also flat behind the berm, called to Kosteczko, "Take a look up there and see what they're doing!" Being a new guy, Kosteczko started to get up, but an old-timer stopped him with snarled words of advice, "Let him look up there! What the hell, you going to look up there and get your head blown off!"

Spirits were draining quickly.

Bravo pulled back too before dusk. It was hot as hell, so before hiking up the trail on Million Dollar Hill, the men flaked out under the trees at the base. About ten minutes later, NVA mortars began exploding along the trail where they should have been. The shelling walked up the path, then blasted a few new holes out of the hilltop. Unreal, Kosteczko thought, shaking inside: the dinks are always watching!

24 August. The ten men killed when Bravo 4–31 started the battle had lain in the bush for six days. They were recovered that afternoon by 2d Platoon of Charlie 4–31 under 2dLt William R. Robinson and SFC Marshall E. Robertson, who'd been in the bush two days and ten months, respectively.

Lieutenant Robinson had been sucked up by the draft from his post-college government job and, neither knowing nor caring, did not really even think about Vietnam until the final hitchhike chopper ride deposited him on LZ West on 22 August. Robinson had completed the combat course at Chu Lai three days earlier and had spent the previous two nights in the unoccupied, air-conditioned trailer of the brigade commander. Things seemed ordered and controlled, although Robinson was shocked by his new, real environment. He'd originally been slotted for Alpha Company, but they were in the middle of a firefight in AK Valley, so he was put on a chopper for Charlie Company on Million Dollar Hill. He joined them two hours after touching ground at West; two hours after that, he got his baptism of fire. Mortar and sniper fire sent the platoon scrambling for foxholes and boulders. Robinson noticed those around him were wide-eyed, mumbling that they were surrounded; they looked like they'd already been through too much. The shooting petered out. It was just harassing fire.

Lieutenant Robinson's platoon found the dead of Bravo Company on 24 August and dragged them back to Million Dollar Hill to be medevacked to Graves Registration on LZ Baldy. Robinson wrote to his parents:

> . . . Tempers were high & moral was low. The area where the bodies were, was in an area that had been previously unreachable; right about in the middle of an enemy stronghold. The company had been out in the field for about a week getting very little sleep and had been hit pretty hard, as the 1st platoon was down to 12 men. The bodies were left behind by a company that was nearly slaughtered there & had to leave their dead behind. We were lucky and didn't get any contact—But we picked up 2 bodies and a large firefight broke behind us in between us and the hill, so we took the long way around in the process we picked ten more bodies. Without going into details I can't possibly tell how bad it was to have to pick up those decomposed bodies. It took six hours to get back. It started raining (1st since Ive been here) and the body bags started breaking open. We finally made it back—but you can't imagine how something like that can kill the morale. The bodies were heavy and the smell sickening. I don't think I'll ever forget it.

The firing Charlie 4–31 heard was the third attempt by Bravo 2–1 to recover their dead man. Another crossfire of mortars and snipers killed one GI and wounded eight. Countermortar fire from Million Dollar Hill crashed around the enemy knoll. The grunts were pinned down in the sunbaked ravine, some taking the chance to raise up and return fire, most just comatose in the heat. Word was finally passed to pull back.

Oh shit, Kosteczko gulped, here we go again.

Kosteczko's squad ran back down the path on the edge of panic, firing and tossing grenades into the underbrush—the dinks are everywhere! The resupply birds had been unable to land due to ground fire, and could only toss supplies out the cabin doors as they buzzed past. The grunts were out of water and the sun was eating up their brains. They crashed down a buffalo trail where they'd previously seen a slimy, green pond. They found it and collapsed to their knees at the rim, pushing helmets under the algae on the surface. The lieutenant was shouting to use purification pills and to give them time to dissolve. Fuck the lieutenant, Kosteczko was thinking. He unhooked his steel pot, spread his sweaty sweat towel over it as a filter, and used the plastic helmet liner to scoop up the water. He threw in a pill; waited a pathetic second; then gulped down the stinking, green-brown liquid. It tasted great. All we've got left, he thought, are animal instincts. The squad set up in a field thick with elephant grass, hacked out spots with machetes, and sacked out atop mats of C ration cardboard, three or four men on each mat huddled against the evening cool. The night moved around them and nervous sentries pitched grenades outside the circle. Artillery rumbled in the distance. In the morning, moving like zombies, they got up to attack again.

PFC Ralph Brantley and PFC Charles Jandecka, who were both twenty-one, arrived on the same day as replacements to 3d Platoon, Bravo Company, 4th Battalion, 31st Infantry. Both originally were draftees but, in their own ways, they represented the very different types who made up the Americal Division.

They originally met at the 4–31 Rear on LZ Baldy before the campaign began. Brantley was being reassigned from a unit in Qui Nhon, and Jandecka had just finished the Combat Center training at Americal Division Headquarters. By then, Brantley had the combat infantryman badge stitched over his left pocket and a 4th Infantry Division patch on his right shoulder, denoting a previous combat tour with them. He was lean, tanned, and long-haired. He'd been ghosting around Baldy for two weeks, not at all anxious to return to the bush. Jandecka was new— so green that when news of the Bravo Company ambush reached them, he commented in false bravado that the streets back home were pretty rough too. Bravo was deep in the bowels of Chu Lai by then, having been trucked in to help renovate some old hootches. The Marines were taking over Landing Zone Baldy, and the 4–31 Rear was moving south to Chu Lai.

Within twenty-four hours of the news, the company top sergeant had rounded up every 11 Bravo he could find. They were herded onto the chopper pad at Chu Lai, about a dozen of them, to catch a Chinook to LZ West. Jandecka was surprised—not shocked, because he'd been to Chu Lai before—to see Brantley lean back on his rucksack and light up a joint.

A couple of other replacements joined in.

The Chinook landed soon after, and it was a thirty-mile hop up to West. The fire base was abuzz with activity, and the replacements were immediately directed aboard several Hueys departing for LZ Siberia. They were hustling across the landing pad when Hoss Gutterez caught sight of Brantley's necklace and bracelet. The sergeant major—a big no-neck lifer—bellowed out, "Get that off, there's no room in this battalion for weirdos or hippies!"

Brantley quickly complied.

Jandecka and Brantley were not best friends, but they were buddies. Jandecka recalled his comrade with a certain fondness: "He never became a driving force within the platoon. Brantley became identified with the Army's subculture instead. Those men in this group gravitated together by the sheer force of kindred interests. They adorned themselves with beads and bracelets, they gathered together to listen to very loud music, proclaim their toughness, and smoke grass. And they did their best to avoid work of any kind, especially the bush. But he was a scrappy little fellow who would fight if so inclined."

As a matter of record, Brantley was wounded by mortar shrapnel on LZ West in September and hit again in December; he was thus nicknamed Cold Steel.

Brantley had grown up poor and fatherless in Jacksonville, Florida. His father was killed with the Marines in Korea and his mother, a child bride, remarried a man the family barely tolerated. Brantley ended up with his grandmother. He dropped out of high school and became a hard-drinking, restless kid who welcomed his draft notice. He was nineteen in September of 67 when he first arrived in Vietnam, joining the 35th Infantry Regiment of Task Force Oregon. They operated near the Batangan Peninsula in a phantom war of snipers and booby traps. By the time Brantley took his R and R three months later, his platoon had been whittled nearly in half without having even seen the enemy. In a fatigued panic after R and R, Brantley reenlisted to get off the line. He ended up as a clerk in the rear, rotated on schedule; but, bored with stateside duty, he volunteered for a second tour. He was assigned to a security guard platoon in Qui Nhon, an area so calm the GIs needed permission to chamber a round when on guard. He lasted four months, until he and a buddy were caught passed-out drunk on post. They were busted in rank and there was talk of a court-martial.

To avoid that, Brantley volunteered for the infantry.

Jandecka, a bespectacled, intelligent kid, did not have a history as colorful, nor was it as unhappy. He came from a close-knit, working family in Berea, Ohio, and left home for the first time to go to college.

His grades were mediocre and, after his second year, he came home and got a job in the local steel mill. He also got his draft call. Jandecka accepted it without protest. He was conservative; the war seemed just; and, where he came from, the Army was just part of life. He never abandoned those views, and he became typical of the citizen-soldiers of America who've always formed the bulk of the combat infantry. When his squad leader decided to fake a patrol, Jandecka didn't mind, but if the man said move out, he moved out. He did not smoke pot; he did not throw away his malaria pill. At the same time, he killed no one and did nothing madly courageous. He followed orders, he did his job, and he endured.

Through no fault of his own, he rotated home unscathed. Because of his outlook, Jandecka survived mentally unscarred as well.

Not so with Brantley.

Jandecka, Brantley, and their fellow replacements joined Bravo Company on Landing Zone Siberia. The company had been pulled to the fire base after the ambush in a state of shock. Since then, though, the old-timers had had some fun with the naive new guys. They'd gotten some hot food and cold drink; and they'd cleaned their weapons, rezeroed them in, and test-fired their new magazines. Most of all, they'd had a chance to sit and clear their minds, and when the word came to saddle up again, it was met with only the normal GI bitching. Bravo 4th of the 31st Infantry CA'd into a cold LZ in the Hiep Duc Valley on 25 August.

25 August. As the sun burned away the valley's morning mist, Kosteczko really didn't know what day it was. He was numb in body and spirit. He felt like a machine—trapped, programmed. Every day was the same. The morning resupply bird brought the same breakfast: powdered eggs swimming in water, toast turned to mush from the steam trapped inside the mermite cans, good bacon. They boiled C ration cocoa over heat tablets or chunks of C4 explosives. The medics passed out the malaria pills, standing in front of some GIs to make sure they didn't spit it out. Stupid fucking hill, guys were mumbling. What are they trying to prove! Kosteczko heard some grunts say they'd waved their hands around during mortarings on Million Dollar Hill, trying to catch a ticket home. He heard one guy shot his finger off.

You had to have a relief from the insanity and pressure, and every morning he was in Vietnam, Kosteczko prayed. He asked the same question every time: will I make it through the day? It gave him some solace, but this morning he felt no answer and it unnerved him. Grunts by circumstance are a superstitious lot.

Sometimes, though, there is reason for odd beliefs.

Bravo Company was weary, but when the order was passed to attack again, they attacked; one more time they fell back to medevac their casualties. This time, a platoon from Charlie 4–31 ducked a few snipers to secure an LZ for them. Kosteczko's squad sat to wait in a tree grove along a path, and he and Foxhole collapsed beside a dilapidated hootch in the tangle. Two Cobras thumped past. No one paid them any attention. They suddenly banked around and dove. Foxhole leaped into the crumbling family bunker and Kosteczko, with no idea what was going on, instinctively jumped right on top of him just as he heard the foghorn wail of a minigun erupt. He felt a flash of heat over his back, then the explosion of the gunship's rocket against a paddy berm.

I'm in hell!

The trigger-happy Cobra pilots were quickly straightened out, but not before Bravo 2–1 suffered three wounded and Charlie 4–31 a fourth. That GI, hit by shrapnel in both legs, was from Lieutenant Robinson's platoon, which was securing the medevac landing zone. It was the first casualty Robinson had. Robinson had no idea what went wrong. He could see no excuse for it.

Meanwhile, B/1–46 continued forward to try to outflank an NVA 60mm mortar position below Hill 381 which was shelling the battalion sweep. Lieutenant Baird and his RTO were with the lead squad while the platoon sergeant, Sergeant Brown, brought up the rear. Baird and Brown were a study in contrasts, the lieutenant an urbane West Pointer new to the platoon, the sergeant a black country boy raised on a cotton farm in Mississippi and drafted away from his construction job. Brown had been in the bush ten months, but did not resent his new second lieutenant; the man was learning fast.

AK47 fire greeted their flanking maneuver.

Brown and his squad dropped among the trees, boulders, and high grass of a hillside. North Vietnamese were firing from a tree line across the paddy to their front. Before long, the squad could also hear the brush moving below their slight hillock. They chopped M16 bursts at the sounds. Chicom grenades were flung back at them. The NVA had crept that close. GIs ducked, then heaved frags downhill. It was sporadic, off and on. Sergeant Brown sat low, trying to peer through the grass. An AK would cut a burst at them and they'd raise a racket firing back. Then there was silence as both sides changed magazines. The NVA mortar crew was firing again, lobbing rounds over the squad's heads into the rest of the company. Brown could hear Baird over the RTO's squawk box: the lieutenant, pinned down with the lead squad, was calmly directing artillery into the tree line from which the ambush had been sprung, and onto NVA who were trying to surround the platoon. Someone near Brown hollered that he saw two NVA running through the trees. A grunt fired a LAW after them. The rest hunkered along the hillside behind spots of cover, trading bursts with the underbrush as the sun beat down.

They too were halted.

As the NVA mortarmen adjusted their fires onto Bravo 1–46 (better known as the Ridgerunners), their sister company, Delta 1–46 (the Vikings), moved to outflank the tube position. Delta Company, 1st Battalion, 46th Infantry, commanded by a black captain named Jesse Sellers, had been airlifted from LZ Professional to LZ Karen the day before.

They had humped to Million Dollar Hill that morning.

SP4 Billy McWhirter, squad leader in the lead platoon, could feel the vibrations when the mortar fired some four hundred yards ahead. He could also hear the flare-ups of automatic weapons fire on the flanks. This was his first big action, but he trusted his platoon and he trusted his officers. That's what kept him moving forward. He thought his platoon was rare it was so good. Yet Delta Company fared no better than any other Americal unit in the valley; what really seemed rare was McWhirter's attitude. He'd been working at Caterpillar Tractor when the draft came, nineteen then and supporting a new bride; that would have made a good sob story, but he was from an Illinois farming community and he knew his duty when he saw it. His patriotism was unshakable, and his only gripe was that the Vietnamese didn't appreciate what the GIs were sacrificing for them. Damn it, he thought, you come in from patrol and here's some gook at the wire peddling Pepsis at five dollars a bottle! He believed in what he was fighting about, but he never trusted the people he was fighting for.

Delta Company's advance across Hiep Duc Valley was covered by the rumble of artillery. They reached a muddy paddy boxed in by tree lines, and halted long enough to recon the far side by fire. There was no response, so the point squad hiked into the field, single file atop a berm with twenty feet between each man. SP4 Victor Silvis went next with the M60; then SP4 McWhirter and his squad joined the file into the open.

The staccato reports of AK47s signalled the ambush.

McWhirter was instantly off the berm, splashing into the paddy, pressing into the dike. Everyone was down in the water and mud and, after the initial shock wore off enough for them to get their bearings, they shoved M16s over their helmets and fired back into the tree line facing them. Artillery impacted into the woods, but it had little effect on the entrenched North Vietnamese. It sounded like there was a company of them.

The firefight dragged on inconclusively all afternoon; the final act was spurred when the NVA shifted their mortar fire into the paddy. The order was given to pull back, and the company retreated in a frantic leapfrog. One man at a time jumped over the dike behind him and crawled to the next as others fired cover. Cobras screamed in. McWhirter was hunkered behind a dike with several others when he suddenly noticed movement in the tree line to his right. With ten months in-country and a Purple Heart to his name, this was the first time he'd really seen the enemy. They had pith helmets and web gear and AK47s, and they were up and moving through the trees, trying to outflank the withdrawing GIs.

McWhirter sighted his M16 on one figure moving behind the screen of trees; he squeezed the trigger, saw the man collapse. The GIs with him were firing too, shouting, spraying the trees. Silvis was hunched sweaty over his M60, firing, expended brass ejecting from his weapon.

The North Vietnamese fell back.

It was time for Delta Company to get out. The men crawled quickly on all fours, splattered with mud. A Hawaiian sergeant was near them, trying to push along with a bleeding leg. McWhirter was an unassuming, down-home kid who wanted to get back to his wife, but his buddies noted he was up front whenever the shooting started. In an unthinking lunge, McWhirter hefted the wounded sergeant over his shoulder and ran as fast as he could, aware of little else but the splashes of AK rounds hitting the brown paddy water. He jogged into the tree line behind the paddy, laid the sergeant down, then ran back to his squad. The last men were coming into the woods, running. One was limping; he was about fifty feet out and, again, McWhirter didn't think as he ran out and helped the grunt hop back into the cover of the trees.

The mortaring and firing petered out as soon as Delta Company disappeared back into the wood line. The retreat had become ragged at the end; weapons that casualties dropped lay where they fell, helmets and ammunition bandoliers sat in the mud.

The NVA recovered much of it—again.

Captain Sellers—slightly wounded by mortar shrapnel—was on the radio getting in the medevacs. As the first Huey settled onto the field behind them, the chilling crack-crack-crack of AK47 automatic rifles burst again. The grunts, hunkered among the trees, pumped fire back into the underbrush as the medevac pulled out of the sun-blasted paddy with the wounded crammed aboard.

Colonel Henry, hunched over his radios on Million Dollar Hill, proceeded with caution in what was his first, large action. He had five companies in the field, four of them in contact, and at the same time his Forward CP was taking sporadic automatic weapons and mortar fire. In the face of the crossfires of the entrenched NVA, Henry was consistently heavy on firepower and short on decisive, frontal assaults. During the course of the campaign, his battalion employed 18,224 artillery and mortar rounds, 191 tons of napalm and bombs, and 24,000 rounds of 20mm air cannons. When his companies couldn't outflank the NVA trenches, he called in his massive fire support. It kept the enemy's head down so his men could break contact with enough time to dig in for the night and to evacuate their casualties. On 25 August, his casualties were:

Bravo 2–1 with seventeen wounded.

Bravo 1–46 with twelve wounded.

Delta 1–46 with twenty wounded.

Charlie 4–31 with one wounded by friendly fire.

The combined companies claimed a body count of seventy-four NVA KIA, a figure which seemed exaggerated when compared to 2/7 Marines' count for the same day. The 2d Battalion, 7th Marines, engaged in heavy combat three kilometers to the east, had suffered thirteen Marines killed and sixty wounded, but the battalion log recorded no NVA deaths (some obviously had been killed, but no bodies had been recovered).

25 August had been a long day for the Marines also, their worst in the valley, and combat photographer Hodierne recounted one of their many problems:

The Army medevacs were flying Hueys, but the Marine missions were being flown by Sea Knights, a larger chopper that required a larger landing zone. And they didn't have enough choppers. Their operations tents were about 200 meters apart [probably at LZ Baldy]. The Army guys, who could monitor the Marine radios, regularly offered to fly missions for them. The Marines never accepted. Bad form to admit that the Marines couldn't handle it alone. And that meant wounded guys lay out in the field longer than they needed to. I remember one scene where the Army air ops guy just absolutely lost it, throwing things around, cursing, furious at the Marines. It was interservice rivalry at its worst.

The Army was very grateful to the Marines for their quick deployment to the valley; some were convinced that it saved 4–31 Infantry from being completely overrun. But all was not cozy. For example, two days later—the size of the NVA finally confirmed—another Marine battalion was helicoptered wholesale from LZ Baldy to LZ West. Almost immediately, the Marines began their hump down the mountainside with full packs. It was over 100 degrees and windless and Major Lee had suggested they leave their flak jackets on the LZ. His advice was ignored and, in short order, the Marines were clogging the medevac chain with dozens of sun victims. It was a common problem. Captain Downey—who admired the Marine Corps—noted, "I'll never forget the silly sight of a Marine unit on the march in full field gear as well as the old heavy flak jackets, having more men fall out as heat casualties then ever hurt by enemy fire. I'm sure even today there are some jackass officers somewhere who can deliver a ringing defense of the flak jacket policy. I doubt if any of them ever humped one in the Que Sons, though."

26 August. The grunts of Charlie Company, 4th Battalion, 31st Infantry saddled up with all the enthusiasm of survivors being sent back into the meatgrinder. After the original ambushing, they'd dug in around Million Dollar Hill. Nerves were still taut, and the men were filthy, unshaven, numbed from lack of sleep. They knew the NVA were still dug in and waiting; but with the loss of their original company commander, their leadership was untested and, thus, untrusted.

Capt John R. Thomas had been in command five days.

Capt Spencer Wolfe, liaison officer, 3–82 FA, was the FO, temporarily replacing Lieutenant Wilson, who'd been medevacked with immersion foot to LZ West on 21 August. Lieutenant Robinson, commanding the point platoon, was now on day four in the bush.

This was to be their first firefight.

As Charlie Company rucked up, Captain Thomas briefed Lieutenant Robinson. The gravity of the situation did not really click with Robinson until he showed his map to the Kit Carson Scout. Twenty exclaimed, "No go, beaucoup NVA!" It was advice, not a refusal. The grunts respected Twenty's experience, and his comment rattled them. When the squad leader picked a man to walk point, the GI said with resignation, "What are you trying to do, kill me?"

But the men followed orders, mostly because of SFC Marshall Robertson, the platoon cornerstone. He was a thin, white-haired veteran with a Virginia accent. He carried an AR15 Shorty, and was aggressive but calmly prudent. He was a thoroughly professional soldier, and most of the company just liked the hell out of him. He had been slotted for R and R but, with a new second lieutenant on hand, had postponed it.

Sergeant Robertson accompanied the rear squad of the platoon while Lieutenant Robinson went with the lead squad. Robinson was fifth man back from the point. The platoon filed atop a paddy berm paralleling a tree line to their left, approaching another tree line that intersected their path. The point man stepped onto the last dike before the trees.

An RPD machine gun abruptly knocked him down.

Lieutenant Robinson instantly dove to the right and scrambled forward to the next dike. He flopped beside the cover man. The RPD was in the trees ahead, joined by several AK47 and RPG gunners and an NVA with an M79 who lobbed rounds into the paddy. The sudden fusillade had fragmented the platoon. Robinson was flat behind a dike with fifteen men near him. The rest had taken cover in the tree line to the rear. The NVA barrage had petered out, firing only when a GI tried to raise up to return fire. The point man was face-down on the berm ahead, unmoving. He did not answer their shouts. Robinson wasn't sure what to do.

He saw Sergeant Robertson appear from a dike behind them. The paddy was wide open between them, but Robertson and the medic made a frantic dash across. Robertson huddled beside Robinson, heads below the dike, and started shouting to the M60 crew to keep the NVA down long enough to drag the point man back. Robertson bellowed out encouragement and direction, taking charge of the platoon. He rolled two feet to the right, just past the dike to get a better look, and waved from the prone, shouting, "Get the pig up here!" In the next second, the RPD levelled a burst into Sergeant Robertson. Pieces of skull and brains splattered onto Lieutenant Robinson and the grunt beside him.

The platoon saw it and froze.

No one tried to raise up to fire their M16s; instead, they fired M79 rounds and hurled frag grenades from behind the berm. Lieutenant Robinson threw several grenades, then took the handset from his RTO. Captain Thomas's calm voice crackled through; he said he had moved up with the reserve platoon and had linked up with Robinson's platoon, meaning those who'd ducked into the tree line.

"Listen," said Robinson, "you haven't really linked up with *us!*"

Robinson never trusted Thomas, considered him a ticket puncher who hung far to the rear of any action. That was not a unanimous opinion, but it explains Robinson's thoughts as Thomas began giving him orders straight from Fort Benning: get your people up and outflank that machine gun with fire and maneuver. Robinson was incredulous. If we raise our heads, we'll die, he thought. Why can't I make the captain understand what's going on! No one moved. Then the NVA did the logical thing, which was to mortar the fish in their barrel. Lieutenant Robinson screamed to pull back, as Cobras flashed in low, pumping rockets into the tree line. The grunts scooted back at each pass, dragging their wounded. They left their platoon sergeant and point man where they lay. Between gunship runs, the NVA RPD gunner fired across the paddy as other NVA moved into the trees on the left flank and took the retreating platoon under even more fire. They sighted their AK47s on the last berm the GIs had to vault to reach the trees.

A grunt clambered over and was nailed.

Robinson and two grunts tumbled over right on his heels. They grabbed the GI's arms to drag him into the bushes, and the two grunts beside Robinson were instantly shot down. The air was thick with an invisible swarm. Robinson rolled against the dike. His RTO lay there dead. He grabbed the handmike but it was out, the radio shot full of holes. The last man coming out, the squad leader, tried to clear the dike. He was dead before he hit the ground.

In seconds, five GIs had been killed.

Robinson crawled into the bushes, confused and frightened and sweat-soaked. The rest of the company was reorganizing among the trees, but the NVA followed them across the paddy and opened fire again. As the Cobras surged in—excited pilots shouting over the radio that the trees were swarming with dinks—Charlie Company shouldered their wounded. Then they ran, and they did not stop until they were well out of harm's way—in another tree line, where they fell in spiritless clumps. In Robinson's platoon, seven were dead, eleven were wounded, and four were in shock. Only fifteen of his men were unscathed, including himself, although his escape had been close: he discovered a bullet hole through the baggy side pocket of his jungle trousers. Twenty, the Kit Carson Scout, had shrapnel wounds.

After nine days of combat, the company mustered forty-eight men. The following day, they were pulled back to LZ West.

The action of 26 August continued.

Bravo 4th of the 31st Infantry was dispatched from its positions between Million Dollar Hill and Wedding Cake Hill; they lugged their recently delivered resupply, including unmanageable five-gallon, plastic water containers. The day was a scorcher and the load heavy. PFC Charles Jandecka, a week with the company and on his first combat operation, described it in irreverent terms:

B Company had been choppered to the outskirts of the Hiep Duc Province Center. From there, we trekked to a barren and flat hill to set up a day laager. I hastily erected a poncho liner shelter to seek relief from the blazing sun; others also erected shelters of liners, banana leaves or whatever. GI camps were easily recognizable to any gook within a reasonable distance. Either they could hear the tent stakes, bamboo or some other piece of vegetation, being pounded into the ground, or if they missed that racket, they had only to look for a spotty collection of poncho liners waving in the breeze. At this present camp, some of the shelters were placed along the side of the hill which made them virtually undefensible from incoming small arms fire that could have been brought to bear from a distant tree line. We stayed there overnight. As we were lolling about camp the next day, we heard the clatter of automatic weapons off to the east. Some company had made contact with a bunch of gooks. Within the hour they called for help so we left our day laager under the guard of a squad and set out for the yonder woods. We soon found them resting in a wooded area along a natural trench. To a man they were scared and thirsty. I recognized a black fellow I hadn't seen since AIT at Fort Dix. He spoke of his wife and children back home. Several weeks later I bumped into him back in the rear where he then had a rear job—a position he was rewarded for reupping.

These battered grunts were Delta 1st of the 46th Infantry, which had pulled back to the ditches along the trail after being ambushed the day before. They were pinned down by snipers and had quickly run out of water. Bravo Company reached them around noon; Captain Gayler moved up the trail until he found Captain Sellers, but was unhappy that the commander seemed as bewildered and fatigued as his men in the ditches. As for himself, Gayler was a confident man and—after a week of rest on Siberia—he at least looked the part of the professional company commander. His hair was close-cropped under his helmet, and he was a handsome man with a full mustache and some bush-time whiskers. He wore leather gun gloves, carried an AR15 automatic rifle, and two bandoliers of magazines were held in place across his chest by the snaps on his web gear shoulder straps. Captain bars and armor insignia were stitched in black on his collar; the Americal patch was on his shoulder.

Gayler's first question to Sellers was, "Where are your security elements? I'll relieve your security elements on your front, right, and left."

All he got was a blank stare.

Gayler quickly moved aside with his RTO, and radioed Lieutenant Monroe to get out security posthaste. Monroe moved one squad to the front while the other two platoons took up the right and left flanks off the pathway. The NVA still held the hill ahead—from where they had originally halted Delta Company—and they responded to the new movement by casually lobbing in a few mortar rounds.

Bravo Company lost one man killed, five wounded.

Delta secured an LZ for the medevac, and other helicopters brought in more resupply. By that time, Bravo had taken over the area and policed up some of the gear Delta had left behind in the open space between the tree grove and the enemy hill; it included more than a few ammunition bandoliers, a PRC25 radio, an M60 machine gun, and five M16 rifles. Noting, in addition, that Delta had not deployed adequate security, Captain Gayler radioed Colonel Henry that the company was no longer battle-effective due to fatigue or morale problems and should be withdrawn.

Gayler had just arrived on the scene, so perhaps his negative observations were not completely justified. Nevertheless, later in the afternoon, Delta Company was ordered out of the area; they humped back to Hiep Duc where Maj Lawrence Remener, S-3, 1–46 Infantry, had been dispatched to handle village security. Meanwhile, B/1–46 moved up to reinforce B/4–31, which moved to a new position—hopefully, one the

NVA had not registered their mortars on—before setting up for the night (within days, B and D/1–46 were airlifted back to LZ Professional where Captains King and Sellers, like almost all company commanders in this battle, were immediately awarded Silver Stars).

The day had been a series of snafus, at least for Private Jandecka. Bravo Company had handed over their resupply to the more depleted grunts of Delta Company, which was proper, except that Jandecka was hungry too. He managed to scrounge up a can of ham and eggs, not a charlie rat favorite. The next day, 27 August, was not much better as he moved along with a growling stomach. Bravo's rucksacks, which had been left near Million Dollar Hill, were choppered in and dumped helter-skelter in the brush. GIs rummaged through them, most unable to find their own and forced to take one at random. That was a real blow to morale. Jandecka, for one, took a pack with the necessary military gear, but in turn lost his letters, camera, film, New Testament, harmonica, sunglasses, notebook, extra food, and Kool Aid.

The rest of the afternoon was spent quietly humping to a new position near the Old French Road. Battalion was realigning its companies for what they hoped would be a final push to the Marine side of the line at dawn. The grunts knew as much about these plans as pawns on a chess board. They did not know why they were sweating from one chunk of elephant grass to the next; they just did what the platoon sergeant said and hoped no North Vietnamese would materialize en route. During the early evening, one of their perimeter trip flares went off and Captain Gayler bellowed to put the damn thing out before the dinks pinpointed their position. Three men quickly scrambled to it—Jandecka the only one quick enough to pick up an M16 first—and they used a helmet to smother it. Actually, their fall extinguished the light: in the blinding, white glare, they all fell over the road embankment, the helmet and flare bouncing with them. They scrambled back to their lines but, Jandecka noted, "it was a couple hours before I could shake that unmistakable feeling of being watched by an unknown set of eyes as we were at the bottom of that bank."

Chapter Fifteen
The Lost Battalion

The dawn of 25 August 1969 spread across the paddies with all the serenity of the inside of a steel mill. Lieutenant Larrison of Golf Company and Lieutenant Vannoy of Hotel Company, 2d Battalion, 7th Marines, brought Phantoms and artillery fire into the tree lines in front of their perimeter.

The battalion was preparing to push west.

Hotel Company, on the right flank, moved out first. They'd been detailed to run a squad recon up the southern slope of Hill 381. Considering the events of the past two days, Lieutenant Vannoy thought two platoons would be safer; Colonel Lugger approved the modification. Lieutenant Vannoy and his command group stayed in place with 2d Platoon while 1st Platoon (1stLt Charles Vallance) moved out on the right flank and 3d Platoon (2dLt William Brennon) moved out on the left. Farther to the left, Lieutenant Larrison of Golf was still bringing the firepower down on the tree lines facing them.

A senior officer cut into the net: "Golf Six, do you realize you're holding up two infantry companies!" Brennon was stunned. Don't they realize what's down here? he wondered.

The situation got worse. Hotel One and Hotel Three began advancing after the airstrikes were stopped, filtering into the trees on the northern half of the battered wood line. A Sea Knight descended behind them, either on a resupply or medevac run, and a 12.7mm machine gun opened fire from the southern half of the tree line they occupied. Brennon could see Vallance and his platoon sergeant moving on his right, and he shouted to them, "I ain't believin' this!" They shook their heads back as if to say, yes, this is suicide.

The two platoons emerged from the trees into rice paddies that stretched two hundred yards across and five hundred yards to the next tree line. It was a little rice bowl right at the base of Hill 381, and jungled fingers rippled through the area and across the platoons' front. Vallance's platoon advanced through napalmed elephant grass at the base of the ridge line into the paddies themselves. They were rough to negotiate—overgrown and terraced, dotted with wild brush and boulders. Point men and flank men were out. Vallance was only a quarter way into the field when Brennon reached the halfway mark. They too were spaced out, ten men in the lead:

Point man
M79 grenadier
Rifleman
Squad leader
Brennon, his radioman and corpsman
M60 team

The North Vietnamese ambushed them halfway into the open paddy, the first burst a jolting thunderclap of at least five AK47s, five RPGs, an RPD, and two 60mm mortar rounds. The M79 man was killed instantly. The corpsman was seriously wounded with shrapnel in his back. The M60 team quickly started returning fire, but the gunner was shot dead and his two assistant gunners passed out with shock or heat exhaustion. The rest of the platoon quickly took up positions behind them; under the direction of the platoon sergeant—who'd been wounded in the sudden fusillade—they sounded like a small army. The point man, rifleman, and squad leader managed to crawl back under the cover fire; together with Lieutenant Brennon, his radioman, and the wounded corpsman, they crammed behind a boulder in the field.

They were completely pinned down. It was 1300.

On the right flank, Lieutenant Vallance had also ducked behind a boulder at the initial shots. But his platoon was out of the most blistering part of the crossfire and he was able to get his bearings more quickly. The NVA, about a platoon of them, were firing from the bouldered slope of Hill 381 up ahead, and from the tree lines on the left flank. More NVA were popping up from behind, in the tree line through which they had just walked. Fire seemed to snap at the Marines from every direction. The NVA were invisible in the vegetation, solidly emplaced with spider holes and trenches. Vallance's men could make out only one muzzle flash and, although they exposed themselves to put M60 and M79 fire into it, it was impossible to tell if they did any damage.

Vallance had men pinned down behind boulders ahead. When they tried to crawl back, rounds chopped the grass above their heads. When the platoon fired to cover them, the NVA rained down AKs and RPGs. But when the Marines stopped shooting and stopped moving, the NVA were content to cease fire and just watch.

Fish in a barrel, fucking fish in a barrel.

Lieutenant Vannoy moved forward with 2d Platoon, and radioed Brennon and Vallance to stay put. Air support had been scrambled again. Brennon, still stuck behind his boulder, got in radio contact with the aerial observer orbiting the battlefield. The Phantoms laid napalm plus 250- and 500-pound bombs, first into the trees 150 meters forward, then—at Brennon's insistence—the reluctant AO brought the fires in 75 meters closer. Brennon and his five grunts crammed tightly against the boulder as shrapnel chunks whizzed overhead.

Vallance, farther away from ground zero, was able to keep his head up. He could see tracers snapping skyward from the jungle canopy even as the Phantoms screamed right at them, letting loose their napalm and bombs. The grunts could see the tracers, too, and their spirits sank even lower. They were sewed up, the air strikes weren't doing much, and the NVA even had the guts to take on jets.

Bullets cracked over their heads and from the rear.

The Phantoms ran eight or nine missions; then Cobras made two more gun runs. The NVA fire slackened a bit, and Brennon told two men to crawl forward and drag back the dead M79 man. It was thirty meters from the boulder to the body, and the two grunts went the entire way on their stomachs, tucked in tightly along a dike, NVA fire nipping overhead. They reached the body, but the dead Marine was a big man— more than two hundred pounds plus all his gear—and they'd have to at least rise to their knees to drag him. They crawled back to Brennon and told him it was impossible.

By then it was 1700.

Before the ambush was sprung on Hotel Company, Golf Company had also been moving west. Lieutenant Larrison was proceeding with extreme caution: he had the platoons of Lieutenants Page and Pickett raise a shattering cacophony of cover fire as 3d Platoon rushed the first tree line facing them. They secured it without contact, and the rest of the company swept in. They prepared to repeat the process on the next wood line facing them.

Then Hotel was hit and Golf was sent in.

Urgency dampened caution as they moved to their right, filing along a stand of trees. The point man was three feet from the first spider hole before the NVA signalled his presence by emptying his AK47. He killed the point man instantly and wounded the next man in line. The wounded Marine squeezed flat behind his dead buddy as a crossfire suddenly electrified the air above him, but he kept his head. He reached over the body to set in his claymore mine, then unreeled the firing wire as he scooted back. When the NVA raised from his hole to fire a fresh magazine, the grunt detonated the claymore. Its one-pound charge of C4 plastic explosive sent out six hundred steel balls like a shotgun blast. Man and brush were shredded.

A squad of entrenched NVA were still firing from the trees, and Lieutenant Page and his radioman ran towards the pinned-down grunts. They made it through a hundred yards of paddy before they too had to hit the deck. Lieutenant Larrison moved his other two platoons into position to provide cover fire; the Marines saw no one to line up in rifle sights, but any suspected firing position was battered with M79 grenades and teargas. The NVA fire did not lessen; Hotel was screaming on the radio that Golf's stray fire was hitting around them. Golf was screaming the same thing back. It was boiling chaos.

Two North Vietnamese soldiers materialized in one of the tree lines and the Marines—almost dead from the heat in the open paddy—poured fire at them. The NVA appeared to go down in the hail of rounds. Or did they only duck into their trenches? The tree lines were honeycombed with slit trenches and spider holes, and the NVA moved along them—below the Marine rifle fire—until they were firing on Golf Company from three sides. The firefight had lasted two hours, and Lieutenant Larrison finally ordered everyone back. They were forced to leave their dead point man.

Hotel Company was still pinned down.

Meanwhile, Colonel Lugger was glued to his radios; his command post was in a tree grove on the northern bank of the Song Lau River, near a crumbling, concrete pagoda which sat incongruously in the high weeds. Lugger had yet to get G and H Companies out of harm's way when F Company—which was providing CP security—was ordered on another mission. Colonel Codispoti (operating from his Forward CP in the 4–31 TOC on LZ West) wanted one platoon from Fox to conduct a reconnaissance a kilometer-and-a-half to the west. The mission was to link up physically with Task Force 4–31, a goal which Lugger could not understand. It seemed to play into the hands of the enemy. There were officers who thought he should have quietly ignored the directive from a distant headquarters. But Lugger did not have the advantage of hindsight, nor was he aware of the tactical situation on the Army side of the line.

So the Fox platoon advanced as ordered. They had gone a thousand yards when a sudden ring of mortar, rocket-propelled grenade, and automatic weapons fire slammed down around them, inflicting heavy casualties.

1st Platoon was surrounded.

At the same time, the 2/7 CP came under heavy fire from an estimated seventy-five NVA just across the Song Lau. Fifty meters separated Marines and North Vietnamese, and Lugger and crew hugged earth as RPGs and AK47s screamed in. Mortars began whistling down on their postage-stamp perimeter. Battalion staff officers and radiomen shouldered M16s and returned fire while Lugger worked his radios, trying to control four fights at one time.

Lieutenant Ehrsam, CO, F/2/7, was a former enlisted man with a handlebar mustache and a fighter's nature. As soon as 1st Platoon was encircled, he ordered 3d Platoon to break through and bring them back. They moved out along the northern bank of the stream.

They too were ambushed.

RPD machine guns, dug in on the opposite bank, signalled the killing. The fusillade was unexpected so close to their lines, and the Marines in the lead fell dead in the shattered elephant grass. AKs joined the RPDs. Everyone tried to hide in the grass. There was no real cover if they were spotted. From behind the immediate crossfire, Lance Corporal Parr pushed forward through the razor-sharp grass with Cpl George Stickman's fire team. They could see a machine gun position across the stream or, at least, the muzzle flash and smoke when it fired. Parr lay flat, pumping his M16 at it. His buddy, PFC Eddie Grusczynski, unstrapped a LAW and pulled out the safeties. He sat up in the tall grass—the LAW on his shoulder—and was instantly shot. Stickman yelled. He rolled through the grass to Ski's body and tugged the rocket from his frozen fingers. He quickly rolled back to his original position, then bobbed up for a quick moment, the LAW flashing from over his shoulder, back-blast whipping the brush, the warhead screaming to impact. The

RPD kept firing, and Stickman flung two grenades across the stream. The NVA machine gun was suddenly silent.

PFC Charles W. Norton was in the part of the platoon line farthest from the river, but when the ambush started, he ran towards his pinned-down buddies. You couldn't even hear shouts over the din of automatic weapons fire; Norton thought they were going to be overrun any second. He ducked from tree to tree, lobbing M79 rounds in the direction of the AK47 fire, then he finally bellied up to a low dike. The platoon's new lieutenant—who would be seen crying with frustration and grief that night—was pressed behind the berm with several men. Norton continued forward on his stomach through the elephant grass. The enemy fire had tapered off, but rounds still nipped overhead. He wasn't wearing his flak jacket, but he had his helmet on. He crawled up to Ski. Ski was the most popular guy in the platoon—probably because he was so naive and bookwormish—and Norton grabbed him to pull him back. Ski's head flopped. There was a blue bruise the size of a silver dollar at his temple, a bullet hole in the center of it. KIA. Herbie Heintz lay nearby and Norton reached out and shook his boot. No response. KIA.

Robert Ryan was still alive. He'd taken a round in the shoulder joint in the first burst—his arm just hung there—and he lay exhausted in the grass, propped up by the radio strapped to his back. Norton edged back to him. So did Stickman. They got the radio off and started pulling him back. Norton was on his stomach, Stickman on his back, and they both had a grip on Ryan's belt, tugging, pushing with their feet against the sunbaked ground. Norton suddenly felt something snap past his wrist. A round punched through Ryan's lungs and slammed into Stickman's leg.

Ryan belched pink blood. KIA.

Parr scrambled over and helped Norton and Stickman drag Ryan's body over a one-foot dike. A grunt named Danny Shields was there, but the rest of the platoon was along a seven-foot embankment to their rear. One of the Marines scrambled down to help drag the casualties up; a sniper nailed him in the legs as he ran.

Marine Air finally rolled in. The four survivors behind the tiny dike tossed smoke grenades, then hugged earth. Norton looked up—right at a Phantom screaming in off the deck, releasing its napalm canister behind them, the silver canister tumbling past and exploding dead ahead. Wump! The snap sucked the air from his lungs, singed the hair on his arms. Bombs were dropped and the concussion bounced him off the ground. He was terrified. He knew he was going to die. But the pilots knew what they were doing, and when they were finished only an occasional sniper round cracked at the knot of Marines behind that dike.

Norton blasted back with his grenade launcher, even as dirt kicked up at the impact of incoming bullets. He'd fire, roll to a new position along the dike, drop another round in the M79, pop up to fire again. He carried about sixty rounds and had fired half when the firing pin was jarred loose and fell out. He tossed down the M79. His holster was empty—he'd lost his .45 pistol somewhere when he was crawling—and he picked up an M16 rifle laying in the dirt.

It was over 100 degrees and he could barely move.

But Norton kept firing. He was raising up with the M16 to fire another burst from the same spot when an AK47 round hit the front of his helmet. The steel pot was blown off and he bounced back, unconscious, blood running from his nose and right ear. Norton awakened only very dimly. When they finally made a break for the high embankment, he didn't know who dragged him to safety.

As 3d Platoon made its ill-fated rush towards 1st Platoon, the rest of Fox Company shouldered their gear and followed closely behind. PFC Lorne J. Collinson, of the company mortar squad, jogged blindly through the elephant grass. There were empty spider holes in the vegetation. The noise ahead was incredible. Collinson suddenly heard a sharp whiz in the air and instinctively threw himself to the ground.

A ragged chunk of made-in-the-USA shrapnel thudded into the dirt behind him. He was instantly back on his feet and moving towards the fire.

Corporal Bass, chief of the 60mm mortar section, was setting up his tubes in a small clearing. Collinson jogged over, dumped his mortar rounds from his pack, then ran to their hasty perimeter. He and his best friend, Ron McCoy, were about the only security the mortars had out there. The rest of the squad set up the two tubes, prepared the ammunition, then waited for firing directions. None came out of the chaos ahead.

A lieutenant appeared from the brush, jogging back with a wounded man leaning against him. The man's trouser leg was stained red.

The lieutenant was shouting to get the casualties back.

Collinson left his pack with McCoy, started running forward, and in short order was forced to low-crawl through the grass as AK rounds whizzed past. He bellied up to the embankment where 3d Platoon had been pushed. Marines were spread along it, firing toward the stream. One grunt lay behind the dike as if asleep. But there was a hole in the back of his flak jacket and Collinson hefted the body into a fireman's hold and took off for all he was worth. He made it back to the trees around the command post. It was a semicontrolled madhouse. Radiomen shouted into handsets, calling for more air, more arty, trying to maintain contact with the pinned-down platoons. Officers and radiomen were clustered near the dilapidated pagoda, a short, older man gesturing instructions and mouthing words that were lost to Collinson in the din. The air was clogged with the whine of jets. Corpsmen rushed among the wounded being dragged in. They had a dozen KIAs and WIAs in a row and Collinson laid his man with them, numbly noticing that blood was smeared on his T-shirt where his flak jacket hung unzipped.

He took off again. Corporal Bass shouted at him as he ran past the trees, "Get your ass back here! Your job's with the mortars!"

"Yeah, I know, but the lieutenant said to help with the wounded!"

LCpl Craig Russel, a battalion sniper, found himself belly down in the high elephant grass. Right across the blue line, NVA were screaming fire over his head. He pumped his M14 into the brush, firing frantically and blindly like everyone around him, then popped up to fling a frag at a muzzle flash. The grenade was tossed right back at him from within the tangle and exploded in midair.

That was right outside the 2/7 CP.

In the middle of the fire, a U.S. Army Huey pilot came on their radio. He was responding to their requests for ammunition, "I'm coming in. Pop a smoke, and get this shit off my bird!"

The helicopter barrelled into a bare patch behind the platoon. Corpsmen had a couple of the seriously wounded ready to go, and they rushed them to the LZ as Marines raked the opposite shore with cover fire. Russell sprinted towards the chopper. He could hear rounds cracking past, some impacting metal against metal, and the door gunner couldn't fire his M60. He could just scream to hurry as Marines hauled off ammo cans, LAWs, a case of grenades, shoved the wounded aboard, then ran for cover as the Huey roared out in a blast of dust.

By the time Fox Company straggled back—unable to reach their lost platoon and forced to leave behind some of those killed in the attempt—the fight along the river had subsided to a cat 'n' mouse.

Among others, Collinson and McCoy took up positions on the slope of the streambed. An AK would chop brush in their direction; they'd trigger a return burst, firing blind into the muggy heat, then duck back behind their trees, change magazines, and wait for the next shot. At one point, McCoy cranked off a hurried burst, then shouted he'd seen an NVA darting from one tree to another. He thought he nailed him. Behind them, up the creek-bed slope, other Marines were firing. A LAW flashed across the stream and was instantly answered by an RPG which exploded inside the lines.

Collinson could hear shouts for a corpsman.

The jets came in again. Collinson must have subconsciously heard their supersonic approach, because he happened to glance up just in time to see a silver napalm canister wobbling down. It seemed to be headed for the middle of the stream, and he bolted from his tree, scrambling up the bank. The sudden heat wave enveloped him, seeming to singe the hair on his face and arms, leaving him breathless. He threw himself behind a tree as a second Phantom rolled in low, splashing more nape among the trees across the thin stream. The air reeked with gasoline and smoke.

The NVA snipers were finally silent.

■ Air support—the Phantoms guiding down the Song Lau and expertly placing their ordnance within fifty meters of the battalion perimeter, close enough for expended 20mm shells to hit the grunts' helmets—is what finally quieted the firing on the command post. Lieutenant Colonel Lugger grabbed a LAW in frustration and strode to an opening in the trees. He aimed at a hootch several hundred meters away. The LAW misfired, so he threw it down and picked up another rocket. It roared off across the paddies.

Lugger had not seen a single NVA soldier, nor could he tell if he even hit the hootch—a combination which seemed symbolic of the entire battle.

Colonel Lugger was simply boiling.

He had made staff sergeant before earning his commission and had volunteered for combat duty in Vietnam, but this battle—his first—was a mess. Lugger thought he was doing as well as any commander could, considering the circumstances, and he was bitter towards his detractors, who were many:

I was up to my ass in alligators with no help from above, and little or no help from below. I was trying to keep together and coordinate what few forces I had left while fighting an escalating battle on four or more fronts against an overwhelmingly superior enemy. An enemy who knew the area like the back of his hand and had prepared positions for years waiting just for this opportunity. Why do you think the Army avoided this area? I had no say in what missions I was assigned after the first three days. Codispoti was commanding my battalion—from a distance. His missions completely fragmented 2/7, sending its units off on wild goose chases to be ambushed by a waiting enemy. Simpson and Codispoti left 2/7 out there because they did not know what to do, or would not admit that they made a mistake in ordering one undersized battalion to get so entangled. Damn it, why didn't they give me some help, or relieve me of command on the spot? Based upon what he wrote about me, Codispoti should have taken over command on the spot from his incompetent subordinate.

The roots of disaster ran deeply, not only in the clashes at command level, but in the character of the battalion itself. The recent history of 2/7 had been a harsh one. They saw heavy combat around Da Nang during Tet 1969, and from that time until they came off Operation Oklahoma Hills, 2/7 had been the division's special landing force. They were sometimes rushed from one hot spot to another so quickly that they didn't get maps of the new AO until well after they were in the bush. When Lugger took over at the end of April, the lieutenant colonel he was replacing looked drained.

The 2/7 Marines had relocated to Dai La Pass; there they worked with the 26th Marines in the Da Nang Rocket Belt to stem infiltration towards the city and the ridge line housing division headquarters. This was the other type of extreme; it was a quiet time, the battalion was stationary—thus, stagnant—and it was only a ten-minute drive to notorious Dog Patch. The more Lugger looked, the less he liked what he saw. The previous hectic pace of operations had left 2/7 in an administrative shambles, and he had to have his CP reorganized and physically cleaned up. He also had to have the drifters rounded up. Dog Patch offered plenty of diversions, from prostitution to a flourishing black market and drug trade, plus Division Ridge had the Freedom Hill PX and other assorted service clubs. It was a real struggle for Lugger to sort out all the Marines wandering around his CP who had no real jobs and get their asses back in the grass.

The battalion's line companies were spread out in independent, wire-enclosed perimeters, running routine patrols and ambushes in the local villes. Virtually all the company commanders and platoon leaders were young lieutenants. Isolated as they were, as far as Lugger could discern, on little hillocks for what became months on end, most fought the war according to their personal interpretation. This meant a certain number were looking for no trouble. That mood trickled down to the grunts. There were some men any unit would have been proud to claim, and a few wild men who took ears from their kills and prodded villagers in front of them during minesweeps. But most were just counting the days until they could get out of the Nam and the Crotch. They were stale and unenthusiastic, fighting a war of "surprise firing devices"—booby traps—in the mind set of withdrawal.

There was another reason for Lugger's bitterness. One of the men's jobs was security for Division Ridge, where the living was quite comfortable. Only a few hundred meters away, the grunts were sweating out night ambushes.

Lugger sensed that his orders were often sandbagged.

He repeatedly requested regiment and division to send his battalion on a defined combat operation. That would have increased casualties, but it made sense. The average Marine in a dangerous situation, where his skills must be sharp and where buddies are depending on him, can be a warrior. That same Marine, when hot, bored, and idle, when exposed constantly to the corruptions of the rear, can respond with the restless immaturity of most nineteen year olds.

So it was in 2/7 Marines. The most volatile problem was race relations. If the blacks' anger could be honed down to one immediate concern, it was that they were being used as cannon fodder in a war that was of no concern to them.

PFC Norton had originally served in the Fox Company mortar squad; he gave up that skating job and volunteered for one of the company's rifle platoons because the racial situation at battalion rear was intolerable. As far as Norton was concerned, the white corporal was the leader only on paper. He had finally acquiesced to the black bullies in the mortar squad; and their only aim was to "get over."

Maj Jim Steele, operations officer at Dai La and one of the most respected officers in the battalion, commented on one of the racial outbursts:

It was just before 2300 and there were rifle shots fired within the camp. I called the CP Security Officer to see if sappers were inside the wire with us. I was advised that the shots had been fired by one of our people—a black soldier—at his platoon sergeant but that he had missed. Shortly after I heard more shots. The next report said that the man was shooting at lights and cans in the company billeting area. This had been going on for approximately thirty minutes so I went down to the company area to see why they hadn't stopped the guy. As I approached the tent area the only Marines I saw were on the ground hiding behind the two-foot high sandbag walls that honeycombed the area. As I approached, voices yelled at me to get down. "He's still shooting," they called as if powerless to do anything. I asked if anyone had been shot. The answer was that no one knew. I really exploded; I told them that if someone might be on the deck needing medical attention while they were all hiding this would be the most sickening spectacle I had ever seen. I moved in the direction they had indicated until I found the guy. He was standing between two rows of tents still holding the rifle, talking to two other blacks. I walked up and the other two became highly agitated and told me to get back because the guy hated honkies and might shoot me. I couldn't believe my ears! I told the shooter I was counting to three and if he hadn't dropped the rifle, I was going to blow half of his guts out of his back with my .45. I assumed the classic movie gunfighter stance; I counted to two and the turd suddenly came back to reality and dropped the rifle just in time.

These were not isolated incidents, and Private Norton, an eighteen-year-old country boy, finally volunteered for the grunts. Out there, they needed each other to survive; hatred was pushed below the surface. Some men forgot it altogether.

In the bush, they were a team.

A marijuana subculture also existed in the battalion; it was a fixture among the support personnel, something which affected the rifle companies whenever they came to rehab at Dai La. It was the race problem or the drug problem which resulted in a fragging on Lugger's eleventh day in command. At 0200, an unknown person or persons tossed two fragmentation grenades under a raised hootch used by officers and staff NCOs of H Company. One grenade was a dud, but the other exploded through the plywood floorboard, wounding a captain, first sergeant, and gunnery sergeant, and killing a staff sergeant under whose cot the grenade went off. From what could be pieced together, the first sergeant—a hard-core lifer who liked to ream out grunts for being unshaven the minute they came in the camp gate from patrol—had been the intended victim. The staff sergeant was an innocent bystander.

The 2/7 Marines had one of the highest crime rates in the division.

Colonel Lugger had indeed inherited a mess, and he busted his ass trying to pump up morale, decipher the troops' discontent, and punish those who refused to reform. His methods would never have won him a popularity contest; he never had a positive word for anyone, only red-faced screaming over the problems he found.

Lugger thought things were improving slowly. Perhaps they were. Others thought the mutiny had only been shoved beneath the surface. There was talk of military justice being meted out by throwing Marines in barbed wire cages or beating them with rifle butts. "The steps Lugger took to help morale just didn't work," said a staff officer. "He used strictness to the point of harassment. This was applied arbitrarily in such a manner as to appear irrational. The troops responded by retaliation. There was a reward on him before we ever went to LZ Ross."

If any one man ould take credit for being the battalion's rock as it sat rotting on the Da Nang line, it was Major Steele, who was on his third tour. Unfortunately for all concerned, Steele was rotated to the Division Surveillance Reconnaissance Center the day 2/7 trucked into LZ Baldy.

The battalion was not a cohesive fighting force.

The men had sat stagnant too long. Too many of their officers were brand new, and too many were considered "crap" by the enlisted men. LZ Baldy was their first real operation in months, and the Hiep Duc Valley was no place to clean off the rust they'd accumulated. They were not prepared for the hornets' nest they'd walked into and, despite the heroism of many of the players, all in all, the battalion was getting its ass kicked. There was no maneuvering, for no matter in which direction a unit moved, it was pinned down. Each platoon of each company—and sometimes each individual—was literally on its own.

1stLt Lloyd L. Lindsey, Battalion Intelligence officer, summed it up when he said they fought the entire battle in a state of shock.

■ At 1800 on 25 August, Lieutenant Vannoy radioed Lieutenant Brennon to pull out of the paddy. It was getting dark and the Phantoms were coming in one more time to cover their retreat. Lieutenant Vallance's platoon on the right flank would also be firing cover, then coming out after them.

The men crawled away from the protection of the boulder one at a time, and the NVA on the high ground opened fire with a renewed fury. The point man and rifleman went first, then the wounded corpsman, the squad leader, and finally Brennon and his radioman. They rolled over the first dike under heavy fire, then crawled through a wet paddy to the next dike. The point man jumped quickly over it, then reached back to help the rifleman hoist the seriously wounded corpsman over the berm.

In seconds, NVA snipers killed the first three men.

They collapsed in the mud, shot through their heads and throats. Brennon, his radioman, and the squad leader crawled back to the cover of the boulder. They crouched, exhausted and dirty, and called in more air strikes. The Phantoms came in low and put their ordnance right on the NVA, but it didn't stop their fire. In the bushes to their left, only fifty meters away, they could hear men moving towards their rear. The NVA were trying to surround them in the dark. Brennon had only two men with him. They'd used M16s, M60s, M79s, Cobras, Phantoms. Well, he thought with a combination of irony and terror, I'm all out of tricks.

There was, however, one more ploy. Brennon radioed the jet pilots to scream in as low as possible, but not drop any bombs. Hopefully, the NVA would duck long enough for the three Marines to jump a dike at each pass. It was slow and scary and some of the snipers continued fighting—one shot the magazine right out of Brennon's M16.

When the last Phantom made its last pass, the pilot radioed Brennon, "Hey, buddy, today it looks like you're just SOL." Shit Outta Luck.

But the maneuver worked; once out of the worst of the crossfire, the three grunts low-crawled the last hundred yards along the dikes into the sanctuary of the tree line behind them that had been secured by the CP and 2d Platoon. They lost the platoon leader lieutenant in the process; he took a bullet in his shoulder. Lieutenant Vallance and his platoon were able to pull back without drawing a shot. Perhaps it was getting too dark for the NVA to see them.

The fight had lasted more than eight hours. Five dead men were left in the field; one man was missing. In Hotel Company, both ammunition and spirits were very low.

The men headed back to link up with Golf Company.

Golf had also pulled back with a dead point man left lying in the dirt. They'd finally consolidated on the main trail and secured the area for Hotel's withdrawal. While they were waiting, there was movement in the roadside brush, then a shout for help. Golf Two's corpsman was about to run towards the call, but Staff Sergeant Clements stopped him, "No, stop doc. Think a minute. Might be some turncoats out there." Clements shouted for the men to show themselves. Two grunts stumbled onto the trail, one shot in the leg and leaning against his buddy. They were pissed. "Those sonsuvbitches! They run off and left us!" The doc bandaged the man's leg in an abandoned hootch, then directed them down the road to where the Golf CP was set up in another dilapidated hootch. It was doubtful that the two Marines were actually left behind. It was more probable that they were separated in the confusing night move, because the main body of Hotel did not pass through Golf for another thirty minutes. The company filed past in the dark, casualties carried in sagging ponchos between bent figures.

At least one thing went right on 25 August: at two hours before midnight, while Cobras buzz-sawed around their ragged perimeter, Sea Knights touched down with Fox Company's surrounded platoon. The survivors, almost out of ammunition, quickly dragged their dead and wounded aboard (leaving only one dead man behind in the darkness); the helos departed with lights off before the NVA could coordinate their fires.

The rest of Fox was still on the firing line.

Lorne Collinson and Ron McCoy were dug into a two-man hole on the battalion perimeter. A hedgerow ran across their front and the ground fell away to the stream. The Battalion CP was behind them in the trees, across a paddy which seemed especially open and wide in the dark. Other Marines were dug in at ten-meter intervals down the line. Collinson and McCoy had their M16 rifles resting on the edge of the hole, ammo magazines and frags spread out within easy reach, knives stuck into the dirt before them.

They were sure they would be overrun.

Collinson was twenty years old; he was a Canadian immigrant who believed very strongly in the Marine Corps and the Vietnam War. McCoy was a rich kid who gave the impression he'd signed up on a lark, and was enjoying the hell out of the experience.

But that night, none of that mattered. It was obvious that the NVA had enough men to attempt an assault, which is exactly what Collinson thought they were going to do—with him sitting in a little hole in the front row. McCoy felt it too and mumbled, ''We're not going to see the sun again.'' In the dark they exchanged glances which did not need words: we're dead so forget it and just kill as many of them as you can when they come through that hedgerow. Their whispered conversation drifted to other things. Collinson was surprised at their calm. The situation was beyond their control, so they might as well just relax.

Chapter Sixteen
Sitting Ducks

Only hours before Echo Company was alerted to move into Hiep Duc, 2dLt William Schuler of 1st Platoon was sitting on their hilltop, watching a Sea Knight trying to land in the river valley. He counted tracers from six 12.7mm positions snapping up at it. Schuler's platoon was north in the LZ Ross AO, picking through the back door of the NVA battalions fighting in the valley. Their order to airlift into Hiep Duc was abrupt.

The company choppered in at dusk, landing a bit east of the 2/7 CP to avoid the antiaircraft guns. As Lieutenant Schuler and his platoon humped towards the battalion perimeter, Lieutenant Lindsey of Battalion Intelligence met them and led them in. Schuler liked Lindsey—an easygoing, humorous guy who'd spent seven months as a platoon leader. Now, though, his voice was edged with fear. He described the events of the day, and said Echo Company had been rushed in because Intelligence was afraid the CP might be overrun during the night.

Schuler had never seen Lindsey rattled before.

As for himself, Lieutenant Schuler had five months in-country; he had killed two men and been recommended for a Silver Star. He was a stocky, pugnacious man, at twenty-two the oldest in his platoon. He had an unauthorized red handlebar mustache, toted an M79 grenade launcher, and was not hesitant to sandbag "unwise" patrols radioed from above. He did not court-martial his men; if someone faked heat exhaustion or was caught sleeping on guard, he allowed the platoon sergeant and squad leader to take care of whatever punishment was required. Schuler thought he did a damn good job and his grunts agreed.

He fit in well with the other officers of Echo Company; they led their grunts through comradeship, not by hard-assing them, and all took their turn on point. Like most of the men, however, although Schuler was proud to be a Marine and proud of the unlettered but gutsy kids in his platoon, he was not particularly motivated by the Vietnam cause.

Schuler had enlisted because the other alternatives his privileged upbringing allowed he saw to be ignoble. He wanted to do his duty, but he had no career intentions. At Basic School, most of the new lieutenants shared his outlook. They became known as the Zoo Platoon because of their unruliness; he lost count of how many times men answered the platoon leader with, "What are you going to do if I don't clean my room? Shave my head and send me to Vietnam?"

Schuler did not lose count, though, of those men who became casualties in their very personal, forgotten war. During the flight into Da Nang with two Basic School classmates destined for the 5th Marines, they joked that, statistically, one would be killed, one wounded, and one would rotate home unscathed. As it turned out, Schuler, who took a blast of shrapnel in the face, was luckiest. Ted, one of the few professionals and a compassionate man, took an RPG in the head in the Arizona. Ken, who also led a platoon in the Arizona, was the one who didn't make the casualty list. Mental wounds weren't tabulated. One friend dead, the other an alcoholic; each name was like a drop of acid in the face of withdrawals. One of Schuler's instructors at PLC, Karl Taylor, was killed charging a machine gun bunker on Go Noi Island. The honor man of his PLC platoon, Bobby Muller, was shot through the chest and paralyzed for life. The distinguished graduate of his Basic School platoon, James Webb, was wounded twice in the Arizona and medically retired. There were more names in Schuler's history.

At first Schuler seemed to lead a charmed life. After several months with various weapons platoons during Oklahoma Hills, he joined Echo Company in June when they were on Hill 22 at the far edge of the Da Nang Rocket Belt. It was an area of villages, cultivated rice fields, rivers, and crumbling French forts; and it was one of the main infiltration routes to Division Ridge. The numerous contacts they made kept Echo one of the sharpest companies in the battalion; as far as Schuler's platoon was concerned, they were kicking ass. They called themselves Schuler's Slayers; their night ambushes and claymores often caught NVA rocket teams trying to slip down the trails. They found a few bodies, lots of blood trails, and bits of flesh. During that period, Schuler lost only two men: a corpsman knocked unconscious when a bullet hit his helmet, and a grunt injured when a claymore blasting cap detonated in his hand. The platoon tripped no booby traps and morale was high.

It unravelled on 15 August when the company convoyed from Dai La to LZ Baldy. During the mortar and sapper attack that night, Schuler and his men had taken refuge under a truck on the airstrip. It was stacked with 105mm artillery rounds; very hairy, he thought. He lost one man wounded that night. At dawn, they stuck chieu hoi passes in the hands of the naked, dead sappers in the wire and posed for photographs. They were trucked to LZ Ross that afternoon—toting liberated U.S. Army gear—then humped to OP Tiger atop a hillock in Happy Valley. Each man had a helmet, flak jacket, full pack, four canteens, thirty magazines of ammunition, six frags, and three mortar rounds.

The company had six heat medevacs in two hours.

The situation was changing for the worse. While the rest of the battalion was piecemealed into Hiep Duc Valley, Schuler's platoon worked Happy Valley. The heat and humidity were ungodly, and their patrols were not as efficient as before. Their successful ambushing around Hill 22 had come about due to the intelligent plotting of Major Steele. He was aggressive, but prudent. His replacement, whom they quickly dubbed Cement Head, was aggressive, but incompetent. At least Schuler thought so and, for the first time, he began quietly sandbagging orders. They still made almost daily contact with the skeleton garrisons guarding the base camps of the NVA battalions fighting in Hiep Duc. Schuler had never seen anything like it—enemy supply trails wide enough for trucks, more rice caches than they could destroy. Even battalion rear on Ross took casualties from shellings.

The most frequent refrain from the villagers when 2/7 patrols moved into what previously had been a 196th AO was, "GI no come." The extent of NVA infiltration was a sore subject in the 7th Marines, and the grunts' angry question was: how in the hell did the gooks dig in so well without being spotted! Marines harshly referred to an armed truce around Hiep Duc, and many men in 2/7 blamed their mauling on the complacency of the Americal Division. To them, the Army had practically abandoned the countryside and hunkered down around their fire bases.

However, it should be taken into account that by any measure, 1969 was an odd year. If Hamburger Hill proved anything, it was that commanders in the U.S. Army were no longer rewarded for closing with and killing the enemy. Their goal, subtly dictated, was to keep casualties down for political reasons.

And, the Americal had more land than troops.

Officers in the Americal Division were quick to defend themselves. To begin with, neither the 1st Marine Division nor the Americal had the resources to secure the Que Sons or Nui Chom; thus, the NVA were afforded a sanctuary overlooking the very lowlands the Army was trying to secure. To the north, the 2d of the 1st Infantry had patrolled actively around LZ Ross until about March; then they were moved to LZ Baldy and an ARVN unit was moved in to replace them. Presumably, support and aggressive spirit were lacking more among the ARVN than in the Americal, and the situation around LZ Ross had deteriorated accordingly. To the south, the 4th of the 31st Infantry mustered a paddy strength of only three hundred men; tied down with static defense, they could not be everywhere in the valley at once. The NVA base-camped along Nui Chom could easily dispatch small groups to scout the valley for suitable defensive positions; when they chose, they could then move down en masse and dig their slit trenches and spider holes in a night or two of ant-like industriousness.

The 7th Marine Regiment was rushed in not because the 196th Infantry Brigade was necessarily incompetent, but because they were spread thin.

The Marines considered themselves to be in virgin territory.

Lieutenant Schuler's platoon of Echo 2/7 made their biggest find near Nui Chom. Intelligence had targeted a hill as a possible base camp and they swept up after the air strikes, sweating hard under the canopy as they divided along the maze of trails running through the thick underbrush. They found several NVA who'd been killed by the prep fire; they were all young and muscular with crew cuts, and their equipment was first rate, their weapons rust-free. Regulars. Schuler and his radioman, Cpl Paul Bowen, walked up the path leading to the top. In the vegetation, they almost bumped into a North Vietnamese who was cautiously walking downhill on the same trail. The NVA had an AK47 slung over his shoulder. He smiled nervously. Schuler smiled back just as nervously. They both started backing away from each other. Sweathog Bowen was frozen, gripping his M16, screaming, "Shoot him, shoot him!"

Schuler motioned the man towards him and called for him to chieu hoi. The NVA, grinning the entire time, started to unsling his AK47 and Schuler instantly shot him just below the chin with an M79 buckshot round.

He tumbled dead down the hillside.

More NVA popped up in the base camp, all of them either hiding or trying to get away. Corporal McFarlan, a squad leader, found one in a cave. The NVA refused to surrender, so McFarlan ducked in and shot him in the forehead. The dead man turned out to be an NVA doctor. Cpl Ruben Rivera, the platoon sniper, nailed another one trying to slip down a trail. When the men searched his gear, they found dozens of snapshots of women and joked that he must have been a big ass man for the NVA. Schuler gave the photos to Rivera but Rivera, one of the bravest men in the platoon, was also one of the shyest, and he was too embarrassed to take them.

As they secured the camp, Lieutenant Schuler and his platoon sergeant, Sgt Tim Lopez, walked up the trail to the summit. Just as they cleared the top, a couple of AKs cracked up at them. It seemed to be a parting volley and the platoon dug in. They popped smoke near a garden at the peak and a Sea Knight came in to a hover. A machine gun suddenly opened fire. The corpsman beside Schuler dropped with bullets in both legs, and the helicopter reared out as rounds tattooed across the fuselage. The GIs kept bumping into NVA the next few days as they worked the trails leading away from the camp. Several men were wounded and one grunt had his bush hat shot off his head. But the NVA always quickly disappeared; their main concern was Hiep Duc, so they let their bases be picked through. That was great for the morale of Schuler's grunts: they found documents, rice, weapons, ammunition. They even chased a man with an AK into a tiny ville which turned out to be populated by only women and children—and which had stacks of laundered and folded North Vietnamese Army uniforms.

Then came the call to Hiep Duc Valley.

While F Company shored up the southern half of the perimeter along the river, E Company assumed positions in the trees along the northern half. The area was uncomfortably small and stuffed with people. Sergeant Major Black—a wiry man known as Old Blue—came up. In helmet and flak jacket, and with a creased, weathered face that most closely resembled an ancient hound dog, Black looked like a Marine NCO. He had a solid reputation, which started when he won the Silver Star as a private first class in Korea and culminated with his selection as sergeant major of the Marine Corps. But even he seemed a bit shaken as he spoke to the M60 crews, "If you see anything out there, open up with everything you have."

Schuler disagreed. The NVA usually probed before an assault, hoping to get the machine guns to expose themselves by firing so they could knock them out first. He stopped the sergeant major with typical bluntness,

"Stay away from my men. When an order's to be given, I give it, not you."

Schuler personally set each fire team and machine gun team into position and checked their fields of fire. They occupied some slit trenches which honeycombed the area—presumably the work of the NVA—and there was a nervous buzz in the air. Everyone remembered the antiaircraft fire and Schuler could see his grunts drawing together, talking about not leaving anyone behind. The feeling was to go down fighting. As it was, they never had that chance.

■ The *1st NVA Regiment* had halted 2/7 Marines in their tracks on 25 August, and many of the officers and men put the blame on Colonel Lugger. With four battles blaring over his radios at once and rounds zipping over his head, the talk went, he did not know what to do. He was in over his head. Such talk was rippling through the battalion; rumors exaggerated at each level until the corporals and pfcs were mumbling about that chicken-shit colonel who froze and got a lot of good dudes killed. There was talk of fragging.

One rumor put the bounty on his head at $10,000.

Colonel Lugger was not aware of such grumblings, and the situation was not so black and white that anyone was really willing to kill a battalion commander. Most men had only the energy to keep themselves alive, and they followed orders. The immediate concern was to get through the night. G and H Companies had withdrawn to the foothills of Nui Chom on the right flank; E and F Companies were dug in around the Battalion CP, and their perimeter was small and bunched up. The concrete pagoda was a homing beacon to preregistered mortar fire. They were a fat target, but a night move to alleviate the congestion was also a prospect inviting casualties. If the NVA assaulted, perhaps it was better to be close in to maximize firepower.

But the NVA saw no reason to expose themselves.

At 0130, 26 August 1969, the first mortar round thumped through the black stillness. The raid was brief, perhaps a minute, but pinpointed, twenty-four 60mm rounds right into the CP and the LZ clearing behind it. It killed four Marines, seriously wounded twenty-six. Many men had been too exhausted to dig more than shallow holes and their equally exhausted lieutenants had not ordered them to dig deeper; many men had removed their flak jackets and helmets in the muggy heat and were simply sleeping on the ground under ponchos. Lugger blamed his junior officers. But in the eyes of General Simpson and Colonel Codispoti, the problem rested on the shoulders of Colonel Lugger.

By dusk, Private Norton had come to. He sat near the CP pagoda, tagged for a medevac, and talked wearily with some other grunts. Then suddenly, swoosh! swoosh! swoosh! Norton sprang to his feet and ran towards a palm tree. An explosion suddenly blasted him through the air and threw him to the ground like a rag doll. He lay there with a gash from his knee to his butt and shell fragments burned in his stomach and intestines.

He did not pass out again.

Lance Corporal Parr was asleep in the grass, wrapped in a poncho. The first explosion slapped him awake, and he put on his helmet, grabbed his M16, and was pushing up to run to a dike when the world exploded three feet in front of him. The next thing he knew he was mashed against a tree and thinking that the tree was fifteen feet from where he'd been sleeping and, oh Lordy, what the hell's going on! He didn't know it, but his entire body was riddled, helmet blown off, right eye blown out, the right side of his skull shattered. Only his left arm was unscathed.

Parr could feel nothing, only a numbness pulsing with hot sensations. The right side of his head seemed hottest of all; he touched his hand to it, feeling neither his head nor hand, thinking, Aw hell, you done it this time!

That was his last thought.

Shields ran up to Norton and got a tourniquet around his leg. Norton was terrified that his crotch had been ripped open, and he argued with his buddy to strike his lighter in the darkness. He finally did. "Naw, man, it's all right!" Gunships rolled in; then a Sea Knight thumped down. Shields and another Marine rolled Norton onto a hootch door, then laid him on the back ramp of the crammed helicopter. As it lifted up, the crew chief sprawled across him to pump his M16 out the open hatch, and burning hot brass bounced onto Norton's neck and chest.

The helo flew to Da Nang and Norton finally ended up on a freezing, steel table in the X-ray room, next to a Marine who'd been hit in the chest. Norton suddenly started shivering and yelled for a blanket; then he realized he was going into shock. He'd seen it before and told himself, take it easy, lay back and let it roll.

Norton woke up three days later, in intense pain, tubes sticking out of him; when it was all over, he'd lost part of his intestine.

Parr woke up twenty-seven days later and, when it was all over for him, his skull and face had been reconstructed with plastic surgery and his right kidney and spleen had been removed, as had parts of his right lung, liver, intestinal tract, and stomach.

It was pitch black when the first 60mm mortar round thunked from its tube, but Collinson and McCoy were still awake in their foxhole. Collinson saw the sudden flash across the stream and, before the round impacted, he was shouting, "Incoming, incoming!" and shouldering his M16. He fired rapid, single shots, peppering the brush all around the mortar tube flashes. But he didn't have tracers and couldn't tell if he was hitting a thing. The NVA kept pumping and the explosions seemed to walk towards his position. The closest one exploded twenty meters short of his hole, then a few more rounds were lobbed in on the command post area.

The NVA mortar crew ceased firing on their own accord.

Collinson could hear shrieks for corpsmen as he continued to fire his M16 into the darkness. He screamed frantically at McCoy to get the M60 crew, and McCoy hollered for them.

An M79 man ran up, and Collinson, in his excitement and frustration, tried to take the weapon from him. The Marine wouldn't let go, so Collinson shouted and pointed across the river. The grunt popped off an M79 round but, in the dark, it clipped a tree limb on their side of the stream. They had to duck under the abrupt spray of fragments. They decided not to try a second shot. Collinson stayed in place in his hole, eating at himself—I saw the bastards, why couldn't I have killed them before they killed my buddies!

Lieutenant Schuler did not hear the thump of the tube, nor was he conscious of the explosion. But he instinctively knew it had been a mortar round which sprayed shrapnel down after hitting the treetops. He grabbed an M16 and tumbled into a slit trench as more fragments stung him, thinking the NVA were going to overrun them. He thought he was dying. He was dizzy from the concussion and blood poured down his face. He realized he was not going to die only when the mumbles and screams of the men around him became intelligible again through the fierce buzzing in his head.

It was black as pitch and blood was in his eyes. Schuler could make out only a few of the faces around him. Sweathog, his radioman, was wounded. Newton, one of Schuler's fire team leaders, was clutching his leg; it was almost severed. Rivera, his sniper, was slumped beside him in the trench. He was dead. No fire followed the shelling, so Schuler took the radio. He told the company commander they'd taken a direct hit and, in short order, personnel from the company headquarters hustled over to help carry casualties to the LZ.

The landing zone was chaos. Schuler staggered to a spot in the elephant grass, sat down, and mumbled to the corpsman bandaging his head, "I ain't leaving." He had shrapnel lodged in his skull, face, shoulders, and back. But he didn't want to leave his platoon if there was an attack that night and, remembering the ring of 12.7mm guns, he didn't want to be a sitting duck in a big, lumbering Sea Knight. Colonel Lugger stopped briefly to check on him. A mustached officer came by minutes later, talking hatefully about fragging Lugger. He said the colonel didn't know what the hell he was doing, and he was collecting a bounty to get rid of him.

It took thirty minutes for the first chopper to arrive.

Five Cobras rolled in first, one right behind the other, pumping 2.75-inch rockets and 40mm rounds around the perimeter, covering the landing of the medevac. The firepower eased Schuler's fears—like the cavalry in a war movie, he thought—and he allowed a couple of his grunts to help him aboard. Spooky came in after the Cobras and the two Sea Knights made it in and out without drawing a shot. The interior of his bird was dark, vibrating, and crowded. Schuler noticed one of the chopper crewmen looking at the wounded with tears running down his face. He couldn't see what that man saw until they unloaded on the flood-lit tarmac of the Naval Support Activities hospital in Da Nang. They were all bloody. Their forward observer stood with a bandage around his face; a corpsman unwrapped it, exposing a hollow, red eye socket with tissue hanging from it onto his cheek.

The wounded were carried or helped into a large room with rows of stretchers over sawhorses. Schuler ended up on one, still dizzy, blinking at the caked blood and the bright lights overhead, hearing screams, crying, orders being shouted. He faded out, then woke up as a corpsman used long surgical scissors to cut away his flak jacket and fatigues. He began shouting when the man clipped the laces of his prized, battered jungle boots. He suddenly started shivering in the hot box, and a corpsman hooked up an IV. Then he realized he was waking up and a Navy chaplain was beside his stretcher, giving him last rights.

"Get the fuck outta here. I have no intention of dying."

The aid station became so crowded that Schuler and several others were transferred to the Army's 95th Evac on the other side of Da Nang. He walked to the Huey, naked, freezing, carrying his own IV.

In the 95th Evac, an Army medic gave Schuler a shot of novocaine, then an Army doctor used pliers to dislodge the fragments in his skull. Another doctor complimented him on his twist; uh-huh, Schuler thought; he must be talking about a good tennis backhand. When the medics were finally done, Schuler looked in a mirror. His handlebar mustache and chest were caked with dried blood, half his head was shaved and marked with stitches, bandages were around his shoulders. All he had on were some pajama bottoms which didn't fit, perhaps because he'd lost almost thirty pounds in the bush.

■ During the night, Golf and Hotel had hiked back a kilometer to the denuded knoll where their battle had started. Lieutenant Brennon sat in the dirt. He had never felt worse. They hadn't put in enough prep fire, they were spread too thin, and five of his men were dead in that paddy field. Another man was missing—dead, wounded, or passed out from the heat, he did not know which. Brennon wanted to go back under cover of darkness and find those men. But battalion denied permission; Brennon thought the denial devastated what little spirit the grunts had left.

What are we doing, everyone was mumbling. No real mission. NVA everywhere. Little food or water. Intoxicating heat. Heavy casualties.

The result was mass confusion and mass frustration.

At first light on 26 August, Lieutenant Brennon asked for volunteers to retrieve the bodies. In nine months in Vietnam, he'd never seen such spirit. Six men immediately stepped forward. That was Brennon's only satisfaction from this battle, that most of his men—even ones he'd previously had doubts about—were courageously bucking up. With Phantoms running more air strikes, the seven Marines moved into the paddy. There were only a couple of snipers this time, and Brennon pumped three M16 mags at one muzzle flash. Others fired M60s and M79s on the spot and the aerial observer radioed that he could see a dead North Vietnamese soldier.

Good, Brennon thought, I hope I killed the bastard.

The men found their MIA unscathed. He'd been pinned down and, when he saw how close the fire was coming to Brennon's escaping group, he thought it best to hunker down and hide. They humped back to the denuded knoll and medevacked him along with the bodies. He was a young, wiry kid named Medina. He ended up at the division psychiatrist; reportedly, the NVA had come out that night to loot the Marine bodies and had kicked him as he played dead.

We're right back where we started from, Brennon thought; every time we gain something, we pull back to consolidate. Three solid days of contact and we haven't gained one inch!

This operation, he thought bluntly, is a fiasco.

While Hotel Company was recovering their abandoned casualties, Lieutenant Larrison of Golf Company brought in his own Phantoms: 250- and 500-pounders at a hundred meters, napalm parallel to his lines at thirty meters. Under that barrage, a squad and gun team rushed forward to retrieve the body of the point man killed in the previous day's ambush. The Marines had just gotten into the trees when four North Vietnamese walked past. They had green pith helmets and fatigues; carried packs, ammunition bandoliers, and AK47s; and they moved through the wood line as though it were private property. The Marines' first volley dropped two of the NVA in their tracks. A short, sharp firefight broke out, but the squad was able to recover the body. They hustled back across the paddy as Lieutenant Larrison brought in the nape again, covering their withdrawal.

Chapter Seventeen

Buzz-Saw

GySgt William N. Yohe of Echo Company, 2d Battalion, 7th Marines spent the three hours before dawn writing casualty reports. Before that, the company had been stumbling in the dark chaos. Some corpsmen had been wounded; the rest worked feverishly. Casualties had to be found in the dark, lit only by the flashing of minigun fire.

The mortaring had shattered Echo Company; choppered into Hiep Duc with seventy-five men, their numbers were nearly halved in the sixty-second raid. All the officers except the company commander, and all the sergeants except the gunny and one staff sergeant were gone on medevac choppers. Gunny Yohe, in fact, was one of the walking wounded; shell fragments had nicked his arm as he'd jumped from the CP trench and headed towards the company lines.

First light revealed the new shape of their lines. Blood-splattered ground, bloody bandages, torn flak jackets, helmets in the grass. Dead Marines were laid on a cargo net spread out on the ground, and other grunts piled up the discarded and lost equipment. Blood and pieces of flesh were plastered to the gear and to some C-ration cases stacked to one side of the clearing. The rising heat wave brought out the smell and the flies. The survivors were hollow-eyed and haggard, battered into numbness.

In that condition, they attacked.

Echo Company, under 1stLt Paul T. Lindsay, was to lead the westward advance. As the men saddled up in the flattened elephant grass, Lindsay had his doubts—one more time, they were walking undermanned into a hornets' nest. He thought it would have been wiser to mass the battalion and advance fifty meters at a time, thoroughly digging out the NVA in that area before advancing to the next parcel. He saw no sense in rushing to some slotted coordinates two kilometers forward of their lines. Lindsay's opinion was worth something. Although he was young and just counting his days, he had plenty of combat time and was highly respected by his grunts. He was like them in many ways; salty, cocky towards his less-exposed superiors.

Lugger and Lindsay did not get along.

But in the recorded history of the Vietnam War, there is not a single instance of a Marine Corps unit refusing a combat mission.

The survivors of Echo pushed into the boiling paddies.

The platoon leader and platoon sergeant of Echo Three had been medevacked, so Gunnery Sergeant Yohe led them. He was up with the lead squad as they entered a clearing, and they got within thirty meters of the opposite tree line before the ambush began. A Marine dropped with a bullet in his arm. Yohe rolled to the kid, grabbed his M79 grenade launcher, and raised up just enough to pump rounds into the woods. He couldn't see anything. Neither could anyone else, but they kept firing. Two Marines were shot in the chest as they did so. Three others also were wounded, victims of the first fusillade. Only Gunny Yohe and three others of the lead squad were unscathed.

Lieutenant Lindsay brought in the air support: Phantoms dropping napalm thirty meters from the squad, Cobras firing white phosphorus rockets into the trees. Under that cover, the lead squad was able to pull back. In the relative cover of the brush behind them, corpsmen pounded on the chests and gave heart massage to the two men with sucking chest wounds. Both died before the grunts could get them to a landing zone.

The push continued.

Echo had advanced five hundred meters. Fox, moving on Echo's right flank, came under only sporadic sniper fire as they continued the push.

Then came the mortaring. PFC Lorne Collinson crouched behind a tree. The company, after having humped to a point along a stream where it thinned to a trickle one could hop over, had been taking a break when the shelling began. No matter. It wasn't a heavy barrage, more a matter of harassment and delay, one round every couple of minutes.

The men could hear the thunk of the round leaving the tube; they were too weary even to be scared as they counted a few seconds, then flattened in the undergrowth. Collinson took off his helmet and flak jacket in the heat and lay on them like a pillow as he kept a watch downstream. A young Marine in the company helicopter support team was not as relaxed. He had been dispatched unwillingly to the grunts from his shore party battalion, and he crouched bug-eyed behind a tree. His hands were sweaty around his M16 and he looked all around him, shouting to Collinson to watch out, man, watch out, the gooks could be anywhere!

Amused, Collinson shouted back, "No sweat!"

Stobie, another new guy, was not as rattled. He trudged past with a mumble, "I gotta take a dump." When he came back from the bushes, he sat to talk. They were being too cocky; they never heard the next mortar round. Collinson was suddenly bounced up and thrown to the ground. He stood up, wobbly, ears ringing so loudly he couldn't hear. The bush behind them was shredded and Stobie was still sitting there, leaning forward, helmet blown off. He put his hand to his head and blood rushed over his fingers. Collinson shouted for a corpsman as he took Stobie's pressure bandage and wrapped it around his head. It quickly soaked red, so he pulled his out too. Then the corpsman who'd run up tied on a third.

There had been other casualties. A Sea Knight landed on a sandbar. Collinson helped Stobie down the bank, rambling on about nothing to keep him out of shock, even though he couldn't hear his own words for the continuing ringing. A body lay in the sand, wrapped in a poncho, face covered.

The Sea Knight pulled up before the NVA could adjust their mortar tube, and the company got moving again single file atop a paddy dike. The grunts were spaced at twenty-five-yard intervals in case of another mortaring. There was a tree line to their right and an NVA was hunkered in it with an RPG launcher. He must have had plenty of ammunition because he started screaming off shells at individual Marines. He didn't hit anybody, but the grunts began running hard down the dike, not even wasting time to fire back, as fireballs sailed between them in line and exploded in the next paddy.

A brushy knoll sat like an island in the middle of the field, where the Marines flopped amid the concealing shrubbery. An opening through a hedgerow led them back onto the dike and they got moving again, one man at a time sprinting out. Collinson got up to the opening when a grunt lying there said something. Collinson's ears were still ringing, so he bent down to hear the man—just as an RPG whooshed over them. It exploded harmlessly in the paddy, but Collinson mumbled, ''Aw, Jesus!'' as he dashed onto the dike.

That had been the last shot. The column returned to a walk.

Fox Company stopped in a tree line that elements of Echo Company had secured; it was approximately where the platoon had been surrounded the day before. Sniper fire kept everyone's heads down, but this time they did not pull back. Collinson was nestled low in the bushes when several grunts moved past. They said they had seen two NVA on their flank and had fragged their spider hole; they showed off a pair of 1942 Westinghouse Rangefinder binoculars and a Soviet infrared sight for an RPG launcher.

Echo 2/7 was stalled.

Fox 2/7 was stalled.

With Colonel Codispoti on the radio demanding they reach the rendezvous coordinates regardless of casualties, Golf 2/7 was thrown into the attack. Previously, when Fox moved out, Golf had humped into the 2/7 CP to provide security; there they had received a resupply of C rations and oranges, plus mail and ammunition. When word came to advance, they left the CP site with two platoons in the lead, followed by Colonel Lugger and his staff, with the third platoon sewing up the rear.

It was 1600.

Lieutenant Page's platoon had the lead. Corporal Skaggs's squad was in front. The Italian kid was again on point. It was the third time Marines had tried to move west on the trail and there was much bitching in Golf Company that the NVA must have it preregistered. They did, because Golf was two hundred meters out of the CP and Lugger himself was fifty meters out when the first mortar round landed only yards from the point man. He disappeared into the paddy below the road.

The rounds started jolting down the trail, and Corporal Skaggs bolted for a tree line almost a hundred feet away. His squad huddled in a ravine in the trees, but the NVA lobbed a few rounds after them. One Marine took serious wounds in his chest and face. Many more had shrapnel wounds. Almost no one had been wearing his helmet or flak jacket; because of the continuing heat wave, command had given them the option not to.

Lugger ordered them back as he called for air and arty.

The platoon began staggering back, carrying their wounded, keeping low along a paddy dike. The mortars followed them. One round landed near a group of men, inflicting more casualties. The retreat became chaotic.

They finally made it back into the tree line secured by Lieutenant Pickett's platoon and Lieutenant Larrison's CP. Larrison was on the horn and, within five minutes, artillery was slamming in. The arty fired for thirty minutes and was followed by air strikes. But in those first five minutes, the NVA managed to walk a few good-bye rounds into the trees. Staff Sergeant Clements saw one explode near his corpsman; however, he was unscathed and calmly continued working on the wounded. Another round landed five yards from the hole where the company headquarters was located. Lieutenant Larrison took some light shrapnel; one man took most of the blast in his legs, inadvertently shielding the rest. Then the artillery pounded in, the medevacs began landing back at the bush LZ, and men rushed back with the wounded in ponchos. One grunt died of his wounds just as they put him into the helicopter.

The chopper crews worked fast. Already that day, two Sea Knights had been forced down near the 2/7 CP with bullet holes in their rotors. A platoon from Hotel Company secured the crews, then ducked as a few mortar rounds thumped in around them.

Altogether, three helos were shot down while supporting 2/7.

Golf Company's advance was thus halted before it even got started. Lance Corporal Russell, for one, had just saddled up and was sitting back on his pack waiting for the word to depart when the mortaring began. He joined a group of Marines working their way up to get the casualties, and ended up as caretaker for one of them. The man lay atop a poncho in the landing zone, face to the sun, calmly talking as if he didn't understand that one leg was gone, the other one shattered. Russell talked with him until it was his turn on the medevac. Russell had taken some shrapnel graze wounds across his leg and arm during the previous night's shower of mortars, but all he could think was how lucky he was.

Colonel Codispoti had watched through binoculars G Company's retreat from LZ West. In his fitness report on Lugger, he noted the incident in thinly veiled terms:

. . . The Marines from one company were clearly observed running from one treeline across about 500 yds of rice paddies and carrying wounded to another treeline. This officer [Lugger] was immediately apprised of the situation by me over the radio and instructed to get control of the situation. . . . Later that evening he reported back that the company was running to the rear because they had been receiving incoming mortar fire and that he considered it appropriate for them to run . . . to achieve the cover of the treeline. . . . He further advised that this company had been moving forward with his small jump CP group and that he had returned them and the CP group to the same battalion CP area occupied . . . for three successive nights.

Colonel Lugger's written rebuttal defended both the actions of Golf Company and his decision to use the same CP location despite the preregistered mortar raid of the night before:

His [Codispoti's] observations were made from OP WEST some 3500 meters from the activity in question. . . . I did not report that I considered it appropriate that this company should run to the rear away from contact, as he infers. I reported that the "running" he observed was the movement of over 15 casualties to an LZ for evacuation. The forward elements of the company had consolidated, were retaining their ground, and fighting the enemy with organic and supporting arms fire.

The LZ was located in the vicinity of the CP we had just departed, but had moved less than 100 meters from. I had no forces for LZ security except the rear elements of the company in contact, which I utilized. It was my intention to continue forward movement after the med-evac; however, in the interim I was ordered by Colonel Codispoti to consolidate in good defensible perimeters for the night. I decided to remain at the CP location I had occupied the night before. This was the second successive night I utilized this position, not the third as stated. . . . it offered a relatively secure LZ for the evacuation of wounded and delivery of supplies; and it was the most defensible terrain in the area with a water obstacle on one flank and good fields of fire on the other.

Whatever the tactics, it was not one of Golf Company's prouder moments. When the medevacs began coming in, Staff Sergeant Clements saw several Marines with minor shrapnel wounds practically trample over gravely wounded men in their eagerness to get on the choppers. One gleefully shouted, "It's my third, I'm going home!" The company gunny stood there aghast, tears in his eyes. Clements too had never before felt such shame and revulsion.

Other men were made of sterner stuff. Golf One made a quick head count and realized that two men—the Italian point and Lance Corporal

Conway—had been left in the paddy. Sergeant Ferguson got together several volunteers and they crept down a dike to where the point man had last been seen. They looked and hollered but, with darkness falling, finally had to crawl back empty-handed.

At first light, the platoon cautiously moved back down the trail. Lance Corporal Conway sat up in the grass; he had passed out either from heat stroke or shock during the mortaring and sweated out the night alone. The point man was dead. He had been hit by shrapnel and crawled back as far as he could before succumbing; a trail of flattened elephant grass marked his torture. Both men were carried back in ponchos and medevacked. Golf One, which had entered the valley with forty-six men, was down to sixteen.

Echo and Fox Companies pulled together near the Old French Road, a dirt trail with a strip of weeds down the middle. That night, NVA crept up and tossed Chicoms into the perimeter, wounding several men. An M60 gunner spotted the NVA's silhouettes, and pumped a burst into them. In the morning, they found a body in the weeds—a healthy Vietnamese kid in khaki fatigues.

It was the only NVA that Echo Company had seen since getting to the valley; it wasn't enough and Gunnery Sergeant Yohe left the perimeter with several volunteers. No order had been given to do so, but they went tramping around for a little revenge. They found a cave opening and one of the young grunts discovered a small hole in the floor. He hollered that he'd found something and tugged at the bush concealing the hole. It suddenly exploded in his face. From what he reckoned was a Chicom grenade rigged to guard the entrance, the Marine got burns and shrapnel from the chest up. The grunts carried the man back to the perimeter, then kept looking.

Another grunt stumbled upon a second hole about fifteen yards away; both led into the same man-made tunnel.

Gunny Yohe said he was going in. He was thirty-three years old, and it wasn't often that an old gunny elected to wiggle into an enemy tunnel. Tunnel rats were usually nineteen and crazy. Then again, Yohe was regarded as a little nuts—and very good. He crouched beside the tunnel opening, took off his helmet and flak jacket, and popped five fragmentation grenades into the black hole. Then he shimmied in head first. It was narrow, but he was a little guy. He crawled in with a .45

in one hand and an unlit flashlight in the other. Almost immediately, he heard a groan in the tunnel. He waited a bit to let his eyes adjust to the darkness, then moved towards the sound as quietly as he could. The North Vietnamese was moaning in what seemed to be an unconscious delirium. Yohe could just make out his silhouette. He decided to drag him back out as a prisoner, but as he reached for the man's ankles he suddenly became aware of a sensation. Whatever it was he never knew, but as soon as he felt it, he aimed his Colt .45 and instantly, instinctively opened fire.

Then he flipped on the flashlight. Just feet from him, two NVA were slammed against the side of the tunnel, shot dead.

A rope was brought down and the dead men and the wounded prisoner were hauled up. Yohe also brought out two AK47s, a rocket launcher, and some documents which the men's Vietnamese scout said described NVA unit locations, supply points, etc. The grunts demolished the tunnel after dragging out the prizes; it measured seventy-five yards and had been unaffected by the previous air and arty strikes. Lieutenant Lindsay chewed out Yohe a bit for his recklessness, then put him in for the Silver Star.

The evening before, Codispoti had given a new mission to Lugger: retain the ground gained, recover and evacuate casualties at first light, then march back to LZ Ross. The company was being replaced by 3/7 Marines which, on the morning of the 27th, was conducting an airlift from LZ Baldy to LZ West, then marching into the valley. Echo and Hotel 2/7 led the way back to Ross. The Battalion CP and Golf remained in place until 1600, when the lead elements of 3/7 humped past.

Talk was the NVA were *letting* them leave.

Fox Company came out last. That morning they had made an attempt to move beyond the wood line they'd secured with Echo Company. But as soon as they left that cover, the snipers opened up and the Marines hustled back to their wooded haven. They were crouched among the trees, returning fire, when Collinson heard the HST man holler he was hit. A corpsman crouched beside him and removed a fragmentation grenade from the baggy side pocket of the man's trousers. The AK round had split the grenade and bent the detonator cap before hitting him; luckily for all around, the frag had failed to explode.

The corpsman secured a bandage, then Collinson and McCoy got the Marine between them and started back. He limped hard and moaned about how badly he'd been hit, and Collinson thought, man, this dude sure wants out of here. As they passed a clearing in the trees, AK rounds began kicking up dust on the trail. The wounded man instantly bolted from their hands. They chased after him but he beat them back to the LZ. Collinson and McCoy finally stopped, looked at each other, and laughed.

Fox Company spent the day nestled among the trees, some men keeping up the exchange with the snipers while others picked at what C rations they had left. They were pulling out and there was little urgency to their actions. One detail had to be taken care of, though; the body from the doomed recon patrol was still missing. Collinson joined the patrol that hunted through the tall elephant grass for him; they finally found the body because of its hot stench. The Marine had been shot full of holes and his wounds were ripe with maggots. It was sickening and sad, Collinson thought; but he was too numb to be truly repulsed. The grunts simply rolled the rotting body into a poncho and carried him back to the perimeter; then they dropped listlessly along an earthen embankment to await the arrival of 3d Battalion, 7th Marine Regiment.

When Fox Company finally saddled up and trudged past their relief column, Collinson noted the 3/7 grunts looked fresh, packs bulging and in good order, loaded with canteens, ammunition, grenades, and LAWs. Grunts from Fox Company began calling to them: the gooks got their shit together here, most places are preregistered with mortars, there's spider holes and trenches every fucking place, keep your heads up! Collinson didn't feel happy or relieved. He really didn't feel anything but tired. The men carried the dead Marine with them as they moved single file back through the old command post area. The brush was ashy from napalm. The stench was intense, of bodies roasted and rotting in their spider holes. Collinson walked among the trees, head hanging, M16 in one hand, the other pressing his sweat towel over his nose and mouth to keep from vomiting.

On 28 August, the morning after 2d Battalion, 7th Marines trudged out of the Hiep Duc Valley, Colonel Codispoti told Colonel Lugger to report to him at LZ West. Codispoti questioned him briefly again about the problems during the battle; one was that, in the five days of combat, 2/7 had lost at least 24 men killed and 161 wounded and evacuated, but could confirm (by actual sighting) only 23 NVA KIA and one prisoner. Not satisfied with the explanations, Codispoti told Lugger he was immediately relieving him and placing his executive officer in temporary command.*

* They had a new commander the next day. As General Simpson noted, "This was no place to insert a green battalion commander. All of my experienced commanders were then serving in command positions. I was in almost daily contact with MajGen William Jones, CG, 3d MarDiv and an old and trusted friend. He made LtCol Joseph Hopkins available. In a remarkably short time he was able to transform 2/7 from one of our weakest battalions to one of our very best and strongest."

Chapter Eighteen

Realignment

I f events had gone according to plan, PFC Charly Besardi of Lima Company, 3d Battalion, 7th Marines would have missed his battalion's redeployment to the Hiep Duc Valley. Two days before the move, Besardi was choppered out of the field, sharing the ride with a wounded NVA prisoner, to attend Mine & Booby Trap School at 1st MarDiv HQ. The chopper was supposed to stop first at LZ Baldy so Besardi could collect his orders from the company office, but it flew directly to Da Nang. Besardi showed up, nonetheless, and was told he had to have the paperwork to get into the school. By the rules, he should have spent the night in a transit hootch at Division Rear. Besardi wanted nothing to do with the lifers and new guys there, so he talked his way into the R and R Center where accommodations were better.

The next morning, he caught a chopper back to LZ Baldy and arrived, showered and rested, at the company hootch. The clerk told him it was too late for the school; the entire battalion was saddling up for a move and he should stay at Baldy. Besardi looked up the company supply sergeant, a good dude, and they bullshitted the night away. They ran a few joints, laughed, told jokes, and for a few hours forgot where they were.

"Geez, Charly," the supply sergeant sighed, "this is one of the first times I've laughed in a long, long time."

Besardi felt the same way.

He'd come to the Marine Corps the summer after high school, a rough truck driver's son who grew up with rats in the backyard, neighborhood baseball after school, and girls in the backseat. War seemed like some kind of rah-rah adventure and he and three street buddies signed up. Parris Island was the first slap of reality. Oh my God, what are these people made of, Besardi thought as the drill instructors raged; they're from another planet come down to kill us! He followed the impersonal conduit to Vietnam; twelve weeks of boot camp, seven weeks of infantry training, four weeks of staging, then the final jet ride.

As the plane descended into Da Nang, Besardi had enough insight to realize that what he was seeing was not really Vietnam.

It became Vietnam to him only after two days of in-processing, of seeing hollow-eyed grunts in weathered fatigues and hearing the steady thump of choppers landing at the NSA hospital. On the third day, Besardi was trucked with forty other replacements to the 7th Marines CP on Hill 55, where a colonel told them bluntly what the area was like and what was expected of them. He ended his talk, "Fifty percent of you people in the first thirty days will be killed or wounded." From Hill 55, Besardi was trucked to battalion base camp on Hill 10; in the morning, a rocket raid sent him diving head first into a bunker, where he thought, I'm here, this ain't Vietnam no more, this is the fucking Nam. Within two weeks of joining Lima Company, he was humping along Charlie Ridge on Operation Oklahoma Hills. He was scared, feeling useless. On his first ambush patrol, he walked tail-end-charlie; as they set in, a grunt whispered harshly to him, "You make sure no one was following us? I'll fucking kill you if anybody was following us." He sounded as though he meant it. Besardi kept his mouth shut and his eyes and ears open; by the time Lima Company came off Oklahoma Hills, he was walking point.

He was a grunt now, and a different person. The killing had done that. He was on point with his buddy Bailey when they heard music in a tree line. Incredulous, they crept up into it and saw some Vietnamese taking a siesta in hammocks; a radio was playing. There were four men and two women; AK47s were leaning against a tree. Besardi and Bailey didn't even wait for the platoon to catch up. They crashed in, screaming and firing. In seconds, two of the men and one of the women were dead, the rest wounded. Besardi stood over one who was writhing with two M16 rounds in his stomach, thinking vindictively, wow, man, you're going to fucking die! Then, mournfully: why? The killing came too easily. Worse, for Besardi, it was as if they killed and suffered in a vacuum, without rhyme or reason. On a patrol in the Que Sons, they had come across an old woman and a little kid who gave them bananas while they paused near their hootch. They had received instructions to destroy the woman's rice lest the NVA confiscate it, so they lugged her rice baskets to a nearby stream and dumped them. When the patrol leader said to burn the hootch, Besardi had exploded, "What, are you fucking crazy!" The corporal had been disgusted too. "It ain't me, it's the people up there." They had torched the hootch with their Zippos and left, no one saying much, Besardi thinking, this is for nothing, what are we really trying to accomplish?

He hardened. He was walking point the day in Dodge City when Terry tripped a booby-trapped frag. Terry collapsed, screaming, and Mayhan the radioman was unconscious, his legs and crotch ragged with red-hot shrapnel. The corpsman, Doc Johnson, worked furiously on Mayhan, tying bandages, using mouth to mouth to keep him alive until the medevac clattered in. They were running patrols off Hill 37 then, between Oklahoma Hills and the move to LZ Baldy, coming back each time dusty and exhausted. They rotated, out for four days and three nights, then back to Hill 37 for an afternoon and night of rest. When they came in, they wanted to rest, to talk, to smoke their pot. The company gunnery sergeant wanted cigarette butts policed up, trousers bloused, jungle boots shined. He screamed his demands. One night, someone rolled a frag under the gunny's hootch. He survived and was medevacked.

Yet Besardi was touched sometimes by the war and a new sense of self respect, but mostly by the people. He barely knew his father when he left; life seemed to offer only some punk job and people looking out for number one. Lima Company gave him something he never had. The grunts were the best people he ever knew. Besardi cursed them. The kindest word he had for his buddy, P. K. Smith, when he saw him sweating along under bandoliers of M60 ammunition, was a laugh, "Fuck you, Smith, you ain't never getting that gun. You're gonna be an ammo humper the rest of your tour!"

He loved P. K. Smith.

In the Que Sons, Besardi came down with malaria, but the company had to keep walking to find a medevac landing zone. One of the new guys—a dude from New York who came across originally as a conniving bastard—voluntarily shouldered Besardi's pack as they walked. A lieutenant from the company headquarters took his rifle and ammo.

He loved them all.

By the time the battalion was saddling up to move into Hiep Duc, Besardi had been with the company, almost constantly in the bush, for a hundred and seventy days. The Hiep Duc Valley was bad, as his friend, the supply sergeant, had been trying to warn him. 2/7 had gone in first, was still out there, and for four days the choppers had been coming into the medical detachment on Landing Zone Baldy. The sergeant had watched from the airstrip as the dead Marines were stacked in trucks. The sergeant shook Besardi's hand, hugged him, looked him in the face. "You take care out there."

■ On the morning of 26 August 1969, Lieutenant Colonel Kummerow, CO, 3/7 Marines, was summoned to Colonel Codispoti's forward command post on LZ West. From there they helicoptered to the 2/7 CP in Hiep Duc Valley. Kummerow once described Codispoti, with respect, as ". . . square in stature, his arms hung to his knees, and he was covered with curly hair, giving him much the appearance of a Neanderthal man. When he attempted to smile, he bared two rows of huge, yellowed teeth in more of a grimace than a grin." Codispoti struck Kummerow as a warrior able to weather the worst. As they conferred, 2/7 was calling in artillery fire and recovering nine of the men left behind in the previous day's debacle. It was shattering to see the dead Marines being carried back into the perimeter. Codispoti decided on the spot to replace 2/7 with 3/7.

Kummerow helicoptered back to LZ Baldy; on the morning of 27 August, he and his jump CP choppered back to LZ West to conduct final preparations as giant CH53 Sea Stallions deposited the rifle companies on the dusty staging point. They were flown in at intervals.

I Company (1stLt R. W. Ramage) was lifted out from a sweep of Barrier Island east of LZ Baldy.

K Company (1stLt T. B. Edwards) was fifteen klicks from Baldy when word came to return. It was midnight; they had destroyed a two-ton rice cache they'd uncovered, then made a forced march. They had walked in the Baldy perimeter at 0800, dropped their gear, and had just sat down in the mess hall when the company gunny said they were saddling up again in one hour.

L Company (1stLt J. F. Bender) was flown in from the field.

M Company (Capt C. W. J. Stanat) had been trucked to LZ Baldy from the bush,* then flown to LZ West.

The Marines gathering on Landing Zone West had been humping hard for weeks on end, and they had no time to rest before being committed to the latest action. They wearily sat in clumps around the Army bunkers, weighted under flak jackets, packs, and ammunition, helmets replaced with battered fatigue covers; they barely moved, but the noontime glare drenched them with sweat and the sheets of dust from the LZ coated them. They had no idea why they were being pushed so hard, and they were pissed off and nervous. Mostly, the grunts were bone-weary.

Because of the 12.7mm AAA fire covering the valley, Codispoti and Kummerow decided 3/7 would have to hump off the mountain rather than risk it in choppers. The hill was 445 meters high; Henry and Lee noted there were good trails down to the valley floor, and lent the Marines their Echo Recon Platoon. They pushed off at noon, but no trails were visible; instead, the point became immersed in high elephant grass. The Army platoon apparently had not been briefed on their specific mission, so Kummerow finally had them pulled back to West; his column, following compass azimuths, kept pushing downhill through the tangle. It was brutal going. Marines who fell out from the heat or who tripped and bruised themselves sat in the brush to recuperate, then tagged along at the rear of their company files. Corpsmen hooked IVs to the heat casualties who could not be revived, and medevacked them aboard the resupply helicopters that landed in clearings along the mountainside. The birds dropped off water blivets, plus helmets and flak jackets for those platoons who'd been on light patrol when scrambled.

It was probably close to 120 degrees under the canopy.

The column, which stretched for almost a mile, was like an accordion and Lima Company was at the end. More specifically, Third Herd was the last one off LZ West. Previously, Lieutenant Ronald and Sergeant Fuller had gotten the men lined up off to the side of the dusty LZ, making sure the ammunition and water resupply were broken down and

---

* M/3/7 lost a man even before their helos arrived. Three Vietnamese children came to the wire with three M79 rounds and two 4.2-inch mortar shells, and the company scout paid them a cash bounty for turning them in. The children ran away and the ordnance exploded, killing the scout. It was unknown if the ammunition had been mishandled or booby-trapped.

passed out evenly. While the men saddled up, Lieutenant Ronald spoke to them. He repeated what they'd been hearing, that the valley was going to be bad. He said he knew Brown and Turner were due to rotate home soon and they now had the opportunity not to go. There would be no hard feelings. The grunts mumbled in agreement; a man owed it to himself not to get killed so close to going home. Decent.

Brown said he wanted to stay on the landing zone.

Turner was P. K. Smith's partner on the sixty. He was a black man from the South who'd already been wounded once, and who talked with hostility about the white man's war. But then he said, "Fuck it, I'm going."

There is a special bond only grunts know.

Third Herd finally got moving through the breaks in the perimeter wire. Ten minutes out, the GIs on the LZ detonated some old crates of small arms ammunition, and rounds cooked off in hundreds of streamers over the men's heads. Besardi sweated his way down beside Vaughn, the squad M79 man, mumbling that this valley was going to be the baddest of the bad. Someone started singing the "Fixin' to Die Rag" by Country Joe and the Fish, and the platoon took it up . . . "What are we fighting for, don't ask me I don't give a damn, next stop is Vietnam, whoopie, we're all gonna die!" Lieutenant Ronald and Sergeant Fuller ignored the mutinous words because they knew what it was, the grunts' way of spitting in death's face.

It took six hours—from noon until dusk—to get the entire battalion to the valley floor. From there, they pushed west down the Old French Road. Another column approached them, headed in the opposite direction, and Besardi hollered to their point man, "Hey, what company you guys from!"

"Well, I'm Fox Company. The rest of these guys behind me are what's left of Two-Seven." Jesus Christ, Besardi thought as they passed. The grunts coming out looked drained and beaten. Noting their relief's lack of gear, they handed over helmets, flak jackets, ammunition; some shook hands, hugged them, beseeched them, "Be careful out there, man. There's some bad fucking gooks out there. Please be careful." The survivors' faces were either blank or set in a horrified grimace.

Third Herd found out why when they crossed the stream. The valley changed there. The smell of death hung in the muggy air, and the downed Sea Knights sat abandoned in the grass-covered paddies. At that sight, the murmurs went up and down the column again.

The grunts knew what they were up against.

They made no contact that night, but it was still touchy going. For one thing, the last of 2/7 had pulled out before the last of 3/7 had conducted the passage of lines. Colonel Kummerow, walking with Lima Company, was unpleasantly surprised when Fox 2/7 suddenly appeared on the dirt road and passed them. "Thus, at dusk," he noted, "3/7 found itself on a route march in no-man's-land, not knowing what lay ahead. I ordered my point company to secure an area suitable for a battalion perimeter defense and to establish guides to bring each of the other companies into their sectors. Every man did a beautiful job of quickly and quietly getting secured after a hell of a day, to say nothing of the preceding several days.''

■ The enemy offensive had indeed brought a frantic pace to 7th Marine operations; even Colonel Kummerow—a low-key Annapolis graduate who had fought as a rifle platoon leader in Korea—couldn't help but be impressed. On 11 August, he had just checked in at the 1st MarDiv CP when the attacks began. There were rockets and sappers against the Division compound.

On the 12th, General Simpson provided a tour of Division Ridge (complete with a look at the freshly killed NVA sappers); then they boarded a helicopter for an aerial view of the 7th Marines AO, and overflew Dowd's fight in the Arizona. Kummerow was dropped off at Hill 55 and, within an hour, was accompanying Codispoti as they choppered into the 1/7 CP for a two-hour observation of the battle.

On the 13th, Dowd was killed.

On the 14th, Kummerow was choppered into the 3/7 CP at an old French fort in a picturesque riverside village; on the 17th, they conducted the official change-of-command ceremony. Within an hour of passing the battalion colors, Kummerow was on a chopper to Landing Zone Baldy.

On the 18th, 3/7 Marines relieved 2–1 Infantry.

It did not take Kummerow long to form his opinion of why his Marines were so desperately needed in the American AO. The 2d of the 1st Infantry was in the process of moving from Baldy to Hawk Hill (where they worked with the 1–1 Cav in the sand-dune country along the South China Sea). The Marines assuming 2–1's positions were not impressed; the bunkers were falling apart and much loose equipment had been left behind, including claymore mines, fragmentation grenades, trip flares with their safety catches missing, and rusting belts of M60 ammunition. The judgement of the Marine grunts about the GIs in the area was that they "weren't worth a fuck."

Kummerow would not have put it in those terms, but he was not impressed either. The 2d of the 1st Infantry had secured LZ Baldy, manned checkpoints on the road to LZ Ross, and conducted local patrolling. But they had not secured the land itself, relying instead on helicopter scouts. When and if infiltration was detected, infantrymen were CA'd into the area and, after several hours of beating the bushes, they were picked up and returned to the mess halls and showers of Baldy. Kummerow's assessment was very subjective—2-1 sometimes did conduct successful extended patrols—but, all in all, he thought the Army was relying on technology and firepower to do what could be accomplished only by men with rifles living in the bush.

So, the NVA infiltrated, dug in, and hunkered down.

While 2/7 Marines were fed into the Hiep Duc battle to the west, 3/7 Marines were committed to Barrier Island to the east. Captain Stanat's Mike Company was choppered onto the island, which quickly turned into a horror show. From the air, the place seemed as flat as a sandy beach; in fact, it was crisscrossed with irrigation ditches and dotted with spider holes. The VC seemed nowhere but were everywhere, tagging along with Mike Company and sniping at will. Kummerow flew out in an Army Huey to talk with Stanat; as they lifted off, an AK47 suddenly opened fire and six rounds punched through the Huey, wounding the copilot and gunner, and wiping out the radios.

A frustrated Kummerow planned a sweep in force to clear out the VC and, after dusk on 20 August, Mike Company humped to a staging point on the south end of the island where India and the jump CP would join them the following morning. On the morning of 21 August, the Marine artillery battery on LZ Baldy registered its fire on Barrier Island. They used survey data provided by the Army battery they had replaced; the data were inaccurate and the company's first two 155mm artillery rounds landed smack on Mike Company. Five Marines were killed, seven wounded. As the men evacuated these casualties, Captain Stanat discovered that a corpsman was missing from the night march. Perhaps he'd fallen asleep on a break, but no one knew, so Kummerow cancelled the sweep and choppered in with India Company. The grunts followed the previous route of march and found the corpsman—dead—his weapon and gear missing, his body booby trapped. VC snipers opened up on them as they recovered the dead man. Kummerow flew back to Baldy with a demoralized M Company.

India Company, under Lieutenant Ramage, continued working on Barrier Island and, on the 25th, they conducted a final sweep with naval gunfire support. They discovered twenty-five VC bodies, rounded up eighty Vietnamese, and ended the sweep on a beautiful sandy beach.

On the 27th, they abandoned Barrier Island.

As soon as 3/7 Marines set up their positions in the Hiep Duc Valley on the evening of 27 August, Kummerow called for his company commanders. The push to link up with 4–31 Infantry would commence at first light. Kummerow was determined not to lose momentum in their attack, and impressed upon his company commanders that, when they made contact, they were to push through.

Kummerow was lucky; his battalion had not been brought in piecemeal.

Chapter Nineteen
And, Finally, Rendezvous

At 0500 on 28 August 1969, 3d Battalion, 7th Marine Regiment, 1st Marine Division began moving towards the objective. The fog on the valley floor hadn't yet burned off, and the men moved across ghostly green paddies. K and I Companies led the way with L and M Companies following two hundred meters behind; they were in a box formation.

They had gone a kilometer before the firing started.

Kilo One, on the far-right flank, came under AK47 fire; company commander Edwards ordered Kilo Two into an adjacent tree line to provide suppressive fire. Among the trees, Kilo Company overran a bunker and captured one of the NVA 12.7mm AAA guns; as the companies consolidated, Colonel Kummerow ordered Mike Company to continue the momentum of the attack.

Mike entered the paddies in front of the woods, 1st and 3d Platoons up, 2d back; then they wheeled to the right. The skirmish line swept towards the bouldered slope of Hill 381; seventy-five meters from the base, the NVA opened fire again. 3d Platoon on the right took the brunt of it and were pinned down behind the dikes when Captain Stanat ordered 2d Platoon into the fire. Mike Two, under 1stLt William Donaldson, moved quickly through Kilo's wood line and across the paddies; they had just gotten tied in with the pinned platoon when the NVA snipers turned their sights on them. At the same time, preregistered 60mm and 82mm mortar fire began landing in the rice paddies.

Donaldson's platoon sergeant was wounded. The lieutenant in command of 3d Platoon was wounded. So was a score of grunts, and the snipers on the high ground added to the toll, opening fire on the two platoons anytime anyone moved.

3d Platoon had taken it bad in the first bursts. An M60 crew up front had been shot, and a corpsman sniped trying to get to them. Donaldson's platoon lay down cover fire to get them back, and one of his grunts shouted he'd seen smoke on the bouldered slope. An M79 grenadier ran up to fire on the spot, and was shot as soon as he raised himself over the dike. Two Marines moved up to pull him back, and one of them was shot. Two more Marines, one slung with several LAWs, crawled up. They blasted out enough fire to allow others to reach the casualties. Artillery began to hammer into Hill 381. Meanwhile, Captain Stanat radioed 1st Platoon, under 1stLt Anthony Medley, to move into the trees at the base of the hill in order to put the NVA on the slope between 2d Platoon's fire and that of the two platoons in the open. Medley's men moved in, yet they suffered the fewest casualties in the company: one man shot through the leg.

The rest of Mike Company had been hit hard—three KIA, thirty WIA—and Stanat called Donaldson for a status report. Donaldson said the snipers temporarily had been quieted, but that the NVA would chop them to pieces with mortars if they stayed in the open paddies. Stanat ordered a withdrawal to the trees behind them, which the platoon conducted in good fashion, bringing back all their casualties and all their gear except the M60 of the most forward team that had been sniped (it was recovered in the morning). Medley's platoon provided the cover fire, coming back last, when they were almost out of ammunition. The NVA had been invisible in the dense vegetation of the slope, which is why Captain Stanat doubted that the air strikes coming in behind their retreat were doing much good. The jets killed at least one NVA, though: a radioman said he saw a body blown into the air.

During the fire, the battalion command post was several hundred meters away on a ripple of high ground. Among those with Kummerow were Maj Dave Whittingham, his S-3; SgtMaj Nick Gledich, his BSM; and Lance Corporal Monahan, his radio operator. They were like family. Whittingham was a sharp, incisive man, very cool under fire. Gledich was a Yugoslavian immigrant who had found his home in the Corps and was—thoroughly—a sergeant major of Marines. A month after Hiep Duc, when the jump CP was humping with India Company in the Que Sons, they had been hit by mortars in a preregistered spot along a ridge. Colonel Kummerow had been standing, his ear to the radio, when Nick

Gledich suddenly shoved him off his feet, tossed his helmet to him, and dove across his legs. Kummerow had cradled his helmet on his head with one arm as a mortar round exploded five feet away; shrapnel punched a hole in his hand, and hit his arm, shoulder, elbow, and foot. But Gledich had absorbed most of the fragments meant for Kummerow—thirty-five pieces in all.

Lance Corporal Monahan was also to become a casualty. Back at LZ Ross after a night patrol, he was unhooking grenades from his flak jacket; the pin on one apparently was corroded, because the safety spoon suddenly popped off, and the explosion blew off his hand. He died of shock. But that was in the spring of 1970, a miserably wet time; this was the summer of 1969, also miserably hot, and Monahan was sweating his ass off. His face was chunky and red under his helmet brim, and his undershirt was soaked under his flak jacket and the tugging straps of his radio, canteens, and equipment. He had a tattoo on one sunburned arm. Monahan was not complaining, though; he was a bright kid from a broken home who had found his place in 3d Battalion, 7th Marines.

Somehow, the CP's flock of antennas drew no fire.

Colonel Kummerow was on the radio with Captain Stanat. Stanat was a handsome West Pointer and veteran of a previous tour with the 5th Marines, and Kummerow had allowed him to use his discretion in pulling back. Kummerow had his doubts, though; Stanat struck him as burned out and he wondered if the NVA had gotten the upper hand because of a lack of aggressive action.

He eventually transferred Stanat to regiment.

Kummerow ordered Lima Company to continue the frontal attack on Hill 381. There were those who called the Marine Corps the greatest invention for killing young American men, but that connoted that the commanders were stupid or callous. Kummerow was neither. There was no way to rationalize what the Marines were doing, he thought; you just have to do the job. Falling back was out of the question. From what he could tell, that's what the Americal had been doing for the last ten days. He called it floundering.

Lima Company had pulled off to the right of the Old French Road. Ahead, the firing had grown into a constant cacophony, compounded by the roar of jets and artillery. Word came for two squads from Third Herd to continue down the trail; as always, the grunts had no idea what was going on and just kept walking until Lieutenant Ronald and Sergeant Fuller waved them off to the right. They hiked down a river bank, waded the stream which stank of napalm, then climbed the opposite shore and proceeded into the paddies. Private Besardi trudged along as his squad hiked through the banana trees and heavy brush, draining with each step. The woods were like an oven. The squad finally reached the tree line where Kilo Company had consolidated. Mike Company was firing ahead of them and they pressed on.

Seven bodies greeted the men in the next tree line. The dead were all Vietnamese, lying side by side and riddled with bullets, shot in the head execution style. There was an old man, a husband and wife, three children, and a baby. What in the fuck is going on, Besardi thought. It appeared to be the work of the NVA, an act of vengeance or a warning to the villagers that the NVA withdrawal was only temporary. The scene did not inspire revenge in Besardi, only revulsion at the cruelty, and fear that they were up against such ruthless bastards.

Ten minutes away, Lieutenant Ronald got off the radio and hollered, "All right, everyone on line!" The two squads swept on a skirmish line towards a brushy knoll on which they could see grunts from Mike Company. A kid grunt was wandering below the knoll.

"Hey, who you with!"

The kid was gripping a .45, dazed and helmetless.

"Where's your company!"

He spoke slowly. "They're around somewhere."

The platoon continued into the tree line, past a large village well tucked among the trees, then walked out into the paddy. The boulder-strewn and forested face of Hill 381 faced them. The mud was knee-deep in the first field and Besardi trudged through it as fast as he could, sweating hard, not wanting to be caught in the open. The paddy rose in terraces ahead of them. His squad was behind a grassy knoll; the other squad was to the right of it. To his left, some of his buddies—Reevs, Bailey, Chico with the M60—trotted down a dry path. Besardi headed towards them and was twenty feet away when Bailey hiked up a berm. As soon as he came into view over the earthen wall, the slope of Hill 381 suddenly erupted with AK47 and RPG fire.

Bravo Company, 4th Battalion, 31st Infantry rucked up as the sun rose; they were to lead the battalion's push west to link up with the

Marines. Captain Gayler held a quick briefing in their night bivouac—the brushy ditches running through the trees near the Old French Road—and Specialist Hodierne, the reporter, just off the morning resupply bird, photographed them. Hodierne looked around the ragged spot of poncho hootches. The grunts looked drained already, he thought; the heat was smothering in this windless valley and the dust from the ancient paddies practically clogged men's pores.

He'd never seen a more miserable place.

Captain Gayler knew his men were wrung out; he knew they wanted only to sit there in the shade. But that's not the way the game's played. He put his helmet back on, and the company began a cautious hump. They stopped eventually in one part of a tree line facing a hillside of elephant grass dotted with overgrown hootches; that was where Gayler thought Delta 1st of the 46th had been halted three days before. With Lieutenant Maurel's platoon on point, Bravo Company began moving into the sun-blasted paddy between their tree grove and the hill. The North Vietnamese—who were still in place—let them get halfway into the clearing. Then an NVA with a captured M60, tucked in one of the hedgerows at the base of the hill, opened fire.

One GI fell dead. Everyone else scrambled for cover. Private Jandecka, under fire for the first time, blindly followed several GIs as they rushed forward and flopped along a bank at the base of the hill, only to find themselves directly under the machine gun which put bursts over them as they pressed against the berm. A second NVA joined in from somewhere on the hill, using a captured M79 to lob grenades across the paddy and into the tree line. Another one of the new guys caught it, a splatter of red-hot shrapnel ripping open his back.

Jandecka had never heard such screams.

The dike that shielded the forward elements of the command group in the trees was about four feet high. Hodierne pressed against it as the M79 rounds began crashing through the branches; he thought, well, at least I don't *have* to be here. That always made him feel better. The North Vietnamese were so close that he could hear the man snapping open the grenade launcher to eject spent casings and load fresh rounds. He sensed that the NVA were playing for time, that they did not plan to counterattack. The GIs around him felt it too. Many tucked themselves behind a piece of cover, heads down, and that was that. Hodierne commiserated with them: it's a bad war; this battle has no point; and why get killed for one more dried out, useless rice paddy?

Other grunts were carrying the fight to the enemy. Brave, he thought, just plain brave.

Jandecka was one of those doing more than sitting it out, although his actions were mostly the result of inexperience and nerves. Pinned down under the NVA gun, he imagined some of the men slipping around the flank. He crawled down the berm to their left to keep it covered, then pushed up to get a good look. Almost as soon as he did, he saw the brush stir ahead of him. In that instant, an AK47 cut loose. Jandecka tumbled backwards as the rounds slammed squarely into his chest; then he quickly swept his hand over his shirt and realized there was no blood. The NVA had fired low and he'd caught only a spray of ricocheting pebbles and rock-hard dirt. GIs beside him were returning the fire; they couldn't see the M60 position for all the brush, but men across the paddy could see the smoke and muzzle flash and hollered directions as the men along the berm blindly pitched grenades. Jandecka threw a few at the spider hole. It seemed futile.

Captain Gayler personally fired two LAWs into the machine gun position, but they had no effect. It was a boiling day and the artillery recon sergeant, crouched with the company headquarters, finally muttered angrily, "I'm tired of this." With that, he scooped up two hand grenades and clambered over the berm. He began easing up to the spider hole along the cover of the dikes. At the same time, Private Brantley—the soldier who'd been chased into the infantry for fear of a court-martial—was also moving forward. Along with his squad leader sergeant, he pushed through the hedgerow and, sweaty and scratchy, pulled the pin on a frag. He could hear the expended brass ejecting from the M60, but when he rose up, another hidden NVA pumped off a burst from his AK47. Brantley flung himself down as his squad leader emptied his M16 at the sound, either killing or cowing the NVA; then Brantley got up again. He was looking right at the North Vietnamese in the spider hole. The NVA was hefting the M60 towards him. In that instant of silence, the recon sergeant made his break; he dashed across the last clearing amid shouts of, "Get your ass down!," then jumped the berm where Jandecka's group was crouched. Brantley lobbed his frag into the spider hole and ducked, just as the sergeant pitched in his and spun around, diving back behind the berm.

There was a muffled explosion. Brantley didn't even waste time to look; he was convinced he'd killed the sniper. Jandecka, however, heard GIs shout that they saw the NVA leap from the hole right after the grenades went off and run bleeding into the thicket behind him. As the grunts discovered later, the spider hole had a slanted floor that led to a small hole in the corner. The grenades had rolled into this angled chamber.

It was maddening.

The NVA may or may not have received a fatal wound. He stopped shooting, which was the break Jandecka's group needed. Jandecka ran with his heart in his throat across the paddy, then jumped the four-foot berm. To everyone's surprise, there was not a shot fired at them.

As Brantley and his squad leader shimmied back through the hedgerow, the NVA with the M79 opened fire again. Brantley crouched with Staff Sergeant Sheppard, returning a little fire, until he suddenly realized they were all alone. He sputtered out, "Shep, the motherfuckers've left us!" to which Sheppard calmly replied, "Yeah, man, it's time we got out of here too." Which is just what they did.

Bravo Company collected itself back in the tree grove; Sergeant Allison of 1st Platoon took a small party back down the footpath to secure an LZ in the elephant grass. The dead man had been left in the open, but thirteen others had shrapnel wounds or heat exhaustion. The LZ was a slight basin behind the trees; the GIs popped smoke, and a couple Hueys were able to come in quickly, take the casualties aboard, and kick out a resupply of ammo. Lieutenant Maurel of 3d Platoon was among those medevacked with light shrapnel wounds, and Staff Sergeant Sheppard took over.

No one was firing, so while the rest of Bravo Company flaked out under what passed for shade, Lieutenant Monroe and the platoon sergeants joined Captain Gayler; they were the only two officers left. They sat amid the trees, helmets off, soaked with sweat. They were going to hit the knoll again, but this time from another angle. The squad that was guarding their rucksacks at their camp was called up to reinforce. No Cobra gunships were available, and air and arty could not be employed because the Marines were only a few hundred meters away and their position was not clearly known.

It had been three hours since the fight began.

Bravo Company moved out again, treading cautiously. They came under fire from the hill as soon as they tried to outflank it. Staff Sergeant Sheppard's platoon had the rear this time, with little to do except wait. Jandecka dragged himself under a small plant with large leaves to escape the sun's blaze; he sipped water from his canteen top, sloshed it around his parched mouth, then spit it back in the canteen. Finally, word was passed to move forward and join the line facing the hill.

Another GI had been killed getting into position.

But the NVA had been quieted, and the lead platoon began its move up the brushy hillside of terraced dikes. The NVA let them get strung out, then laid down a withering fire which knocked down two GIs in their tracks and pinned down the fifteen men in the lead. The platoon sergeant was up front with them; he found himself pressed against a dike as the NVA with the M79 fired grenades down at him. M79 rounds spin-arm after fifteen meters of flight; the NVA was so close that his grenades were slamming against the dike above the sergeant's head and ricocheting off without exploding. The sergeant threw grenades back at the thumping blast of the grenade launcher, but the NVA was crouched invisibly among some vines and the frags did not reach him. The sergeant hollered for more grenades.

Sergeant Allison collected frags by going from man to man in his platoon, which was watching the flanks. He carried the frags up a small rise; the crest was too exposed to get over, but he was able to toss the grenades to a GI on the other side. Allison did not see what happened next. Hodierne did. The GI nearest the stranded group was told to crawl to them with the grenades. He refused and moved back to where the medics had dragged the newly wounded. He was moaning to a medic about his nerves when an NVA M79 exploded nearby and he went down with a piece of shrapnel, a Purple Heart, and a ticket out. Nothing's fair.

In the tree line, Brantley lay with his squad RTO as Captain Gayler polled his platoon leaders on the radio. Their consensus was that it was time to get out; there were probably only a dozen NVA, but they were dug in and held good fields of fire. Gayler wanted men from each platoon to flank the hill and provide cover fire so the stranded men could crawl back. Brantley got off the radio and called to the GI nearest him, Private Doughty, to join that group. "Keep your ass down and if you guys can't do the job, get the hell back!"

Doughty was a steady dude. "Fuck it," he shouted back, referring to the NVA fire, "it don't mean nothin'!"

Doughty tagged Jandecka and they decided to crawl forward to the right of the point platoon. There was an old French hootch, with a sniper in the rafters. Doughty borrowed a grenade launcher and pumped two rounds into the hootch; then came the distinct clatter of a weapon hitting the hard-packed floor. They pushed off, Doughty in the lead as they crawled along a hedgerow that led up the hill. They reached a clearing. Jandecka slinked into a spider hole, feeling too exposed for comfort, but Doughty kept going and disappeared into the brush. A minute later, there was a burst of automatic fire, then the terrible racket of fire being exchanged. Then it was quiet again. Jandecka had squeezed a couple of bursts at the sound of the NVA weapons, then sat tight, weapon ready in his hands, glancing nervously into the thick vegetation around him.

Suddenly, Doughty dragged himself out of the bushes, yelling, "Charley, I'm hit, Charley, I'm hit!" He collapsed in front of the hole. Jandecka hollered back for help and Frank Eates ran up with two GIs; they grabbed Doughty and dragged him back, running in a fast crouch, while Jandecka came out last covering the rear.

Doughty had about eight rounds in him.

They were still trading M16 for AK47 bursts in the tree line when Brantley hustled back to where Doughty lay. He was on his back in the brittle grass, stripped of all gear except an M16 bandolier around his waist, breathing shallowly, eyes open but unfocused. He should have died on the spot; Brantley wondered if he'd forced himself to crawl back so he could die among his friends. A buddy knelt beside him, shirt off, cigarette jammed in his mouth, face streaked with sweat; with one hand, he clasped Doughty's hand, with the other he held a piece of C-rat cardboard over Doughty's face to shield him from the sun. There was little the medics could do. Hodierne kneeled there, photographing the scene.

Brantley said he was sorry. Doughty's eyes were open, but there was no way to tell if he heard.

No medevac was immediately available.

It probably wouldn't have mattered. Doughty was dead within minutes. He just stopped breathing, his eyes still open, and Brantley slumped into the grass, eyes brimming with tears. He was awash in hurt and guilt, and anger.

In the big picture, Private Doughty might have died in vain; but he and the few others who'd moved forward had put out enough fire to allow the fifteen men pinned on the hillside to crawl back. They had left the two who'd been shot, and no one had been able to check on them. Captain Gayler didn't want to pull back until he knew for·sure there was nothing else for them to do. Several troopers donned gas masks, heaved CS grenades at the knoll, and rushed forward into the cloud. They ran back within minutes to tell the captain that both men were definitely dead.

Gayler passed the word to withdraw.

The medics rolled Doughty into a body bag, zipped it up, and a strung-out Brantley helped carry it as they straggled back down the trail.

PFC Tom Bailey stepped atop the berm and instantly collapsed in the sudden torrent of AK47 fire from the facing hill. In the next moment, his squad leader, Cpl John Reevs, bounded forward to pull him back. He too was blown down. Their corpsman, Doc Johnson, scrambled up next and helped get the two Marines to cover behind the berm. He hunched low and wrapped bandages: Bailey had an AK round through his neck, Reevs had two in his gut.

The rest of the two squads frantically ran from the open paddy as dust kicked up around them. The bouldered slope ahead seemed to be blazing with a thousand rifles. More rounds cracked through the air from the tree line to their left. They threw themselves down along the grassy green dike.

They were pinned.

Besardi and his buddy Sterling found themselves to the left of the mound—where the worst of the crossfire was hitting—trying to practically burrow into the berm. The air above them was electrified. RPGs slam-banged in, shrapnel whizzing in all directions, and Besardi thought simply and horribly: Jesus fucking Christ. Marines along the berm returned fire, shoving M16s and, maybe, helmet and eyes over the dike; they'd squeeze off a second's worth of fire, then tuck back down as the AK rounds cracked back. Besardi and Sterling emptied magazines in two or three bursts, getting quick glimpses of the NVA among the boulders, but having no time to aim at them. The sun was hard over them.

Besardi was hunched back down when a terrific explosion suddenly bounced him and Sterling back into the paddy. Besardi lay there, out of touch with his senses, ears ringing, eyes closed, his entire body numb. Only his mind was clear. Am I dead? His buddy Joe Johnson was screaming and it cut through the fog, "You guys all right, you guys all right!"

Besardi realized he was alive.

He also realized he was uninjured, and made a dash on all fours back to the protection of the dike. Chico was firing his M60, and Turner and P. K. Smith were firing theirs; Besardi noticed several men trying to bring back the wounded Bailey and Reevs. They were to the right of the mound, shielded somewhat from the crossfire.

Ball, Dean, and a third Marine were laboring with Reevs in a poncho, and they were hollering to Besardi, "C'mon, Charly, we gotta get John back!" To reach them, Besardi would have to scramble away from the cover of the dike and rush around the knoll. He froze. His buddies were stooped with their comrade, shouting for help; their faces were a mixture of anger and pleading. Well, fuck it, Besardi thought, here I go; and he jumped into the paddy, landed painfully, and scrambled up.

It should have been a five-minute walk back to the tree line with the village well, but it turned into a death march. Even with four men dragging the poncho, it was a load, and the paddy mud slowed each step. The sun soaked them. Reevs grimaced from within the poncho, his voice a strained mumble against the pain, "Leave me alone, leave me alone, I'm gonna die, go back and help those guys out." They answered in labored gasps, "Naw, John, man, you're gonna be all right. . . . We're gonna getcha back, we're gonna getcha back."

They had just reached the trees when Reevs looked up and said calmly, "It was really nice knowing you guys."

The tree line had been secured by other elements of Lima Company, and the corpsmen had set up a hasty collection point among the trees and terraced paddies. They hustled Reevs to a corpsman and set down the poncho; the man quickly went to work. He ripped off the bloody shirt, exposing the two small entry holes in Reevs's side; he hooked up an IV and tied bandages. His four buddies stood in a huddle around the corpsman until he stopped and looked up.

"I'm sorry, but your buddy's dead."

Besardi couldn't accept it. He just stood there in a daze until one of them mumbled, "C'mon, let's go back up and help out the rest of the guys." They started plodding back towards the dike. The first person they saw was Turner, the machine gunner who didn't have to be there. He was stumbling back between two grunts, arms over their shoulders, blood running from shrapnel wounds in his eye and throat. The entire line was falling back with them.

By the time Besardi got back to the tree line, the casualties of Lima and Mike Companies had been dragged there and the corpsmen were working frantically. Besardi slumped into an exhausted stupor by the well. Four Marines were coming back, carrying the body of a fifth Marine by his arms and legs, chest up, head hanging and flopping grotesquely as they walked. There was a gaping hole in his chest. Naw, it can't be, Besardi thought. He looked closer. Aw, no. It was Big Red Davis of Alabama, a buddy from boot camp and infantry training. Besardi had just talked to him the day before on LZ West: he was with Mike Company and in good spirits because he was under the impression that his company was to be the reserve. Besardi wandered back among the casualties. One of the corpsmen, a kid, leaned in a crouch against a berm. He was sobbing hysterically. There weren't enough corpsmen to help all the wounded, and for a second Besardi had the evil impulse to shoot the bastard. Instead, he tried to coax the kid back to reality. The corpsman couldn't, wouldn't, didn't respond.

Two NVA 12.7mm AAA positions were firing from the vicinity of Hill 381, mostly at the Phantoms flashing past. The grunts of 2d Platoon, Kilo Company, 3d Battalion, 7th Marines—resting at the base of the ridge line after their bout with snipers that morning—had the misfortune of hearing one of the gun positions. The platoon leader, 2dLt Arnold C. Nyulassy, radioed the company commander and the report followed the chain of command, until it came right back to the platoon.

They were to find and destroy the gun position.

The grunts were fatigued to the bone, murdered by the heat. But when Lieutenant Nyulassy said to saddle up, they pushed themselves one more time with a courage born of pride, discipline, and numbness. They advanced towards the ridge, then slumped into the underbrush as Phantoms ran another mission against Nui Chom and the suspected location of the gun. The grunts didn't know it but their attack was visible from Landing Zone West, and the command staff of the 7th Marines Regiment trained their binoculars northward. Colonel Codispoti, the ever-present cigar jutting from his jaw, was one observer; so was the reporter, Sterba, who'd hitched to West on the 196th InfBde C&C and who described the air strike:

Let me tell you a little about Marine pilots. They supported their grunts. I had never seen fighter pilots come in so low and stare down the .51s like these guys. The Air Force seemed to have a rule about not going below 2,000 feet to drop their napalm and bombs. These guys came in right on the deck. Or they'd dive straight into the .51 fire coming from the side of the ridge and unload their napalm at the last second. But each time, when they made another pass, at least one NVA would start shooting his .51 at them again. It must really have been dug in.

The last jet screamed over by 1400—the 12.7mm delivering a parting volley—then 2d Platoon of K/3/7 got moving again, trudging uphill through the thick vegetation of the ridge line. Fifty meters up, the AK47s commenced firing and everyone flopped in place as the bullets chopped the high brush above them. The fire seemed to be coming from one spot straight ahead. Lieutenant Nyulassy, who could have been no less tired than his men, was up shouting encouragement and directions, and the grunts fell into a ragged line again. They fired and threw grenades, and scrambled uphill. The NVA fire stopped; they found an abandoned bunker, a couple spider holes, and bloodstains, but no bodies.

The squads maintained their line, then bogged down in a field of shoulder-high elephant grass. Ten meters into the briar—as the grunts were shouldering through the sharp rows of blades, increasing their frustrated exhaustion, getting disorganized in the tangle—the North Vietnamese ambushed them from higher up on the ridge.

The 12.7mm and several AK47s scythed the grass.

Everyone scrambled for cover.

LCpl Danny R. Emery had wandered off to the right before the shooting started, humping his M60, his partner tagging along, humping the ammunition. When the NVA fire hit the center of the platoon, Emery and his partner were able to crawl uphill. The 12.7mm was firing from somewhere to their left, invisible amid the vines and trees; Emery cut loose at it from a crouch, raking his M60 back and forth, his assistant gunner keeping the ammo bandolier from jamming; both men were soaked with sweat. A piece of shrapnel hit Emery. He kept firing.

The 12.7mm kept firing too, keeping the platoon pinned. LCpl Jose Francisco Jimenez, a small, wiry fire-team leader, got up. No one had ordered him to. He simply crashed through the elephant grass, rushing uphill right into a North Vietnamese who popped from a spider hole to shoot him. Jimenez cut him down in an instant with his M16, then was upon two more of them. He blew them away in their spider holes. He was near the 12.7mm, and he dropped on the tangled slope; yanked the pins from one, two, then a third grenade; and hurled them into the spot of brush from where the gun seemed to be firing, rushing up after the explosions, firing on the run. The 12.7mm gun was in a shallow pit on a tripod, its gunner slumped dead. Lieutenant Nyulassy was on

Jimenez's heels, shouting the platoon up the fifty meters to the gun pit. Then another group of AK47s screamed from the right flank. Lance Corporal Emery fired his M60 at them as Lance Corporal Jimenez charged again. He threw frags, then ran up to pump his M16 into two North Vietnamese.

In a matter of moments, Jimenez had killed six NVA regulars and silenced the machine gun. He paused for a second near the last two victims when an AK47 suddenly cracked from the left, hitting him in the side of his head.

Jimenez was killed instantly.

Under the renewed fusillade, Lieutenant Nyulassy got most of his men back behind a knoll. He tried to sort out the situation. The parched elephant grass had caught fire, probably from their tracers, and burned out of control. The NVA were firing from above them; they seemed to have a slit trench along the ridge which allowed them to avoid the Marine fire and pop up anywhere along the hill. The NVA were not using tracers, so it was virtually impossible to zero in on them. Jimenez's body was sprawled by the gun bunker, and the Marine Corps does not abandon their dead. Nyulassy silently cursed the Americal Division for allowing the NVA to dig in so well, then called for volunteers to get Jimenez back. He was mightily impressed by the response. Seven men joined him.

Campos
Bosser
Sherrod
Davis
Jones
Dirken
Doc Sampson

They crawled uphill on their hands and knees, Nyulassy up front and Doc Sampson coming last, heads down under the AK fire and the hot smoke of the brush fire. The NVA went mad behind their guns as soon as the Marines neared the clearing where Jimenez lay, sending everyone down except Sherrod. He fired into the snipers—it looked as though he got one—then tumbled with an AK47 round through his neck. In the next moment, Chicom grenades were thrown downhill onto them. The explosions bowled over Nyulassy, tearing his right arm with shrapnel; Campos was also wounded. They scrambled back. The AKs and Chicoms kept coming. Their return fire seemed to have no effect.

Bosser tried again and was shot in the head.

Sherrod was hauled behind a spot of cover and Doc Sampson patched him. He was dying, and Jones and Dirken sat with him talking simple, reassuring things to him.

Davis was killed trying again.

The fight was in its second hour when they finally pulled back, leaving Jimenez's body under the guns. An M60 team on the right flank suddenly opened fire; the gunner hollered that he'd seen two NVA creeping up on them. He had nailed one, and chased them both off.

2d Platoon consolidated on the slope as two squads from 1st Platoon, under Sergeant Frank, came up. Lance Corporal Emery and another M60 team blasted uphill, while two men with M79 grenade launchers crept forward and lobbed HE and CS rounds along the ridge. Sergeant Frank led his men up through the burnt patch of elephant grass. Then the wind suddenly shifted and the blaze sprang up behind, driving them forward. They stumbled confused in the smoky tangle right into the snipers' sights; two Marines were killed and one was wounded in the sudden popping. They fell back, dragging their casualties, as soon as the fire burned down. Another Marine was wounded during the retreat.

Lieutenant Nyulassy noticed that the corpsmen with the re-act platoon seemed stunned. They hid in the deep grass and treated only those who were dragged to them. Doc Sampson, however, was rushing out to help carry back the wounded. Nyulassy got in radio contact with an aerial observer in a Bronco, who fired WP rockets along the ridge. They exploded in a smokescreen of thick, white clouds, and the Marines raised a cacophony of M16, M60, and M79 fire as another team rushed forward. Jimenez's body was on fire; a grunt got close enough to grab him but Jimenez tore loose in his hands.

1st and 2d Platoons finally fell back as Phantoms came in; between each pass, they could hear one or two AK47s firing into the sky.

The men had shown a lot of guts taking out that 12.7mm, and they'd paid the price. Six Marines were dead, nine wounded. Although the subsequent morning sweep found two NVA in a shallow grave, the platoons were credited with a total of only twelve kills. The sweep also found the burnt body of Jimenez. For their valor in dying to recover a dead buddy, LCpl Johnny S. Bosser and PFC Edward A. Sherrod were posthumously awarded Silver Stars; PFC Dennis D. Davis was awarded a Navy Cross. LCpl Jose Francisco Jimenez—who was from

Mexico City and nicknamed JoJo by a squad that considered him one good dude—was posthumously awarded the Congressional Medal of Honor.

For a moment, as he sat atop the paddy dike, Besardi thought he might be going insane. He slumped head down, his weapon heavy in his hands, hair soaked with sweat, face dripping. The heat was incredible. So was the stench. The corpsmen had lined the wounded and dead below the berm in preparation for the medevacs, and Besardi stared at the bodies. They'd been covered with ponchos, so only battered jungle boots showed, but he knew Big Red and John Reevs were among them, and they'd been good dudes, damn good men. A group of villagers tramped down a nearby dike, herded along by Gunny Martinez. The company gunnery sergeant, a ferocious-looking and respected man, had cleared them out of the family bunkers of some hootches discovered in the woods. Besardi looked at the bodies and the villagers, his mind burning up. Oh what the fuck, what the fuck are we doing, all these dead and you fucking cocksuckers are helping the NVA! Besardi was eighteen and couldn't cope with what he was experiencing. He wanted to blow them all away, shoot them off the dike. He didn't.

A wounded grunt walked up and told him, "Hey listen, Bailey wants to talk to ya." Bailey lay in the paddy, a thick bandage around his neck. His voice was scratchy. "You were right, I should've listened to you," he whispered to Besardi, who was kneeling beside him. Bailey was a spunky kid who always wanted to walk point. He was too reckless, though, and Besardi had tried to slow him down. Now he lay there, tears in his eyes, thinking he had somehow walked his platoon into the ambush on the dike. His voice cracked. "You told me to go slow, you told me to go slow."

Most of Besardi's squad were casualties.

Reevs was dead. Bailey was shot in the throat. Turner had shrapnel in his eye and throat. Roy Lee Hammonds from Texas had a bloody, ten-inch gash down his arm. Vaughn was hit by shrapnel. So was P. K. Smith. P. K. had taken a blast while he and Turner were manning their M60 on the dike. He moaned, sounding very frightened and very homesick, "This is it, this is it, I'm going home, this is my last one, I'm going home, I'm going home." It was P. K.'s third Purple Heart and everyone was glad he was going home, but grunts aren't very maudlin and Besardi chided him, "Fuck you, Smith, that's just a little scratch. You ain't goin' nowhere!"

The truth was he wasn't out yet. Mortar rounds began exploding around their position. Grunts and corpsmen rolled for cover and the wounded lay terrified and immobile, but the NVA didn't have their exact location. None of the rounds hit home.

Finally, a Sea Knight came in behind the tree line and landed in a dry paddy, rotor wash swirling dust high; the back ramp was down and grunts hustled through the whirlwind, humping in the loaded ponchos. No sooner had they gotten the last casualty inside than the mortar tube began thumping again. The overloaded Sea Knight pulled pitch, then banked to gain altitude and passed too near the side of Hill 381. Green tracers began whizzing past the helicopter, but somehow it rose through the fire and flew out of sight.

Besardi stood rooted, amazed, thanking God.

Lieutenant Ronald came up with the platoon's reserve squad. He'd taken some RPG shrapnel but had refused evacuation. He told Besardi he was the squad leader and that they were moving back towards Hill 381. Besardi didn't have much of a squad left—only Ball, Dean, Johnson, and Sterling—but they scrounged what ammunition they could from that left in the LZ by the casualties and got going.

Lieutenant Ronald said to move out.

"Okay," Besardi replied, "I'll walk the point."

"No, I'll walk the point."

Lieutenant Ronald led the way, Private Besardi walked slack, and they worked their way into a tree line about forty yards back from where they'd been mauled. They set into some dugouts that appeared to be abandoned NVA positions. The grunts in the reserve squad asked questions while the survivors of the first two squads sat shocked and silent. The sun was orange along the ridge line as more Phantoms crashed their bombs and napalm into the crest. Artillery rounds slammed against the bouldered slope. Between salvos, the men could see NVA moving along the face in groups of six or eight, toting AK47s and RPGs, leaves secured to their pith helmets. Oh shit, Besardi thought, don't tell me they're going to assault. But they didn't.

In fact, the *1st NVA Regiment* was pulling out.

Chapter Twenty
Finish

By the time the men of Bravo 4th of the 31st Infantry straggled back to where they'd dropped their rucks, the valley was dark. Fearing an ambush or booby trap, Captain Gayler had the company set in thirty meters east of their campsite; only with daylight would they retrieve their gear. As a perimeter was being organized along the terraced dikes, Private Jandecka noticed a dark clump in some bushes. He walked over, stuck the barrel of his M16 into the cushy object, and made sure to note its location. It was one of their rucksacks and, by morning, the canteens on it would be refreshingly chilled by the night air.

At daybreak, Jandecka walked over to get his drink. The ruck was gone, which was not too startling, until a sentry said he'd seen something crawl away from that bush during the night. Jandecka suddenly realized the thing he'd prodded with his M16 was probably an NVA straggler doing his best to hide from the American company setting up around him.

At first light on 29 August, Bravo 4–31 prepared to retrieve their four missing men. Before they moved out, Colonel Henry radioed Captain Gayler to delay his sweep until the arrival of Alpha 4–31. Alpha Company came up the road shortly, and Gayler was amazed to see two USMC M48 main battle tanks from the 1st Tank Battalion raising dust with them. Captain Mantell was grinning to him as he came in the perimeter, "Well, I knew an old tanker like yourself would be interested in these iron monsters." They advanced on the hill from another angle; Gayler stood on the tank deck and the Marine section leader asked if he minded if they reconned by fire. Gayler replied, "Sergeant, I think you'd be foolish if you didn't.'' He had just jumped from the deck and had not yet passed word that the tanks were going to fire when both let loose with a shrieking canister round. He looked around and realized he was the only one still standing; everyone else thought it had been incoming and they were down behind the tanks, the dikes, or the trees. As the tankers put .50-caliber fire into the hill, Gayler jokingly chided his men to their feet and they advanced.

Jandecka had been sick at heart with worry. His first firefight the day before had been like nothing he'd expected. He wasn't sure he could take a repeat. The sight of the tanks was comforting, but more reassuring was the mail brought in by the morning resupply bird. He got a letter from his father which made reference to Psalm 4.8. "In peace I will both lie down and sleep for you alone, O Lord, do make me to dwell in safety." It brought tears to his eyes and he did his best to swallow his fear and hump along with his comrades.

There was no NVA fire.

A cautious sweep of the knoll turned up numerous spider holes, four reinforced bunkers, a 60mm mortar base plate, seventeen 60mm shells, two NVA packs, and an old carbine. There were blood stains in some of the spider holes, but the only bodies were those Bravo Company had left behind.

It took awhile to find the two men who'd been killed in the second attack, mostly because one may not have been dead when they'd retreated. He'd taken a head wound but apparently woke up in the night and crawled deep into some bushes. He died alone sometime before the sweep arrived; at least, that's what it looked like. Gayler noticed that, when a helicopter arrived to drop off body bags and take the dead back out, a few GIs shied away from the body detail; they'd shared C rations with those men, but in death they were some kind of bad omen.

The bodies weren't the only passengers on the medevac. Brantley's squad leader, one of only two sergeants in the platoon, complained he'd cracked a rib during the fight. He left on the Huey and managed to swing a job in the rear.

Brantley himself went out with torn back muscles. He returned to the company, but not before he and a couple of Bravo walking wounded left the hospital for a week's siesta in a Da Nang whorehouse. What are the lifers going to do, send us to Nam? they speculated. As it was, they were reduced in rank. So what?

PFC Marion Feaster soon reupped to get out of the bush.

So did two of the FNGs.

After the medevac, the sweep turned around and returned to their night laager. There was much bickering when they discovered that the Marines guarding their rucksacks had fingered through them. One GI was relieved of a prized bottle of whiskey and he wanted blood. They did not get their satisfaction; the Marine tanks and infantry soon headed east to rejoin their battalion. Bravo Company moved out at dusk too, humping west to assume security outside the Resettlement Village. Jandecka's squad had the drag position. Eates was walking last. He was sick with fever, stumbling, barely keeping up. He toughed it out, though, only asking Jandecka, who was just ahead of him in the line, to look back occasionally and make sure he hadn't passed out on the trail. Jandecka did so gladly, remembering the rucksack incident. There was something claustrophobic about the valley, as if the NVA were everywhere, ready to ambush two straggling GIs. If imagination could kill, Jandecka would have been a victim that night.

■ On 28 August, A/4–31 Infantry and I/3/7 Marines had made the linkup without contact. On 29 August, the Battle of Hiep Duc Valley was essentially over. That morning, the grunts of Lima Company 3/7 slumped sluggishly in their holes as eight mortar rounds exploded among them. That was a departing volley from the NVA pulling out of Nui Chom; medevacs took out fifteen wounded men. Word was passed to move onto Hill 381. Lieutenant Ronald had been medevacked—finally ordered out by Colonel Kummerow—and the orphans he left behind were on edge. Spencer was bitching to Besardi that he was a corporal, while Besardi was only a private first class, and he shouldn't make them go back up that hill.

"Hey, listen," Besardi snapped, "if you wanna be the fucking squad leader, you go right ahead. I'll give it to you right fucking now, if you want the responsibilities!"

"No, no, no."

"Okay, then shut the fuck up."

He turned to Johnson. "Joe, I need a point man."

"What the fuck, Charly, I'm . . ."

"Yeah, man, I understand where you're coming from. But I still need a fucking point man."

"All right, I'll walk it for ya."

With Johnson on point and Besardi walking slack, the platoon finally hiked up the bouldered slope. The NVA were gone. They humped most of the afternoon, searching the abandoned dugouts, until the acting platoon leader called a break near a stream. Besardi was loaded under extra M60 ammo he had scrounged from the medevacs, and a U.S. Army flak jacket one of the casualties had previously liberated from Baldy or West and left lying in the dirt. He was really dragging and his good buddy Dean took his canteens to fill them up.

They set up atop Hill 381 for the night, then hacked through some thick brush to rejoin the rest of the company. They found them on one of the knolls of the ridge line, and from there they eventually were choppered to LZ Ross for a rest. A lot of replacements were milling on the LZ. Besardi noticed one of them and thought shocked, oh my God, this can't be. It was a hometown buddy.

He grabbed him. "Pizza Paul, what you doing!"

Paul stared at Besardi for a long second. He finally recognized him and blurted, "Charly, you look fucking terrible."

"Don't worry about that, pal, you'll look the same way in a few months too."

Lima 3/7 had disembarked at Ross in the late afternoon, then erected tents in the rain. The monsoon was beginning. Around 2100, word came to saddle up. The battalion was taking to the bush again in order to thin out the congestion atop LZ Ross in case of a rocket attack, and to investigate a sighting of North Vietnamese in nearby foothills. Besardi trudged bleary-eyed through the mud, his helmet cover soaked, his uniform soaked, his gear soaked, his skin shrivelled from the constant dampness. He rounded up his squad; they were bitching as they reshouldered packs and bandoliers, too tired to accept any rationale of why they were moving again. The acting platoon leader finally addressed them, "Listen, people, this is a W-A-R and we got fucking things to do. So, let's go do it."

They filed out of the fire base gate and down the muddy slope in the rainstorm, humping from ten at night until five in the morning in the direction of LZ Baldy. When they stopped, Besardi wrapped himself in a poncho liner, put his helmet over his face to shield the rain, and slept in the wet grass for two hours. Then they were up again, shivering and soaked, back on patrol.

Chapter Twenty-One

Continuum

To cap the victory, Colonel Codispoti presented Colonel Henry with a silver bugle. According to MACV's very subjective distillation of prisoner statements, Hanoi did not consider their campaign in Hiep Duc a success. Some said that the commander and executive officer of the *1st NVA Regiment* were relieved after pulling back into the mountains. Others said that a B52 arc light along Nui Chom had found the *2d NVA Division* Headquarters and pursuing units killed dozens of North Vietnamese. It was impossible to verify the prisoners' statements. Scores of NVA stragglers were picked off by the pursuing units. An NVA battalion commander was captured by M/3/7 Marines; he was found in a cave with three soldiers, all of whom surrendered after the Marines fired in a few rounds. The enemy colonel would not budge, so they tossed in tear gas and had to drag him out physically.

An ARVN battalion was brought in to help with the mop-up, and they spotted a withdrawing NVA column. U.S. artillery was brought to bear and by some accounts a hundred bodies were found.

The NVA were hurt more severely in retreat than in battle.

In the spring of 1970, when Colonel Henry was senior advisor, 5th Regiment, 2d ARVN Division, the ARVN troops overran an NVA hospital south of LZ West. The hospital records were translated and, according to Henry's memory, they indicated 1,500 NVA casualties between 11 and 31 August 1969. Thus, if the campaign was honed to a simple matter of debits and credits, it was another American victory. The enemy had retired from the battlefield before they could put the torch to the Hiep Duc Resettlement Village, and General Ramsey called it "a successful pre-emptive battle . . . one of the greatest battles and victories my men have fought.''

Records are not comprehensive regarding U.S. casualties in the Hiep Duc and Song Chang Valleys, but it appears that the 4th Battalion, 31st Infantry was bled the most. In twelve days, 17–28 August 1969, the battalion suffered 39 KIA and 204 WIA. They claimed 406 NVA KIA, 8 prisoners, and the capture or destruction of 36 individual and 11 crew-served weapons. For this defense of Hiep Duc, the Polar Bears won a U.S. Presidential Unit Citation and an RVN Cross of Gallantry.

The lulls and peaks continued.

On 12 September, an NVA attack on LZ Siberia was repelled by B/4–31 and C/3–82. The battle signalled a week of heavy fighting in both the 4–31 AO and 3–21 AO; casualties were heavy. Two months later, the 7th Marines rooted out numerous base camps and caches in the Que Sons; the NVA decided to slug it out and both sides were bloodied. They were bloodied again on 6 January 1970, when fifty NVA sappers penetrated 1/7's perimeter on LZ Ross; thirty-eight of them were killed and three captured, but thirteen Marines died.

The Americal did not see prolonged action in the area until 30 April 1970, when NVA sappers slipped the wire on LZ Siberia two hours after midnight. The attack was repulsed by D/4–31 but, meanwhile, other NVA units rampaged through a section of the Resettlement Village. Fifty homes were burned and twelve civilians killed; most fled to LZ Karen. In fighting which continued into the first week of May, the 5th ARVN Regiment with Americal gunship support retook the village; 4–31 with reinforcements regained the valley. Two reasons were suggested for the NVA attacks: to confiscate the rice then being harvested and, as an Army officer commented, ''. . . just to demonstrate they could do it.''

On 6 May, 2/7 Marines repelled a ground attack on Que Son District Headquarters. There was another series of mortarings and ground attacks in the area in June, then another lull, then another flurry of attacks in July, most of them weathered by B and C/1–46 Infantry.

The next lull for the 196th Brigade lasted until 28 March 1971, at which time Charlie 1st of the 46th Infantry was overrun by NVA sappers. They were on stand down atop LZ Mary Ann, a remote mountain south of the Song Chang Valley. Although the company commander had an outstanding reputation, a couple of bunker guards could not resist getting stoned; even sentries doing their duty could see practically nothing because of thick ground fog. The NVA sappers were able to wiggle through the wire under the fog. When a mortar barrage sent the GIs ducking, the North Vietnamese sprinted the last few meters into the perimeter. The sappers destroyed the B-TOC bunker (wounding the BnCO), cut communication lines, and tossed satchel charges into as many bunkers as they could before running down the opposite side of the hill.

Twelve NVA bodies were found; of the 200 GIs on Mary Ann, 33 were killed and 79 wounded. The battle was an indication of the state of demoralization of the U.S. Army in Vietnam, and resulted in the removal of the Americal Division commanding general.

The war was getting very old.

The Marines were also still in the area, conducting patrols which successfully dug out many of the enemy's mountain hideouts. On 31 August 1970, 2/7 conducted Operation Imperial Lake in the Que Sons. It was the 7th Marine Regiment's last operation; they were withdrawn in September. The 5th Marines CP then moved to LZ Baldy with 2/5 and 3/5 (1/5 was still in the Arizona, reinforced by the 1st Marines and the Vietnamized ARVN). In February 1971, the 5th Marine Regiment was withdrawn to Da Nang for further redeployment to the United States, and the 1st Marine Regiment became the last USMC infantrymen in South Vietnam. They held the Que Sons until the ARVN were ready, and on 12 April the last battalion, 2/1, terminated Operation Catawba Falls. Four NVA were killed in six days.

On 7 May 1971, 2d Battalion, 1st Marines stood down (they left Da Nang nineteen days later) and two companies of the 196th Infantry Brigade assumed the bunkers on Hill 327 and the rest of Division Ridge. At that time, the ARVN assumed completely the Que Son-Hiep Duc-Song Chang AO, and the 196th, Americal, joined the 101st Airborne Division in patrolling around Da Nang and the An Hoa Basin (in the new defensive terminology, "areas of responsibility" were now "areas of interest").

In the fall of 1971, journalists again caught up with the 4th of the 31st Infantry. One correspondent tagged along on patrol with Bravo Company and reported that, although unenthusiastic, the men had a good captain and did a good job. It was also noted that Bravo had not made contact in six months. The morale was entirely different at 4–31 Rear, Da Nang. The story there centered on the battalion exec, a perceptive and strong man, and his war on drug abuse among the support personnel. By then, the GIs had graduated from marijuana to heroin and they did not limit themselves to private bitchings about the lifers. Fragging threats had been made against the exec; the major commented, unbluffed, "It's like war, you take chances."

It was a bad time for the Americal Division.

Fraggings. Drug abuse. Combat refusals. They seemed to be epidemic, and the trials for My Lai never seemed to end. "The press at times seemed eager to publicize only the most negative stories about the Americal," commented Captain Downey of the 196th, who finished his second Vietnam tour in November 1971, "but remember this. In the midst of Nixon's great Vietnamization program it wasn't the 1st Cav, the Big Red One, 101st Airborne, nor the 1st Marine Division that was holding the NVA at bay. It was the Americal Division and not much more. My own very subjective opinion is that the Americal Division, after My Lai, was unofficially but purposefully designated as the sacrificial lamb to a war everyone knew would end in tragedy."

The troops felt the same way. In April 1972, Alpha and Charlie 2–1 were airlifted to Phu Bai, north of Da Nang, to protect U.S. installations in the face of the 1972 Easter Invasion. Of the 142 troopers in Charlie Company, 50 temporarily refused orders to move outside the Phu Bai perimeter. It wasn't even big news anymore, just a couple of paragraphs:

> "Excuse me, colonel, but as accredited MACV correspondents we are entitled to talk to these soldiers."
>
> The colonel blocked the way. "Well, I'm not going to let you talk to them." He was as good as his word. The trucks carrying a company of the U.S. 196th Infantry rolled away moments later. In a conversation over a concertina-wire fence, other soldiers explained there had indeed been a misunderstanding and a temporary refusal by a company to go into the field. The soldiers are reasonable and rational, and after a two-hour appeal by their commanding officer they all agree to go. But the soldiers make it plain they feel no obligation to fight for Vietnam and will accept only such action as is necessary to protect themselves and other Americans.

The colors of the Americal Division were folded in November 1971 (taking with it the 11th and 198th Brigades), and the 196th Brigade followed in June 1972. In four years in South Vietnam, about 100,000 men had served in the division; more than 3,400 had been killed and

22,500 wounded. They won eleven Medals of Honor. The last battalion of the last brigade, 3d of the 21st Infantry, remained on the Da Nang perimeter. Six years after its first operation in Vietnam, the Gimlets conducted the last U.S. infantry operation of the war. Two men were wounded by booby traps during the four-day patrol; then Hueys landed ARVN in their place in the bush and flew the GIs out. Thirteen days later, on 23 August 1972, the battalion deactivated as Increment IX of the U.S. Army withdrawal from the Republic of Vietnam. It was noted that the last ground combat units, 3d Battalion, 21st Infantry, and G Battery (Provisional), 29th Field Artillery, ". . . departed from Da Nang without ceremony."

■ Major General Simpson (CG, 1st MarDiv) won his third star before retiring in 1973; he recently retired from a university administrative position and lives with his wife in Bryan, Texas. Lieutenant Pidgeon (C/11th MTB) is a reserve lieutenant colonel; he is married, with two children, and is general manager of a wine and beer distributorship in Kent, Washington. Corporal Dill (B/1st Tanks) served eighteen months in Vietnam and lives in Baltimore, Maryland. Corporal LaRue (D/1st Recon) is a police detective in Olathe, Kansas.

Colonel Codispoti (CO, 7th Marines) retired to Los Gatos, California. Lieutenant Colonel Dowd (CO, 1/7) won the Silver Star for his first Arizona operation, and a posthumous Navy Cross, Legion of Merit, and Purple Heart for his second. Major Alexander (S-3, 1/7) won his second Silver Star for the Arizona; in 1984 while a colonel on active duty he died of a heart ailment. Captain Clark (CO, A/1/7) owns a hardware store in Ellicott City, Maryland. Lieutenant Weh (CO, B/1/7) won the Bronze Star in the Arizona, then his second Purple Heart from a mortar round in the Que Sons; he also held five Air Medals from his NAO service, and rotated in November 1969. He is now a reserve lieutenant colonel, and president of an airline contracting company in Albuquerque, New Mexico. Lieutenant Hord (CO, C/1/7) received the Silver Star; he has since married and is a lieutenant colonel commanding an infantry battalion. Captain Fagan (CO, D/1/7) earned the Navy Commendation Medal his first tour, two Bronze Stars for his two Arizona operations and a third for his assignment as S-3, 1/7. He also picked up a Purple Heart during the LZ Ross sapper attack; moving towards the command bunker, he ran into a sapper with the same idea and was downed with AK47 rounds through the cheek and neck, and across the shoulder. He is now a colonel. Captain Beeler (CO, I/3/5) won the Silver Star and finished his tour as Battalion S-4 because of his wounds; he is also a colonel now. Lieutenant Peters (D/1/7) was the S-1A during the LZ Ross attack and rotated soon after with a Bronze Star. He was divorced in 1984, shares custody of his two children, and is a major. Sergeant Major Awkerman (BSM, 1/7) earned the Bronze Star and Navy Commendation Medals for his two Vietnam tours; he is retired and lives with his wife in Mount Holly Springs, Pennsylvania. Gunnery Sergeant Richards (D/1/7) had his face reconstructed after being shot in November 1969; he retired in 1974 as a first sergeant to Rawlins, Wyoming. Sergeant Lowery (C/1/7) won the Silver Star and his third and fourth Purple Hearts in the Arizona; the bumpy road of his present life has included a divorce after three children, and employment at the post office in Clarkstown, Washington. Corporal Brundage (D/1/7) is a gunnery sergeant. Corporal Cominos (D/1/7) made sergeant before rotating; he also came home with a Purple Heart earned during an ambush sprung on a party of NVA. He shot an NVA to death as the man threw a grenade at his feet. He is married, with two daughters, and owns an independent insurance agency in Schererville, Indiana. Corporal Valley (I/3/5) is a political consultant in Mass. Lance Corporal Bradley (C/1/7) was medevacked from the Que Sons in November 1969 when, as a squad leader, he took an AK47 round across his back in an ambush. He stayed in the Corps, usually serving embassy duty (thus winning a Navy Achievement Medal in Afghanistan during the 1979 Soviet Invasion), and is presently a master sergeant. Lance Corporal Nelson (D/1/7) earned a commission and is now a major. Lance Corporal Zotter (H&S/1/7) rotated in March 1970 after eighteen months in-country. After two divorces, he is engaged again, and he is a sergeant on active duty with the Army National Guard in Charleston, Arkansas. Lance Corporal Wells (H&S/1/7) was medevacked with malaria from the Que Sons in November 1969, but was back in time for the January 1970 sapper attack. He then returned to his hometown, Middletown, New York; put away his campaign ribbons with pride; married and had two children; and drives a truck for the city.

Lieutenant Colonel Lugger (CO, 2/7) retired in 1972, his only personal award a Navy Commendation Medal for the DomRep. He lives with his wife in Pittsburgh, Pennsylvania, where he has a successful career in consulting and computers. Lieutenant Colonel Hopkins (CO, 2/7) retired as a brigadier general. Major Steele (S-3, 2/7) retired as a lieutenant colonel with three Navy Commendation Medals and a Purple Heart; he is a security consultant in El Toro, California. Lieutenant Pickett (G/2/7) was KIA after Hiep Duc. Lieutenant Schuler (E/2/7) rejoined his platoon in October 1969 and rotated in February 1970 with the Bronze Star and Purple Heart. He is married, with two children, and is administrator of the Portsmouth Hospital in New Hampshire. Gunnery Sergeant Yohe (E/2/7) won the Bronze Star and his second Purple Heart at Hiep Duc. He retired in 1973 as a first sergeant, is married, and works for the post office in Longview, Texas. Lance Corporal Parr (F/2/7) won the Bronze Star, two Purple Hearts, and a 100 percent disability after reconstructive plastic surgery. He has since married; has three children; and, after graduating with a degree in design engineering, was hired by a gas and electric company in Georgetown, Indiana. Lance Corporal Russell (H&S/2/7), divorced three times and a college graduate, is a crane operator and a lieutenant in the Air National Guard in Anchorage, Alaska. Lance Corporal Sirianni (H/2/7) rotated in June 1970 as a squad leader with sergeant stripes and a Navy Commendation Medal. He was discharged in 1972, has since married, has three sons, and works in a VA hospital in Buffalo, New York. He earned a B.A. in art from the University of Buffalo (his speciality is drawing) and is involved in art shows dealing with Vietnam veterans. Lance Corporal Stickman (F/2/7) is a superintendent with a construction company, and lives in Harpers Ferry, West Virginia. Private First Class Collinson (F/2/7) rotated in February 1970; he is married, has two sons, and is an assistant vice president of a bank in Federal Way, Washington. Private First Class Norton (F/2/7) got out from Hiep Duc with a Navy Commendation Medal and Purple Heart, plus an 80 percent disability for wounds and post-traumatic stress disorder. He is in his second marriage and works for the post office in Morgan, Vermont.

Lieutenant Colonel Kummerow (CO, 3/7) was medevacked from the Que Sons in September 1969, but returned in October 1969, and earned a Legion of Merit and Purple Heart. He retired as a colonel and lives with his wife on Bainbridge Island, Washington. Captain Stanat (CO, M/3/7) resigned his commission in 1970 and reportedly moved into the mechanical engineering field. Captain Rider (CO, L/3/7) commanded a recon battalion before being promoted to colonel. Lieutenant Ramage (CO, I/3/7) entered the business world after the service. Lieutenant Orefice (M/3/7) was released from the hospital with two Purple Hearts in October 1969, and completed his tour with B/1st Shore Party Battalion, An Hoa. He was released in 1971 with a 30 percent disability for his arm and leg; he has married, has three sons, and is manager of a golf country club in Simsbury, Connecticut. Sergeant Major Gledich (BSM, 3/7) is a convenience store manager in Casselberry, Florida. Corporal Jones (K/3/7) is a captain and counsellor in the U.S. Army Medical Service. Private First Class Besardi (L/3/7) was medevacked in January 1970 when he injured his knee running to a bunker on LZ Baldy during a rocket attack. In seventeen years, he's worked seventeen different jobs for a total of four years. He receives a 30 percent disability for his knee and another 30 percent for post-traumatic stress disorder. He lives alone in Milbury, Mass. Private First Class Hammonds (L/3/7) was returned to the bush in November 1969 when his wounds healed, and was KIA in January 1970. Private First Class Smith (L/3/7) was mustered out with three Purple Hearts and is now working in Schwenksville, Pennsylvania. Private First Class Turner (L/3/7) lives in Alexandria, Virginia.

Major General Ramsey (CG, Americal Division) retired with almost four years of WWII duty and an extended Vietnam tour, earning three Silver Stars and five Purple Hearts; he gave up command of the division in March 1970 after being injured in a helicopter crash. He is a bank executive in McLean, Virginia. Colonel Tackaberry (CO, 196th InfBde) won his third Distinguished Service Cross during the September 1969 attack on LZ Siberia. As a company commander in Korea and a two-tour man in Vietnam, he also netted five Silver Stars and a Purple Heart, and retired with three stars. He is now a businessman in Fayetteville, North Carolina. Captain Downey (196th InfBde) is a business executive in Los Angeles, California. Specialist 4 Keefer (A/1–1 ArmCav) won a CIB and ARCOM,* then a BSM and his fifth Purple Heart during a 1970–71 tour with his old cavalry troop. It has been a rough mental road since his discharge as a sergeant platoon leader, and he is now a laborer in Ridgely, Maryland.

Lieutenant Colonel Henry (CO, 4–31 Inf) won a Distinguished Flying

---

*Abbreviations used to clarify the lesser end-of-tour awards.

Cross for his resupply flight to D/4–31 in Song Chang, and a Silver Star and Purple Heart for his on-the-ground command in Hiep Duc. From January to June 1970, he was an ARVN advisor, and he retired as a colonel in 1981 to a cattle ranch in Amity, Arkansas. Major Lee (S-3, 4–31), after two combat tours, won three Bronze Stars for Valor and three more for service; he is now a colonel. Captain Gayler (CO, B/4–31) gave up the company in October 1969, served as Battalion S-1, and rotated with the Silver Star, Bronze Star, and Army Commendation Medals for Valor, and the Purple Heart for a small punji stick wound. He is now a National Guard lieutenant colonel commanding a tank battalion; he lives with his wife and three children in Arlington, Texas, where he is starting an advertising and photography business. Captain Murphy (CO, C/4–31), Captain Thomas (CO, C/4–31), and Captain Mekkelsen (CO, D/4–31) are active-duty lieutenant colonels. Captain Whittecar (CO, D/4–31) earned his third Silver Star and Purple Heart for Song Chang. He retired as a major, is now a management analyst with the Department of the Army, and lives with his family in Salina, Kansas. Captain Kinman (HHC/4–31) is practicing medicine in Vincennes, Indiana. Captain Thomason (CO, C/3–82 Arty) is now a major. First Lieutenant Monroe (B/4–31) commanded the company during the sapper attack on LZ Siberia since Gayler was on R and R; after his discharge, he joined the New York City Police Department. Second Lieutenant Robinson (C/4–31) was WIA at Banana Tree Hill in September 1969; by the time he was rotated and discharged in August 1970 with a BSM, AM, and Purple Heart, he was the company commander. He is divorced and works for an accounting firm in Birmingham, Michigan. Second Lieutenant Wilson (C/4–31) won an Army Commendation Medal for Valor at the Banana Tree Hill fight, and finished his tour as an ammunition officer in Chu Lai. He married his fiancee in May 1970, and was discharged a captain in February 1971; they now have two children and he is a programmer analyst in Greensboro, North Carolina. Sergeant Allison (B/4–31) earned an Army Commendation Medal for Valor and a Purple Heart for Hiep Duc, and rotated in November 1969. He is a reserve captain and, after reenlisting in 1975, is a regular sergeant first class. Specialist 5 Kralich (HHC/4–31) served a second tour with the 101st AbnDiv, and is presently a professional counsellor in a chico hospital in Calif. Specialist 4 Ferris (D/4–31) was discharged with an ARCOM and two Purple Hearts; he lives with his wife and three sons in Woodbury, New Jersey, where he is a police officer. Specialist 4

Holtzman (A/4–31) won a Bronze Star for Valor for Song Chang and rotated as a sergeant in November 1969. He is married, with two children, and owns several coffee trucks in Islip Terrace, New York. Specialist 4 Parsons (A/4–31) rotated with an ARCOM and was discharged a staff sergeant. He is now a major in the Delaware National Guard and a safety consultant for an insurance company; he lives with his wife and two children in Folsom, Pennsylvania. Private First Class Bleier (C/4–31) won a Bronze Star for Valor and a Purple Heart, and wangled an early-out in July 1970. Despite a 40 percent disability, through a program of disciplined exercise and legal steroids, he played in the 1975 Superbowl with the Pittsburgh Steelers (an achievement chronicled in a book and television movie). He has two children, runs a small advertising firm, and lives in the suburbs of Pittsburgh, Pennsylvania. Private First Class Brantley (B/4–31) lives in Gainesville, Florida. Private First Class Jandecka (B/4–31) was mustered out as a Specialist 4 with an ARCOM. His wife owns a health food store, they have three children, and he is a police officer in North Olmsted, Ohio. Kit Carson Scout Twenty Ly (C/4–31) was KIA in 1969 when a GI beside him tripped a booby trap; he was posthumously awarded a U.S. Silver Star.

Second Lieutenant Baird (B/1–46) served in Vietnam from 1969 to 1971, won a Silver Star, and is now a major. Sergeant Brown (B/1–46) is divorced and working in a steel mill in West Point, Mississippi. Specialist 4 Hodierne (*Stars & Stripes*) was a civilian correspondent in Vietnam in 1966–67, then received his degree in political science, enlisted in the Army, and was a military correspondent in Vietnam in 1969–70; he now works for a television station and lives with his wife on a thirty-two-foot cutter in San Francisco Bay. Specialist 4 McWhirter (D/1–46) earned a Bronze Star for Valor at Hiep Duc. He has two sons and is an authorizations analyst for Caterpillar Tractor in East Peoria, Illinois. Private First Class Kosteczko (B/2–1) rotated as a sergeant with the BSM. He still lives at home and is a bank loan officer and collection supervisor in Chicago, Illinois. Private First Class Tam (B/1–46) co-owns a Chinese restaurant with his father in San Diego, California.

Lieutenant Colonel Bacon (CO, 3–21) retired as a colonel to Columbia, South Carolina. Captain Chudoba (CO, A/3–21) served two combat tours with the Gimlets between 1966 and 1969, won a Bronze Star for Valor and a Purple Heart, but then resigned his commission in 1980 after failing to make major. Captain Wolpers (CO, A/3–21) is still on active duty. First Lieutenant Shurtz (CO, A/3–21) was rotated and discharged in July 1970 with captain's bars and an end-of-tour BSM and ARCOM. He is a senior commercial sales and service representative, and lives with his wife in Oregon, Ohio. Captain Carrier (CO, C/3–21) is married, with a daughter, and is an independent oil and gas businessman in Sugar Land, Texas. First Lieutenant Browne (A/3–21) and First Lieutenant Maness (D/3–21) both wear Silver Stars and the oak leaves of lieutenant colonel. Sergeant Cuthbert (B/3–21) was KIA after the Song Chang battle. Specialist 4 Curtis (A/3–21) rotated in November 1969 with the Silver Star, BSM, and sergeant stripes; he is married, has two children, and works in a paper mill in Kelso, Washington. Specialist 4 Hurley (A/3–21) was WIA in the September 1969 battle and medevacked; he lives in Broomfield, Colorado. Specialist 4 Niebuhr (A/3–21) was reportedly killed when a car hit him in 1971. Private First Class Goodwin (A/3–21) is married, has a son, and is a computer operator for a bank in St. Louis Park, Minnesota. Private First Class Kruch (A/3–21) spent seven months in the hospital, was discharged a Specialist 4 in December 1970, and testified two months later at a sensational hearing on war crimes conducted by the Vietnam Veterans Against the War. He has since married, has two daughters, and is a building inspector in Williamston, Michigan. Private First Class Lasso (B/3–21) was rotated and discharged in April 1970; he is married and a computer programmer in Bethlehem, Pennsylvania. Private First Class Shimer (B/3–21) was mustered out in August 1970, is married with two children, and is an attorney at law in Bethlehem, Pennsylvania.

Bibliography

BOOKS

Bleier, Rocky and O'Neil, Terry. *Fighting Back*. New York: Warner Books, 1975.

Boyle, Richard. *Flower of the Dragon*. San Francisco: Ramparts Press, 1972.

Jury, Mark. *The Vietnam Photo Book*. New York: Grossman Publishers, 1971.

Mills, Nick, ed. *The Vietnam Experience: Combat Photographer*. Boston: Boston Publishing Company, 1983.

Scruggs, Jan and Swerdlow, Joel. *To Heal A Nation*. New York: Harper & Row Publishers, 1985.

Simmons, Edwin H., BrigGen, et al. *The Marines in Vietnam 1954–1973, An Anthology and Annotated Bibliography*. Washington, D.C.: Headquarters, U.S. Marine Corps, 1974.

Webb, James. *Fields of Fire*. Englewood Cliffs, New Jersey: Prentice-Hall, Inc., 1978.

Westmoreland, William, Gen. *A Soldier Reports*. Garden City, New York: Doubleday Company, Inc., 1976.

Zalin, Grant. *Survivors*. New York: W. W. Norton, 1975.

PERIODICALS

Babb, Wayne, Capt. "The Bridge: A Study in Defense." *Marine Corps Gazette*, June 1971, pp 16–23.

Bowen, Bob, SSgt. "Barrier Island." *Leatherneck*, January 1970, pp 34–41.

Buckley, Kevin. "The Alpha Incident." *Newsweek*, 8 September 1969, pp 17–18.

Crawford, Bill, SP4. "The Valley is their Home." *Americal Magazine*, October 1969, pp 14–17.

———. "In Defense of Hiep Duc." *Americal Magazine*. January 1970, pp 18–21.

———. *West of West* (Newsletter of 4-31 Infantry). 3 August, 3 September, 3 October, and 3 November, 1969.

Delzell, Robert. "Night Attack on Landing Zone Siberia." *Soldier of Fortune*, August 1981, pp 42–44.

"Incident in Song Chang Valley." *Time*, 5 September 1969, pp 22–23.

Jandecka, Charles. "It Happened to Me." *Soldier of Fortune*, October 1982, pp 12–13.

———. "Hiep Duc Valley 1970 Winter/Spring Offensive." *Soldier of Fortune*, August 1981, p 44.

Sloan, John, Sgt, ed. *The Professionals* (Newsletter of 1-46 Infantry), 13 September 1969.

Sterba, James. "Close Up of the Grunt: The Hours of Boredom, the Seconds of Terror.'' *The New York Times Magazine,* 8 February 1970, pp 30–31, 91–96.

DOCUMENTS

"Combat After Action Report, Headquarters, 4th Battalion, 31st Infantry, 196th Infantry Brigade, Americal Division, 170001H August to 032400H September 1969."

"Command Chronology, 5th Marines, August 1969."

"Command Chronology, 1st Battalion, 5th Marines, June 1969."

"Command Chronology, 7th Marines, August 1969."

"_____, September 1969."

"Command Chronology, 1st Battalion, 7th Marines, August 1969."

"_____, September 1969."

"Command Chronology, 2d Battalion, 7th Marines, August 1969."

"_____, September 1969."

"Command Chronology, 3d Battalion, 7th Marines, August 1969."

"_____, September 1969."

"Operation Order: 522–69. Patrol: Puppet Show, Co. D, 1st Reconnaissance Battalion, Da Nang, RVN, 201220H June 1969."

"U.S. Marine Corps Oral History Program/Interviewee: LtGen Ormond R. Simpson, 25 May 1973."

1ST MARINE DIVISION HISTORICAL TEAM IN-FIELD INTERVIEWS

Brennon, William, 2dLt, H/2/7 (6 Sept 1969)

Clements, Alfred, SSgt, G/2/7 (10 Sept 1969)

Codispoti, Gildo, Col, 7th Marines (6 Sept 1969)

Donaldson, William, 1stLt, M/3/7 (9 Sept 1969)

Emery, Danny, LCpl, K/3/7 (8 Sept 1969)

Evans, Donald, Maj, S-2, 7th Marines (29 Aug 1969)

Grimes, F. J., GySgt, 1st MAW (N/A)

Hollingshead, Glenn, Cpl, K/3/7 (10 Sept 1969)

Huber, Vernon, HMCS, 7th Marines (9 Sept 1969)

Jones, Alan, Cpl, K/3/7 (10 Sept 1969)

Krulak, William, Capt, S-3, 7th Marines (6 Sept 1969)

Larrison, Jack, 1stLt, G/2/7 (11 Sept 1969)

Lindsay, Paul, 1stLt, E/2/7 (8 Sept 1969)

Lindsey, Lloyd, 1stLt, S-2, 2/7 (7 Sept 1969)

Lugger, Marvin, LtCol, 2/7 (1 Sept 1969)

Medley, Anthony, 1stLt, M/3/7 (9 Sept 1969)

Morrero, Felipe, LCpl, K/3/7 (10 Sept 1969)

Nyulassy, Arnold, 2dLt, K/3/7 (7 Sept 1969)

Pickett, John, 2dLt, G/2/7 (11 Sept 1969)

Skaggs, Travis, Cpl, G/2/7 (11 Sept 1969)
Stanat, Christopher, Capt, M/3/7 (9 Sept 1969)
Vallance, Charles, 1stLt, H/2/7 (6 Sept 1969)
Vannoy, P. E., 1stLt, H/2/7 (6 Sept 1969)
Wilson, B. M., HM, E/2/7 (7 Sept 1969)

11-12 August 1969

Index